Selected Letters

Olson at Enniscorthy, Keene, Virginia, summer 1946.

Selected Letters

Charles Olson

Edited by Ralph Maud

University of California Press
Berkeley   Los Angeles   London

PS
3529
.L655
Z 48
2000

The publisher gratefully acknowledges the contribution provided by the General Endowment Fund, which is supported by generous gifts from the members of the Associates of the University of California Press.

University of California Press
Berkeley and Los Angeles, California

University of California Press, Ltd.
London, England

Library of Congress Cataloging-in-Publication Data

Olson, Charles, 1910–1970.
  [Correspondence. Selections]
  Selected letters of Charles Olson / edited by Ralph Maud.
      p.   cm.
  Includes bibliographical references and index.
  ISBN 0-520-20580-4 (cloth : alk. paper)
    1. Olson, Charles, 1910–1970—Correspondence. 2. Poets, American—20th century—
Correspondence. I. Maud, Ralph. II. Title.
PS3529.L655 Z48 2000
811'.54—dc21
[B]   99-048424

Manufactured in the United States of America

08 07 06 05 04 03 02 01 00
10 9 8 7 6 5 4 3 2 1

The paper used in this publication meets the minimum requirements of ANSI/NISO z39.48-
1992 (R 1997) (Permanence of Paper).

This volume is dedicated in advance
to the yet unknown benefactor who will
ensure that Charles Olson's home from 1957 to 1970

28 FORT SQUARE, GLOUCESTER, MASSACHUSETTS

can be preserved from the ruins of time as a fitting
monument to the memory of the poet.

Contents

Introduction

Charles Olson believed in letter writing. It was honest communication. He believed in it as a true political act that might create a polis, if anything could. It was a means of establishing polity, of registering what he believed the postmodern (as he defined it) should give us: a sense of belonging. For Olson letter writing was an everyday thing; it made the world more of a home.

The *Maximus* poems were, he always insisted, literally letters. The model available to him was Maximus of Tyre, a philosopher of the second century A.D., who traveled to centers of learning and sent disquisitions back to his home town. At the outset Olson wrote the poem-letters to his friend Vincent Ferrini in Gloucester from Washington, D.C., Yucatan, and Black Mountain College. Later, himself in Gloucester, he wrote from there to the world at large and at times to his fellow citizens. He once called these poems his "dailies."

The title essay and several others in the *Human Universe* volume began as letters and retain that informality. "I believe a man talks best straight and going out to another," Olson wrote to Robert Creeley on 5 July 1950, when he had the problem of revising his formal essay "Projective Verse" for publication (letter at Stanford). "I sort of imagine some of the things I put to you recently on breath and line and the backwards of same, are worth all this crap i see in front of me this morning that i wrote once, when, who was that dope?" He rewrote "Projective Verse" utilizing a great deal from his correspondence with Creeley. When some years later he wanted to add to "Projective Verse," he did it with a letter, "Letter to Elaine Feinstein," published in *Selected Writings of Charles Olson.*

Several notable poems outside the *Maximus* series, brought together in Olson's *Collected Poems,* came from letters. Some of them retain their letter form, for instance the notorious "Letter for Melville 1951," which Olson sent special delivery to where it was needed, a conference of Melville scholars. In short, letters were not a secondary activity for Olson but the preferred way of conducting himself as a writer.

Letters were, in fact, his normal work. I once was on Fort Point returning to the center of Gloucester, having found Olson not at home, when I saw an automobile coming up the street very slowly, almost, I thought, meandering. It stopped, the driver leaned over to open the passenger door and waved me in. "I bet you think I'm drunk." It was the poet himself, beaming as was his wont. "No, I've eaten and I'm just exhausted." And he added by way of explanation, "Today I wrote eight letters, all of them of some consequence." I had run into Olson coming off his shift.

That word *consequence* was as exact as one had learned to expect Olson's words to be. How many of his letters do not make points that ask to be answered with further thought? Not many. Most of us write letters to fulfill some kind of duty: we do not know what correspondence is. At its best it is thinking aloud so that the recipient also has to think. Oh, I suppose we know it all right, but we shy away from devoting the energy and attention we know are required to begin and maintain such an exploration, which is both intellectual and personal. Only certain exceptional people among us have the equipment for it, and when the letters of those individuals have been saved and can be made available in such a volume as this one, the rest of us are shown our possibilities.

The "consequence" was not only in what the recipient had to do but also in what the letter did for the poet himself and his cosmology:

> putting things together
> which had not previously
> fit

as he expressed it in *The Maximus Poems* (p. 327). Olson would sometimes beg a correspondent to return a letter; this was disconcerting until one realized he just wanted to see what he had written. What had been penned in the heat of the moment and mailed was now needed for reflection. In one instance, Joyce Benson typed out for him the best parts of a requested letter; Olson wrote back asking for the whole letter: "I do believe you aren't yet enough of a *victim* of life to know that all or context has the meaning . . . it isn't only the quotable"; adding, "It's like fishermen say the set. Which gets the fish" (letter of 11 November 1967 at Storrs). Only by reviewing the whole letter, he believed, could he know whether he had, to use an image from *The Maximus Poems* (p. 264), been able

> to shake off his cave-life
> and open an opening
> big enough for himself.

The only time in Buffalo I was in Olson's classroom was when I found him there long after the class had ended, sitting in the front row of the seating and surveying the surround of blackboards that he had filled during the previous three or four hours. He was fixing in his mind where the journey had taken him and determining if he had opened a big enough opening. It is the same with these selected letters, some of which may seem impenetrable at first glance. One has, as it were, to sit in front of them for a while, pull out a mental notepad, and see how they are set.

The letters in this volume are not, however, meant to show off Olson's genius all the time at its highest pitch. On the contrary, the selection seeks a rounded picture with the inclusion of family letters, job and grant applications, letters of recommendation, Black Mountain College business correspondence, letters to sweethearts, and letters of the normal course, as well as those at the boundary of a poet's experience.

It befits a volume of selected letters to include letters to as many different people as possible, even at the risk of slighting somewhat the more important correspondents. This is one reason why the passing of the years has been of benefit to this enterprise. If a *Selected Letters of Charles Olson* had been produced in 1971, immediately after the poet's death, as was originally planned, it would perforce have been dominated by letters to Robert Creeley, Edward Dahlberg, and Cid Corman. Because the correspondence of these three key figures in Olson's career has been published (Creeley's now in its tenth volume from Black Sparrow Press, Corman's complete in two volumes from the National Poetry Foundation, Dahlberg's available in one volume from Paragon House) the present *Selected Letters* is relieved of the burden of proportional representation. Further relief of the same kind comes from the publication of Merton Sealts's *Pursuing Melville*, containing many of Olson's letters on Melville

matters, and by the recent appearance of the Frances Boldereff correspondence. Editions of Olson's letters to Donald Allen, Ronald Mason,
Robert Duncan, Edward Dorn, and Robin Blaser are either in preparation or are destined to be. All this publishing activity means that the
main correspondents are well taken care of and thus have in this edition
what amounts to token representation only. The advantage gained is in
seeing how interesting was the extent of Olson's acquaintanceship, how
very far his airmail stamps took him.

It is the wider story, the whole life, that is aimed at here. The letters
have been largely chosen because they are self-explanatory, allowing the
story to flow without the intrusion of scholarly apparatus. There is un-
deniable charm in the early letters, where one clearly sees a sensitive and
bright young man trying to find his way in the world. If one reads in sequence one will slowly become accustomed to the poet's so-called difficult style as it develops. A trust will be generated to carry one forward, a
trust that Olson may be idiosyncratic but not uncreatively perverse. His
advances into a new syntax of experience are then not unattractive. Included in the present volume is Olson's reply to a request by David Ignatow for an essay for *Chelsea* magazine's special issue on politics. His letter
(letter 87) is a full response, with historical and mythological allusions as
well as contemporary concerns, a reticulum of leaps of thought. "My
own experience," Olson writes at the end, trying to persuade Ignatow to
use the letter itself as his contribution to the issue, "is that such 'forms'
coming via the occasion carry a drive into discourse that the older formalisms (of paragraph etc) don't." There are enough later letters in this
selection to enable the reader to test this proposition.

But it is not only that one can get a feel for Olson's later style by proceeding with deliberation through this volume. What one also gets is the
sense of a lifespan, in itself one of the more moving gifts that a forebear
can leave behind. Given the linked sequence of these vibrant letters, from
college in 1931 to hospital in 1969, a few weeks before Olson's death at
fifty-nine years of age (about two hundred letters out of a known three
thousand), this edition enables us to have a life presented as a whole: that
uncommon common thing, a whole life.

As to editorial procedures: all the letters in this volume are given in
full from their manuscript or printed source (with one indicated exception, letter 44, where a great deal of Melville minutiae was being dis-

cussed). Not all postscripts have been included, and marginalia have either been absorbed into the body of the letter at the appropriate place or ignored. Idiosyncracies have been retained, although misspellings and typing errors judged unintentional have been silently corrected. The format of the letters as Olson wrote them has been followed, within reason. One deliberate change is in respect to the square brackets Olson began to use in later letters: these have been silently converted to normal parentheses because they are truly equivalent to parentheses and because square brackets are reserved for their usual use, to indicate editorial interpolation.

It has not been necessary to censor any remarks. Olson was self-reflective and candid, but he was not sloppy with his secrets. The letters show proper containment. He loved to gossip as much as the next person, but he did not libel (at least in the letters selected) and therefore there are no omissions of that sort. Olson's use of abbreviated names was not meant to hide identities, which are usually clear in context. These abbreviations can be found in their alphabetical place in the index to the volume.

Performing the function of footnotes, the index gives brief annotations for persons, places, written works, and some concepts. The extent of any particular annotation depends on what might be puzzling in the letter. Headnotes are tailored to provide context for individual letters. A chronology of Olson's life as it relates to the correspondence is included in the introductory matter, and each section of the volume has its own short biographical introduction. Additional information about Olson's work and life can be found in George F. Butterick's *A Guide to the Maximus Poems of Charles Olson* and Ralph Maud's *Charles Olson's Reading: A Biography.*

I am chiefly indebted to Richard C. Fyffe and, subsequently, Rutherford W. Witthus as curators of the Literary and Cultural Archives in the Archives and Special Collections Department of the Thomas J. Dodd Research Center, University of Connecticut Libraries, Storrs, for making available to me copies of letters and, as administrators of copyright for the University of Connecticut Library and the Estate of Charles Olson, for giving permission to publish the letters and other passages from Olson's writings. Assistance was received from Charles Boer, the first executor of the estate, in the earlier stages of editing this volume of letters, when the book was to have been a collaboration between myself and the late George F. Butterick, then curator of the Olson Archive under Richard H. Schimmelpfeng, formerly director of special collections at the University of Connecticut Library. I am indebted, too, to the present reader services coordinator at the Dodd Center, Tara L. Hurt.

I thank the libraries that have made available the letters published in this volume. They are listed separately as part of the introductory material. The following libraries responded to research requests, although letters from their holdings have not been included: Kenneth Spencer Research Library, University of Kansas; the George Arents Research Library, Syracuse University; Elmer Holmes Bobst Library, New York University; Fairleigh Dickinson University Library; Goddard College Library; University of Chicago Library; Pennsylvania State University Library.

For making available to me Olson letters in their possession I am indebted to Joyce Benson, Robin Blaser, George Butterick, Paul Cardone, John Clarke, Albert Cook, Edward Dorn, Robert Duncan, Albert Glover, Mac Hammond, Robert Hogg, James Laughlin, Harry Levin, Michael McClure, Kenneth McRobbie, Frank Moore, Suzanne Mowat, Charles Peter Olson, Kate Olson, Robert Payne, Frances Boldereff Phipps, and Ken Stuart.

I wish to express my appreciation of the kindness of all the above, and of the following individuals for responding to enquiries: Richard Emmet Aaron, Donald Allen, Peter Anastas, Melissa Banta, Jonathan Bayliss, Robert Bertholf, Richard Blevins, Enikö Bollobás, Michael Boughn, George Bowering, Harvey Brown, Gerald Burns, John Cech, Ann Charters, Clark Coolidge, William Corbett, Matthew Corrigan, Robert Creeley, Andrew Crozier, Guy Davenport, Frank Davey, Fielding Dawson, Charles Doria, Helene Dorn, Monroe Engel, Clayton Eshleman, George Evans, Thorpe Feidt, Vincent Ferrini, Rolf Fjelde, Skip Fox, Benjamin Friedlander, Robert Fulford, Joseph Garland, Greg Gibson, Allen Ginsberg, Lyle Glazier, John Granger, Donald Hall, Geoffrey Hargreaves, Mary Emma Harris, Lou Harrison, Jack Hirschman, George Hochfield, Norman Holland, Anselm Hollo, Tim Hunter, Kenneth Irby, Roderick Iverson, Jean Kaiser, Lionel Kearns, Robert Kelly, Harry Keyishian, Madeleine Kierans, Burt Kimmelman, Bryant Knox, Gerrit Lansing, Harris Lenowitz, Bruce Loder, Tom McGauley, Duncan McNaughton, William McPheron, Peter Magnani, Harry Martin, Ronald Mason, Frederick

Merk, Paul Metcalf, Thomas Meyer, Linda Parker, J. H. Prynne, Peter Quartermain, William Radoslovich, Jed Rasula, Tom Raworth, Harry Redl, Richard Reeve, Klaus Reichert, Peter Riley, Jerome Rothenberg, Michael Rumaker, Ed Sanders, Herbert Schneidau, Merton Sealts, Gavin Selerie, Bernarda Shahn, T. Leverett Smith, Raymond Souster, Marion K. Stocking, William Sylvester, Ellen Tallman, Warren Tallman, Nathaniel Tarn, Sharon Thesen, Gael Turnbull, Fred Wah, Charles Watts, Philip Whalen, John Wieners, Richard Wilbur, Jonathan Williams, Seth Yorra, Jery Zaslove.

Financial help for visits to libraries holding Olson letters was provided through the years by the Simon Fraser University English Department and the President's Research Fund. I was the recipient of fellowship aid from the Social Sciences and Humanities Research Council of Canada. I appreciate the privileges extended me in my present capacity as emeritus professor of English and associate of the Institute for the Humanities, Simon Fraser University, Burnaby, British Columbia.

The kindness of my hosts during the research trips undertaken for this volume surpasses any attempt I could make to express individual thanks. I can, however, make a list in gratitude: Jim and Sue Garrard, Stanley and MaryAnn Mailman, John and Jeanne Hackett, Richard and Elizabeth Ohmann, Katka Hammond, Joseph Cambray, Carol Cook, Marilyn Hochfield, Jim Wheatley, Dan Barrett, Rust Hills, Joy Williams, Mary Weissblum, Lee Halprin, Abby Rockefeller, Peter Hay, Dorthea Attwater, Susan and Vilmos Zsigmond, James Haining, Torsten and Paivi Kehler, B. J. Katz, Kit and Sue Lukas, Helen and William Mulder, Peggy Kelley, Jeremiah Kelley, Steven Carter, Rosetta Raso, Leslie and Kitty Norris, Thomas Moore, Peter Bayliss, Linda Sutherland, Carolyn Zonailo, Stephen Morrissey, and Lilia Aaron.

*Library Sources for the Charles Olson
Letters in This Volume*

The sources are listed alphabetically by the abbreviated placename used in the headnotes. (Numbers in parentheses refer to the letter numbers in this volume.)

Archives of American Art   Archives of American Art, Smithsonian Institution, Washington, D.C. (39, 40, 53)

Berkeley   Bancroft Library, University of California, Berkeley (47, 75, 77, 124)

Buffalo   Poetry/Rare Books Collection, University Libraries, State University of New York at Buffalo (76, 96, 100, 105, 110, 138, 141, 146, 152, 170)

Columbia   Rare Book and Manuscript Library, Butler Library, Columbia University, New York, New York (38, 83, 84, 139, 160)

Concordia   Concordia University Library, Montreal, Quebec (69)

Delaware   Special Collections, University of Delaware Library, Newark, Delaware (93)

Harvard   Houghton Library, Harvard University, Cambridge, Massachusetts (28, 89, 95, 125, 155)

Indiana   Lilly Library, Indiana University, Bloomington (20, 31)

Iowa   University of Iowa Libraries, Iowa City (140)

Kent State	Special Collections, University Libraries, Kent State University, Kent, Ohio (148)
Lakehead	The Chancellor Paterson Library Archives, Lakehead University, Thunder Bay, Ontario (74)
Manitoba	Department of Archives and Special Collections, University of Manitoba Libraries, Winnepeg (91)
Minnesota	Manuscript Division, University of Minnesota Libraries, St. Paul (23)
Newberry	Special Collections, The Newberry Library, Chicago, Illinois (15)
New York Public Library	Henry W. and Albert A. Berg Collection, New York Public Library, New York (29)
Northwestern	Special Collections Department, Northwestern University Library, Evanston, Illinois (24)
Pennsylvania	Special Collections, University of Pennsylvania Library, Philadelphia (9, 10)
Princeton	Princeton University Library, Princeton, New Jersey (9)
Raleigh	North Carolina State Archives, Raleigh (35, 70, 71)
Reed	Special Collections, Eric V. Hauser Memorial Library, Reed College, Portland, Oregon (82)
San Diego	Archive for New Poetry, University Library, University of California, San Diego (64, 87, 166)
Simon Fraser	Contemporary Literature Collection, Bennett Library, Simon Fraser University, Burnaby, British Columbia (104, 106, 118, 154)
Southern Illinois	Morris Library, Southern Illinois University, Carbondale (33, 36)
Stanford	Stanford University Libraries, Stanford, California (107, 143, 158)

Stony Brook   Frank Melville Jr. Memorial Library, State University of New York at Stony Brook (36, 51, 92, 123, 129)

Storrs   Special Collections Department of the Thomas J. Dodd Research Center, University of Connecticut, Storrs (passim)

Texas   Harry Ransom Humanities Research Center, University of Texas, Austin (33, 48)

UCLA   University Research Library, University of California, Los Angeles (44)

Utah State   Special Collections and Archives, Merrill Library, Utah State University, Logan (41)

Vassar   Special Collections, Vassar College Libraries, Poughkeepsie, New York (22)

Washington University   Olin Library, Washington University, St. Louis, Missouri (135, 137)

Wesleyan   Olin Library, Wesleyan University, Middletown, Connecticut (3, 168)

Yale   Beinecke Library, Yale University, New Haven, Connecticut (7, 8, 14, 72)

A Chronology of Charles Olson's Life and Correspondence

1910   Born 27 December in Worcester, Massachusetts; son of Charles (formerly Karl) Joseph Olson, who was brought as an infant from Sweden, and Mary Theresa Olson (née Hines), daughter of immigrants from southern Ireland. He was raised as an only child in a "three decker" tenement in Worcester. From 1915 the family spent summers in the seaside fishing town of Gloucester, Massachusetts. Very few of Olson's letters to his parents are known; see letter 2, to Homer and Viola Barrett.

1917–1928   Attended Abbott Street Grammar School and Classical High School in Worcester, graduating president of his class. He then took a ten-week trip to Europe as a result of a national oratorical contest. See letter 62, to the school, and letter 159, to teacher Anna Shaughnessy.

1928–1932   Attended Wesleyan University, Middletown, Connecticut, majoring in English. For Olson's intellectual and extracurricular interests, see letter to the Rhodes Scholarship Committee. He met Barbara Denny during the Christmas holiday of his freshman year. His sole existing letter to her was copied into a notebook; see letter 5.

Summer 1931   Spent this summer—and the subsequent three summers—as a substitute letter carrier in Gloucester. This is the subject of letter 1, to his father.

1932–1933	Spent M.A. year at Wesleyan under the direction of Wilbert Snow, professor of English. Almost forty Olson letters to Snow, spanning a lifetime, are archived at the Wesleyan library; see letters 3 and 168. Olson's M.A. thesis, "The Growth of Herman Melville," acknowledged help from an interview with Carl Van Doren. Several subsequent letters thank Van Doren for continued support; see letter 9.
1933–1934	Supported by research funds from Wesleyan, contacted Melville's granddaughters, Mrs. A. D. Osborne, of East Orange, New Jersey, who supplied crucial Melville volumes, and Eleanor Melville Metcalf, of Cambridge, Massachusetts. Many letters from Mrs. Metcalf exist at Storrs, but, except for occasional carbon copies (see letter 25), Olson's letters have not been located. During spring 1934 Olson roomed in Cambridge with ex-Wesleyan John Finch. Olson's letters to Finch have not been preserved, except for letter 4.
1934–1936	Taught English at Clark University, Worcester; see letter 6, to Anne Bosshard, which also mentions the memorable three weeks Olson spent as a member of a swordfishing crew out of Gloucester.
August 1936	Met Edward Dahlberg in Gloucester; see letters 27 and 33. Both sides of the emotional and confrontational Olson-Dahlberg correspondence from 1936 through 1955 have been published in *In Love, In Sorrow.*
September 1936	Entered Harvard University as a graduate student in the English department; hired as a teaching assistant to William Ellery Sedgwick. No letters to Sedgwick are known to exist at present.
December 1936	Visited New York City and met Alfred Stieglitz (see letter 14) and Waldo Frank (see letter 10). Sixteen letters to Frank are housed at the University of Pennsylvania library.
Summer 1937	Finished paper on Melville and Shakespeare for F. O. Matthiessen. Through a smattering of letters, the

	teacher and his student kept in touch until Matthiessen's death in 1950; see letter 8.
September 1937	Returned to Harvard as a graduate student in the new American Civilization Program and a tutor in John Winthrop House. Olson took the famous "Westward Movement" course from Frederick Merk, professor of history. Carbon copies of three letters to Merk exist at Storrs; see letter 67.
November 1937	Met in Cambridge with Dorothy Norman, who was preparing the first issue of *Twice A Year,* in which Olson's essay "Lear and Moby Dick" appeared. Yale has many Olson letters to Norman up to 1946; see letter 7.
September 1938	Started final year at Harvard. Olson was awarded a Guggenheim Fellowship with the backing of Van Wyck Brooks (see letter 9); he spent it in Gloucester, working on a major book on Melville that he later discarded.
May 1940	Met two people of future importance to him: the artist Corrado Cagli (letters are unavailable at present) and his wife-to-be Constance Wilcock; see letter 11.
November 1940	Moved to New York City to look for work. Met Melville scholar Merton Sealts; see letter 57. The correspondence between Olson and Sealts was published and discussed by Sealts in his *Pursuing Melville, 1940–1980.*
1941–1942	Worked in New York for the American Civil Liberties Union and, subsequently, the Common Council for American Unity; see letter 13, to the Office of Strategic Services, for details.
1942–1944	Worked for the Foreign Language Division, Office of War Information, Washington, D.C. Here he met, among others, Ruth Benedict (one letter is in the Vassar archive; see letter 22) and Adam Kulikowski (some copies of letters survive; see letter 21). Olson collaborated with Ben Shahn on a pamphlet, *Spanish Speaking Americans in the War* (Office of the

Coordinator of Inter-American Affairs, 1943), and became a close friend; see letter 39, selected from the eleven letters to Shahn in the Archives of American Art.

July–
December 1944

Worked as an employee of the Democratic National Committee, first at the national convention in Chicago, then on the "Everybody for Roosevelt" election rally in Madison Square Garden, then at the party's winter headquarters in Key West, Florida. For Olson's work on party matters, see letter 19, to Senator Hannegan.

January 1945

Decided on a career as a writer; wrote the poem "The K" celebrating that decision. In April 1945, Olson moved from Florida to a permanent base: 217 Randolph Place N.E., Washington, D.C.

August 1945

Finished *Call Me Ishmael*. "First Fact" was written during a visit to New Bedford and Nantucket. See letter 17, to William H. Tripp, curator of the Old Dartmouth Whaling Museum.

January 1946

Through publisher James Laughlin, made the first of twenty-two visits over the next two years to Ezra Pound at St. Elizabeths; see letter 18, to Winfred Overholser and Mary Rudge. Olson had worried about Pound's arrival (see letter 15, to Malcolm Cowley) and had written his piece on Pound, "This Is Yeats Speaking," which was published in *Partisan Review* (winter 1946). Pound expanded Olson's contacts, including short-term connections such as John Berryman (see letter 23) and Douglas Fox (see letter 26), and long-term friends such as Caresse Crosby (see letter 36) and Laughlin himself (see letter 164). See also letter 20, to Pound.

March–
April 1946

Visited New York, with Connie, as a lobbyist for Polish interests; see letter 16, to Oscar Lange. Signed a contract with Reynal and Hitchcock for *Call Me Ishmael* (officially published 17 March 1947), and formed a lasting friendship with Monroe Engel, editor for that book and the later unfinished "Red,

	White, and Black"; see letter 28, one of the many letters to Engel at Harvard.
June 1946	Began correspondence with Jay Leyda on Leyda's *Melville Log;* see letter 44, one of twenty-five Olson letters in the Leyda archive at UCLA.
June 1947	Visited Gloucester. A lunch with Alfred Mansfield Brooks, the local historian, is taken to mark the beginning of the *Maximus* poems (letter 94).
July–September 1947	Invited to the Northwest Writers' Conference in Seattle. Olson, with Connie, shared a ride to the West Coast via Yellowstone Park. They then went to San Francisco, meeting Muriel Rukeyser (one letter is known; see letter 29), Kenneth Rexroth (no letters are known to exist at present), and Robert Duncan (over fifty letters are at Buffalo; see letters 68 and 149). Olson then traveled to Hollywood, meeting Robert Payne, who later visited Olson at Black Mountain; he published "The Kingfishers" in *Montevallo Review* (summer 1950). Letters to Payne are available mainly at Stony Brook; see letter 36.
October 1947–January 1948	Stayed on to research Gold Rush manuscripts at Berkeley and Sacramento. Olson's edition of *The Sutter-Marshall Lease* was published in 1948 by the Book Club of California. From California, Olson submitted a proposal to the Guggenheim Foundation for a project on the American West; see letter 28, to the Guggenheim Foundation, and letter 30, to Monroe Engel. During this period, Olson wrote his first letter to Frances Boldereff (29 December 1947) in reply to her inquiry; see letters 46 and 162. Both sides of this emotional and intellectually productive correspondence are at Storrs and are now published.
February 1948	Returned to Washington, D.C., by train, and made two visits to Pound before their final break-up; see letter 31.
May 1948	Received proofs of *y & x,* a volume of Olson's poems and drawings by Cagli, from Caresse Crosby's Black Sun Press; the official publication date was 1 February 1949.

July 1948	Stayed in Philadelphia for the Democratic Party's national convention, which was Olson's last fling in politics. At the Art Gallery he was impressed by the work of Sienese painter Giovanni di Paolo, as described in letter 33, to Edward Dahlberg and Caresse Crosby.
October 1948	Received help from Henry Murray toward a doctor's fee for treating Connie following a miscarriage. Nineteen letters to Murray dated from 1946 through 1953 are deposited at Storrs; most address Murray's psychological approach to Melville. See letters 34 and 55. Olson's first appointment as a visiting lecturer at Black Mountain College (BMC), 12–16 October. This was followed by seven more monthly visits during the academic year; see letter 35, to Josef Albers.
March–May 1949	Worked intensively on "The Kingfishers" and "The Praises." Glimpses of this effort appear in letter 36, to Crosby and Robert Payne, and letter 37, to Kitue Kitasono.
June 1949	Met Vincent Ferrini, on a visit to Gloucester; see letter 42, to Ferrini.
July–August 1949	Taught a summer session course at BMC titled "Verse and Theatre." Olson wanted Michael Lekakis to orate in the original Greek as part of a summer production, but this plan failed; see letter 40, from the eleven in the Archives of American Art.
October 1949	Was the best man at the wedding of his friend Jean Riboud. See letter 39, to Shahn; no letters to Riboud known at present.
April–May 1950	Wrote first letters to Robert Creeley, which helped with the revision of the "Projective Verse" essay; see letter 43. The exchange of letters—Olson's are now deposited at Stanford University—is being published in multiple volumes by Black Sparrow Press.
October 1950	Began correspondence with Cid Corman, which led to Olson's being "featured" in the first issue of Corman's *Origin* (April 1951) and several others; see letter 48. Olson's many letters at Texas have been

	joined with Corman's at Storrs in *Charles Olson and Cid Corman: Complete Correspondence 1950–1964*.
January 1951	Departed for Mexico. The death of Olson's mother on Christmas Day 1950 delayed the trip by several weeks; see letter 49, to Rainer Gerhardt.
February–July 1951	Contacted a number of experts about glyphs and sites while in Mexico, including Tulane University's Robert Wauchope; see letter 50. Olson kept track of his Washington house through Frank Moore (letter 56 is from about half a dozen in possession of the recipient), and he kept in touch with Black Mountain College mainly through Fielding Dawson (letter 51 is from the archive of over twenty letters at Stony Brook). From Olson's correspondence during his five months in Lerma, Campeche, Creeley selected a number that were published as *Mayan Letters.*
July 1951	Returned to BMC. He contacted Shahn, resident artist at the college, and through him approached a foundation about funding the college's future; see letter 53, to Shahn and W. H. Ferry.
August 1951	Composed *Letter for Melville 1951*, which was printed at Black Mountain and sent to a meeting of Melville scholars in Pittsfield on Labor Day. Henry Murray's talk on that occasion produced a strong reaction from Olson; see letter 55, to Murray.
October 1951	Daughter Kate born on 23 October; see letter 55, to Murray, letter 133, to Constance Bunker, and letter 161, to Kate Olson.
May 1952	Began plans for the Institute of the New Sciences of Man by inviting Carl Sauer to lead it; see letter 47. Nine Olson letters to Sauer, now at Berkeley, were published in *New World Journal* (spring 1979).
October–November 1952	On leave of absence from BMC, at the Washington house; Connie stayed at Black Mountain in a trial separation. Olson wrote almost daily; see letter 59.
December 1952–March 1953	Invited Carl Jung to the Institute of the New Sciences of Man; Marie-Louise von Franz came; see letter 60. Christopher Hawkes and Edgar Anderson were

invited, but could not come; see letter 61. In the midst of the institute lectures, *In Cold Hell, In Thicket* arrived from Mallorca, published there by Creeley to Olson's complete satisfaction.

April 1953 — Vincent Ferrini's magazine *Four Winds,* nos. 2/3, published "Maximus Letter 3" and set Olson off on a flurry of activity on the *Maximus* series. The manuscript for *Maximus 1–10* was completed and sent to Jonathan Williams in Stuttgart, Germany; it was published there in November 1953. See letter 63 to Williams, from about one hundred letters deposited at Buffalo.

June 1953 — Began correspondence with the British Melville scholar Ronald Mason, an exchange that continued through the end of the year. Ten substantial letters are archived at Storrs; see letter 66.

September 1953 — Began correspondence with Canadian poet Irving Layton, who was invited to BMC but whose visit was prevented by U.S. immigration laws. Olson was to have been invited to Canada (see letter 69, from the nine at Concordia; these were printed in *Line* in 1989). He did not have that opportunity until April 1960. See letter 74, to Raymond Souster, selected from fifteen letters at Lakehead. See also letter 91, to Kenneth McRobbie.

March 1954 — Evicted from his Washington, D.C., house. He was appointed rector of Black Mountain College; Creeley arrived to teach. Great efforts were made to keep the college viable; for example, Olson sought approval from the U.S. government to enroll Korean veterans under the G.I. Bill; see letter 70, to the Department of Public Instruction, letter 71, to Gerald van de Wiele, and letter 72, to William Carlos Williams.

September 1954 — Traveled to Boston to read at the Charles Street Meeting House. John Wieners was there, and he later came to BMC; see letter 86. The next day Olson gave a reading in Gloucester; see letter 73, to Ferrini. Olson had with him copies of *Maximus Poems 1–10* and the first two issues of the *Black Mountain Review.*

May 1955   Charles Peter Olson born on 12 May to Betty Kaiser, a student at BMC.

July–
September 1956   Continued as rector for BMC's last quarter; see letter 76, to Edward Marshall. *Maximus Poems 11–22* arrived from the publisher.

January 1957   Wrote "The Librarian." Olson kept in touch on the subject of dreams with former BMC student Michael Rumaker; see letter 79, from over twenty deposited at Storrs.

February–
March 1957   Traveled by train with Betty and Charles Peter to San Francisco; here he gave a lecture titled "Special View of History" and read at the Poetry Center. Returned via Albuquerque, to visit Creeley. See letter 77, to Ruth Witt-Diamant.

August 1957   Finished closing down BMC, then moved with his family to 28 Fort Square in Gloucester. Olson began afresh on new *Maximus* poems; see letter 80, to Ferrini, letter 81, to Betty Olson, and letter 99, to Wesley Huss.

November 1957   Met Robin Blaser in Cambridge; see letter 78, from about twenty-five letters in Blaser's possession.

February 1958   *Call Me Ishmael* reissued by Grove Press through the agency of Donald Allen, who printed "The Lordly and Isolate Satyrs" in *Evergreen Review* and many of Olson's later works; see letter 90, from about 130 letters to Allen deposited at Storrs.

March 1959   Met Allen Ginsberg and Gregory Corso at their reading in Boston; see letter 83. The ten letters to Ginsberg at Columbia span the years 1957 to 1966; no letters to Corso are known at present.

April 1959   Answered query from English poet Elaine Feinstein; this letter was published with "Projective Verse" by LeRoi Jones. An addendum was written, although it may not have been sent; see letter 85. Columbia also has eleven letters to Gael Turnbull, the Scottish

	poet and editor of *Migrant,* from about this time; see letter 84.
November 1959	Received visits in Gloucester from Michael McClure (see letter 88), Philip Whalen (see letter 82, from the collection at Reed College), and LeRoi Jones, a very close associate until 1965 (see letter 104).
May 1960	Included in *New American Poetry* (ed. Donald Allen). *The Maximus Poems* (the Jargon-Corinth edition) was in preparation; see letter 84.
September 1960	Gave a reading at Hammond's Castle, Gloucester. A local artist, Harry Martin, was present; see letter 111, from the six letters at Storrs.
December 1960– February 1961	Joined in psilocybin experiments with Timothy Leary; see letter 101. *The Distances* published by Grove Press.
February 1962	Gave a reading at Harvard University; see letter 95, to Harry Levin.
December 1962	Sent first letter to *Gloucester Daily Times;* see letters 120 and 151. Olson's seventeen letters to the editor of the local newspaper are collected in *Maximus to Gloucester.*
July– August 1963	Taught summer school at the University of British Columbia, Vancouver, along with Creeley, Ginsberg, Duncan, Whalen, Denise Levertov, and Margaret Avison; no letters to the latter two exist; see letter 98, to Vancouver poet George Bowering.
September 1963	Joined the English department of the State University of New York at Buffalo; see letter 119, to the chairman Albert Cook, letter 105, to Mac Hammond, and letter 103, to Ralph Maud. Olson organized summer teaching for LeRoi Jones, Edward Dorn, and Robert Kelly (see letter 100). He wrote a review of Eric Havelock's *Preface to Plato* for *Niagara Frontier Review,* no. 1; see letter 102, to Havelock, and letter 110, to Harvey Brown.
March 1964	Betty Olson died in an automobile accident near their residence in Wyoming, New York; see letter 107, to Robert Creeley and Vincent Ferrini.

April 1965	John Wieners and Ed Sanders gave a reading in Buffalo. Letter 129, to Sanders, is one of two at Stony Brook; nineteen exist at Simon Fraser.
June–July 1965	Traveled to Italy for the Festival of Two Worlds, Spoleto, where he met the guest of honor, Ezra Pound. Thence to Bled, Yugoslavia, for a P.E.N. conference. Olson returned to the United States via Rome; see letter 113, to Mary Shore and Vincent Ferrini.
July–August 1965	Traveled to California for the Berkeley Poetry Conference; here he met Suzanne Mowat (see letter 114, from the collection of seventeen deposited at Storrs). Olson's recorded lecture was transcribed and published as *Causal Mythology* in 1969, and the evening reading as *Reading at Berkeley;* see letter 139. *Human Universe and Other Essays* was published in San Francisco by Auerhahn Press (it was published later in paperback by Grove Press).
September 1965	Returned to Buffalo, but was back in Gloucester within two weeks. Olson left John Clarke in charge of his seminars; see letter 116. Students who kept in touch included Albert Glover (see letters 115 and 116), Andrew Crozier (see letter 118), George Butterick (see letter 152), and Robert Hogg (see letter 127).
March 1966	Film crew from National Education Television shot a segment of "Poetry: U.S.A." in Gloucester for broadcast 4 September 1966.
August 1966	The small, beautiful volume *'West'* arrived in Gloucester from the editor of Goliard Press, the poet Tom Raworth; see letter 132.
October 1966	Left for Liverpool and London with Panna Grady; see letter 141.
December 1966	Traveled to Berlin for a reading organized by Olson's German translator, Klaus Reichert (letters not available).
February–March 1967	*Call Me Ishmael* was reissued by City Lights; see letter 124, to Lawrence Ferlinghetti. *Selected Writings* was edited by Creeley and published by New Directions;

see letter 147, to Donald Sutherland. Olson visited Jeremy Prynne (see letter 130; the mass of this correspondence is in possession of the recipient) and Edward Dorn, visiting lecturer at the University of Essex (see letter 131, from the collection of over one hundred deposited at Storrs). He also made a five-week trip to Dorchester, Dorset, for research on the *Maximus* series.

June–July 1967   Flew back to the United States and went on to Oxford, Ohio, to see Joyce Benson; see letter 134, from some twenty-seven deposited at Storrs. He returned to London for the International Poetry Festival on 12 July.

October 1967   Gave a reading at Cortland, New York; see letter 146, to Harvey Brown.

December 1967   Entrusted to Cape Goliard in England the publishing of *Maximus IV, V, VI;* see letter 154, to Barry Hall.

January 1968   Visited by George Butterick in Gloucester researching his *Guide to the Maximus Poems* (University of California Press, 1978). Olson was working on "A Plan for the Curriculum of the Soul," which was published by Butterick in *Magazine for Further Studies,* no. 5 (Buffalo, July 1968); see letter 152.

March 1968   Visited Beloit College, Wisconsin, to present a series of lectures; see letter 145, to Beloit professor Chad Walsh. Olson's lectures were edited posthumously as *Poetry and Truth.*

April 1968   Last visit to West Coast; returned via Tucson as a guest of Drummond Hadley (no letters are available at present).

June 1968   Hospitalized for two weeks. Ann Charters visited Gloucester for her book *Olson/Melville: A Study in Affinity* (1968), in which she quotes some letters.

July 1968–
August 1969   Spent his last months in Gloucester. Olson had many visitors during this period. During 1968 they included Alasdair Clayre from the BBC on 27 July; Inga Lovén from Sweden in mid August (see letter 171); and Jack Kerouac on about 17 August (no letters). Visitors in

1969 included Barry Miles in late January, who recorded a tape for Apple Records, London, that was eventually released as a Folkways LP (see letter 160); an M.A. student, Andrew S. Leinoff in early April (interview was transcribed in *Olson*, no. 8 [fall 1977], pp. 66–107); Gerard Malanga for a *Paris Review* interview on 15 April (transcription in *Muthologos*); Elsa Dorfman, to take photographs, on 25 May; Ralph Maud on 6 June; Edward and Jenny Dorn in mid August; and Charles Stein in late August.

Gloucester companions of these months included Gerrit Lansing (no letters are available at present), Joseph Garland (see letter 156), Thorpe Feidt (see letter 153), Vincent Ferrini (see letter 165), Peter Anastas (see letter 169), and Harvey Brown, who had taken up residence at nearby West Newbury (see letter 170).

September 1969   Arranged to meet Charles Boer in Cambridge and was driven down to Connecticut. Letters to Boer are quoted in his *Charles Olson in Connecticut* (1975).

October–November 1969   Taught a graduate seminar for eight weeks at the University of Connecticut at Storrs. He was admitted to a local hospital on 1 December. See letter 172.

January 1970   Died in a New York City hospital on 10 January from cancer of the liver. Buried in the cemetery in Gloucester after a memorial service on 13 January.

I

The first letter was written in June 1931, at the end of Olson's third year at Wesleyan University in Middletown, Connecticut. He graduated the following year and stayed on to complete an M.A. on Melville in June 1933. His first teaching job, from 1934 through 1936, was at Clark University, in his home town of Worcester, Massachusetts.

Olson's father, Charles (formerly Karl) Joseph Olson, had come from Sweden as a babe in arms. Olson's mother, Mary Theresa Olson (née Hines), was the daughter of Irish immigrants. Annually from the age of five, Olson spent summers with his mother in the fishing town of Gloucester, Massachusetts, while his father continued his post office work in Worcester, coming to Gloucester on weekends and for his two weeks' annual holiday.

Olson, an only child, was born 27 December 1910. He was therefore twenty years old at the time of the first letter.

To Charles Joseph Olson (1931)

Except for dutiful letters from Europe during his trip upon graduating from high school in the summer of 1928, Olson's letters to his parents have not generally been preserved, apart from occasional Mother's Day and birthday missives and the letter to his father presented below. This letter celebrates a significant milestone: the son is following in his father's footsteps by becoming a summer substitute letter carrier in Gloucester, the job that Charles Joseph Olson did full time in Worcester, Massachusetts.   *Letter at Storrs.*

[letterhead]
The Wesleyan Argus, Charles John Olson, "Editorial Writer."

June 9, 1931
Tuesday night!

!Dearest Dad!

!!! I was baptized into the service today—and what a baptism!! Talk about the doctrine of immersion! Why, this baptism was a dousing!! Yup, I went over the route this afternoon! In the worst downpour ever known around these parts! Gosh, was I soused!! But it's just as well to get the worst first—and the rest will follow. I got here and Homer, Mrs. B and Mother met me at 12:30. Up at 7:30, pouring cats & dogs, I got over the office about 8:45. Drohan showed me around and of course they all had a laugh over my height. Then, when the P.M. arrived I got the certificate for my physical and went over and saw the doc, who made it out in 10 mins, and gave me "First Class." Then I had my finger prints taken which was a horrible job. And I was through at 11. But I was to report back at 2:00 to go over the route with a regular named Charley Noble. Can you guess? A summer route! It's first delivery today! Fernwood—over back of West Gloucester Station, Winniahdin and Little River. Long walks between stops but a good route for me for the summer, I think—outdoors, good leg training and I can work the route out myself instead of stepping into a regular's place. My desk is next to Billy Maister's. They gave me a new bag. Net pay down here learning the route. I punch the clock tomorrow for the first time at 7:30.

And I go out alone! Oh, boy, what a time I'll have trying to find these summer cottages and the people in 'em. But it'll be great fun anyhow.

And they require a white collar—so Mother's going to fix one tomorrow while I wear the blue. Drohan said it would be O.K.—I kicked around with the carriers today. The fact that they know you're a carrier makes it easier for me, I think. Poor Freary Hodgkins has to relinquish his title of tallest man in the last 25 yrs! They put us up to each other right off.—Tomorrow morning I breeze out in my new uniform!

Things are O.K. here—Mother's got over the depression she was in, like all general business conditions. She wishes you could get that clothes tree up in the attic and send it down—it would be a great help on rainy days like today. The bed arrived and it's a honey, although there were no bolts & I'll be damned if I see how it goes together.

It was great of you to come down last night. I hope you didn't mind the cahoots.—And Dad, those three books in the box are Worcester Public Library—will you bring them back immediately? Thanks a lot. And if you could send the rest of the stuff in there I'd appreciate it.

Well, I only got 6 hours sleep last nite—I think I'll go and knock some off now—it'll be a great experience tomorrow—and pray to God it stops raining—oh, oh, oh—

Your loving son,

Charles

The bolts—4—should be $\frac{3}{8}''$ to $\frac{1}{2}''$ diameter and about $2\frac{1}{2}''$ or more long—nuts also necessary—huh-huh.

C.J.

According to George Butterick in his introduction to Olson's *The Post Office,* Olson's father later that summer "secretly arranged it that he might appear unexpectedly in full uniform in Gloucester to help make the rounds with his son, to the delight of their friends and patrons" (p. ix).

2

To the Rhodes Scholarship Committee (1931)

This application for a Rhodes Scholarship is undated, but must have been written at the beginning of Olson's senior year at Wesleyan, probably in October 1931. Olson was unsuccessful, a runner-up to his classmate John A. Wells.

Letter (carbon copy) at Storrs.

Gentlemen of the Committee:

The tangible reality of culture in itself still remains an ideal which I cannot—nor do I wish to—cast aside. I have desired not narrow "kultur" but culture in its wider sense, the all-embracing culture that makes a man broad minded but critical, intelligent but democratic, aesthetic but not effeminate. This has been the fountain head of my desire for education. It has carried me this far and it is what, when everything else is stripped off, impels me to seek a Rhodes Scholarship. Even from the first day in high school the idea of not going to college never entered my head in spite of the fact I had no finances to expect. So it has been in college—although I have supported myself almost entirely, by scholarships and work, the thought of not doing graduate work never seemed to receive any consideration. My aim in life is to secure a cultural education and then spend the rest of my life imparting that knowledge and interpreting other knowledge to other young men.

Because of that ambition I have never restricted myself to studies. I have not even restricted myself to one other activity. It may sound like trite and sentimental blubbering to say that I have always loved school, but it is the only way to express it. I have never found a subject, in arts or science, that has not held some kernel of interest for me. So it has been in my extra-curriculum activities. But this general interest and love has always pointed up, so to speak, the English language and English and American literature as my particular field. It has been my "major" in college and it would be my course of study at Oxford. I would take my finals in the Honour School of English Language and

Literature, taking the course of study marked (2) on page 94 of "Oxford of Today." College teaching is the vocation I have chosen.

It is interesting to trace, then, the way the general desire for a cultural education and the more specific interest in English led my activities. My pursuits in high school were extended into all lines of extra-curriculum work with the emphasis on public speaking and debating. The latter was practically the "football" of the school and through it I achieved the presidency of the Student Body and of the senior class. In my last year there I competed in the National Oratorical Contest, winning the Northeastern States Zone championship and placing third in the national finals in Washington. This speech training, obviously part of any professor of English's equipment, I have continued in college not because it is part of my "work" but because it holds more fascination to me than any other activity. I enjoy—perhaps to a fault—any good argument. Whether it is on a platform or in the opprobrious "bull sessions" I like to argue. There is no better training of the mind in clarity of thought and expression than public speaking. Wesleyan has given me experience and coaching. I have debated two years on the 'varsity team. We were undefeated last year, winning the Eastern Intercollegiate Championship. I engaged in contests with Yale, Princeton, Oberlin, and Williams. Offices have come along as a result: the Vice-Presidency of the Eastern Intercollegiate Debate League, the Presidency of the Wesleyan Debate Council, and Secretary of Delta Sigma Rho. Seven years of this work have only increased my desire to go on with it.

As a result of this voice practice in high school I was cast as Sganarelle in Molière's "Le Médecin Malgré Lui" the first month I was in college. Dramatics has been second only to my debating in college. I have engaged in eight productions. Two summers ago I attended for ten weeks and received a degree from the Gloucester School of the Little Theatre. Since then I have handled make-up for the dramatic organization here, the Paint and Powder Club, directed shows and last spring was made president of the Club. Here again is a field for cultural development. The future of the American theatre lies in the college dramatic groups. With a view to making some small contribution to the American scene we have planned four productions this year, solely indigenous plays starting with "Fashion" of 1854 and ending with one of O'Neill's.

Of course the spoken word is only one half the story. I have endeavored not to neglect the written word. I have been editorial writer of the Argus, the bi-weekly college newspaper, since last February which has given me another chance to "let off steam" and, at times, to perpetrate some intellectual atrocities. With no deliberate purpose, therefore, my intellectual pursuits—debating, dramatics, news writing and editorial work—have conformed in great measure to my desires.

On entering college one side—and an important one—had remained undeveloped. In the high school I came from physical training resolved itself into cutting the air with wands and dumb-bells for five minutes and playing helter-skelter basketball for ten. I had never received any serious body development. I resolved to get it in college. Lack of coordination and a slow reaction time has to be overcome. Freshman year I went out for track and basketball with no success. Sophomore year I made the soccer and swimming squads. Last year I played 'varsity goalie in soccer, winning my "W" and remained on the swimming squad. I enjoy competitive sport not only for the development it gives you but also for the chance to meet men eager to win, clashing not only physically but also emotionally and mentally. I have always been out-of-doors. My father early ingrained a love of walking into my nature. Last summer, as a letter carrier, I used to tramp fifteen to twenty miles a day. I have played golf and tennis with average proficiency for years.

This recital of facts has been distasteful to me. I beg your indulgence if they have been "trivial" to you. They are important parts of my life, but I can see where they would be otherwise to you. Even in my own mind they cannot indicate what I have given and what I have received from college. For instance, they do not take into account my fraternity life. The chance to carry on and build up the ideals of my house, the chance to get to know and to gain the respect of my brothers, especially of my own delegation has been invaluable. I have had false pride knocked out of me. I have had foolish and small ideas cleared away. I have known the beauty of friendship and comradeship. It is with what I term a healthy pride that I tell you that I am chairman of the senior delegation which under our constitution governs the house. A fraternity becomes *the* community group in a college the size of Wesleyan and it is there that the college life and government centers. There is, however, a governing group known as the Senate of which I have been a member since last spring. This has resulted in two positions, the chairmanship of the Parley Committee and one of the two senior members of the Honor System Committee which tries all cases of dishonesty and, in conviction, recommends that men be dismissed. But student government here is on the wane. It seems to be a mark of our times. It can be tied up, I think, with the deplorable lack of interest on the part of American students in politics. Of course the obvious contrast is such an institution as we are applying for—Oxford. There it becomes in Union debates the very heart of the country but here the trained men turn aside into business law, the professions, and education. Students have no desire to train themselves in government. If it were not for my great love for teaching and the college community I should like to do something to remedy the situation. Obviously something has got to be done.

I have slighted my intellectual hobbies, I note. Probably the greatest one I have is reading. All my spare time I give to it, picking up whatever fits into my mood at the moment. A second interest that I have pursued since my contact freshman year with Jere Abbott, Assistant Director of the Modern Art Museum in New York, in a course he gave has been art in the stricter sense of painting, sculpture, and design. I have not sought the manual skill but rather the development of a critical and appreciative faculty. A third hobby has been writing for writing's sake, as a literary love rather than as a task. I have much to learn and far to go before I reach even a superior ability. And so on almost ad infinitum. Everything absorbs my attention. It is a tendency I have to fight against. I seem to want to "fly all over God's hebben." The last year has seen the more important things in my life precipitating out and I know the future will further this transition. I am determined to teach English in college. It is one of my most cherished ideals that married happiness is more truly possible in that society than in any other in our modern world. At Oxford I would aim at the B.A. in two years and go on for my B.Litt, Deo volente.

Gentlemen of the Committee, I rest my case. This self examination has been both a pleasure and a pain. I can safely say it has been one of the most difficult tasks I have ever attempted. It stands or falls by its own intrinsic worth. As Robert Emmet said as he closed his famous plea, "I have done."

Respectfully yours,

3

To Wilbert Snow (1932)

Wilbert Snow, a professor of English, a Democratic Party candidate, a published poet, and quite a character himself, was the mentor whom Olson was lucky enough to find waiting for him at Wesleyan. Snow, in a memorial of Olson, "A Teacher's View," in the *Massachusetts Review* (winter 1971), expressed himself as the lucky one:

> Few students ever made on me the impact that Charlie Olson did. He was an original thinker, a stutterer to the stars, and an endless dreamer. I knew him first as a debater when I coached the debating teams of the college. With his height of six feet eight inches, and his booming voice, he was so overpowering on the platform that the judges didn't dare give the decision to anybody else! In three years he lost only one debate. That was at Brown University in Providence, Rhode Island. He was so humiliated by this defeat that he refused to return to Wesleyan that night with the team. Instead he hired a taxi-driver to take him to his home in Gloucester, Massachusetts. He told the driver that Wesleyan would pay the bill. The price was a huge one, fifty or sixty dollars. The driver came to me. I went to President Mc-Conaughy. "Jim," I said, "he was workin' for the college, and you ought to pay this." But McConaughy teased me and needled me—for three weeks. Left me in hell for three weeks, purgatory anyhow. In the end McConaughy paid the bill.

The Brown debate was in February 1932. Olson wrote the following letter after his graduation and after a lethean summer in Gloucester. He was now beginning his work for an M.A. Snow would eventually see the Melville thesis through, but at the time of this letter, 16 October 1932, he is on sabbatical in Maine, at Spruce Head, his vacation home. Snow's *Down East,* published in 1932 by Gotham House, was preceded by two books of poems from Harcourt, Brace: *Maine Coast* (1923) and *The Inner Harbor* (1926). These and Snow's subsequent volumes are contained in *Collected Poems of Wilbert Snow* (1963).   *Letter at Wesleyan.*

Wesleyan—
Sunday, the 16th—
In a new stride

Dear Bill,

I have commenced a critical year with hope—and the trepidation of the child finding its first tottering steps—"sweet, small, clumsy feet." The past summer brought me "a change of life." I use the phrase advisedly—for it really was a creation of the new from the old. I have mulled over many of your ideas and your ideals. I have realized that for four years I have bolted my intellectual food. My intellectual I.F. (commonly known in modern advertising as "Intestinal Flora") has spread apace. What I needed—and I got gallons of it this summer!—was the acidophilus milk of contemplation. I've resolved upon a steady diet! I have been happier in my three weeks here—in spite of orientation to the new position of graduate student—because of a resulting slower pace.

Frankly, however, I miss you. There are no talks over "cokes." The inspiration of your intense interest is missing. Above all I wanted to work on my Master's thesis with you. This summer I got acquainted with a person by the name of Herman Melville, introduced to me through a story called "Moby Dick" and some short "Piazza Tales." Now I burn to know, to possess the man completely. With Woodbridge's rather enthusiastic approval I have decided to do my thesis on him. Homer is so burdened with work—owing to the sickness of Farley—that he cannot take me under his wing until you get back. He accepted the idea of Cowie acting until you return—presuming, of course, that you are willing to work the thesis on Melville out with me. You are, aren't you, Bill?

But, in your absence, I have had the warm, intimate touch of your eyes through the new book. It has been a beloved haven for me. "Down East" is far greater than either "Maine Coast" or "Inner Harbor" and I take up arms against a sea of critics that have so far let it pass unnoticed. It should send the belittlers of your poetic power scudding like yawls before the wind. With the strong local color of your first two books becoming the background, in the development of the personal, reflective poems of "Down East," to a more universal expression of your emotions and philosophy, you reach maturity. The most striking growth is in your ability to describe the sea and its effect on you. In your earlier work you often failed—there are metaphors and similes in such poems as "The Gulf Stream" and "Ocean Liner" that grate on the mind like a dory bottom on a rocky beach. To describe the sea to other people is the task of a genius. You achieve that power in "Down East"— "Coast Cathedral" is one of the most beautiful lyrics in the English language. That last line still sings through my head. The most significant part of the volume is the sonnet section. Your four earlier poems in this form were all of an extremely personal nature—particularly the lovely "Restoration" and the poignant "Margins." It is not without significance that three of the great personal poems of your new volume—"Clean as These Rocks," "Groundswell," and the superb "Valediction" are also in the sonnet group. It strikes me that the sonnet, allowing simplicity of language, personal revelation, and a meditative twist at the end is peculiarly fitted to your poetic genius. That is not to say that you will be confined in the "Sonnet's scanty plot of ground," for you will thrust aside the form as in "Poet's Knowledge" and in "Visitor" in "Inner Harbor" and as in perhaps your most beautiful poem, "And Must I Say Farewell." Oh, Bill, it is an incomparable volume—I love it. I return to it constantly.

Debating will get under way as soon as the E.I.D.L. gets the question arranged. Peter has been very kind in accepting whatever help I can offer. I've got Wood, Huntress, and White out for the first tryouts. We'll do our best, Bill.

And I've accepted the challenge of the Department—and my other critics! I am taking Dodd's composition course as six hours credit toward my M.A. I shall drive the stick through the vampire that has been sucking the life-blood of my reputation for over two years! It's a great class—Finch, Willson, Rome amongst others—and Dodd is excellent. He has the gift of not only perceiving what's wrong but also of being able to point it out clearly to the writer.

The year that is spread out before me calls me like our sea. I am anxious for February and your return. I look forward to the completion of my work. I fervently pray every night on retiring for a college job next year—the eternal optimist, Bill! I "itch" to teach. I long for the chance to let my mind mature. But I suppose the hope is futile.

Please remember me to Mrs. Snow and the boys.

Yours,

Charles Olson

4

To John Finch (1935)

From the platform of the Honors College, Wesleyan University, John Finch joined others on 18 November 1970 to remember his former roommate Charles Olson. He entitled his piece "Dancer and Clerk" when it was published in the *Massachusetts Review* (winter 1971) because his compatibility with Olson rested not only on literature—Finch went on to be professor of English at Dartmouth College—but also on vaudeville and ballet and a mutual sense of what Olson would later term *proprioception:* roommates knowing how to move in their interior spaces or enjoy hitchhiking together. The following is an extract headed "Letter to John Jl 25 35," as copied by Olson into his notebook at the time.

Notebook at Storrs.

God, how right, how goddamned right, achingly right you are about form, about control. Let's write a book about this America called "The Great Omission." Is there this great omission because there just ain't no "great tradition"? Is it because we're all what Wolfe insists we are, page after page after thousand page, strangers, without a home, restless wanderers, who squander all the richness of our land, who can find no angel, no leaf, no door to enter into, to find and know ourselves, our land, this red question mark called life, and mold it all into form by control and restraint until we have dignity, something called beauty, something good? Are you so sure it's acquired by one man all alone? Sprawl, that's been America. It's been Emerson, Melville, Whitman, Twain, Wolfe. When the best America's got comes out, it bursts and spatters like black oil struck in the Oklahoma fields. By the time it's harnessed and piped, controlled, the terrible fire, the lovely power, somehow, is gone. Perhaps it just *has* been that way and now we're old enough to get a code on our spiritual as well as our social forces. I don't know. I don't know any more what I think about it than I do what I think about Wolfe or about myself. One thing's sure: we see the lack and we better try to get control ourselves and pray to some sweet Christ we have something to control.

5

To Barbara Denny (1936)

Olson met Barbara Denny in Worcester in 1928, while home for Christmas vacation during his freshman year at Wesleyan University. She became, in the words of Tom Clark in *Charles Olson: The Allegory of a Poet's Life* (1991), "his first big flame" (p. 17): "Socially, she was of a totally different world, with a bloodline extending back to one of New England's oldest families, the Connecticut Griswolds (another member of the family owned an expensive Worcester jewelry shop)." They shared books and plays, but by the time of the letter below, dated 21 January 1936 in Olson's notebook (the letter itself is not extant), the relationship has wound down, though Olson is now back in Worcester, teaching at Clark University. *Notebook at Storrs.*

Jan 21, 1936.

You know the sluggishness in me too well to wonder why I haven't written before. I've kidded myself too long about how busy my work keeps me. If I can nurture conversation with anybody I'll nourish it to any hour; of course I talk better than I do anything else and when my tongue is loosed my brain rides briskly and clearly and with destination, and it's a truism that we enjoy doing that which we do best—in that is our ego-satisfaction. But I'm now painfully but happily aware that I often talk just to avoid making decisions, reading themes, writing letters—thinking.

This lack of will I've noticed for two years. At first I luxuriated in it, feeling that it was the natural reaction of my system to the pressure of the previous five years; but when it became worse and when I began to remember incident after incident, even during those previous five years, of decision-ducking on deeper issues than whether I should go after that job at Hazen's or apply for that Rhodes scholarship, I became worried. I guess it has been this worry over my will that has been at the bottom of my melancholy for the past year. It prompted those letters I wrote to you last summer. I know that now. I know also now that your answers were hard on the truth: I was indulging in the worst of all sins, self-pity. It's not two weeks ago I came to see this cheap, disgusting pity clearly; intuitively, out of love, you saw it long ago.

Nor am I out of the woods yet. I think (you see, I no longer "fear" and that's good, because when we fear we run and hide and I would, typically, hide in myself); I think I have naturally a weak will—Mary T. gave me that along with life. Moments like this (and they increase every day) I can look this fact square in the eye without blinking (as I could into your eyes before I hurt you). I can look at this natural glass chin of my will without going soft and sorry for myself. I no longer confuse my physical and mental energy with what we vaguely call will. A discipline from without has always been a necessity for me, a priming to get me to move and flow. That's what college was; that's what Melville was; that's what teaching is. Once started I can depend upon my physical and mental energy; God bless my father for that. But energy alone never made a whole man and to be a whole man, a rich human being, is my desire in life. The spaces in my backbone keep me from wholeness now.

Whether my marrow will toughen or not is up to me. I don't know whether I've got the guts to thicken that marrow. But I'm seeing myself more clearly every day; it's not a pleasant sight, especially to one of my egotism; the years of self-pity make it harder not to turn my eyes away, because it was so easy in those moods to adopt as myself the delusion so many people think is C.J.O., simply because of his personality and his tongue and his energy. But I continue to look now, falteringly, sometimes to turn away, but to come back again to stare steadily in upon myself. This encourages me. And something else encourages me. It is a discipline growing from within. This very discovery of the last two weeks—how long I reveled in self-pity—is a ring of growth. You know how slow I mature: I give the impression of seeing and being things long before I feel and am them. I was not truly disciplined before. But this new inner order sharpens my mind, sharpens my sight of contemporary life, of life itself, and sharpens my emotions. I could write of many things I perceive, that the cataract on the eye of self kept me from before.

But I'm still stumbling and this last month has been a struggle. I've sat for hours trying with a tough mind and heart to see this thing through, not in a maudlin way keening over myself and building wish dreams on my blown-up abilities as I used to. I haven't even allowed myself to escape into the false discipline of correcting papers. (This is mid-year, with 85 blue-books to be collected in half an hour; 85 research papers to be read, and 1000 back themes benignly squatting on their white asses in my office.) Only my sharpening sense of values directs me.

You can understand why I had to write to you like this. You're the only one to whom I could write all this. And I suppose it seems to you just another proof of what you've been writing me—that I'm cold, fishlike, self-centered, emotionless. Oh, God, I've been ahead of you on that. I sometimes startle myself at my hardness. But I think I'm honest to myself when I believe that rather than cutting down my emotions I've given them richer, stronger life by pruning away synthetic parasitic feelings, by lopping off dead sentimentality. It is quite true, for example, that my love for you is much finer, deeper, stronger now than ever. I knew that Christmas day. I know, too, that I can say it to you now without the irony of it hurting you.

To come to see and feel all this I had to get off by myself. I'm a lonely beast. I've had to lick my sores away from the pack. In that way I am, as I think you put it, "self-sufficient"; and because you are a woman and because you love me, you wanted to take me in your arms and help me; and my withdrawing into myself set your natural, beautiful desire and need at nought and you were hurt and you thought I was become a fish. Oh, God, I think not. It's a law of my being, this loneliness. It's probably my tragedy; certainly it's the tragedy of my existence with other humans. There's a check in me that keeps me from communicating with other people; and only by confessing can you get help. I have troubles, sex troubles you know of, out of which I know a good psychoanalyst could help me rise; but I cannot bring myself to it. I'm unnaturally fastidious about what is me. The presence of other people makes me competitive; usually I can dominate them, say, in conversation or reasoning, and then I feel good, afterwards to realize how easy the achievement was and how cheap my pleasure; sometimes I lose and then I am shattered, because my high regard for myself is destroyed. (I hope as I slough off the false conception of my abilities I spoke of above, this disappointment will no longer be so pathological.) But there is no doubt I'm always pitting myself against other people and comparing myself with them. Thus only when I'm alone can I get anywhere—and I've only been getting somewhere since I stopped sitting by myself, brooding, moaning over myself.

I've tried honestly to open myself tonight. This letter is the saying of what I've been thinking for a long time. If it were said to anyone but you, it would be a disgusting display. I've wanted to try to show you I'm not the bastard I've seemed to be. I couldn't have written it a month ago—I didn't see it; and before that I couldn't because I had reserves, even toward you. My fear of saying anything which would hurt you was a repression; that's what I mean by branches I've lopped off; if our love couldn't stand the hard-headed truth, it wasn't love. But tonight I've written straight, adding nothing to pump up the emotion or the expression of it, holding back nothing.

6

To Anne Bosshard (1936)

Anne Bosshard befriended Olson during his first year's teaching at Clark University, 1934–1935. She was the wife of a professor of German, Butterick informs us in his introduction to his printing of Olson's "Journal of Swordfishing Cruise, July 1936" in *Olson*, no. 7 (spring 1977), where he quotes part of this letter.   *Letter at Storrs.*

[letterhead]
CLARK UNIVERSITY
WORCESTER, MASSACHUSETTS

Monday, July 6

Anne—
    They call it luck. I don't know. My feelings are mixed. I know I'm excited. For tomorrow, or rather *this* morning, the hankerin' of years

ends—I ship as a hand aboard the Dora M. Hawes, to swordfish for at least two, probably three weeks down Georges Bank 300 or more miles to the east'ard of Boston. Swordfishing is the sportingest left, and the most dangerous. It's as close as you can come to old American whaling, what with a pulpit on the bowsprit with a harpooneer and his naked arm, masthead sights, and the chase. I got the chance to go only a few hours ago—thus the haste.

But it does mean that I shall not see you until the first of August and the postponement of your visit. Even in my excitement I regret this.

The apartment and its problems got settled on the Fourth—beyond my expectations. I sublet it to four old maids from someplace in Ohio, Softsands, I think, for the six weeks of summer school for more than we'd expected in rent for the whole summer! And how they quiver over your china, Anne. I think they'll eat off the table with their fingers they admire the china so and fear to chip it. You became so much a part of my apartment so generously it makes me happy.

Until August then, Anne. Remember me deeply to Hairi and thank him for his help, too, in the apartment.

With love,

Charles

Soon after his return, Olson reported to Anne Bosshard on his trip. He copied part of a letter to her into his notebook of the time, dating it 9 August 1936 (notebook at Storrs):

A full three weeks fore and aft, fore and aft, yes, on and under the plankings of a deck, sleeping in the peak of the fo'c'sle on a flat hard, pillowless mattress, walking the deck with legs which became prehensile, climbing the rigging with a body become all grip, to a masthead where the suspension is after five hours more than a gull-like clinging of the body to a wooden crosstree 75 ft from a wooden deck, when slowly, subtly, the body has slid away and I am extended infinitely, mystically in a sway over sea in air.

II

Olson's work on Melville's reading attracted the attention of F. O. Matthiessen, who brought Olson to Harvard University in the fall of 1936 for graduate work in English and American literature. In his subsequent years at Harvard, 1937–1939, Olson joined the newly created American Civilization program and completed coursework for a Ph.D. He was awarded a Guggenheim fellowship for 1939–1940, spending the year in Gloucester writing a book on Melville.

Having met in May 1940, the twenty-one-year-old Constance Wilcock, his wife-to-be, Olson decided he must look for a job, and he obtained short-term employment in New York City.

7

To Dorothy Norman (1938–1939)

The writer Edward Dahlberg, whom Olson met in Gloucester in 1936, introduced him to people in New York City, including Alfred Stieglitz, the renowned photographer, and Dorothy Norman, who was planning a new cultural magazine to be called *Twice A Year*. At the time of the first letter below (about 1 March 1938) Olson is in his second year at Harvard graduate school and moving in circles where he could be of help to an editor. Ralph Barton Perry might make available unpublished work from the papers of Charles S. Peirce. Alfred North Whitehead might be persuaded to write for the magazine. The second letter, of early October 1939, is not so heady. Olson has made solid progress. His seminal essay "Lear and Moby-Dick" had been included in the first issue of *Twice A Year* (fall–winter 1938), and he is now enclosing "Dostoevsky and the Possessed."   *Letters at Yale.*

                                        Cambridge
                                        March

Dear Dorothy Norman

   Thank you for the pleasure your letter gave me. It helps to know you liked the essay. To know you are heard is such a rare thing, God knows especially here in Cambritch. I am anxious to see the mss. and learn what youandEd suggest might be changed.

   I made a hurried trip to N.Y. this weekend. Don't think it strange I did not see you. My chance to see you was a visit to American Place and I had thought to find you there. I did find the Marins and Stieglitz and Stieglitz at one break in our conversation (as he revealed to me when he had put the receiver down) talking to you. I decided to wait until I had a real chance to see you. I hope to get back soon.

   Edward told me your plans for the magazine and it seems to me to shape itself around your original intensity beautifully. I am very excited about it. As I am about Dahlberg's triatic essay on the Poet and State. I read it as a whole and it seems to me his finest work. The three parts have each their own fluency. I think the "Thoreau" part the only true reading of the man which has been written. Of course this is so right, that

Dahlberg should touch the true tincture of Thoreau. The embrace is primary, out of time and space, for their temperaments are significantly consonant. Dahlberg has delivered Thoreau from the American scholars and their cheeping discord and established him in his context and concord with humanity. The ending of the Thoreau piece and the ending of both "hate and war", "superstition and image" sing the subtitle Dahlberg has planned to give the whole book "A Vision of An American Culture." I like to think of the "hate and war" section as a preamble; its compactness is artistically as subtle a form as Dahlberg has achieved. The form-idea-and-language, elliptical and stranded, is to me completely realized. Ultimately I feel it will prove to be actually the finest of all the three beautiful parts of this essay that seems to me one of the best I have ever read. In this essay of three parts—the man-symbol, the parable and the fact—Dahlberg's prose has a challenge of acclivity which is quite wonderful. His prose has now his own personal orbit. I found the reading of the essay very exhilarating.

But I found Edward himself torn. It worries me very much. He is deeply shaken, isn't he? Thank God he has the magazine you have made possible. It gives him a context with both tradition and the present which he as all of us needs but he more than most because of his intransigence. You should be blessed for bringing that magazine about. I myself am deeply happy to be a part of it.

I'll keep at Perry whenever I see him about the Peirce stuff. And oh, yes. I had dinner with Whitehead last week and talked for a couple of hours with him. He has asked me to see him again. At table I spoke to his wife about getting something from him. As I did to him. I shall hope to have a piece if the book he's working on is not too demanding or to him too solid a unit to be broken. If you plan to republish the Mosses essay of Melville Constable & Co have the rights. I explained all that to Dahlberg.

Well, I'll help in any other way I can. Just write me. And again thanks for your letter. I'll plan to see you soon and if you are in Boston please have dinner with me or something.

Sincerely,

Olson

Oceanwood Cottage
Stage Fort Ave
October

My dear Dorothy,

I wrote you a long letter a month ago, but the only thing I can con-
clude is that it got lost. I'm sorry, because in it I told you why I had
seemed abominably silent. For six months I was quite stupidly ill: actually in April suffered a nervous breakdown which put me to bed for
three months. But I've been working in spite of it. You see I have this
year free. In fact because you were so interested and because the publication of the Melville essay was so important to it, I planned to let you
know personally that I had received the Guggenheim, but it was the very
day it was announced to me that I went to the hospital! Oh, it was all so
stupid and really so unnecessary. I hope I'm out of it now and I want to
forget it. But I can't have you think my silence had any other cause.

And I did receive the spring copy of TAY: it was splendid. I fed upon
the architecture section. But of course what interested me most of all
was Williams' weather thing: I call it the best piece of aesthetic I've
seen. The word aesthetic is mean to put upon it. I shall be in N.Y. soon
and I should like to call on you, if I may. I have two or three friends
who are writing stuff I think you might be interested in. And I have a
couple of ideas for the magazine you might think worth something. I
do hope things are going well with it.

Out of the morass of the last half year has come a couple of chapters
of the Melville book—and this enclosed essay on Dostoevsky. This
Dostoevsky thing is the first writing I've sent out and I wanted you to
have it, if you could use it, for the fall number. I have like jobs as that in
the section on The Possessed, on the other ignored novels of D: Notes
From Underground, The Idiot, Diary of A Writer and The Raw Youth
especially; and if you were interested in this you'd not be publishing
something in a vacuum, for the others might follow. The present essay
is a kind of testament of my own faith and I'd like to get it in print this
fall, if possible, and I'd be terribly grateful for your answer about it.

I've just looked back into my files to see when I last heard from you
and I'm shocked to discover that still that ugly incident was present.

And so I'm more sorry than ever you did not get my letter a month ago, and sorry that this, my first word to you in so long, bridges a silence which goes back to that unfortunate thing. Please, Dorothy, do not think my silence was due to that.

I should like to be remembered warmly to Stieglitz when you see him. And take my warmest best wishes to yourself and the magazine.

As ever,

Charles John Olson

8

To F. O. Matthiessen (1939)

It was Professor Matthiessen who sought out Olson on hearing in the spring of 1934 that one of Melville's granddaughters had entrusted Olson with ninety-five of Melville's own books to use and then give to Harvard library. He borrowed Olson's notes on the annotations in the Emerson and Hawthorne volumes, for which favor Olson received a substantial footnote in Matthiessen's classic critical study *American Renaissance* when it came out in 1941. Meanwhile, Olson arrived at Harvard, and in one of Matthiessen's graduate courses he completed the first draft of what became "Lear and Moby-Dick," which was published in *Twice A Year* in 1938. Alone in Gloucester during his first Guggenheim year, Olson was thinking back on all this.   *Letters at Yale.*

Stage Fort   Gloucester
September 23

My dear Matty,

I have wanted to say hello to you many times, and now I shall, for September has had for many years a resonance of you for me. Your book's been in my mind, and I have a feeling it's done, and I wished you to know I welcome it. My own's a slow thing, and I still strive to give it wings. I find my method, and lose it again. Shakespeare usually recovers my prose: I found him again this summer as I did when I worked for you. But myself is still to be discovered, and I spend my days divulging me to myself! Who was it said "I know not myself what I shall sing, But only my song is ripening"? If it be a song!

I wanted to come to Kittery, if you would have me, but I've stayed on here in this room for months and worked. I was in Boston for a Sunday and saw John, and Ellery came in one night. Otherwise, like Virgil, I'm hoarse from long silence. The war's got confused with the Atlantic's spill upon the beach, down the hill from my window.

Do give me news of you, and of the book. And remember me to Russell,—and to lovely Kittery. I look forward to seeing you again.

Your friend,

Charles Olson

Oceanwood Cottage
Stage Fort Ave
Gloucester: Nov 11

My dear Matty,

Because I am sorry I did not follow my last note, I write you another, for I have missed seeing you. So many things come up, working like this, and I keep thinking of you and wanting to talk about them with you. The truth is the book's been moving so I decided not to move myself. For three months I've been working as I never have before, except that time I did that job for you, and it being two years later perhaps there's a little hope what's coming out of that work may be better. I'm at it night and day, and loving it. Everything is so concentrated and confining here it makes for that strait jacket you and I both know I need. Yes, my mother and I are still here in this winter-fragile cottage, with more air inside than out when it blows from the northwest, and, now the city has decided to fear a freeze, the water is gone!

I've been at those last thirty lean years of Melville's most of the time. I decided to see just what I thought and felt about them and write what I could make out of it. So it has been Battlepieces, Clarel, the Poems, and Billy! I hope to have a section done in a few days and then I shall be in Boston to do some work on the Mss. I hope then I may see you.

I almost phoned you one day two weeks ago to draw on your union knowledge when a strike I've interested myself in here threatened to break out, but the workers finally got a lawyer. That's been a fruitful part of these six months here, a closer participation in the life of the city than I've ever known before. As a letter carrier, of course, I knew the streets and the gossip, and fishing a bit likewise. But I've had occasion to help some of the workers here, especially over in my part of town, which is locally called "The Cut," and it, too, has helped steady me. And what a bad labor town it is! The Gorton-Pew Co and their slime of a president, Tom Carroll, have easily frightened a naturally conservative people into a fear of organization which is wide. But there's a strike on now amongst the Italian seiners which is strong: the Italians have a much more alive sense of right and fight than what are locally known as the "whites". That review I did of that Babson's book on Gloucester—the Wellesley "white" wise man of money—may have seemed libelous to Stewart Mitchell but as I go further into the economics of this poor town it becomes truer and truer!

Well, I see the fight goes on in Cambridge, and I've wondered what you were doing and wanted to hear the dope. And Matty: isn't the Dies Voorhis the Jerry I met at your place at Eliot House: if so, what about it? And I think and feel a hell of a lot about this war, and Mr Roosevelt's foreign policy—and Mr Streit's new Buchmanism: the class in this country that's going for Union Now is enough to set your teeth on edge like a radio.

I wish I'd had sense enough to ask you down earlier, but I did think I'd not hold this stride so long. And now I'm afraid, with the rugs up, the curtains down, and the water off, I've no hospitality to offer you. But I'd like so terribly much to see you. And I shall very soon. For no matter how good it is to work here, winter must break me out.

My regards to Russell, and best wishes on the book and everything you're doing.

As always,

Charles

9

To Carl Van Doren
and Van Wyck Brooks (1940)

In the acknowledgments in his 1933 M.A. thesis on Melville, Olson thanked Carl Van Doren, who had "added to the writer's understanding of Melville by graciously sparing him a few hours from a busy life." Van Doren became someone from whom he could beg letters of recommendation, and he did so for his Guggenheim application in November 1938. It was at this time that Edward Dahlberg recruited Van Wyck Brooks to the cause. On 23 March 1939 Olson was able to write to his first sponsor, "We won" (letter at Princeton); to Brooks the next day he wrote: "I have the year I wanted . . . your wish to sponsor me was more important to me than anything else" (letter at Pennsylvania). In a Christmas greeting that year he told Brooks that he had confined himself in Gloucester to write night and day on the book: "It's joy and work and that's all I ask" (letter at Pennsylvania). On 11 January 1940 Olson sought Van Doren's advice about requesting a renewal of the Guggenheim, and accordingly he reapplied to Henry Allen Moe of the foundation, enclosing a carbon copy with letters to both his sponsors.

Letter to Carl Van Doren at Princeton
and letter to Van Wyck Brooks at Pennsylvania.

Stage Fort
Gloucester
Feb 14

My dear Carl—

God knows whether this reaches you—but I was wholly thankful for your advice about a renewal of the G., and wanted to put before your eyes the product of your encouragement, no matter what most lovely things those eyes are now looking on. I'd rather offer you the 20,000 words of mss I sent to Moe last week—but they, God help us, might blight anything as lovely as Honolulu!

Anyhow, all joy!
Charles John Olson

Stage Fort Ave
Gloucester
Feb 14

My dear Van Wyck Brooks—

Your encouragement last year meant so much to me, I'm writing now just to keep you informed of what I am up to. The enclosed speaks for itself. It does not speak of what means more to me—a part of the book I sent off to the Guggenheim last week, 65 pages in two pieces, the first in the nature of an interlude on the trip Melville took to the Mediterranean in 1856-7 and the second, consecutive to the first, an initial attempt to say why Melville deserted prose for the verse of *Battle-Pieces*. Both pieces I regard as drafts to be rewritten in the fall, but they do tell something about the nature and shape of the book.

After a short trip to New York I plan to pick up again the second section on myth and *Mardi*. To that end I have written to your brother-in-law in Tahiti. Being a writer you will, I hope, understand why it is now and not earlier that I have followed your most generous hint about Stimson. Only when I had plunged into *Mardi* again did I feel all the questions and promptings to justify a levy on him. And I was able, before writing him, to read some of his own work, particularly on the distribution of Polynesian languages as a key to Pacific migrations. What he has done has already fed me and I am most grateful to you.

Thank you for the Picasso card! And I'm glad your own work moves well. I expect that work keeps you too busy for any interruptions, but if, by any chance, you should like some evening to sit down with these two sections on Melville and judge what I am about, I should be most pleased and thankful. I have a clean copy ready to send you if you would not find it a burden. Perhaps you'd drop a note to me care of the Hotel Albert, University Place & 11th St, N.Y.C.; I shall arrive there Friday and bear the mss. with me.

In any case, *please* do not find any of this an imposition. I want only to thank you for your friendship.

Most warmly,
Charles John Olson

The renewal of the Guggenheim was refused. Olson wrote to Brooks on 6 April 1940: "I had Moe's noe this week" (letter at Pennsylvania).

10

To Waldo Frank (1940)

Because the writer Waldo Frank was more of an intellectual leader in his time than any present attention to him would suggest, Olson's letters to him may seem now to smack of strained adulation. And perhaps there was some strain, for the letters ceased after 1940 for reasons at present unknown. Nevertheless, the evidence is that the correspondence with Frank sustained Olson during the trying Guggenheim year of 1939–40 when, mostly alone in Gloucester, he was pushing himself to write the big Melville book that was never to be finished.

Letter at Pennsylvania.

Gloucester
March 25

My dear Waldo

I got up one morning and suddenly had left N.Y. in an hour, distracted by it, and hungry for Gloucester and for work. And yesterday I knocked off after 25,000 words and that section on myth was done, one of those wonderful strides we strike once in a while in life. God knows it may seem nothing to you, possessed as you are of one of the finest working capacities I know; but for me such a stretch is the beginning, and I must one day equal your beautiful commitment.

Gloucester is breath stealing, sunned and wind, its color suddenly open to my eyes after the drab of N.Y. Yesterday I walked against a bitter wind miles along the coast alone with the gulls. I am living in a house which sets on a jut of land between the river which ebbs and floods under my eye out the east window and the sea which moves and pushes and breaks against the window to the south. I don't know when I have been so open to life here. Today I've been in the bars with my friends the fishermen, the skipper Cece Moulton, an old mastheadsman Walter Burke, Jim Mason, and an old striker (Gloucester for harpooner) whom we call Long Ranny—he has two inches on me but he's been so stowed in the peak of so many vessels he's bent like a cadaverous Atlas. A good deal of excitement in the talk, 'cause the biggest schooner, the "Thebaud," went fast aground today in the inner habor when Moulton was trying to work her out to sea to avoid the lowest tide remembered here in years—the spring equinox ebb's the longest of all and on top of that there's a northwest wind, so the harbor's a crick.

Thanks for your good letter which reached me and for our enriching evenings in N.Y. Mumford had to cancel our tentatively arranged meeting and I left too quickly to see Benardete. Isn't the news of Dora's operation unhappy? I pray to God she's all right: I've heard nothing from Rosa; do stir her for me if you see her.

I hope you don't mind my continuing to read Muriel Rukeyser. I keep turning to her book with deep pleasure even if, sometimes, phrases and lines come to me contrived. But if you should want it immediately of course I shall send it pronto. And if, by chance, you can send me the Tillich I shall be grateful.

Do write. And do take my faith and love—

Charles

And do take your vacation—you deserve it.

11

To Constance Wilcock (1941)

According to Tom Clark's biography of Olson, it was Connie who initiated their relationship by accepting an invitation to Gloucester in place of her sister (whom Olson had met through Dahlberg). In May 1940 Connie was a serious and precocious twenty-year-old, ten years younger than the man she had seen but not met. Quickly, as the letter below puts it, they became "two Buddhas of desire." They parted temporarily when Olson went to New York City looking for a livelihood; this was in late October 1940, and the letter below was probably written 3 April 1941, after some commuting back and forth. Olson has made a dinner date with Melville scholar Raymond Weaver. He has proposed his big Melville book to Harcourt, Brace. He has had an interview with David H. Stevens, director of the Division for the Humanities, Rockefeller Foundation, which had been arranged by Francis Henry Taylor of the Metropolitan Museum of Art. He is reading a library copy of William H. Prescott's *History of the Conquest of Mexico;* he will pick up his own copy the following month. It was to be an enduring influence. As was Constance Wilcock.   *Letter at Storrs.*

Wednesday

My beloved,

   Well, today I made it! Yesterday I didn't. I tried. I shaved. I had my pants pressed. I put on a clean shirt. I trimmed my moustache and those sideburns. Before I had left here I was afire with nerves and by the time I got to Rockefeller Center I was ill, and missing him I sought, fled back here and took to bed and aspirin! As I lay dying! I fought back to sanity and today I mounted the world again, insisting calm upon my pores. And it worked! I gave Stevens of the R's a half hour performance as good as I ever gave any executive. He promises me an answer on the gold in a week to ten days! He was most open, but I remind myself Taylor warned me Stevens was like that, sanguine, but his trustees another fish: shellback! Said Taylor, "Before those birds give up the change they want a deposit in the Chase National Bank!" But I'll chance it—I can do nothing else—and wait that week to put my nose into the other feedbag, the Carnegie. To-morrow, however, I go to Ascoli, the boss of the Italians, and propose a job for myself I have worked out: as a nurse for refugees! And I don't think I'll be on my back tomorrow! I think the precious circle I have lived and written in is broken, and I can now manage to settle the world and, if luck is good, return. In fact, of course, the circle cannot be broken, as I discovered talking to Stevens: I found myself speaking with private authority, mincing no words, and I'm damned if I don't think he took it! I was sharp as hell about education and stubbornly pure when he, astutely, asked me why I did not seek an advance from Harcourt instead of coming to him. I told him frankly I did not regard the prose as good enough to chance losing publication with them! That's pretty snotty, and I may pay for it, but I mean to win where I stand and no place else. I think you believe in me and know I measured the situation accurately: when I finally exact poise of my pulse I don't make the wrong mistakes!

(I had to go out to phone Murray—you 'member, he's the victim!—
but again he slipped through my fingers: I cannot see him for two
weeks. But I got Weaver and am to have dinner with him. And just
now as I squeezed myself some orange juice in came Santillana, on
from Boston, and that's good for he'll give me the dope at dinner
about Ascoli—and I'm going to pump him for more dope on something he mentioned last time, a wealthy writer in Buenos Aires who
backs writers.)

So I play squirrel in the cage of the world, and ride the wheel all the
ways it runs!

Your special came last night but the fat letter has not arrived today,
unhappy me! O darling I miss you so. Last night was hard to pass over
without you. I had to drug myself to sleep by reading Prescott until
the eyes were too tired to stand more. O yes, I now have a library card
here, and I shall have the Nun's letters so that we can read them together, darling of mine. In the branch where I got my card they did
not have them. (The 42nd St will.) Instead I got a bad book on the
Mayans with which I amused myself last night before I turned back to
Prescott as nembutal! When you come I'll have the best thing on the
Mayans, the Conquest of Yucatan, by Blom. A few lines did come yesterday on the Indian! Not good enough to send you, really only notes
groping along. But they show that what is going to be central is
GOLD, perhaps as image only, maybe as subject too, for the greed of
the Spaniards for it and the Indians confusion of the S as the breed of
the Sun, the sons of white Quetzalcoatl do join somehow, and ironi-
cally.

Today it was your hair again which tangled my heart! and your long
legs which snared my body! Do you feel a treasure house of moments
and sharp sensations which our love has gathered into which, lonely
and hungry, to dip and recall? Suddenly you will stand or move a certain way, your arms will raise, inside where he is you will feel afire, your
lips will kiss in a way they have not kissed, you will look at me out of
your eyes anew, you dive into the water different, it is that graveyard at
Barnstable and the voices below us, or your hand held is all the world,

or it is beside the bed at Ipswich when quickly we were in each others arms two Buddhas of desire. These things happen to me. It is always a birth. I love you, Constance.

Please, love, have nothing to do with that auto, please. Everything in me tells me it's bad. Be assured it's no aid to our love. It is only enemy, the machine. You and I hold something *against* the machine, against the world of the machine. The very thought of it cuts across me like a rip saw. I could not bear to have you drive to me in an automobile. Our love is clean of it, and if our love had nothing else, it would be a miracle because of that. No darling no. Cleave to your instinct here, as in everything: thank god you do hate to drive and dislike autos. I love that very hate. That prime spontaneity of yours, which makes my heart seep with love, exists because of hates in you like that for an auto and a subway. Never betray it, woman of mine.

God knows to lose this weekend is harsh, beloved, but again I trust your senses, love. I know what you mean. O Constance, whenever you work from your organs, organically, I am strong, take composure, live steady, endure. I toughen when you toughen, and that chemistry makes me very sure of us. Do you know, beloved woman, that initially you are rare, rare, love? The given of you is exact and fine. That also has to do with what I meant by the fastidious, the delicate as it is the strong. your arms, your arms, your arms. your womb. all of you. oh oh sweet, sweet love of mine I want you. You were born beautiful, and all either of us do to live up to love is to remember our innocence. People and the world scale and cover beauty until beauty remembers itself: then they can be experienced and known and no longer mar us, actually even then add to us. But love's the secret. I don't know whether I ever showed you those lines I wrote a long time ago and have never made anything of, though I suppose some day they may spring into something:

> Die out of the world
> Die into the self
> Live in the self
> Live in the world.

I love the seed of you. May God at last be good and make the weekend beyond, ours! For in heaven and hell's name I want you, my woman. I await and abide you, love.

for I am yours, your Charles
Charles

for god's sake tell me
if you are not well,
sweet heart.

12

To Homer and Viola Barrett (1941)

Olson was five when the family had their first summer at Stage Fort Park in Gloucester, Massachusetts. After his father's death in 1935, Olson helped his mother keep up the annual visits. In fact, "Oceanwood" cottage became Mary Olson's main residence, and she retreated to relatives and friends in Worcester only for the winter months. Homer and Viola Barrett were the owners of the cottage. The following letter can be dated 1941 by the reference to the famous Valentine Day's storm of 1940. *Letter (carbon copy) at Storrs.*

86 Christopher St
New York: April 6

My dearest Homer and Viola,

Greetings at long last again! Mother wrote me you found it a harsh winter, and I am sorry. But now I can greet you with spring, and may it gladden you both! A year ago, Homer, I was watching you tender your seedlings under the little glass hot house each morning: I hope you are already at it again! And how does the cottage look? It wasn't snowed under this year like the Valentine storm last, was it? And if my little buggy's in the way of the spring, get Philip to remove it!

Mother writes me she wants to go to Gloucester after Easter. I sense she feels some embarrassment, for it is the first time in twenty-five years that she has returned to the cottage with money standing between our family and you people. I am terribly sorry that that is so. I think you know me well enough to know that if there had been any way I would have removed our obligation to you. And shall, the moment I have the money.

You see, for a writer, everything depends upon his first book. Upon it depends both reputation and income. On the other hand, because he has not published, his name is worth nothing and a publisher will not advance him money before publication. I was lucky in having been awarded that Guggenheim Fellowship. That helps me. For example, one of the biggest publishers in N.Y. is interested in my book: Harcourt, Brace & Co. Because the book is so important, I have had to give all my time to it. This year, and these months now passing are the critical ones of my life. By them I am establishing myself as a writer. I have worked steadily on my book since I left Gloucester. Right now is the squeeze. The Guggenheim Foundation are holding the renewal of my grant which, usually, a fellow of their foundation can expect, up for another year until my book is published. I am at the moment hoping that the Rockefeller Foundation will tide me over until I am able to put the manuscript into the publisher's hands. If that fails, I shall turn to the Author's League. I want to put the manuscript in the publisher's hands by summer, for fall publication. I tell you these facts to assure you I am not neglecting my debt to you and to indicate to you how I am struggling to make this passage, the most important and difficult of my life, into the writing and publishing world.

All the money, of course, which the cottage earns shall go directly to you, as it did last season. I think again that Wiley Lantz and Meredith will be there a month as last year. And I plan to write letters after Mother is there to all the people who have ever been customers reminding them that the place still exists, that Mother is there, and asking them to tell any friends of theirs about it. This is mainly good in Worcester, but amongst my Cambridge and Boston friends I shall also spread the word. That goes to you, all. And the moment I have an income I shall send you the money I owe.

Do, please, write me frankly if such an arrangement is not satisfactory to you. I hope it will, for Mother wants to go and I want to make it possible for her to go. If I do not hear from you to the contrary, Mother will come on as soon after Easter as she feels it is warm enough. I'm sure she'll let you know. I shall not be able to afford the trip and I'm afraid she'll have to make it alone again. But Philip will help her shake things down. I shall write to him about the car and about working around the house for my mother. And about putting the double bed back in the big room on Morrison's side upstairs: that will make more rental space.

My love to you both, and all health. Remember me to the Cut.

Yours

13

To the Office of Strategic Services (1942)

In 1941 Olson got a job for a while with Dorothy Norman's friend Roger Baldwin of the American Civil Liberties Union, but he quit to go to Gloucester for the summer. Returning to New York City, now in a common-law marriage with Connie, he worked for six months for the Common Council for American Unity, an immigrants' lobbying group. In September 1942 he was again looking for a job. The letter below is one of his applications.   *Letter (carbon copy) at Storrs.*

206½ West 13 Street
New York City
Tuesday, September 1, 1942

Mr. Wallace Duell
630 Fifth Avenue
New York City

My dear Mr. Duell,

When we spoke yesterday you suggested I set down my story on paper, brief. Here it is—for what it may be worth to the Office of Strategic Services.

My special experience is with the press and politics of the foreign nationalities in this country, gained as Chief of the Foreign Language

Information Service. (FLIS, originally a part of the Committee on Public Information of World War I, since 1940 a part of the Common Council for American Unity, has for twenty-five years serviced the 1000 odd foreign language publications in the U.S. with news translated into 27 languages.) My job was to administer a staff of 2 editors, 25 advisors and translators in 27 languages, and a half dozen special readers of the foreign language papers, to make surveys and reports on that press, to maintain contact with foreign language editors and to direct and edit the preparation, translation and release of copy to the press. Since Pearl Harbor the work involved as well reports of political developments in such a group as the Finns for the State Department and the translation and distribution of material for the Office of War Information (as OFF), the Office of Government Reports, WPB, OPA, FSA and the Depts. of Treasury and Justice.

Previously, under a grant from the Guggenheim Foundation, I was at work for two years on a book about Herman Melville, largely to set the maritime story of America off against the more familiar land story. The Pacific area was central to the book and it was in this connection that Joseph Barnes offered me the position with the COL I mentioned to you.

Professionally I was trained as a specialist in American civilization. In that capacity I was three years a member of the Harvard faculty, the last year under a direct appointment from James B. Conant as Counsellor in American Civilization.

References: Alan Cranston, Chief, Foreign Language Division, OWI, Washington; Roger Baldwin, Director, Am. Civil Liberties Union, 170 Fifth Avenue, N.Y.C.; F. O. Matthiessen, 87 Pinckney St., Boston, Mass.; Dorothy Norman, Editor, *Twice A Year,* 509 Madison Ave, N.Y.C.; Raymond T. Rich, Organizations Division, O D, N.Y.C.; Francis H. Taylor, Director, Metropolitan Art Museum, N.Y.C.; and Carl Van Doren, 41 Central Park West, N.Y.C.

My thanks to you.

Sincerely,

Olson was not given a job with the OSS: it is generally considered that he would not have made a good spy. His wartime career was with the Office of War Information, under Alan Cranston.

III

Olson's time at the Office of War Information ended in 1944, when he devoted himself to Roosevelt's election campaign as a paid member of the Democratic Party staff. He and Connie then went to the Democrats' winter headquarters in Key West, Florida. Roosevelt's death in April 1945 put any thoughts of a political career out of his mind, and he and Connie returned to their small house in Washington, D.C. Olson, now a committed writer, finished *Call Me Ishmael* by the end of 1945 and started publishing poems.

Visits to Ezra Pound at St. Elizabeths hospital dominated 1946. Olson got clear of Pound only after making a trip west in the fall and winter of 1947.

14

To Alfred Stieglitz (1945)

While staying with Edward Dahlberg in New York on a quick trip down from Harvard the last weekend in February 1938, Olson was taken to meet Stieglitz at his gallery, An American Place. Stieglitz and Olson were also brought together as contributors between the covers of Norman's magazine *Twice A Year*. Olson's notebook of the time indicates that this birthday greeting was sent on 20 March 1945. *Letter at Yale.*

> 624 White St
> Key West, Florida

My dear Alfred Stieglitz—

I have wanted to greet you in another year of your magnificent life. And now I do, raising myself out of a sloth of sun. And a sluice of work: three months here, after three years of war, gave me a chance to let go.

I think of you often, and feel strong.

> Yours,   Charles Olson

Please remember me
to Dorothy Norman

15

To Malcolm Cowley (1945)

Malcolm Cowley, long an eminent man of letters, must have seemed the right person to whom to address questions about the literary establishment's attitude to the treason charges against Ezra Pound. Cowley had known Pound in Paris, and he subsequently came out in favor of Pound's receiving the Bollingen Prize in Poetry; but we do not know what he said in reply to the letter below. If he did reply, there is no trace of it at Storrs. *Letter at Newberry.*

217 Randolph Pl NE
Washington, 2, D.C.
April 26, 1945

Mr. Malcolm Cowley
Gaylordsville, Conn

Dear Mr Cowley:

I wrote to George Mayberry a couple of weeks ago from Key West enclosing a poem on Pound and asking him if any writers were taking any steps in the Pound case. George knows I have been connected with the government since Pearl Harbor and understood I might be of some use if there was anything that could be done to save the scoundrel's skin. For any day now Pound will be in custody and soon, I assume, tossed into a trial with the bunch of propaganda hacks he had the misfortune to be indicted with.

George suggested you could give me the facts about what, if any activity there is in re Pound. I shall, of course, take it in confidence as you will me. Just so you can gauge me I am enclosing a copy of the thing I sent the New Republic.

I shall be grateful to hear from you and if there is anything afoot I might be able to front for it with the Justice Department. You will understand, therefore, the pseudonym "John Little."

Respectfully,

Charles Olson

"Lustrum" is the piece conjectured to have been sent to the *New Republic* and rejected by them. It has been printed in *A Nation of Nothing But Poetry* (pp. 26–27, with George Butterick's notes on p. 173). "Lustrum" represented a stage in Olson's thinking about Pound leading up to "This Is Yeats Speaking," published in *Partisan Review* (winter 1946) and in *Collected Prose*, pp. 141–144.

16

To Oscar Lange (1945)

Olson's friend Adam Kulikowski, an exiled Polish landowner and colleague at the Office of War Information, introduced him to a fellow patriot, Oscar Lange, a professor of economics at the University of Chicago and author of such books as *Price Flexibility and Employment.* As the new Polish government's chief friend in the United States, Lange hired Olson to lobby his old Democratic Party friends in New York on Poland's behalf. The present letter indicates there are plans to send Olson to Poland as a communications and media expert.

Letter (carbon copy) at Storrs.

Friday, Sept 14, 1945

My dear Oscar:

I thought I'd set down for you and me the upshot of our telephone conversation yesterday.

First, your idea of the invitation coming from a writer's group is excellent. It obviates most of the problems. It would be best, from my point of view, if it were a group of creative men. I could get from such men a quicker, deeper sense of what stirs and motivates the people. It would establish the visit, here, as creative, not political.

Second, my services. They would be to the government, on information and its communication to the U.S. It seems to me at this distance that it would involve two steps on my part: (1) a look-see at the information set-up, including the arrangements of U.S. news, radio, newsreel, and photo outlets; and (2) as wide as possible an acquaintance with Poland and its people, to mark out materials for news export. For the most dramatic source of news is what people do and, in the long run, the most healthy objective of an information policy is to make graphic to the American people what the new Poles are like, not just what their government is up to. That is why I emphasize the *graphic* and call your attention to the importance of newsreel and photo service as well as radio and correspondents.

Comment: such a double-edged arrangement makes the best use of me. As a writer I have a long bow, and what I experience I deliver only after a good pull. That is why it would not be fair to myself or anyone else to go as a correspondent, even for a magazine. On the other hand I can deliver fast, because of the nature of my experience, on the public relations side.

Third, time. I hope you will find a writer's group in existence so that such a visit may come very soon. For the way things are shaping, with the book about done, I shall have to make a move, both for financial and creative reasons.

Fourth, finances. As a gauge, the Democrats paid me $860.50 a month. I have now no personal means, or capital. I should have to have the expenses of such a trip (over, that is) advanced to me. The salary, however, need not be an obstacle. My principal concern on salary is the arrangements of my family.

These are notes, Oscar. I wanted to do them so that you and I keep our scrupulous relationship.

All that is left is that mysterious TIMING of ours—which has itself proved so scrupulous! May it continue!

So this gives me a chance to wish you again the very best of fortune on what you have stepped forward to! It is a healthy sign, when men of your perception, are called and accept leadership. I am confident of what's ahead because I am confident of you. (Irene will call this a love letter, too—tell her she's right!)

Yours

Charles Olson

The proposed trip to Poland never came off, but the following year Lange, now Poland's ambassador to the United Nations, called on Olson to do more lobbying in New York City.

17

To William H. Tripp (1945)

This letter is a follow-up to a visit Olson made to the Old Dartmouth Historical Society and Whaling Museum in New Bedford, Massachusetts, during August 1945. "Friend Tripp," as Olson refers to him in *Call Me Ishmael,* was the curator there, and he gave Olson a copy of the society's pamphlet, *A Visit to the Old Dartmouth Museum* by Zephaniah W. Pease, which included a photograph of the *Acushnet*'s "Crew List with Melville's Name." Olson is writing for help in deciphering some of the names on this list, double-checking Melville's own list of "What became of the ship's company . . . ," which Olson had inserted into *Call Me Ishmael* just finished.   *Letter (carbon copy) at Storrs.*

217 Randolph Pl NE
Washington 2, D.C.
September 18, 1945

My dear Mr Tripp:
    It was delightful to have a card from "The Lookout"! It surprised and pleased me.

    I hadn't known I'd be in touch with you so soon again. But I sat here today over my manuscript puzzled and blocked. And I thought, I wonder, if William Tripp were around, what he'd have to say, he'd have some ideas. For it concerns the crew of the "Acushnet"! About which I dare say you've been troubled many times too often!

    Some of my trouble comes from being so sure, that day I visited with you, that I could read the reprint of the List in the copy of "A Visit" you generously gave me and my friends. Would you confirm the following?
    name 4: is it David Smith
    "   5: what is Stedman's first name and height? 5′2½″? (I am interested in his height, and him, in an attempt to identify who was what Melville, in his list of "What happened to the Crew" (as Henry Hubbard told him in 1850), described as "Little Backus" and "Black." Only three Negroes are named on your list, but Melville lists this fourth one, Backus. In looking for him in Stedman, or possibly Barnard, the other small man, 5′½″ (for he is listed as "light"), I am going on the assumption that he might not have been identified on the Crew List as "Black": is that, from your experience, a possible assumption? Stedman is "Dark," with "Black" hair.)
    name 14: what is John Wright's place of birth & residence?
    name 17: Wolcut's first name, place of birth?

name 22: Hubard's place of birth? Charleston, S.C.?
name 23: Williams' first name, and place of birth?
name 26: Banne's place of birth? Charleston?

This looks like an awful chore. It just occurs to me I could save you it, if I had a photostat. But that might be more trouble for you. I should of course be glad to pay the cost.

I'm wondering if it wasn't you that did the identifications from your Crew List of the names as Melville gives them in his list for Anderson? His note on it reads peculiarly, doesn't quite say you did it, but gives me the feeling you did. Can you tell me the reason for identifying William Maiden as "The Old Cook"? because he is the oldest man in the crew?

One more and I'm done: Melville says that both the "Blacksmith" and "Backus—little black" ran away from the Acushnet at "St. Francisco." I can't believe that this is California. As far as I know *sperm* whaling, there was no reason for the Acushnet getting up there. I figure it's another port, but I can find no such on the coast of South America. And know none in the Pacific Islands. Do you know of any other record of a port of this name at which sperm whalers might have touched?

Well, I'd feel guilty about all this, if I didn't figure you can answer them, because of your knowledge, so easily and fully!

And maybe, just by chance, I can offer you a little thing in return. I have brought together, on the basis of all I can gather (and it includes at least one new fact) a substitute for a Log Book of the Acushnet, a list of her cruise points. Would it interest you, and the Museum? If so I shall be pleased to send you a typed copy.

So I now add more thanks to those that went before. And again my warmest greetings!

Cordially,

Charles Olson

Tripp's reply is not extant, but it may have been the basis for annotations that Olson made in pencil on this carbon copy. Tripp received a copy of *Call Me*

Ishmael upon publication and wrote to Olson on 11 March 1947: "it shows what a lot of research you have done. I know of no other book which so carefully interprets Melville. I am very glad to add it to my collection" (letter at Storrs).

18

To Winfred Overholser
and Mary Rudge (1946)

"I saw Pound today," Olson reported to publisher James Laughlin on 4 January 1946. "With a guard present we talked a half hour. And I shall go back Tuesday." There was red tape and some delay, but Olson persisted.

Letters (carbon copies) at Storrs.

217 Randolph Pl NE
Washington 2, D.C.
January 5, 1946

Dr. Winfred Overholser
Superintendent
St Elizabeth's Hospital
Washington, D.C.

Dear Dr Overholser,

Dr Griffin has asked me to make this formal request of you for permission to visit Ezra Pound occasionally while he is in your care.

It was at the suggestion of Mr Pound's publisher, James Laughlin, of NEW DIRECTIONS, that I called yesterday during what I took to be visiting hours and had the privilege of talking to Mr Pound. I should like to continue to come so long as I can be of service to Mr Pound, if you will grant me the right.

My motive is the simplest: I wish to proffer a helping hand to him, and a sympathetic ear. I do it out of respect for his published work and to do whatever chores one writer might do for another. I happen to live in Washington, and because of that, in the absence of his immediate family, I thought I might serve. I had also the idea that Mr Pound might like to talk to someone from the outside. Mr Laughlin had the same thought when he suggested I go over during visiting hours. That is all.

I think that both you and Mr Pound will want assurance, because I am a writer, that there is no hidden motive of publication. I should not wish to abuse his confidence, in our conversations.

Dr Griffin asked me to indicate to you how often I had in mind to come. I should imagine that at the beginning there would be more things I might do than when things had settled down a bit. Mr Pound yesterday asked me to send cards to people, as soon as he got his address list from Gallinger, telling them he would like to have them write to him. I stand ready to come each week.

Let me add that I have been a Fellow of the Guggenheim Foundation to do a book on the American novelist Herman Melville. I am in the process of finishing it now.

I look forward to hearing from you.

Respectfully,
Charles Olson

---

217 Randolph Pl NE
Washington 2, D.C.
January 16, 1946

Dear Mary Rudge,

I visited your father yesterday for the second time at St. Elizabeth's Hospital. He asked me to write to you, to say he had heard from you—an October letter, I believe, and to suggest that mail be sent to him via England. He thinks it will come faster that way.

He looks fine. The rest he had at Gallinger Hospital the three weeks between his arraignment and his transfer to St. E. has restored his physical vigor. "Tell Mary," he said as I was leaving, biting a smile, "I am not repulsive!"

His repeated request is, have people write to me, but tell them I cannot answer, I am only able to concentrate on a few lines. Perhaps you will be able to get his friends in England and on the Continent to do this. (Mail in to the hospital is uncensored.)

It is his family of whom he speaks with most anxiety.

Cordially,

Charles Olson

It was after this second visit that Pound added a postscript to a note to his lawyer: "Olson saved my life." See the facsimile letter in Julien Cornell, *The Trial of Ezra Pound* (1966, p. 71).

19

To Robert Hannegan (1946)

It was Robert Hannegan, senator from Missouri and confidant of Harry Truman, who gave Olson a job in 1944 as director of the Foreign Nationalities Division of the Democratic Party. Olson's task was to get out the big city immigrant vote. "Dear Charley," Hannegan wrote soon after the election, "I want you to know that I think your work during the campaign was great and was very effective in bringing about our great victory. All I can say to you is—'Many thanks.' Kindest personal regards, Sincerely yours, Bob" (letter at Storrs). It is on the basis of this track record that Olson, in the letter below, is reminding Hannegan that the same vote needs to be wooed again. "I spent twelve hours the other day on a memo for Hannegan," Olson wrote to F. O. Matthiessen on 2 February 1946 (letter at Yale), "and most of it, trying to contrive ways of making the point without mentioning foreign policy, not to speak of fascism! God love him, he knows it was the name Wilson that brought these people in to the Party and it was the magic of 'Roosevelt' that kept their vote despite the years the Italians were mussolinied and the Poles were londonized. Yet he doesn't know it that way" (letter at Yale). *Draft letter at Storrs.*

January 23, 1946

LETTER
& MEMORANDUM
to: Hon. Robert E. Hannegan
fr: Charles Olson
re: the Party, the '46 Campaign, and the Foreign Nationality Vote

My dear Bob:

I want to try once more to convince you there is a need for the Party to operate full blast from national headquarters on the foreign nationality vote, and not leave the job to the local organization. It is more urgent than ever now that the Administration has lost such war-time activities in the field as Justice, FCC Intelligence, OSS Foreign Nationalities Branch, OWI's Foreign Language Division, and those members of the White House staff who had got hep to what goes on.

The whole front is broken and where, before, the Party, as in '44, could cash in on the general advance of the above Administration Agencies, we will now in '46 and, more seriously, in '48, lose the gains all down the line. And take my word for it, in the foreign language business such controls as these agencies represented meant more than you'd guess: with them gone, forces out to get us are already running wild, aided and financed not only by old foreign interests but *by the Republican Party itself.* (Evidence when you want it.)

It is for these reasons that a few of us who are most concerned have unsuccessfully sought to salvage via State some of the old operations, and I cannot too strongly urge you to help us through the White House to restore the old front as far as possible so that we will not be at this disadvantage in '48. (Proposals ready for you.)

But your immediate concern, and mine, is '46, and the Congressional elections. I recommend that you put two men on the job as soon as possible the *1st* to do what is *basically the publicity end:* (I have talked this over with Sam O'Neal)
  (1) to keep a flow of news, selections from The Democrat and
      original stuff angled for f.l., in translation to Polish, Ger-

man, Italian, Hungarian and Yiddish papers and radio pro-
grams;

(2) to concentrate news and pamphlets in districts where Congressmen lean heavily on f.l. vote, translating where the group
predominates;

(3) to keep a constant eye on the big groups—press, radio, &
organizations—via the f.l. Digests we purchased during the '44
campaign in order to prepare reports on f.l. reaction to Administration policies and individuals for advice of Comm.;

and (4) to do routine cooperation of the Committee with f.l. organizations and individuals who are working with us—speakers,
legislation, fundraising, etc.

The 2nd man to do what is to my mind the *most necessary* and *most
neglected* job of all:

(1) *contact with the Hill.* Several of our own Congressmen are as
much at crosspurposes with the Administration's foreign policy
as the Southerners are on domestic issues. They get away with a
hell of a lot of mischief because nobody wise to the foreign nationalities watches them in relation to their foreign nationality
constituents. There was no reason, for example, why Ryter, whom
we at Nat'l Hdqurs damn well did a lot to elect in Conn., should
have shot his mouth off on UNRRA. Ditto others. Or that Sad-
owski right now should, perhaps innocently enough, be recom-
mending men to UNRRA who are out to wreck our foreign policy. All of such harm has to be eventually undone, and there's no
reason why it should happen in the first place. It would be the job
of our man to keep the boys in line;

(2) *liason with the White House, State, UNRRA, Justice* and *wherever
in other agencies foreign nationality Americans are involved.*
Vital, now that the war-time controls are gone. Somebody has
to watch sharp where foreign governments come in contact
with Americans from their homelands. It is an old problem in-
tensified now with both the new nationalism and international-
ism consequent to the War. I could quote you chapter and verse
for hours on what the Republicans are up to right here. Let me
just say this: here the fight against the Administration's foreign
policy is at its darkest and dirtiest. And on foreign policy the f.l.

American is most vulnerable. We got his vote with Wilson, and held it with Roosevelt, because both personally stood for a new deal in Europe. Thus the undermining of confidence in our foreign policy, which has been going on amongst Germans and Italians since the Nazis and Fascists came to power, amongst the Poles since the death of Sikorski, and now amongst the Jews, was offset. But now, with the magic of Roosevelt's name among the f.n. Americans gone, we will have to explain, defend and protect the Administration's foreign policy day by day right down to Nov., '48. That goes everywhere we can reach the f.n. American. But one place to begin is inside the government on all delegations to Poland, Greece, Italy, Jugoslavia etec., on all personnel on UNRRA missions, on State Dept. observers, etec., etec.;

(3) *coordination of national policy on f.l.* groups with the *local party organization* where any given group is concentrated. This means Chicago, Detroit, Pittsburgh, New York as the front line, and Boston, Connecticut, Buffalo, Utica, Syracuse, Cleveland as second line etc. We still get into a lot of unnecessary trouble because we do not handle foreign language groups and leaders as they are organized in fraternal, political, benefit societies, in their press and radio—which is *nationally.* The result is the blackmail Rozmarek pulled on us in the Polish situation in '44. Or the series of situations the President's War Relief Board has been confronted with, due to the way local Party people have been used by anti-Administration interests in almost all of the foreign nationality groups. The whole business discredits us, and now will hurt us in votes. It's the Congressmen all over again;

(4) and last, the coordination of f.n. politics to Party policy generally. This is obvious, but without such a man as I have suggested, whose job it is to do just this at Headquarters, it won't get done.

Well, Bob, there it is, for what it is worth. And if I can be of any help, I am, of course, at your call. My address remains what it has been: 217 Randolph Pl NE. And I can be reached by phone through my wife's office: EXecutive 3533.

Cordially,

Charles Olson

Hannegan replied 30 January 1946: "Stop by at the Post Office Department some time at your convenience" (letter at Storrs).

20

To Ezra Pound (1946)

Olson made eight visits to St. Elizabeths Hospital to see Ezra Pound between 4 January and 26 March 1946. This regularity was broken by a trip Olson made to New York to negotiate a contract for *Call Me Ishmael* with the publishers Reynal & Hitchcock early in April 1946. The three letters he wrote to Pound while he was away are given below. The first, undated, was probably written around 8 April 1946; the second is dated "Sunday" (probably 14 April 1946); the third is dated "Wednesday" (probably 24 April 1946).   *Letters at Indiana.*

[letterhead]
Hotel Commodore "New York's Best Located Hotel"

My dear Ezra Pound:
  (1) N.Y. just now is Paris, and I stay on
  (2) Saw Adamic, but no leads on Mazzei
  (3) Have La Salle book in mind
  (4) Reynal & Hitchcock will buy Melville if I expand & elucidate
  (5) Laughlin was gone to Utah, a place for Sandy Boys
  (6) Many people ask for you, I miss you
  (7) A very pleasant note from your daughter Mary
  (8) Write if there is anything I can do, or get for you
  (9) UN is nothing but tragicomedy

Yrs,

Charles Olson

[letterhead]
The Commodore New York

Sunday

My dear Ezra Pound:
  Feel bad not to be there to see you. But this thing is running out. Will go to Gloucester to see my mother, then back.

Constance and I called on Mary Barnard today. She asks that you excuse her, she will write the moment she frees herself from an index she is doing.

Your daughter Mary wrote what I think you know—that she is back on the farm in Tyrol, making wool and spinning. She hopes to see you there soon.

We all think and speak of you, send love. You are the active principle.

Yrs,

Charles Olson

Tomorrow I shall know what changes Reynal
& Hitchcock will want. I said N.Y. was
a some time Paris: it ain't.

Gloucester, Mass
Wednesday

My dear Ezra Pound—

This is home. I got here, and thought to turn right back. But the place, the sea, and the wide light which it also has in October won't let Connie and me go. We shall refuse it though. Money will drive us south, in a day or so.

I signed a contract for the Melville book with Reynal & Hitchcock Friday. They have had their man talk to Eliot, and there is a chance Faber may take American sheets. I thank you.

I shall be glad to get back, to see you, and to work.

Do you recall a conversation we had about my friend the Italian painter Cagli? I found him in New York last week, and he asked to come to Washington to visit you. He will, if you are willing, stopping with us.

I wanted to send you respect from this latitude.

Yrs,

Charles Olson

21

To Adam Kulikowski (1946)

Olson's Enniscorthy suite of poems (*Collected Poems,* pp. 24–33) celebrates a country estate in Jefferson's Virginia where Charles and Connie found refuge in the summer of 1946, and the poem "Trinacria" (pp. 45–46), originally published in *Harper's Bazaar* with the title "For K," was a tribute to their host, Adam Kulikowski. Kulikowski had worked with Olson at the Office of War Information (see letter 16) and remained a compadre in spite of such ups and downs as are exhibited in the following letters. "Good place here," Olson wrote to Pound from Enniscorthy on 13 July 1946. "But am in clash at the moment with host." (The first letter below is dated on the basis of this remark.) Olson will regret leaving, he says, "for active physical life after five years doing me good. Went swimming in rapids of creek yesterday. Played two sets of tennis. Also harvested last of oats. Getting lean" (letter at Indiana). There is a snapshot confirming this (see the frontispiece to this volume). The first letter is a draft, which may indicate that no letter was sent; the second was definitely not sent: the envelope—addressed to "Adam Kulikowski Esq. c/o American Express, Paris, France 'To be forwarded Polandwards' "—was not postmarked. *Letters at Storrs.*

A LETTER TO A FRIEND

My dear A:

I regret we had to lock horns, and I dare say, because we are both bulls, that our passage of words may be mortal. I admit I am licking my wounds, and am full of bitterness.

The way we rushed at each other suggests to me that the words which passed between us sprang up out of a state of antagonism which has existed between us all this week. I have been puzzled and troubled about it, and should like to give you my sense of what is the cause of that antagonism before we lock again or each pass from the field. For the greatest danger is that we shall not speak, and thus let silence widen the gap.

When you heard the word "loveliness" last night you rushed in, and the split second you jumped on it I jumped back at you. It was all too fast to be actually a part of the argument then on about Wright's Black

Boy. When you struck at the word I used you were striking at my sense of life, and I was as swift as you to the strike because I am ready to defend it.

But I should like to tell you more of what I take to be reflexes which drove us into this sharp animal conflict. I understand now that you wanted your son's remarks to prevail. Good. I knew it, but not enough to keep silent, and once I had spoken, and you had taken exception, I hope you will grant, because you too have a strong sense of amour propre, that I had to speak out. For it was more than a son that was involved to me, it was myself. I regret I did not sense how strong your need now is to reinforce your son, or I would not have entered into the discussion at all.

---

217 Randolph Pl NE
Washington 2, D.C.
September 18, 1946

My dear Adam:

I left Enniscorthy Saturday to conduct a course in the New Jersey political action school. I shall not return, and I wanted to write you my thanks this first day I am back at my desk and base.

For your original largess in inviting us was a splendid thing, has still for me a splendor I shall always associate with you. I think I told you once you have the size in which Cleopatra dreams of an Antony. You keep it in my imagination, and my heart.

You might say, it is a little surprising, we did not define things better, you such an active man, and I who believe in accuracy. Together we could have kept things clear, if we had spoken. It is important we should speak, (we have in the past), for we are not little men, are big enough to grip like Romans, and sound against each other, to make echoes.

I shall say this. I have the sense that you and I both, since April, have, quite independently of each other, been undergoing an upheaval of our lives, from bottom up. I believe you have gone to Europe to seek a fresh start, and it is my profound wish you find it. I have been following my courses, too. I should hope that you might respect that, for I have valued your friendship. I was the more bewildered you talked to others, and not to me. Men have a way of holding confidences, and meeting each other in the large. That's why the ancients called friendship love no. 1. It still goes, with me.

So here's love, and best wishes on the trip. I myself begin anew.

Yrs,

Charles

22

To Ruth Benedict (1946)

The famous author of *Patterns of Culture,* Ruth Benedict, had impressed Olson when they were coworkers in the Office of War Information. It was to her that he wrote from Key West on 12 January 1945, at the moment of his resolve to leave politics for poetry: "I am alone again working down to the word where it lies in the blood," and adding what is possibly his first statement of a postmodern position: "I continuously find myself reaching back and down in order to make sense out of now and to lead ahead" (as copied by Olson in "Key West—January 1945," notebook at Storrs). Ruth Benedict's death in 1948 meant the loss of any further letters beyond the one below. *Letter at Vassar.*

217 Randolph Pl NE
Washington 2, D.C.
November 24, 1946

My dear Ruth Benedict:

It was such a delight to have your letter, forwarded from Key West. We are too rational to pay it mind, but the day it left Key West here I sat with you very much in my mind outlining a book I have started into, how much so you will gather from the 6th and central item: "the Cochiti tales"; and the last and climactic, which reads: "Kwakiutl"!

The book I started in Key West was bought last spring by Reynal & Hitchcock and will appear, in the slow fashion of publishing these days, around March 15, coming up. Its title: CALL ME ISHMAEL. Contents? well, for quick, let me give you what they insisted on for a sub-title: a book about Herman Melville, *Moby-Dick* and America, Their Power— and Price. That's close, I guess. I tried out in it a method of narrative I shall want to go much further with in this next work. It opens, for example, on a FIRST FACT, a telling of what happened to the 21 men of the crew of the "Essex" sunk by a sperm whale in the Pacific in 1819. They ended, as you may know, by eating each other, Nantucket men on Nantucket men. It serves me as prolog to a statement of us as Americans.

It is my feeling that *the record of fact* is become of first importance for us lost in sea of question. (Here I touch on why your work has meant so much, and why, I would say, you find, as you write me, that your students are ever so much more ready for the kind of thing you have to give them.) Excuse me if I go further with this, for I think you can help me. I do not mean Aristotelian fact. "Progress" itself involves an attitude, and has for my purposes invalidated much record. Plus the Christian moral frame as it has been a sociological wall. I tried in the "Essex" story to be as cold as tho I were in the Cochiti Ice Mountain Inferno. No interpretation *within* the story, no position. In New History the act of the observer, if his personality is of count, is before, in the selection of the material. This is where we will cut the knot. There has been, is too much of everything, including knowledge, because it has not been winnowed. And is it not because the West coming down to us from A, and C, has been a slow rifling of the assurance of person, of human power in the individual? so that we lose the courage to select? I think if you burn the facts long and hard enough in yourself as crucible you'll come to the few facts that matter. And then fact can be fable again.

It is fact as fable that I am after in this new book. I propose to open with Cabeza de Vaca, to get the first swift land weave of white, red and, via his companion Estevanico, the black. From there out I plan to tell about a dozen "facts" as simply and directly and as "scholarly" accurately (this is paramount) as possible, all to bear historically on the first or essential meetings of white, red and black with the land America, all at the same time, if they are correctly chosen, to read the keys to us as we are today. (This last end has a fatuous sound plans have a way of having. I should wait until you have had a look at the "Melville," and tested me. But you will guess, from the length of this answer to your lovely note, that I have need of your advice now, and make bold to assume your confidence.)

The advice I should be grateful for is this. I cannot pretend, nor can I accomplish, in the field of anthropology, a scholarship comparable to Melville, the whaling industry, and the Pacific. You were generous enough to say you would like, when I am in New York, to pick my brains. Yours I have already picked, and should like to, more. For example, some three or four years ago I ran into an Indian myth of the origin of the race in caves three levels down, and of the brutal issue of the people into the sun by ladders, making their way to the surface of the land stepping on each other, pushing down the weak to mount. The translator, if I remember right, was Cushing. I shall want to use that story, as I shall use yours. Now it occurs to me that you might be willing to put me in the way of such essential material as this, as your Cochiti hell, as your and Boas' Kwakiutl, which, in my ignorance, I would miss.

I think it is largely a matter of directing me to the other individuals of high quality who have worked and written in American anthropology, or to the singular myth or artifact. Do not, please, see any burden in this. I think it comes down to this: I have told you a little of the direction towards which I am finding my way. I throw this letter at you. When you have a moment, and can write me a note, my letter may have reminded you of things you have run across which seemed to you singular—as singular as you made the Kwakiutls—which you think I should read, if only to refresh and give shine to what I do use. Be assured that anything I provoke from you shall be fertile to me, as your work has been.

Let me add a couple of things to fill in the outline. I may cut back, after the de Vaca, to Folsom man, a portrait. After the Aztec and Cochiti I shall want to inject LASALLE, particularly that last tragic move to find the mouth of the Mississippi. He will come in as "coda," de Vaca again. I think also to use that crazy Beckwith on the Plains Indians before I close with your Kwakiutls.

I am full of curiosity to read your Japan book. Will it give me the clue to what you plan ahead—of European countries? Is all this a development out of the valuable if unrequited work you did here for the G?

You ask of Lew Frank. I had a letter from him this week. He has been doing a fine job for PAC, during '44 and '45, as Publicity Dir. for National Citizens PAC. Now he gives them all the time he can spare from running his father's paper business in Detroit. He and Patsy have a baby daughter. Come to think of it I believe I saw you last in their house here across the garden from me. I do believe we Olsons are the last of the lost Roosevelt tribe to be left squatting on this Washington ground!

My deep pleasure, and my fullest respect.

Yrs,

Charles Olson

By way of warning I wish I had in hand
to send you as present a little book
of 4 of my poems, plus 10 drawings by
Corrado Cagli, called *y & x*. But it's
been held up in the printing—Black Sun
Press—and shall not be ready until the
new year, when you shall have one.

Olson's progress with the unfinished book titled "Red, White, and Black" is laid out by George Butterick in *Olson* no. 5 (spring 1976); see especially the notes dated "November 20, 1946" (pp. 20–21) as pertinent to the above letter.

23

To John Berryman (1947)

In 1947 John Berryman was not yet a widely known writer, but Ezra Pound had gained an impression of him, and his name went down in the notes Olson made while visiting St. Elizabeths on 23 February 1947. Pound had been proposing a Committee of Correspondence, and the next day Olson wrote to Berryman at Princeton about it.   *Letters at Minnesota.*

217 Randolph Place NE
Washington 2, D.C.
February 24, 1947

Dear John Berryman:

That guy Pound!

We had it out again yesterday: "Damn! yr. generootion must find its own . . . Hang together or . . . Set up correspondence, committees of . . . (public safety?) . . . circular letters, we did, London, 1912, Louis Zukowski. . . ." He badgers.

I bang back, dig—"we who stay here to fight climate . . . skin, hair, and stay in private holes."

But crave polemic (got none from job on E.P. you may have seen PR last winter), and grant to myself the rightness of his tactic, agitator he is, contriver, still spry agent of the lit. revolution. Am of another breed myself.

Sez he: now Berryman, 1 of 4, 5 serious.

Granted. Know work, respect.

I have not opened 'cause the Olson hand is little played as yet. And I would lead, have any man lead, with his work. Will now, though. Berryman can judge—book (Melville etc.) "Call Me Ishmael," Reynal, out this month, and poems coming up soon from Black Sun Press.

So—for papa—this opener.

Cordially,

Charles Olson

---

217 Randolph Place NE
Washington 2, D.C.
March 19, 1947

Dear John Berryman:

I should much prefer to wait on an answer from you to my previous letter but Pound has asked me to answer your letter of Friday to him.

It's a plot of the wily man. He craves letters from you and a few more but he also wants you and me to make five with Allen, Spencer, West, and circulate letters, robin round or otherwise, among ourselves. Says he to me, and I to you, are you a man to write five lines at the end of the day, have you the energy left?

Frankly, I'm sounding you out before any step to the others. You say, students claw away your time. I claw my own away, and have other directions. Nor do I see anything else common to these five but one fact: each in his fashion has given Pound the sense, in the year and a half he has been back, that they are friendly to him. Is it enough?

Saw you him here you'd see that letters 1-1 are not enough, and I for one would like somehow to give him this other thing, a Sam Adams in Boston-Cambridge, you Charles Thomson in the middle colonies, and others (West? Allen?) in the new territories.

I dare say, from him, you catch the program: fight the fake wherever, viz, the public print, EXCERNMENT. Promote the "serious": "his" men Kung, Frobenius, Ford, Gesell, Fenollosa. You'd add Fenichel, I'd not know Gesell. Ford, Frobenius, Fenollosa I'd willingly war for.

But is this the way? I tell him we who've stayed here have not the habit of polemic. But maybe we should learn, and this is a start. In any case it'd be a present to, an action for, an honor of a most civilized guy locked up in St Elizabeths.

In five lines, what do you say, sir?

Mrs P is sending you the five mss Angolds Leite never gave me an answer on. And go ahead on the others you excerned from NEW. A is dead, killed in crash, and only his widow plus the Pounds have him in memora.

E.P. was most gratified at your precision re contemporaries. Myself, I'd except M. Lowry.

Word of you from Bob Giroux was good.

Yrs,

Olson

To the second letter, Berryman replied to Olson in five lines that he declined to participate in producing a round robin to gratify Pound (postcard of 22 March 1947 at Storrs). Needless to say, Olson, half-hearted anyway about a committee of correspondence on Pound's model, did not pursue the idea.

24

To Harvey Breit (1947)

Harvey Breit worked for the *New York Times Book Review* and was therefore an influential friend. He was instrumental in getting "A Lion Upon the Floor," Olson's first published poem, into *Harper's Bazaar*. However, the retrospective review of *Twice A Year* (TAY) mentioned in the letter below never made the pages of the paper, and *Call Me Ishmael* went for review, unhappily as it turned out, to Lewis Mumford. Perhaps Breit wasn't so helpful after all.

Letter at Northwestern.

3/1/47

Harvey!

Most gratifying to have note from you: do do it again, and again, and again. You can't imagine how much news of you can mean here in the desert. Desert comes to be the word because I got out for the first time in a month Sunday, and had a gab with Poundie, and talked about you to him, and retold your story of Bunting. Bunting, it seems, is now such an expert on Persian and Persia he is able to turn down all offers from the British Foreign Office and still have them coming back with more!

And do come for that weekend any time you want to. It was such a disappointment when the wire didn't come, and I couldn't use the answer, and you didn't come, and there warn't no Harvey to have around.

It was just about that time that that gland which lies sou-sou-east of the left ear suddenly ups and turns into a molehill, with the god-damned mole inside. And he's still there. I'm waiting now for spring. But the worst of the infection seems over.

I figure you have the Melville book by now. I got my first copy yesterday. I asked them, as you know, long time ago, to send you an advance copy. By the way, excuse, please, the dust jacket: had nothing to do with it, and am dismally upset about it. Hate this personal business: and such a puss! Do hope Weaver obliges you. But still want most to hear what one H. . . . . B. . . . has to say. Am nervous! (Such a funny business it is, to be all outside there, anywhere, whoever reads, looks at you!)

And am curious as all get out about the mysterious galleys you say you will send on TAY: what? do.

All o's this morning, good round O's! For you. So Connie tOO—
Love,
Charles

25

To Eleanor and Harry Metcalf (1947)

It was while working for his M.A. that Olson first entered the home of Melville's granddaughter Eleanor Melville Metcalf in Cambridge, Massachusetts, and was so welcomed by her and her husband, Harry, that he became like one of the family. Many research leads were subsequently discovered, for which Olson must have expressed thanks in many letters. At the moment, however, only a very few drafts or carbons retained by Olson are available; the one below was written at the appearance of *Call Me Ishmael.*   *Draft letter at Storrs.*

3/1/47

My dear Eleanor and Harry Metcalf:

This should have been a note enclosed in a copy of a book by one c. . . . . . o. . . . which two people who have been so much to me had so much to do with. BUT I was not in New York when that book came from the bindery because a sub-maxillary gland turned into a mountain a month ago. And am still pretty much house bound. But if Reynal & Hitchcock are functioning properly the advance copy I asked them to send to you should be on its way to you now. I got my copy special yesterday. If you do not get it reasonably soon please let me know. For I am most anxious that you should have it first.

I was so glad to have your letter, and to know that Jay Leyda was back, with you, and at his most valuable work. Please, when you see him, give him my warm regards, and say to him: write Olson. You might tell him how much I appreciated his lead on the ship Chase was skipper of when Melville saw him in the south pacific. I checked with friend Tripp, and the mystery remains, for the *Nassau,* with Chase as master, returned to New Bedford May 13, 1841. Thus, if the *Acushnet* did speak her, it must have been early in the year in Atlantic waters or, as Tripp points out, in the neighborhood of the Horn, a most unlikely place for a gam. And when the *Nassau* sailed again in September it was under another master, Weeks.

Connie is fine, and joins me in love to you both. Do write and let us have all the news. It is mostly a desert here, and letters in the box are a god send. We are like country people, on an rfd rte, snowed in, whom only the mail reaches! So do say hello, and give us that pleasure.

Yrs,
Charles

26

To Douglas Fox (1947)

Leo Frobenius was one of Pound's men that Olson felt he wanted to study seriously for himself, but most of Frobenius's work was still in German. One thing readily available was Douglas Fox's translations of folktales published in 1937 under the title *African Genesis.* Olson was so taken with some of these that he recast them to form a proposition about origins. However, the resulting piece, "Origo," was never published.   *Letter (carbon copy) at Storrs.*

217 Randolph Place NE
Washington 2, D.C.
April 19, 1947

My dear Douglas Fox:

Regret very much you are not here. Called, wanted to see you, to bring you a copy of my book, CALL ME ISHMAEL, just out: will hold until I hear from you, for one day I should like very much to have your analysis of the stuff on Space in it (written, as you may recall, before I knew of your work, and your colleague's).

Wanted also to get a permission of you. Finished the first draft of a piece last night which gives me a chance I have long waited for, to make what I take to be a novel use of two of your tales, the Kabyl First Man, Woman and 50 Chillun and Gassire. I shall enclose on a separate page the opening of the article and the way I acknowledge you, in order that you may have a sense of the intent and present form of the piece. The Kabyl, due to the design, is condensed and somewhat rewritten, and Gassire I break up some at the beginning but from the partridge on use pretty much as you have so finely translated it.

Now I don't, of course, know where the thing will land. Harper's Bazaar, who have bought a couple of my verse, has asked to see something else and I am thinking of trying this out on them. But in any case I wanted to get this letter off to you in hopes that it will reach you quickly and that you will be able to let me know if the whole idea meets with your approval, if you will grant me permission to make what use I have of the material and, if you will be so kind, what the copyright situation is and what terms would be agreeable under it.

At the moment I am somewhat excited about the thing, for it is the first break in some of the things we talked about last year, and I have hopes more might follow from it. Do let me know any developments along these lines from your end.

And how are you?
And what are you up to?
Our friends and I speak of you often.

Yours,

Charles Olson

27

To Edward Dahlberg (1947)

The letter below sums up the changeable and aggravating relationship Olson had with Edward Dahlberg, ten years his senior, whose interests and style of writing were for a time so embarrassingly close that periodic repudiations became a prerequisite for Olson in order to develop his own way. This meant that ingratitude was an accusation Dahlberg always had to hand. For instance, Dahlberg wrote, in the letter to which Olson is replying here, "In our friendship I labored for you and not for myself. . . . If it will give you more felicity to have the newspaper Barabbases, the Van Dorens and Brooks call you genius rather than I, I will try to bridle my tongue" (letter of 25 April 1947 at Storrs). The full correspondence from 1936 to 1955 is presented in *In Love, In Sorrow* (1990). It reveals that though much was written after 1947, the nature of the relationship was fixed pretty much as Olson describes it here.

Letter (carbon copy) at Storrs.

April 29
217 Randolph Place NE
Washington 2, D.C.

My dear Edward:

I want to be clear with you, and without the humping of the blood when I last wrote. Yet you anger me, when, in pieties, you wrap and hide your greed. Now you would eat my book as you would diet of my father's death and curse my mother for the food she gave me!

Why don't you ask of me my name? I'll give it to you, and you'll have it all. I am Nobody, he said.

Cut away these holy wrappings, cease to play Christ and to quote me Chester plays, so we can speak together, now, for I am unread by you and do not wish to wait for posthumous Christian places imagined by literary men. If you were able to distinguish between us you would know from ISHMAEL, especially the CHRIST, what a lie I take a path to be which leads a man to make himself a Cross and cry, "I hate the world."

It is thin of you to think I go the way of the world because I stay in the world. Or that comfort is the alternate to a Cross. It is mechanical conclusion. Your Essene rite of self blinds you, it would seem, and makes your fine ear dull. I miss active thought, and intent, when you speak as you now speak. You repeat, and in incantations which do not speak but hypnotize— yourself. Brooks   Van Doren   Pound, repeat, Brooks   Van Doren   Pound. But what do you know? You miss now as you so flatly missed seven years ago, the meaning of events, of who and why I see. For behaviour is a long bow. It can only be confused with identity by those who confuse the ritual in life with ritual in individual behaviour.

If you would play Christ, to succor yourself, do. I said as much, and wished it, with the heart, for you. But when you come down and seek to flagellate others with these outworn rods, these pitiful weapons of a literary religion, it won't work. "Sacrilege", "betrayal", nonsense. You kill a friendship when you make yourself so pious. I do wish you'd left things as they were, contained, despite our disagreement, for I took pride in you, valued the many things you'd given me, had learned, as a young writer might, from your critique. Now you must regurgitate.

Have you no sense of another man's memory? Do you know memory as anything other than a rosary of your own acts which you tell over as you walk with yourself, you and yourself in long monkish robes? It's a crazy business, friendship with you, a game, I'm damned if I do and damned if I don't. You offered me many things. I accepted them. Obviously I could not give them back in kind. How I give them back is, is it not, to be my way, not yours? If you gave them, now only to blackmail me with them, then, surely, anyone would wish they had not been given. That is why I say I regret you have chosen to misread my note in answer to your gracious letter on the book and to judge me, judge me, judge me, three times down the wind, with dead leaves.

Yrs,

28

To Monroe Engel (1947)

The novelist Monroe Engel began his career as an editor with Reynal & Hitchcock in New York, supervised the production of *Call Me Ishmael* (1947), and commissioned a second book from Olson. The subject was to be the American West. The first postcard presented below, written on 13 June 1947, records a significant reattachment to Gloucester, just prior to Olson's trek with Connie to Seattle and California via South Dakota (second postcard, 8 July 1947), a literal engagement with the Wild West. The longer letter of 27 December 1947 describes the research on the book, now to be Viking's, as Engel has moved to that publishing house. *Postcards and letter at Harvard.*

                                            Stage Fort Avenue
                                            June 13

E's:

   1st time Gloucester clear & not home town. Very exciting. Ears wide open.

   Have been asked to Northwest Writers Conference, Seattle, 1st week August. Have accepted, & are now figuring ways and means.

   Busy as hands in a storm, Connie fishing the Cut, I listening to wharves & men.

   Here a week or two more—let us hear the news.

                                            Yrs, the Olsons

                                            July 8

Research, brother, research! La Salle on the 4th, this wonderful place, Jim Beckwith coming up today on the Bozeman Trail. Ain't I surprised!
   Address: Trout Lake
            Route 1, Box 548,
            Puyallup, Washington.

                                            Love fr both of us.

                                            Cal. State Library
                                            Dec 27 Saturday

My dear Monroe:

   Connie just read me yr letter over the phone. Been waiting since Tuesday for word from you, happy things are at last straightened out.

I think this one overwhelming fact will answer yr question: for 4 months I have been living from pillar to post up & down this coast doing research for the book & discovering such material that I have been led on, first day to day, then week to week, until I invested everything, our fare home, & then some. It started at the Huntington, led to the Bancroft (Berkeley) then here to Sutter's Fort & Cal. State Library. The results are so good I have been asked to publish a couple of the finds in the Cal. Hist. Soc. Quart., & I propose to take other steps to enable me to continue the research. I have been at it night & day and let all else go to hell—one reason you didn't hear. You know my method. This phase is the hardest, slowest, and, especially on the road, most expensive.

Now things are very serious, have been all this week. Connie must return to Washington & I must go down to Berkeley to the Bancroft to relate new material there to what is here. I was hoping all week I might hear from you by phone or wire, for *these moves have to be made Monday.* (It was just because I couldn't see how the switch could be made fast that I asked R&H for funds strictly on the Ishmael, with no mention of the West book which you & I had agreed to settle on my return east.) The delay of this week forces me to make this extraordinary request of you: will Viking be good enough to deposit the 250 to my checking account, The National Bank of Washington, D.C. 7th & Pennsylvania Ave, by Tuesday (or Wednesday), accepting the fact that I have already signed a contract for the book as earnest of my responsibility to them.

If you could wire me Monday I should be most obliged. Otherwise I shall have no way to know, mail is so very bad. Things (family et al) are most serious. I have to have money—or know I will have it—*Monday night.*

Much is left unsaid. But I must rush this off to you. Please allow me to depend upon you.

Connie & I are both so very anxious to know about Brenda—& when the baby is expected. And about yr work. Please write—& I promise to do the same.

Do let me have word Monday. I assure you it is crucial.

Love,

Charles

The address the same, until I hear from you:
> c/o Gildersleeve
> 4360 23rd Ave
> Sacramento 17.

P.S.

At Post Office. I want you to understand the *urgency.* For example, Connie has to go within hours or we lose house & jeopardize belongings.

Desperate—

Disaster averted, Olson was able to stay in California another four weeks.

29

To Muriel Rukeyser (1947)

The poet Muriel Rukeyser was one of the people Olson met in San Francisco as he moved down the coast from the writers conference in Seattle. Rukeyser gave him the address of the writer Robert Payne in Hollywood, who introduced him to the poet Edwin Rolfe. And so it went. Olson writes here from the Los Angeles beach community of Venice about almost breaking into films.

Letter at New York Public Library.

> 220 Sunset Avenue
> Venice
> Oct 1

My dear Muriel Rukeyser—
You are a starter.

1st, greetings to you & yr baby now that I imagine the child is come. I called Robert Payne yesterday, figuring he'd have the news, but he was in the business of moving, & I could catch him neither place. (Glad to know him, by the way—& Ed Rolfe, too.)

This past month has a trace back to you, to yr encouraging remark CMI is a shooting script. I have no impression Hollywood agrees—

which leaves you bracketed with Eisenstein (if I read him right). But John Huston has asked me to do a critique of his script of a Moby-Dick movie, if he & Blankery, his producer, can get Jack Warner to agree to it on his return next week. Jack Warner, it appears, is haunted by another whale—a $365,000 job made for the Sea Beast, which sounded in 50 fathom the day they launched it, & did not come up. Result: he has not yet agreed to allow Huston to do a Moby-Dick, & may not ever.

I shall, thus, be here a further 10 days, & shld like news of you, & another beginning.

Yrs,

Charles Olson

Muriel Rukeyser replied on 7 October 1947: "I hope they will have some sense at last about the whale" (letter at Storrs). When Olson told this anecdote to Pound on his return to Washington, Pound wagged his head and said, "Well, seven months, one story, not bad . . ." (*Charles Olson and Ezra Pound: An Encounter at St. Elizabeths,* p. 98).

30

To the Guggenheim Foundation (1948)

The trip to the West Coast was unplanned, but seems in retrospect to have been preordained as the necessary fuelling for the book on the West that had been commissioned by Monroe Engel. The various stages of Olson's thinking on this theme are presented in *Olson* no. 5 (spring 1976), including the Guggenheim Fellowship proposal that followed H. A. Moe's positive response to the letter below. *Letter (carbon copy) at Storrs.*

Berkeley, California
January 10, 1948

Mr. Henry Allen Moe
Secretary General
The John Simon Guggenheim Memorial Foundation
New York City, N.Y.

My dear Mr. Moe,

The way the work on this new book has developed I am led to ask if you will consider me an applicant for a Guggenheim renewal.

I have been out here since July, when I came to do the lecture on poetry and criticism at the Pacific Northwest Writers Conference at the University of Washington. I had a letter from Miss Leighton at that time and, in answering her, brought the record up to that date. (If I remember rightly I listed two books which were due before this from Paris—the Gallimard Melville and the Black Sun poems. They have not yet come to hand.)

Since then things have developed. I had started last spring the book I had been muttering about to myself for years. It is a successor to the Melville, to be based on the same method of total research, the end the questions about this land and people. But this time I proposed to publish the research as it was made and, in the book itself, to increase the narrative. The idea is to take what I see as seven archetype persons and events, and put them together turning on the table of the land:

Cabeza de Vaca—Estevanico   Cortez—Donna Marina   LaSalle;

Jim Beckwourth, emerging from preceding Indian interpolations
        and Negro sub-plot;

the Donner-Sutter complex, (the book's climax) anthropophagy-gold.

I worked Cabeza all last spring. Out here I started at the Huntington to investigate manuscripts, particularly on the last part, and what has happened since should not happen to a man with home and family. It has led me up and down the coast. Most of the time I have been in Sacramento, at the Sutter Fort and the State Library Collections. At the State Library I turned up the unsorted and unedited papers of George McKinstry. He was the recorder of the Donner story as sheriff and one of Sutter's managers, and new material on it and the whole '46 crossing is there, Sutter is there, the story of the Fort and the mill, the gold discovery and a good deal of the whole story from 1846 to 1850. I am at the moment preparing some of the things for publication by the California Historical Society Quarterly and by the Book Club of California.

All this has increased the reference the last part of the book will have, I think, and has done the same for the Indian material (which is to be used in a similar fashion to the "Facts" of the Melville book). As of the work ahead on the rest: I shall, for awhile, depend on Barlow in Mexico City to keep me straight on Cortez-Marina. The LaSalle is another matter and may, in the end, lead to France. But I am launched, Viking will publish, and staked me to an advance to keep me out here up until now.

Beyond such a letter as this to you I am not quite sure about procedure on renewal. Shall you want a more complete plan of work? I have the project the publishers accepted and can reshape it for you. Shall you want a panel of sponsors? There is one man who knows more about the book than anyone else, Carl Sauer. As a matter of fact he is the only one to whom I have confided the full scope, for his own imagination has brought a lot of it alive in me.

If you should find it possible to honor me again I would be grateful if the work is denominated creative. As you know I rest and believe in scholarship. The record of fact is, in my method, the root. It is what I take time for. But that method ends in narrative and image and it is a gain, I think, if all concerned expect that.

Mail now is reaching me care of the Bancroft Library here, Dr George Hammond, Director. My permanent address is, of course, unattached writer, Washington, D.C.

My personal greetings

Cordially yours,

Charles Olson

Olson received the Guggenheim fellowship (his second), but the commissioned book was never written, except as metamorphosed into the volume of verse titled 'West' (1966). A small amount of Olson's work for the California Historical Society appeared in his introduction to The Sutter-Marshall Lease (Book Club of California, 1948).

31

To Ezra Pound (1948)

The following letter, the first letter to Ezra Pound in which Olson presented independent views (and, not unexpectedly, the last), was typed on Santa Fe Railroad stationery, Olson having just crossed the country by train. He had, from the West Coast, kept in touch with Pound as much as anyone, and within three days of returning he went to St. Elizabeths to report. But he was edgy and ready to be irreverent. The visit was described by Olson in notes published posthumously in *Charles Olson and Ezra Pound: An Encounter at St. Elizabeths* (1975), so we know the background to this letter, which was written later that day, Sunday, 8 February 1948. Olson told Robert Creeley that he "came home, got drunk, and hammered off the note did break it" (letter at Stanford, 17 June 1953). It was Pound's racial slurs that Olson by this time was not prepared to let go by. Olson, bridling, reports Pound on "immigrant America": "Ya, they'll end up in sterilization. I was against passports a long time ago" (*Charles Olson and Ezra Pound*, p. 93). Olson could not resist posing his own recent European ancestry against the *Mayflower* strain that Pound liked to say he came from.

Letter at Indiana.

[letterhead]
Santa Fe   El Capitan

EP: You're right sterilization is the upshot. But to tie to immigrant Amurrika is post hoc etc. I am thinking of B. Franklin, and others of the Middle Colonies. Carl O Sauer is right, yes? to see the M C as the root of the Middle Class kultur (New York recognized as such). The bracket Adams and Jefferson were politically and intellectually defeated almost simultaneous to their presidencies?

I'm agin you on this passport policy. (or am I, stop to think of it) Erase this. I'll not stop now. See yr point. Maybe, to start somewhere, yes.

BUT you do have to deal with us Olsons, Leite-Rosenstock-Huessys; your damn ancestors let us in. (AND AS ABOVE I DON'T THINK THE BATHTUB WAS SO CLEAN WHEN THEY DID.) We're here, and to tell you your own truth, you damn well know anglosaxonism is academicism and shrieking empire: LIFE out of Yale, CULTURE out of Princeton, and THE BOMB out of Harvard.

Don't get me wrong. I'm as much against Bill W's dramatizations of stocks as my father was (before the USGovt went out to get 'im and forced him back into Svenska dagblat localism, both of which he died young). Contra also I hate the sterilization of foreign nationality Amurrikans: Greeks and Negroes who go "white."

I would bring yr attention to bear on Leo Frobenius Olson: the morphology in loc. cit. is not as easy as it appears, Europewards.

The proposition: wrong from the start. Take a space and hurl economic, religious and 18th century derelicts in, and you get a pot. So far as Prince Jefferson goes, ever read his letter on the education of his daughter? He was contaminated.

The hard core to stand invasion may never be arrived at. But what do we know about China before Chou? Ya, I know, people don't get time these days. And agreed: the only way to get a core is what you tell us. But brother: we get decomposed here. We are not decomposition via the Atlantic. The frontier here is where you are—also where my father arrived. And my grandfather, to get the date back before the post hoc fallacy. He rolled in his red underdrawers on green grass, something about the time of Grant's 1st administration. (Adams is so powerful he has confused me into reading two administrations.)

The breakdown of the cells: the Indians of the Northwest used to call all whites "Boston men." Yr gd damn Europeans (I speak of my ancestors) (and yrs) acted from the start like a fucking bunch of G.I.s on leave in invaded country. Holiday. (Exception: Cabeza de Vaca. He knew.

      His grandfather had conquered the
      Canaries, and C de V was raised by
      "colored" folk.)
Aristotelian VD bastards.

I'm with you. You got to start somewhere. Ok. We're starting. But let's you see what yr people are. Truculent ummugrunts.

Yes sir.

one of em

CHARLES JOHN HINES OLSON

Pound replied by return mail, with a customary postcard (at Storrs, postmarked 12 February 1948), that Olson should sit down with Confucius and not bother him with secondhand, mass-produced "bricabrak." "Goddamn him," Olson wrote to Creeley (letter at Stanford, 17 June 1953) that "he cld let such a note have such an easy answer." Olson went to St. Elizabeths on one further occasion, but got more of the same—this time innuendo about William Carlos Williams's mixed blood (*Charles Olson and Ezra Pound*, p. 101). For Olson, this was the end.

IV

Olson came into his own with the publication of *y & x,* the first copies of which arrived from Caresse Crosby's Black Sun Press in October 1948. Five Olson poems were printed alongside five drawings by the Italian painter Corrado Cagli, a special friend. Other friends—Frances Boldereff and Robert Creeley—strengthened him at this time with daily correspondence.

Olson also established himself as an extraordinary teacher with visits at Black Mountain College beginning in October 1948.

He was released by the death of his mother in December 1950 to make a journey with Connie to the Yucatan in Mexico.

32

To the Western Playing Card Company (1948)

In lieu of letters to Carrado Cagli (not available at present), we have the following evidence of their collaborative spirit.   *Letter (carbon copy) at Storrs.*

217 Randolph Place NE
Washington 2, D.C.
July 7, 1948

Mr. W. R. Wadewitz
President
The Western Playing Card Company
Racine, Wisconsin

My dear Mr. Wadewitz:

   I am writing to offer you direct a playing card project, the joint work of Corrado Cagli and myself, both of us Guggenheim Fellows, he the American and Italian painter, I the American writer and poet.

   For some years Cagli and I have been collaborating in the use of the Tarot pack for painting and writing as well as projects in the field of music and the dance. I am enclosing, under accompanying cover, copies of HARPER'S BAZAAR and TOWN AND COUNTRY in which some of that work has already appeared. (In the last instance you will note that one of Cagli's drawings appears in the same issue with one of your full-page advertisements.)

   The interest of these magazines is only one sign of—what I dare say you have noticed yourself—a growing curiosity on the part of Americans in the Tarot cards as the most dramatic and mysterious of all playing cards. That is point 1.

   Point 2 is, we have found that the moment the names of the characters and suits of the Tarot are translated for Americans and the meanings of the numbers and the arcana related to the western pack as they know it, the Americans are most fascinated to know more about the Tarot and to use a pack for themselves.

Now despite these two points not only is there no pack available in English to our knowledge, but no American playing card company is taking advantage of the curiosity in the Tarot to call attention, by the fresh and most unusual illustrative materials the Tarot offers, to playing cards in general.

We have, therefore, blocked out a project which we should like you to be the first American playing card manufacturer to consider. It is the design of a new pack of 78 cards, an AMERICAN TAROT, the face designs in color by Cagli and the translations, interpretations etc. by Olson.

The project is three-fold. It offers immediately

(1) a wholly new and dramatic series of designs and devices for magazine and display advertising on playing cards in general

and, the moment the 78 cards are completed,

(2) a new and novel pack for prestige attention to your company, as well as some immediate sale for fortune telling and future sale as a new American game;

(3) an unusual and dramatic folder-book (made up from the interpretive material of each card) on the mystery and history of the tarot as the oldest of playing cards, which would serve both the purposes of general card promotion as well as serve as an introduction to the AMERICAN TAROT pack itself.

What we would propose, if you are interested, is to lay the work out for some such period as a year, starting to supply you as soon as possible with what we regard as the foremost immediate value of the project, the series of advertisements dramatized by the use of such figures of the major and minor arcana as "The Fool" or the "Bagatto"—"the Man of Magic" (a copy of Cagli's plate of which I have also included with the magazines.)

I shall look forward to hearing from you. And do, please, hold the accompanying material for return to me.

Cordially yours,

Charles Olson

Cagli: (shows) Knoedler, New York, 1948, 1947; Hugo, NY, 1946;
San Francisco Museum, 1946; Arts Club, Chicago, 1946
La Palma, Rome, 1948, 1947; London, Paris etc
(stage) The Triumph of Bacchus and Ariadne, Ballet Society
New York, 1948, and others
(books) TRENTI DISEGNI, Studio d'Arte Palma, Rome, 1946
y & x (Cagli and Olson) Black Sun Press, Paris, 1948
Olson: (books) *y & x*   "   "   "
CALL ME ISHMAEL Reynal & Hitchcock N.Y. 1947
(stage) *The Fiery Hunt,* dance-play, Graham-Hawkins, NY, 1948
(verse) The Atlantic Monthly, Harper's, The Partisan Review,
The Western Review, Harper's Bazaar, Portfolio etc.

On 14 July the company returned Olson's submission: "We already have a Tarot
deck on the market and sales during the last ten years have not been more than
a few thousand decks per year" (letter at Storrs). Cagli's drawing "Bagatto" was
included in the brochure of *Charles Olson—Corrado Cagli,* an exhibition
sponsored by the University of Connecticut at the William Benton Museum of
Art, March–April 1973.

33
To Edward Dahlberg and Caresse Crosby (1948)

Olson was drawn to Philadelphia for the Democratic Party's national convention,
12–16 July 1948, but this was his last effort in party politics. Indeed, he played
truant from the convention to go to the Philadelphia Museum of Art. The letters
he wrote on his return to Edward Dahlberg and the flamboyant patron Caresse
Crosby, proprietor of the Black Sun Press (BSP in the letter below) are less
concerned with politics than with Giovanni di Paolo and the Sienese school of
painting.   *Letter to Dahlberg at Texas; letter to Crosby at Southern Illinois.*

Tuesday, July 20

My dear Edward:
    I am going to make this a note deliberately: I must get out of this
humid house and go to the gallery where it is cool and a man's head
can be Duccio Buoninsegna's sea, which is grass, and the fish are fish

in grass, and Jesus and Peter and James are fisher men and Siena was a christian place when spirit was alive as fish are alive, and grass.

(Which has not been true since? I picked up a book of Dostoevsky's short stories the other day and read it on a train and was not interested as I once was interested and was struck again with the accuracy of your discussion of Dostoevsky's ennui, and the root of it in sex.)

Saying these things I am suddenly aware of why I am interesting myself at the moment in Giovanni di Paolo. It is a double search, against suavity in art and spirit. I prefer his "St Clare" and "St Nicholas of Torentino" to Sassetta (I do not know his "St John the Baptist" in Chicago). I take it, his awkwardness is a clue. He, and Domenico Veneziano. And the insistence on the small subject. All quantity has sickened, and suavity is the Picasso of that big and competent world. I begin to see why I want small plays, 2, 3 people, woodwinds, no sets: chamber theatre, music, painting. It is a point of beginning.

I said a note. It is two weeks late. Something told me I should have shot off to you a card, even, to say, do send the FLEA when you have it. I await it. (I thought to write a letter and, instead, went off to Philadelphia to rub against the beast and make my own fur rise.)

Yrs,
Charles

A propos Keats:
have you noticed the hidden poem called
an Epistle to Reynolds?

(It is in the 1925 ed. of Poems & Letters, Houghton Mifflin, p. 241)
(March 25, 1818) (Also see letter, p. 295, & note, p. 461)
I honor him as much for that as anything.

Friday—the 23rd July xlviii

CAResse!
More. More. Your letters come like a breeze into this humid house. Washington is unbearable this summer, testify others as well as hot me. Yr letters are like kisses of life.

And such news of *y & x!* Result: I now list it as among my publications, BSP, 1948! Had occasion to make out a "life" for lecture next week
at Am. U. Intersession (they call it! sounds sexual to me) and so did.
Came about at P. Blanc's the other night: a Jack Tworkov is here for six
weeks as painter-on-visit with Calfee. Am now making "Notes on the
New Dimension": idea, why we critters take Duccio, Sassetta, Giovanni
di Paolo, etc., even up as far as Piero and Uccello, as more interesting
than the big and suave boys. The coins I'm handling, the counters,
are: awkwardness (as permanent cloth of spirit), the oblique as a via to
confront direct,—as guerillas, maquis—the enemy. The enemy being:
quantity, materialism, the suave: Chiang Kai Check.

And as for that lovely white horse's ass: AGREE, AGREE! Only you
had me stopped for a minute. For Giovanni di Paolo to paint a horse,
I couldn't figure out. Now I know. And are you right! Don't you mean
Paolo Uccello's lovely horse in the Uffizi ROUT OF SAN ROMANO?
There was also a like tender blooming behind in the German Show, but
that, I think, was in either Masaccio's or Domenico Veneziano's Adora-
tion of the Magi.

Had lunch this week with Huntington. Also talked to John Walker.
You were very much present to both. H showed me the proofs of his
most curious anthology of 1400pp.: The Limits of Art, Hyperion. If we
had polemic in this country he'd get gone over, for it is a most polemi-
cal idee: the selections are based on the superlatives of critics, those
creatures who live off the host. Walker is at work on his "paper" on
Bellini's Feast of Gods. (In that connection take a look at Wind's job
on it, Harvard, this year: as clean as scholars can be, and alive.)

See Ruf-us save-us Saturday. (He may not get away: French will take
weeks to give him permanent visa.)—I am on the spit vis-a-vis politics
at moment. Both the New and Old Party propose I deliver my "votes",
my hunky, wop, spick, canuck, pole-schitz, svensk, dutch mongrels, out
of their offices. But damned if I want to give up four months, much as
I need their dough. Or perhaps the real trouble is, I can't go for any of
their positions. We citizens of the woooorrrlllddd—the plain pippul—
"IIIII ggggive you a mmmman" "IIIII ggggive you a mman WHO . . ."
find their ends and means rotted. It was curious in Philly to see how

broken the whole political front is, how mixed up the good men are
in each camp.

Delighted you'll be back soon. We'll have much to talk about.
The "piece" on G di P was meant to be ambiguous. Whether it's prose
and/or verse I could not say, cannot.—Say, can you tell me in what way
peintura tonale does describe a different palette from that which followed after Piero, right down to now? Or who is a painter disciplined
enuf in this here town to tell me? It is one big unanswered question for
me at the moment.

You did not enclose the letter (the intersecession) to the—was it
"Progressives"? Do.

Hail the BSP "Painter-Poet" It could be handsome, and important,
now that nobody here pays the relation mind. Open on Eluard. And remember Baudelaire—at least one on Delacroix. And what about Gau-
tier? And Keats on Claude's Enchanted Castle—which is the finest thing
K left, and nobody knows it. It's hidden. Look at it. It's in his "supplementary verses", called "An Epistle to James Reynolds", about March, I
think, 1818. Such lines as:

> Lost in a purgatory blind
>   the Robin
> ravening a worm
>   I saw
> too far into the sea, where every maw
> the greater on the less feeds evermore

It is the last reach of him, the promise of what he might have done, that
Masaccio he was (almost). The pome on Claude is unKeats.

Further idea: why not follow it with tuppenny pamflets of painter-
poet now: each issue a poem and drawing or repro: Eluard-Picasso,
Lorca-Frances, Pound-Cagli, De Chirico-Olson, St Perse-who?,
Montale-Morandi, etc. etc. Eliot-Lowell! etc

Must run. Keep 'em flying, o Caresse, o citoyen du monde, o bellisima!

> Love from us both
> yrs for more life
>
> Charles

The "piece" on Giovanni di Paolo does not seem to have survived; it was presumably a forerunner of the poem "Siena," which Caresse Crosby received in due course. See *Collected Poems*, p. 78.

34

To Henry Murray (1948)

Olson met Henry Murray at the fireside of Eleanor Melville Metcalf, and the bond between them was that of a pioneering fraternity. Murray, whose private wealth enabled him to consult Carl Jung about *Moby-Dick* as well as set up his own psychology institute at Harvard, was a patron as well as a friend of the Olsons—"ready, at any time to give a lift where there is an utter emergency," as Olson once put it to Frances Boldereff, adding, "I have myself only called on him twice, and the total about 350 in ten years" (letter, 10 February 1950 at Storrs). This is one of those times. *Letters at Storrs.*

> October 1, 1948
> 217 Randolph Place NE Washington

My dear Harry:

It is ridiculous that at this stage of my life suddenly I am snarled in difficulties. I'll get out of them, and have spent the last few days seeking a teaching job here to get the ship righted before winter. But food and this house are immediately threatened and I write to ask if you could help me. You have often asked me if you could, and on two occasions have, but I have never before asked you myself, and tender this letter to you as the most fragile thing.

For nearly three months Constance and I have lived on our nerves. Almost from the start of a pregnancy she bled. Her gyn wanted nature to take its course. She had to give up her job as manager of the Nat'l Inst of Practical Nursing, her first real success in the world, and just got weaker and weaker. The doctor finally put her in Columbia Hospital and after a week did a d & c. Or what he said was such, for the next day, to my consternation, I found them giving her a quart transfusion: that day, as she put it, she had had the labor of seven births, had aborted the foetus *after* the operation. I have not yet ventured to ask the full story of her and as for the doctor, supposedly the No 2 man in town, I have a horror of seeing him again. It was last week, her third month. I imagine you will know whether or not there was anything more than merely the worst kind of miscarriage, but it has left us both severely shaken.

The doctor's bill came today, and the amount of it makes me the more suspicious: only $50.

Well, enough of the cause. The upshot is this: the butcher has carried us on food, but he asked me yesterday if he could have the $125 we owe him by next Wednesday when his note with his bank comes due. On top of that I had to hold the rent off and use it to pay the hospital bill of $147. These two are the immediate pressures. With some teaching I can start to take care of current expenses but except for an advance of $50 I raised yesterday as a final advance on *y & x* (which is now, at last, in press, and I shall be able to send you around November 15, that's the poems, with drawings by Cagli, published Black Sun, Paris) I am without funds.

There it is. But do, Harry, give this letter not a second thought, please, if it in any way comes as a burden. Your generosity is already a singular thing in my experience.

I said this whole business is ridiculous. It is. It stems from this course, started last spring, of plays for the dance and verse theatre. That work has left me where I now am, yet by spring all things promise to be jumped way ahead. *The Fiery Hunt* should then be published (as well as *y & x*), for Viking are considering it now and I have another offer if it is too small and fancy for their commercial purposes. The second play, a mask called *Troilus,* which I had a quarter done when all this hell broke out, ought to be finished, plus the third, a ballet of Ulysses.

Do let me know what, if any effect *About Space* had on you, and news of your own work. And come to Washington soon. I have not been away since I last tried you in New York but shall have to make a trip to find my mother a room in Worcester for the winter soon. Shall I be able to see you then?

With love from us both,
Charles

Sunday
October 10, 1948

My dear Harry:

Your gift is a talisman: this morning Josef Albers called and has asked us down to Black Mountain College for a week, I to lecture, Constanza to take the mountain air. Her doctor says, all to the good, and it comes on the very prick of time. But for us the turn came Friday with your letter, and I thank you deeply, Harry, for the deliverance. You have enabled us to start back to life.

Your news of yourself is distressing. What *was* the Leyda-Morewood incident that gave you such trouble? In any case, do not feel bad at slowness. It is the ripeness that is all, and that men of feeling purchase slowly in this narrow place. Muench made a remark after his first months here which gave me a clue: "In America you have to spend so much of your time reacting you don't have the time or energy to act." I think any of us halters know that, but it was a palliative to my slow soul to hear it. I distrust those who rush ahead. They come to me always thin.

Constantine Poulos, back from Greece, put in my hand a novel this week I think you would feed on: CEPHALU, by Lawrence Durrell, published by Poetry London. It handles a theme I have interested myself in, blocked out a ballet or dance-play of (the 3rd ahead): the labyrinth. Durrell does it as of 1950, a handful of Englishmen and women who get lost in a newly discovered, war discovered cave on Crete. (A propos that, can you direct me to the most pertinent papers or passages of your fellows, on the image of the labyrinth? I shall want to examine them as I work on my THESEUS.) What interests me is as much Theseus' women as his deeds: his lost mother, Aethra, left in Asia, his effeminancy, his stepmother Medea who tries to have his father poison him, Ariadne who gives him the thread, Helen whom he was the first to seize, his marriage to the Amazon Antiopa and—the return to Crete—his marriage to Ariadne's sister, Phaedra, despite, because, eh? of his desertion of Ariadne. Would it not make a company happy? a man's passage through the labyrinth, woman.

We leave in an hour. I will do one lecture on space and I'm thinking it might be best to read the text of About Space as a point of departure. I have an earlier version of it but if the mss is where you can put your hand on it without thinking twice do drop it to me c/o Josef Albers, Rector, Black Mt College, Black Mt, NC.

And I'll hope to see you soon. I'll have to move my mother before it gets much colder and, if you could spare it, an evening with you in Boston would take the curse off the trip.

> Fr us both, our love and gratitude,
> Charles

In the letter of 10 February 1950 to Frances Boldereff (at Storrs), Olson also says of Henry Murray: "He is Melville's chief biographer now alive. And that is both how I know him, and why, because of a certain rivalry he feels towards me, that I go gingerly with him. For he is more than a patron. He is our friend, both con's and mine." Murray's letters to Olson reveal only open admiration; perhaps the rivalry was more on Olson's part.

35
To Josef Albers (1948)

Edward Dahlberg suggested Olson as his replacement when he left Black Mountain College in September 1948. Olson could not commit himself for a whole semester, but when it was suggested that he come down for a few days each month, he felt the proposal made sense. The first visit was 12–15 October 1948. Although totally different in temperament from artist Josef Albers, who was the rector of the college, Olson admired him, and he sided with Albers in college battles. *Letter at Raleigh.*

217 Randolph Place NE
Washington 2, D.C.
November 6, 1948

My dear Josef Albers:

I too was longer on the road than I had expected to be, am back a day. I made it a point to spend an evening with Dorothy Norman. As you suggested my role was simple, to prepare ground. My visit and interest in Black Mountain came up naturally in the conversation and I was merely adding another person whom she knows to those who speak enthusiastically of you and your place. I did key the present situation by protesting that such work should not have to go with its hands out when it offers a gift of importance to society. When we are together I can go over approaches to her if such a course still interests you. If there is earlier action required I suggest that John Cage is very much in her mind and favor at the moment.

Thank you for your letters. I accept the arrangement for November and December and shall await any further plan you and the Board may choose to offer. It looks now as though I can stick to our plan of a month ago: come on the train next Sunday and be with you Monday, Tuesday and Wednesday, November 14, 15, and 16. If you should like it I would continue the previous plan thus:

Monday	2:00	writers
	8:30	lecture on non-Homeric myth
Tuesday	2:00	writers and readers
	8:30	readings from contemporary verse
Wednesday	2:00	writers

with individual conferences to be arranged.

But it may be that you might wish the evening lectures in the dining hall not continued. I shall leave that to you, as well as the afternoon hour, in case it should conflict with any other classes.

Both Constance and myself deeply enjoyed our stay and I look forward to this return. Do carry my greetings to all.

Cordially,

Olson

36

To Caresse Crosby and Robert Payne (1949)

We do not have many words from Olson on the composition of "The Kingfishers," which was written on and off from February to June 1949. Thus the following letters have particular interest. He sends a draft of part III (with notable variants) to Caresse Crosby in London on about 10 March, and, at about the same time, reveals to his friend Robert Payne (also in Europe) that "The Kingfishers" was meant to supplant T. S. Eliot's "The Waste Land."
  Letter to Crosby at Southern Illinois; letter to Payne at Stony Brook.

Thursday

Duchessa Caresse!
  This was a telegram, a long distance telephone call,—and now a letter, to wish you a good arrival!

  It all was, what was Laura's address? Nor did Suzy know, nor find out.

The day's work today began thus:

> I am no Greek,
> hath not th'advantage.
> And of course no Roman:
> he can take no risk that matters,
> the risk of beauty least of all.
> Thus, and only thus, no tragedy.

> But I have my kin. Despite the disadvantage,
> it works out this way. I have an epigraph. I quote:
> si j'ai du goût, ce n'est guères
> que pour la terre et les pierres.
> In other words, on this continent,
> what was slain in the sun.

> I invoke one man, he who was shipwrecked on this shore
> lost Europe's clothes, was naked how many winters,
> lived on shell-fish, was lacerated feet and skin, was slave,
> first trader, learned what tribes these were, walked,
> walked, found deer skin, clothed himself, walked

as the doe walks, white man, white
a second time

a second time, and he only, of all, no one else, reborn!

WHICH I SEND YOU AS GREETINGS ON YOUR DEPART-RETOUR
á EUROPE!
To tell you
        this place already declines
                  as do our hearts
                         constanza sharle

———————————

                          same place Wash some time later
Robert:

I beg to be forgiven. And yesterday I decided my excuse was wasted.
I had locked myself in for three weeks in an attempt to do a 1st long
poem. Yesterday I put it together, and looked it over, compared it to
THE WASTELAND, and decided, as a practicer of the gentle craft, I
better do more work at the last. Which leaves me with only bones to excuse my silence. Still I ask yr pardon, and of all gods of good workers.

And I must catch you before you go off again. That you go disturbs
me. I must have some geotropic complaint. It's hard enough for me to
move, and when my friends do, I get as frantic as tho I were the one. I
made a major effort (by beating the front of the head with the card Le
Stelle 1000 times) to get you located, and continuous, in Lunnon town.
And now you go to Paris. I shall now beat my head twice as many times
with the Cavallo de Spade, and keep the connection, I hope.

You will see I am empty-headed today, but I have certain things to
report. I took up this matter of an agent with Caresse. Hers is BERTHA
KLAUSNER, and good, I'd judge. But what the hell did I do with her
address. Yes, here it is: 130 East 40. Caresse is now some sort of "finder"
for Klausner, and has asked me to ask you to use her name in opening
business with La K.

La C herself is now in London. Went off this week. She can be
reached thru the American Embassy: I gather her daughter works there?
It is a loss, she is gone. She gave me a milieu, something I never had

here, and previously only in Key West, and, of course, among my people, Gloucester. (I have never forgiven Eliot for stealing Dry Salvages from me: if his "poetic" use of same, and of the Lady of Good Voyage, and of the longshore fisherman in T W, is a measure of his use of other experience, then he lacks economic root. And he will turn out to be romantic.)

My deepest thanx for yr generous letter. Shall try to keep you out of hell, though why you should want to, with persephone to come down each year, and ulysses to look across a bloody trench every time a poet drives him thither, I do not know. Also, to shift ahead, I offer a quote to propel your play: You are in hell. Or can't you bear Goethe?

And continue to trouble yourself over the title to the dance (which is a meanness, for already your troubling has made me most grateful). You have led me to this, with yr emphasis on Ahab. Obviously my next step is to title it so: CALL ME AHAB (!). Seriously, THE HUNTSMAN holds the seed, though if I could get a modifier for THE TEMPEST, I'd send Shakespeare where you do not want to go. Either need a modifier other than that queerer "fiery."

As to the dedication: yr beautiful passage on Pan left me, as you knew it would, disarmed. All I have left is my shield, with which I now confront you. And behind it you must allow us to hide. You cannot be pan. Do you want to be delphic? You know how Plutarch tells the virtue of numbers. Would "for the Two" be of use (I capitalize for no egregious reason, merely to make it a number). Perhaps "for two"—but then, you certainly write for many, and that won't do. I'm damned if I see a way out of your difficulty, mixed up, as you are, with sheep!

Constanza is home, to join the love of this letter. I go again tomorrow to Black Mt. Shall find out about any opening re in stead. But no word out of him. Is he all right?

I await all yr news. Do write, and I promise more, in the juvescence of the year came dogwood, shadblow. And it is almost here. In North Carolina I'll meet it.

Yrs

Charles

Of the concerns of this letter: (1) Payne's proposed play about hell was a passing thought; (2) Olson's attempts to find another title for his dance-play came to naught, and it was left as *The Fiery Hunt;* (3) Payne's request to dedicate his book *The Tormentors* to Connie and Charles Olson was sidestepped, but he finally pinned them down as the dedicatees of his *Zero: The Story of Terrorism* (London: Wingate, 1951); (4) Olson failed to get Rexford Stead, Payne's friend, appointed at Black Mountain College; and (5) it was, in the end, Robert Payne who first published Olson's poem "The Kingfishers," in the inaugural issue of *Montevallo Review* (summer 1950), a magazine he began when on the faculty of Montevallo College, Alabama. He was host to Olson there for eight days in May 1950. See Ralph Maud's *What Does Not Change: The Significance of Charles Olson's "The Kingfishers."*

37
To Kitue Kitasono (1949)

Written on the completion of "The Kingfishers," this letter was probably Olson's first try at identifying for himself what he had done. He was testing his ideas offshore by consulting Kitue Kitasono, a poet and magazine editor in Japan (his *Cendre* would print "La Préface" later in the year). Kitasono had translated Pound in the 1930s, and Olson thought he could be a sounding board for projective ideas that would go beyond Pound. The "Projective Verse" essay, which Olson would be working on a year hence, speaks of Seami, the famous playwright of the Noh theater. Here Olson urges Kitasono to make available Seami's autobiographical treatise on dramatic method. Presumably Olson copied out for his own use this portion of what was a longer letter.   *Notes at Storrs.*

to KITASONO April 14, '49 arguing he do SEAMI auto, thus HERE it would mean a jab in the arse to verse

There is a deep change on the front of Amurrikan werse (Old Ez would protest he wouldn't know—"what dog sees his tail"). The "known men" (the eliotics?) have done an about-face, are going back along the line of british verse, are learning from Wordsworth, Milton and now Pope—are doing what used to be called here in the colonies "back-trailing." I'd hunch it is in search of some larger form than the lyric but that form not to be dramatic (where Eliot was defeated, despite a tremendous dramatic line, they also fear).

The contrary path, which would seem to me to be a continuation of, not a reaction from, the developments post-1908 (arrival Pound London age 23) is THEATRE, the re-invention of the union of SPEECH & SOUND, the making of the language new by PROJECTION & PERCUSSION, by undoing the tyranny of instruments & diatonic harmony, by pushing beyond the CANTOS out where even EP refused to take his LINEAR COMPOSITION (you know his hate for the "drahmah").

NOW: what this does is to take amurrikan werse out from the british (even the Elizabethans are *not* the clue) to

(1) THE GREEK (Homer & Ovid to be seen as greek, as well as the drahmahteests—I am thinking of Ovid's Heroides, and his lost MEDEA)

& (2) the NOH and the Chinese.

Which brings me (& you, if I have made the point thus stenographically) back to SEAMI, who has more to teach current invention than Will Shax ((and than aescylos-spophkles-evripedes, given the recognition that the ODYSSEY is actually three plays, the best of the three THE TALES AT THE HOUSE OF ALKINOOS)

Or so I have found. AND STAY CURIOUS to have the text of SEAMI *in circulation* here (my own guess would be that, if you did this chore, the publication of it here would be the jolt that neither YEATS NOR EP'S attempts of 1917 WERE).

38

To Albert Erskine (1949)

Olson received from his friend Albert Erskine of Random House the newly published *Complete Stories of Herman Melville*, edited by Jay Leyda, and on 22 April 1949 wrote of his pleasure in having such a reliable and beautiful volume. Two days later he is writing again, on behalf of the son of his long-standing patron Eleanor Melville Metcalf. *Letter at Columbia.*

217 Randolph Pl NE
Washington 2 DC
April 24, 1949

My dear Albert:

I am surprised myself thus to be writing to you again this soon, but yesterday morning, I was awakened by Paul Metcalf out of North Carolina hills, on his way to the big city, it turned out, to sell his first novel, finished finally, after three years, Wednesday. He stayed overnight, and is now on, citywards.

I have known him for years, as he grew up, but only in the orbit of his mother, Eleanor Melville Metcalf. Even when he was on his own as an actor and writer at Hedgerow, before the war, it was still the same. I didn't get through to him. But this winter, on these trips I take each month to lecture on verse at Black Mt, I have been going to his house for dinner at Skyland, some twenty miles off from Albers Education Institute, and have begun to know him on his own. And like his growth. And a sharply risen perception.

I say these things, because I imagine you know I cannot read or judge novels, and even if I'd read his novel, I'd know nothing to say about him more than what I take in for myself.

So this is to introduce him, if he comes your way. Knopf seems to have taken a lien on his work; but I said to him, if and when the mss is free, go down the street to Albert Erskine; SO

Thus greetings again to you and Peggy

yrs

Olson

39

To Ben Shahn (1949)

Olson dedicated his short essay "The Resistance" to Jean Riboud. Riboud had been in the French underground, was captured in 1943, and spent two years in Buchenwald. He is the figure behind Olson's poem "La Préface." They met when Riboud came to New York as a representative of a French business; but, as no letters are available, knowledge of their meetings remains sketchy. This letter to the artist Ben Shahn indicates the high esteem in which Olson held Riboud. The feeling was mutual: Olson was best man at Riboud's wedding on 1 October 1949. *Letter at Archives of American Art.*

> 217 randolph pl ne
> washington 2 dc
> may 10 xlix

Ben!

There is a fine friend by name Jean Riboud, yes, French, Lyon, now NY, though soon back to France. Have known him some two years since he has been here. Has great eyes in his heart. Is one of the rare ones.

A month ago, on a trip here, he tried, at my suggestion, to call you at Hightstown. No answer (a Saturday) (no, a Friday).

Now, fresh from Buffalo, where he tells me, a Shahn slew him, he wants, yes, he wants to own a Shahn.

Because he is a man, and of yr kin, I suggested he get in touch with you direct. (He goes to Boston tomorrow, and it should be next week you will hear from him.) I sd I imagined you did still go into Manhattan during the week. I think you will enjoy each other.

Miss you very much. Have stayed put for a year (in fact since I saw you all last summer) except for lectures once a month at Black Mt. But no New York. For some reason wanted none of it. (Have a copy of *y & x* for you, Bernarda, Suzy, John and Abby, which I will deliver one day.) Wish I might see you all. Hope the blessings are, as they should be, showered on you, one & all.

Can hardly hope to hear from you but surely expect to see you if you are here. Please.

All love,

Charles

Something of Olson's long-standing and deep friendship with Ben Shahn can be seen in a later letter, letter 53.

40

To Michael Lekakis (1949)

Michael Lekakis had his first one-man show of sculpture in 1941 at Artists' Gallery, New York. Olson may have attended; their friendship went back a long way. The extant correspondence begins with a highly charged postcard of 24 May 1949. Olson, in Washington, is asking Lekakis to comb the New York bookstores for certain titles destined to be of great significance to Olson, especially the book by Jane Harrison. Olson appreciated, among other things, his friend's ability to declaim Homeric Greek, and he wanted to use him in the productions he was planning for the summer session at Black Mountain College. The third letter below is undated, but Olson had sent Lekakis a typed carbon copy of "The Kingfishers" on 20 July 1949, so the letter must be dated soon after that.   *Letters at Archives of American Art.*

                                                        tyoosday
Michel:
    yr list
                        THEMIS miss harrison
                    EPILOGOMENA same miss
        (THE PRAYING WHEEL) or (THE WHEEL IN MAN)
                            by simpson
    MAXIMUS OF TYRE (T. Taylor's translation) 2v 1824)
                                my thanks
                        this card I sign for both of us   Olson
                        NIKOY KAZANTZAKH

                    ————————————————

                                        Wash Mon June 13 xlix
Michael L:
    The full-and-not-so-bright business: did you think of Cagli as rec-
ommender? Another idea I had was Shahn, tho I do not know that he
knows yr work, and it may be that now he is no. 1, he may want to see
before he sez even on my say-so, but I am seeing him Thursday night,
and can ask him to speak for you if you will allow me   And myself, I'll
speak, if it would do any good

I am just back from Black Mt (all yesterday was spent at a most delightful Stathes-Chacos-Wills picnic in Rock Creek Park). And the summer productions mentioned to you have gone ahead fine: I plan a three part evening around Aug 25 in this order:

(1) a 15–20 min passage in the best American transposition of the Odyssey (possibly the Cyclops story) with Buckminster Fuller as Odysseus, whom I shall direct to act the part as it was writ by one Omeros

(2) Pound's Canto 1, ditto, with an actor if one turns up (olson otherwise?), the verse used as score, with dance and color on top

(3) either a piece written by one of the group, or a piece of my own, definitely non-Homeric in substance but re-invention in feeling, verse, music dance

the whole to last no more than 45 minutes, all parts; therefore, to be rehearsed until they come out most professionally.

Tho I know you felt you could not come down there for the summer (and the Board of BMC was not willing to stake any coagitators of mine) I did raise up another question, whether they would stake you for a visit of two to three weeks to lend yr taste and knowledge to the above. I shall pursue that further when I am there, you willing.

Well, Constanza has just come in and I must feed her her lunch. This was a note anyhow. We so enjoyed seeing you here. Our love.

Yrs,

Charles

Had a letter fr Bill Williams last week, in which he sd he had not called you because he had not yet been in the city.

---

black mt college
summer session
black mt nc

michael:

sunday is the only time around this black hill i can get to this machine   which is definitely a point not in the place's favor   (a passage shortly after THE KINGFISHERS as you have it includes these lines:

My Sunday morning people, here
the snake-bird hiss:
"jugex, jugex"
to empty ears

all yr several delights, including the BOOK, have come, and have
given me the illusion that my own work was possible to continue   (actually all i have been able to do is a great deal of reading, and some re-
writing of THE KS)

and not because my project for the summer has gone ahead as i
planned   which is why i write   the time i have lost has been largely
attrited by conflicts here due to the anti-albers administration   i am
being balked because i respected the man & make no bones about it
(or the right faces with the new)   i think it is clear that that is why they
would not opt for you when i proposed it in June, & why there is no
chance now   they only last week, when it suited them, came across
with this, my study

i should have written you this earlier, could have, for the hostile situation was pretty clear from the day we arrived   but i wanted to try it
out   i hope you will not be disappointed, & will excuse me for raising
up the possibility   but i could not have known the shift of power
would so go against me   they would even charge full rate if you were
our guest, the bastards!

despite it, committed as we were, i decided to stay and get what i
could done   i have gone ahead with plans for a production, and will at
least put a piece of mine on, to try out some ideas of language & the
theatre   but it will not be what i wanted   (not what i could have done
with these characters if they could have heard you read Hippolytus'
prayer!)

O! an IDEA!!   do you have a friend who has a recording machine,
and could could you do, even ten lines, at the piercing intensity you did
that prayer that night for Con & Frank and me? and ship it to me
pronto? that would be wonderful   LOOK even if you do not have a
friend who has a recording machine, perhaps you could go & do it

commercially, and have me pay the costs (if they wouldn't go above 5 bucks?)   i should be most happy if you find this possible, & can do it: i could give these people a jolt   in fact, i have a 2nd idea   if you do have a friend, & we could do it for the materials involved, how would you like to make a record of the whole CYCLOPS passage fr the O in Greek with yr reconstruction of how the rhapsodists sounded it?

my, all this is very exciting, & please consider it seriously, and see what you can do about it—the CYCLOPS PASSAGE I could use directly for demonstration

(& possibly, it occurs to me, for production, with yr Greek cutting it on my American translation as voiced by Bucky Fuller)

Do let me hear back as soon as you can manage it how this alternative to yr being here sits with you, & if you can go right ahead with it, i should be most pleased

love fr con

Charles

The program for "Exercises in Theatre 28 & 29, August 1949, Black Mountain College" indicates that Olson had to abandon many of his plans. The productions were mainly small ones done by students.

41

To Ray B. West (1950)

"There Was a Youth Whose Name Was Thomas Granger," published in *Western Review* (spring 1947), was Olson's first poem in a literary magazine. Olson failed to meet the young editor Ray West on his trip to the West Coast in 1947, but their relationship maintained its cordiality. The poem "Siena" was accepted for the winter 1949 issue of *Western Review,* and Olson's discussion of F. Barron Freeman's *Melville's Billy Budd* appeared in the fall 1949 issue. With a letter of 28 January 1950, however, West returned Olson's "The Praises." Though he liked the poem himself, there had been opposition from his board. We know from other letters that Olson thought it had been vetoed by the new advisory editor Paul

Engle, a power within the writing department of the University of Iowa that now sponsored West's magazine. In the letter below, Olson does not name names, but West would have known who was meant. Olson's quarrel with Engle was over Pound and Engle's scoffing at the hospitality he received while visiting Pound at Rapallo before the war. *Letter at Utah State.*

217 Randolph Place NE
Washington 2 DC
January–February 1, 1950

My dear Ray:

I should like to try to tell you how very very unhappy your letter (& returned mss.) have made me today. And I think, because I believe in the act of writing and of such publishing as you represented, I ought to spell the thing out a little. For I have valued you as though you were a friend, and have so cherished and praised yr existence that I am worried by what happened to "The Praises". (I like yr saying you send the "The Dry Tempest" back for executive reasons, but if I say my enemies have a clean sweep, you will not misunderstand.)

You see, you couldn't know maybe, how singular you have been, that, as I had occasion to say to a New York friend only two nights ago, "What's fine about West is, my impression is he trusts his own taste, does not, as almost all the others, go around the corner to get corroborated—or buy only the boys who are already institutions." This, in the present moment of magazines in America and England, unusual.

Nor could you have known that what happened today I predicted would happen, if you were not strong, the moment I learned last summer that the magazine was going to Iowa. That is why, believe me, I was so proud of you when you fired back, you liked & thought you would use, "The Praises". For it was more than the poem. It meant that I was wrong, that there was not a dividing line, almost as precise as the continental line of rainfall, in this country now.

I was too long a man of public affairs not to guess professional & economic reasons why you have to include others as advisory and contributory editors (look how even now I leave out any need for your taste to be corroborated!). But I shall say this. I know the finger man (it was why I predicted you would need to be strong). And I know why he put the finger on me, because he once had occasion so to speak of a finer poet than either of us, that, if I were a man, he had to take my scorn for him, and my contempt for his verse, which he did. This is now in the nature of a pay-off.

That I say to you simply that you may be warned. For I do not worry for "The Praises", or "The Tempest", or other things. You would not have published me if you had not felt likewise. And for that I thank you.

The only thing I want to say, is, please, West, fight for yourself. You are too valuable, too free of that cultural disease which has spread out from Eliot, through the universities as they took him up as a measure in the '30's, and now, through the generation that was so educated which is now editing most magazines and writing most verse which finds its way into print.

Of course I am partisan, of course I believe in you because you published olson. But that is only the indicator. West of Iowa it has stayed true that the sons of, say, Williams, Pound, those few who are continuing the revolution those men started, of the oral in verse, say, of the non-literate in culture (the intelletto as opposed to the school-mind) have had a hearing. (We should not be confused that the Eastern and the English magazines publish Pound & Williams gladly. For it is not they that are now the tests of taste. They are too easy to publish, with their reputations. It is us younger fry who take courage in the reader.

Or put it a substantive way, which is better, just because the formal remains still the instrument, not the matter. You may have noticed Hyman's joining of me to Lawrence, in the current "Hudson". It was no accident that, in the RMR, and WR, one found Lawrence, and his chillun.

The fact is, the whole front of art right now is crucial, and that the literary quarter is so dominated by the eliotics, the false formalists (which explains the current hawthorne, the previous james fads), is a disaster. (The neo-Christian movement is already a force in critique).

((God, god, that you are gone to me, that the WR is no longer there to invoke me. Or I could be sending you what has got written these days on this very subject. You see what I mean, how full of sorrow the possibility that you may be giving in, makes me!)

O, West, do not let practitioners seem valuable merely because they are professionals in a form or are "known". Take the risks of what moves *you*. And we who keep at the job with no hope of any return but the job done, who do not straddle, who want only to put it out straight and clean, will be gratified. Because we will know we can say, point to one magazine, "There, the Western anyhow exists, because West has made it free."

I better shut up. I'm too tired now, after the day's work, to put this all as well as I might. And I am already discouraged. But I had to lay this one home to yr heart. For you have honored me. And I would be letting value and feeling go by the board if I did not honor you back, and ask you to resist, to resist. And if you cannot hear me now, you will before either of us is much older. The truth is, the issue is already there, right in front of us, even it is not yet easy to see.

I give you my love, and the hope that I can again give you my faith.
Affectionately,
Olson

42

To Vincent Ferrini (1950)

In the spring 1949 issue of *Imagi* Olson read a poem he liked called "The House," by a Vincent Ferrini, and he discovered from the contributors' column that the poet lived in Gloucester. "So," as Olson tells the story to the NET film crew (*Muthologos* 1, p. 182),

the next time I come back to visit my mother—you know, you say, "Hello, Ma,"—and that's it. I mean, you eat one meal and think, "Oh, Jesus, I got to go back to——." Well, you can't leave, you know. Your mother wants you to stay overnight at least. So I went out. I said, "Look, I've got to go over town . . ."

"I liked him right off," recalls Ferrini in "A Frame," an autobiographical account published in the Olson issue of *Maps* in 1971, in which he prints "The House" and describes Olson's "manner of ease and his candid quality," which made him quickly at home "as though he had been a member of the family" (p. 48). These, then, are Olson's "family letters," with shared understandings and mutual caring often kept hidden under a jocular surface. Then there are the other "letters," the *Maximus* poems themselves, where Ferrini provided "a frame" for at least the earliest segments of a long epic of Gloucester. "Deeply pleased you invoked it from me," Olson wrote in a letter of 2 June 1950 to Ferrini (printed in *Origin* no. 1), referring to the first *Maximus* poem.   *Letters at Storrs.*

                                                    wash 2 dc april 22 '50
dear vinc.:
    yr boy creeley sure gets 'imself around   Had a letter from Bill Williams friday, saying c. had ideas and wants to USE 'em, and suggesting i write 'im
                    so i did, saying, how de do, telling him it was you who had told me abt him, and how pleased i was you are, and shipping him one thing i was holding for you and the New England poets you conjured up to print some months ago, and also a rough one, done a month ago, long, called THE MORNING NEWS

    (you know, i wish i had thot of that remark i made to you on post card about language vis-a-vis each poem earlier: it belongs properly in the PRO VERSE piece In fact it is the core of "composition by field", I now reckon)

    so now there are two houses lived in in Gloucester close to me: for my mother returned to stage fort ave this week!

    i am terribly depressed, and to correct it I quote you Blake:
        Art is the Tree of Life, Science
        is the tree of death

    Maybe it is the prospect of war

                                    write to me, and tell me how
                                    my streets

are, what
gulls are up your way, do you
& peg walk
up to Dogtown Common, go
to dreadful
St Ann's, or
the Portygee's church, shout
down dreary Sundays, play ball
in Burnham's field?

(the old man's homesick)
   obviously, too, he ain't
  got words
  in his balls

       (did i correct text in yr copy?
       (1) *preface:* cancel "in vita nuova",
       excise "cunnus in" and continue
       "crotch gashed of a green tree" (2)
       K: out "then" 1st line

        love to you both, and spring: O

what abt
   injuns?
      have
you ever interested
yrself in
     our predecessors?
One thing:
     they knew
how useful dreams
are—(one
horrendous one of O's
concerns a schooner
I park on the old family
doctor's porch, & the
smell is of Al Gorman
(he was known to all Gloucester

as "the Wharf Rat" at
the time I was a
cart-pusher on
Gorton-Pew's wharf)

another one: two
kids die, on my hands,
down back of Lufkin's
diner, between it (which
was a Chinese Rest.) &
Roger's St!

Dreams are
an amulet
    we have
forgotten how
   to wear 'em

Are you interested in B. Bunting? translations from Persian? Dilly Dally Simpson 41 Island City Homes, Galveston, offers Bunting $1.50

Same struggle in "art" comes out: the NON-REPRESENTATIONAL vs the Representational for the economics of it, try Brooks Adams *The New Empire* (his best)

———————

                                                tuesday may 23 L
my dear vinc:
    let me see.   obviously ferrini is down in the dumps.   how in hell can i tell him, there's any number of reasons why—and good ones, right straight out of him—he needn't be.   besides, it's SPR-i- ng agAIN.

    and he's done a lot of work this winter.   'course, publishing, getting stuff published. . . . But then, this rejection business. Christ, my *impression* is he's had less of it than most of us.

    And anyway, a guy who wrote HOUSE of ME, just has to go on and write more of same. He's stuck with it. He's got it—whether he chooses at given moments to call it a curse or a bless, he's in there

    i guess, probably, the pressures are sociological, he wants to get to a landing where he can give his time exclusively to his proper business

    but on the other hand he must know the uncertainty wavers (gutters in the wind, in another sense than
*t*ough *s*hit)
forever wavers, the soul
(what we call guilts—or pleasures—remain, forever
  ambiguities,
            the only object is
a man, carved
out of himself, so wrought he
fills his given space, makes
traceries sufficient to
other's needs

(here is
social action, for the poet,
anyway, his
politics, his
news)
     O my friend

                      in short, this is, the bird overhead is
                                  anthony of

This letter represents the inception of the poem "In Cold Hell, In Thicket," the first draft of which was completed the same day. See *Collected Poems,* p. 155.

43
To Robert Creeley (1950)

It was through William Carlos Williams that Olson contacted Robert Creeley on 21 April 1950. Creeley, then twenty-three, was frustrated by his remoteness and poverty in Littleton, New Hampshire, and by most of what passed for current literature. Olson struck him immediately as different, and he embarked on a dialogue at the furious pace of two letters a week. It was in his eighth letter that he used the phrase "single intelligence" (*Olson-Creeley Correspondence,* vol. 1, p. 57), which impressed Olson so much that he injected it into the final version of the "Projective Verse" essay, along with another of Creeley's formulations, "Form is never more than an extension of content." Olson's letter below (as published in *Olson-Creeley Correspondence,* vol. 1, pp. 91–94) demonstrates that it was the excitement of the new correspondence with Creeley that made "Projective Verse" the more powerful force it became in its second draft.

Letter at Stanford.

                                  fri. june 9   50
R. Cr.:
    the vulgarizations: too much (in the old sense)   the opiate, for ex.,
of the ray-deo worse, much worse, than what historically shrinking
lenin talked his mouth off, about   ((do you know gorky's days with
lenin, AND his reminiscences of tolstoy? excellent, both))

a streetcar, which used to be (especially in Worcester when, they
were open, and made like French trains, and ran down freeways in back
of people's houses), or since, are now, here, with o people, the NEWS,
the latest, and mu-sick, mu-sick, mu-sick, worst than war, worse than
peace (both dead), and the people's faces like boils

well, not the point   which is, to tell you how moved i am by yr
plea for the heart, for the return of, into the work of language: i figure
myself the *via* is from object, back in (for it has to be got back by
form (form, given yr definition only) not by the ways of the likes of
Mill. or Patch. (or EE, for the matter—nor do I mean Elderberry
Eggnog)
   rule #1: it is not to be talked about, to be descriptive of, or explode
   all over the place: that makes for the old pile of grease and shit,
   gurry, we calls it, where i hale from

I still believe the Path of Ezra is the 'oly won, even tho I do not believe
him capable of fronting to that which is thuggish abt the 'eart. (Is it not
true, that Ez, is more fine than strong, that it is such gentilities as rain,
grass, birds on a wire, 5, now 3, Metechevsky or whatever, tents, the
trillings, rather than the thrustings, that are where he scores? He goes
literary with lynxes, Dioces, and fuckings, and can only stalk thru the
heart-lands by the wit of attack, attack: attack on USURA, attack on,
by Artemis, PITY, cleanings, yes, but WE WANT SCOURINGS
                                                                      where
the right is, is, that he goeth by language: this we must do, and do, and
do, otherwise we better go into, say, politics

Bill, good Doc, I think is now the more seen, because, from the beginning, he has gone for his images to the running street of, to the Passaic
of (water poisoned with the dead   (cats win, in the urbe)   and stained
with dyes   (cats, & industry)   the brutal, but fruits, he has (has he?)
wanted beauty so hard
                                          (AND WHO CAN BEAT LIFE INTO
FORM, who is
so foolish?

                              (is it no only language, for the likes of
                              uss?

If I were to put it another way—to expand upon the text, Beaute is
difficult, Mr. Yeats—it would come to a matter (the heart would) of syllables: measure our masters by 'em—

> miss moore merely mathematical
> mr cummings, quite vulgar (broad) abt 'em
> mr bill, getting 'em fr the scrupulousness of his attention to
>   the objects of which words are to him the nouns (he
>   is in this sense a beginner, gets back to, the *naming*
>   force/function of language (folk, city folk, his)

> Ez, i honestly believe (despite all his chatter abt
> mu-sick, & harmonics) does it (he does it grandly, as
> dante, sure) without thinkin' about 'em, does it, like
>   —In the drenched tent/ there is quiet
>   Sered eyes/ are at rest
> does it, because, he has absolutely, single-mindedly
> (is that SINGLE INTELLIGENCE?) GONE BY LANGUAGE

> ((Let me throw in, for the gander of it, for yr lookins, and thinkins
>   back, a sort of an arty piece done some time ago, and only recently
>   stumbled on, for yr opinion: shall i, is it worth, bothering to publish?
>   (the trouble with what was done (even yesterday) is, today, . . .)
>   (will look it over, 1st)

I think this whole matter of heart is, at root, content (again, in the precision of yr FIRST PRINCIPLE: form is never . . .) IS a matter of
ploughing in, from the man, his content (& it better be good) and forcing, always forcing on, not by way of it as statement, but it as it brings
abt its form, ONLY THUS, not by the talkin of it, the posture of O
LIFE, & O ME

                                                    (REPELLENT,
ILL., or whatever city, state, the LOVERS come from, the tenement
boys, the O LET'S OBJECT, LET'S PLAY AND FUCK, THE LET'S BE
QUAKERS AND ANGELS ABOUT ALL THESE HORRORS
                                                    "o, let

us just believe in beyootie")

crist

(*note:* there must be, somewhere, a word/concept/putsch the extension
     of *claritas*   (better than olson's "*est hominis confusio*") for
     that
IS WHAT HAS TO BE ADDED

          sd R. Cr:
                    form is never more than an extension of content
                                   June, 1950

                                  amo

                                    o

44
To Jay Leyda (1950)

In 1942 Jay Leyda translated *The Film Sense* by his friend Sergei Eisenstein. Olson
wrote to him at that time from the Office of War Information. He thought the
book "a gonfalon," and on Eisenstein's premature death he commiserated: "It is
such a loss. The vulgarization of the movie is so complete we needed his battle
flags stuck down in the dump of it" (letter of 1 March 1948 at UCLA). With
Leyda's entry into Melville studies, a letter-writing comraderie developed. At one
point it even seemed possible that Olson's *Call Me Ishmael* and Leyda's *The
Melville Log* might be published in tandem. Leyda was one of the few Melville
scholars with whom Olson could be candid, as the following letter shows. Leyda
had challenged Olson on the question of his having obtained exclusive access to
certain Melville source materials—rather ancient history by this time, but still
apparently a sensitive matter.   *Letter at UCLA.*

                                           wash june 14 50
my dear Jay:
    I am sensitive over this question of "rights" simply because I am
burned, burned, my friend, at the carelessness about *facts in time.* It is
not a question of "rights" as it is a question of THE RECORD. For a
man's hours are his fate, and when a man put the hours into Melville
research *at the time I did,* one gets pretty god damned sore that, with

the conspicuous exception of F. Barron Freeman, not one Melville scholar has had the courtesy to record what Olson did, as of when he did it.

I have deeply admired your openhandedness, and you have been acknowledged. But simply because I did my work in 1932, 33, 34, and did not rush it into print,—in fact, did not even use it any more than a ground behind ISHMAEL—is no reason, to my lights, why, in the places where I actually opened up areas of research, the fact that I opened those areas is not added to the record, is not acknowledged by those who have followed me in.

I should be a fool if I did not expect others to have gone over the same ground after me. And it is equally true that, at any given time thereafter, if I had not done my work, the same ideas of leads would have unquestionably occurred to others. (You, for example, with yr alacrity, have not only swept the boards, but have—and this delights me—found light where the rest of us were blind.)

And at no time, when I saw that material in my hands was not going to be used by me have I, I think I can accurately say, blocked any-one else. Yet I have ruthlessly—the marked example is the *Essex* book—tore in and took away, when, as in that case, I had been hunting the book since 1933! (I could not take seriously, that, by accident, it was Vincent who disclosed to me that it had come out of the Hogan sale. For it was Swann, in the first place, in 1934, who had disclosed to me that the "Bentley" who purchased it was, in fact, the owner of the An-derson Galleries, Cortlandt Bishop himself. And I watched that book pass into equity court proceedings, and out, to Hogan, long, long be-fore Perc Brown bought it. And yet, I was scrupulous, and went to Swann, and it was Swann who sent me to Brown 1945-6.)

I respect scholarship, and because of that respect I ask that, as in sci-ence or in writing, a man's priority of invention or "starting" is still one of the values on which civilized men build a humanitas. I have been made fun of for it, but I ask you to call back into yr mind the page in ISHMAEL in which I record my predecessors. They are conspicuously my *predecessors*: Mumford is not there, for obvious reasons, Mat-thiessen, Sedgwick, Thorp. (I could date the day Matty came to Mrs Metcalf's door, and I, who had been for months taking down a card file

of all annotations, from hers, from the Osborne books—which I had
fetched, more, had actually "found," in the sense that I had gone to New
Jersey Dec-Jan 1933-4, had separated from the whole library the scat-
tered volumes, and had carted them off to deposit them in the Harvard
Library—, from Mrs Thomas in Boston and at Edgartown, and the
other granddaughters,—and I handed, as you would, I'm sure, over to
Matty, the cards on Hawthorne, Emerson, etc.)

   Which brings us, to my present beef. Sealts knows, so I can speak of
it to you, though he is a very sick boy, and I see no reason why it should
be added, now, to his burden. But I was deeply wounded that, in his
Check-list, one would never gather that it was I who

   (1) had the idea of such a list, in the first place
   (2) was the first to reconstruct the library
   (3) by the Osborne books, caused Harvard to buy the Shakespeare,
         was, as a matter of fact, agent (with DeLacey) of the sale,
         the 1st Harvard purchase ($250!)
   (4) spent weeks, spring, 1934, in NY, flushing the story of the sale
         of the books (it was Anderson, and thru him, I who got
         Wegelin out of NJ, and yet, in his article, you would not know
         who provoked his memories!) ((Saw Farnell myself (the son
         of AB), and started the Brooklyn business.))
& (5) who, in Twice A Year, 1938, 1st used in print the methodology of,
         M's markings   (I think this is right, tho Braswell, on Emer-
         son, may precede me in printing time, due to the way I mull!)
  ((6)), or an aside: I still have that card-file of all annotations done
         before you and Sealts and whoever added the other books to
         what was the base, and is, of the Check-list: have you any sug-
         gestion abt its disposal? It is crazy, that anyone else should do
         what I then did. And it may be, that now that the Harvard
         Collection exists, and the NYPL, etc., there is little point to it.
         I don't know. Can you think of anyone or place, where it
         might be of service?

All the above I can document from my papers—or, and this is some-
thing I have never seen in the record, despite the boring repetitions of
Phd Theses on deposit, there is, on deposit, at the Wesleyan Library, the
MA thesis of Olson, 1933, which lays out the origin points to his work.

(This will amuse you: the MA was done at Wesleyan and Yale, under an Olin Fellowship, and part of the work was a course with S. Williams, in which I was refused the right to do a paper on Melville because he was so unimportant, and had to contrive a thesis on Hawthorne & His Friends! Later, when I was the 1st candidate at Harvard for the Phd in Am Civilization, and was on the faculty, I received a letter I still have fr same Williams, begging me to let his locusts in !)

No, Jay, with you I have no quarrel. And if I write out the story to you, it is only because I think there is more in the "rights" question than you allow. (I dare say, if I had worked at the time you have, that I would be as pissed off.) But I have been astonished at the smallness of the Melville people generally.

On the Shaw question I am, I guess, almost as vulnerable as I am on the *books.* I imagine that is why I allowed myself to get into such a fracas with Allan Forbes, in, was it, 1945. (I can send you carbons of that clash, if you shld be in any way involved, or interested.) For the day in the spring of 1934 that it suddenly dawned on me at chez Metcalf that the Shaw papers might include Melville things (I think the lead was provoked by Philarete Chasles' reference to the cousin) was one of those moments I imagine you, too, have been lifted by. I was at the MHS before that afternoon was over, and, with the help of the old librarian, whose name I have, but can't at this moment remember, I was started into the boxes. For—and it is this sort of thing which, to me, is a part of humanitas—the collection was then AS IT HAD BEEN RECEIVED. I even took a room nearby, and for some time spent each day culling and arranging the whole business. That is why Stewart Mitchell and that librarian respected me, and were so ready to allow me priority. (Allan Forbes only came in some time afterwards.)

I am prepared to say that I erred in allowing the years to pass without publishing that material— and I am glad, welcome, the fact that you now do that very thing (as it worked out, I only used part of one of the HM letters in ISHMAEL, and did not, there, bother, because I had decided form was more important, to claim the discovery of it).

But that I was the one to conceive that the Shaw Papers might include Melville material, that, in fact, until that afternoon, there was no knowledge of the existence, even, of the

Shaw Papers, to Melville workers—this seems to me something which a man ought to be credited with, no?

Well, it is hot, and I am spent with these recollections. But I am in a fighting mood about this whole courtesy question, and you must excuse this documentation. You see how seriously I do take the RECORD of WORK (the WORK of the DAYS, in Hesiod's beautiful title, which, by the way, he acquired from the Hebrews!)

To the other questions:

> [Olson spends two pages on questions about specific details
> of Melville research raised by Leyda.]

Well, see what that does, what USE it may be. And let me hear if there is anything else.

Yrs,
Olson

P.S.: please, Leyda, consider seriously, and deeply, this question of the courtesy of, the RECORD;   do not confuse it with, "rights," in the sense of, the publication of, the material;   the distinction I draw is of some certain consequence, in a much broader sense than Melville scholarship, to our civilization;   yet it is no accident that it arises, most sharply, out of the continuing WORK on HM, for he is ROOT MAN, test,—and you & I are honored, that we have done a *document* & a *LOG* on him.

"Forgive me for my insensitive lashing letter," Leyda replied on 20 June 1950. "As I wanted to right some wrongs in the notes for the Log, I'll try to make amends there, in a small way" (letter at Storrs).

45

To Robert Giroux (1950)

Robert Giroux of Harcourt, Brace was once described by Olson in a letter to Robert Creeley, dated 16 August 1950, as "the only sort of sensitive character i know among that lot"—that is, New York publishers (letter at Stanford). Hence, this letter of introduction on behalf of someone with whom he was now quite close. *Letter at Storrs.*

217 Randolph Place NE
Washington 2 DC
June 16, 1950

My dear Bob:

This will introduce to you Frances Motz, of Woodward, Pennsylvania. She is the book designer, Mrs Frances Boldereff, and I have urged her, out of the fullest kind of belief in her and her work, to go to see you, when she can be in New York.

I think if she carried only one single piece of her design, the Pennsylvania State College Catalogue for this year, you would need to see no more to know how rare and how thorough she is. What impresses me, is, how grounded her work is, how her sense of printing is not type alone but a profound understanding of the space which a page is, and what breath—to speak like a writer!—leading can give. I dare say it is a clue, that she learned her trade in the hardest kind of discipline, the Jersey City house that does the N.Y. telephone books. For she knows her business (like a good writer knows syllables!).

But she will tell you, and show you, more, for she has, in her position as Publications Production Manager at Penn State, done an immense amount of work, of all the kinds of paper on which print goes, including the most beautiful posters, in which she shows as high a sense of color as she has of space, and of the union of color to type and to cut.

There are also books of her own, one *of* her own (using Michelangelo plates) and one of Whitman, which is just done.

Mrs Boldereff wants, now, I understand, to work in New York, and I suggested, that of the men I know, you are the one I should want her to see.
Greetings, and shall see you myself, shortly.
Affectionately,
Charles

Olson had been impressed by Boldereff's self-published *A Primer of Morals for Medea* and by a scholarly book on Whitman that she had designed (*Walt Whitman of the New York* Aurora, *Editor at Twenty-Two: A Collection of Recently Discovered Writings* [1950]).

46

To Frances Boldereff (1950)

At times, letters passed between Frances Boldereff and Charles Olson daily. Although they met on only a very few occasions (or perhaps because of that), the letters are powerful and emotional, both informative about day-to-day events and soulful in the examination of their lives. In contrast to much of the correspondence, the letter chosen here is a quiet one. It is postmarked 21 August 1950 from Washington D.C.   *Letter at Storrs.*

monday

with quiet pleasure i have spent the afternoon, wasted it, in a way i have not used my ambience in a very long time, in, I guess, two years:

i have walked, sat in the sun, talked, mostly along the railroad yards
which are a block and a half away (my woods, or sea shore, even
the freight wheels waul like gulls: I'm not much to walk, as you used
to walk in Woodward, I think: somehow I drift best as I did today,
amongst people, when they are working, keeping their attentions on
something like a meal, or groceries, or the shifting of cars: they are usually so much richer at their tasks than they are if something is expected
of them, when they go out, say, or are even in passage home)

imagine, it is two years since i have spent any time in my yards, where i
used, actually, when i was that kind of a poet, to do my composing, sort
of, walking around (they are lovely lonely sun and wind swept lanes
with only the awkward cars with the crazy chalk hieroglyphs, and
maybe a truck, and ice running where a refrigerator car has been
cleared, and crates, smells—wharfish (or the surprise of the guard, of
the r.r. dick, who didn't like me there during the war, and asked me why
I was there, and i sd, because it reminds me of the sea!

it was a convalescent act, shall we say, a gathering by letting go. i was
sure, anyhow, i didn't intend to work. don't. am through, for a spell.
through. am gathering. stock. shipment. "don't hump". repairs. scream.
loaded. Eckington Yard.

at the store, what was the conversation: the Bonus Marchers, and
MacArthur! first time I'd ever heard washington natives tell tales of it.
stumbled on something: it's their "Flood", their "Quake", their War. how
everyone rushes up on every one else, to tell, to tell, to tell! anecdotes.
And, of course, disclose themselves. Fascinating, to me, who does
gather in such crazy places, as you know, lady mine.

this did take time from say, a letter to you, but you must not mind: i
was busy about you, at the same time! And i am enclosing a lump the
equal of what i sent the first day to T, (because tomorrow is the day, is
it not; and a spot more, just so you and Lucinda can feel a, have a, do a
spread, lady)

and here i am jammed up against the last collection, due to my lovely
folly   the mood is still on me, or i'd go to the p.o. later   but i want to
see that the enclosed is off to you, and so i'll shoot this on, with yr
understanding

   (funny.   no word in me.   but no regrets.   like sliding, in winter,
   down hill,   on to a iced meadow, with that slipping and tossing at
   the bottom.

love,
Charles

47

To Carl O. Sauer (1950)

Bob Callahan presented "The Correspondences: Charles Olson and Carl Sauer"
in his *New World Journal* (1979), quoting Sauer as telling him that "your Mister
Olson can ask some very difficult questions and yet he has a most unusual and
interesting mind" (p. 137). Olson's letters to Sauer indicate that the respect was

mutual. After their first meeting in December 1947, Olson wrote from Washington about "the gracious days in Berkeley you enlivened." Sauer had not written, and Olson complained: "You are my university, but I can't even get a correspondence course out of you!" He asks to be put on Sauer's mailing list: "There must be some way you can deposit droppings on my doorstep" (letter of 20 October 1949 at Berkeley). Sauer responded, and he sent the offprint Olson refers to in the letter below. *Letter at Berkeley.*

217 Randolph Place NE
Washington 2 DC
October 26 1950

My dear Carl Sauer:

You have been much in my mind. (I have even writ you in to a piece—an aggressive piece on knowledge, as of now—which, if it ever sees the light (Boston light, in this case, due, a new mag, abt march), i pray you shall not think i did it in vain.) For, as I told you, that day, I walked in on you, you are one of the rare & native forces. (What I tried to do, in this last job, was to remind these hyar amurrikans, that their energy hath expressed itself in much more important things than engineers & machines, that such men as you are, round the world, re-basing knowledge, and that, from such knowledge, if its particularity is carefully seen, its drive for a total bearing not for mere sanctions of an older humanism, there is plenty of reason to expect fresh culture from same.

(Keep turning, over, by the way, that shot of yours, that middle culture in the States issued from the Middle Colonies.)

I am sending you, under separate cover, an issue of Poetry New York which has just come to hand, a little in the hope that the piece on verse may suggest the ways i take it the poets are also pushing toward that kind of bearing which i see in you, but really to try to smoke out of you some more of your own pieces. You see, you have the advantage over uz kerekters, for you do get offprints, and I am trying to kadge some of same from you. I have had one, yr job before the Am Phil Soc, on Environment and Culture in the Last Deglaciation. One day, maybe, you'll have a chance to see how I have drawn up from it. So I am hungry for more, for *all* Carl Sauer says, in print. Please, please. (I don't know a man whose work I want more to keep abreast of.)

I do miss you, wish you were not always there, but were here. Did I tell you I did not go south last year, but elected to stay at this table (an old kitchen table) and cut away at prose & verse instead? (The New Englander, or whatever. Anyway, to get it down seemed, then, the thing to do. And now I have no funds. But, I do have one thing to show for it, a book coming out, soon. So . . . the way it is. Alas.) No regrets.

Also keep eye on Edgar Anderson. Any new such solid workers come to yr attention? (How does Barlow thrive? Recommended him to the attention of this new Boston editor.) Who else is there? Shld like it, if you'd drop me a penny post card whenever any work jumps up to your own eyes, in any of those areas that yr own center is center to. (It is this concept of the CENTER as the thing knowledge goes for, or its not worth its keep, that I was pushing, of late: THE GATE & THE CENTER.)

Do write, when you can. And send, o send!

Charles Olson

48

To Cid Corman (1950)

In 1950 Cid Corman was twenty-six, but he seems from his letters to Olson to have been very much younger, almost boyish. No wonder that Olson suspected Corman's ability to pull off the proposed magazine *Origin* and felt he had to lecture him on the subject (see especially the first two letters in *Charles Olson and Cid Corman: Complete Correspondence, 1950–1964*). Olson put a lot into this effort, which left him open to disappointment: his third letter, after several of Corman's, begins, "each sentence you write breaks my heart" (p. 57). This letter in turn flustered Corman, who defensively countered with: "NO assurances. . . . Deal is to get the best we can: of what we want. Along the PROJECTIVE trail. The issue will be as I want it or there won't be any" (pp. 60–61). Here is Olson's reply as published, pp. 61–64. *Letter at Texas.*

tuesday
november 14
50

my dear Corman:

So, it was that easy to smoke you out, was it?

Well, well.

Look here: I don't at all care to be addressed
in such terms as this letter of yrs. And I shall keep same
for whoever or whatever use, it is called for.

In yr first
letter to me, you allowed you did not think I needed you. That remains
quite, quite it.

You are a great fool, Corman. When a man—or two men—are ready
to pitch in, to throw all their work your way, and you make such pos-
ings you drive them off, that is foolishness, bug foolishness.

You are really quite stupid. You do not know the difference between
any of us just as writers who will *use* you and your mag to get things
published, and quite another will & drive, of some such writers who,
recognizing the deep use a magazine can be to all who read, would be
willing to go along with you in a project to put a magazine out which
would be of that kind of USE.

You had nothing to fear, and all to gain.
That is, if you did not so palpably fear you have no taste at all. But
where do you think taste & judgment come from? They are *earned,* and
it is not the least wise way to earn taste than from your betters—
especially, when such are ready to give you the best of themselves.

But that takes a little mod-
esty. I am embarrassed, by your lack of it. Such preening, that "the issue
will be as I want it or there won't be any," is simply a silly try to plug a
space which is empty, empty, my boy.

Or this: "Deal is to get the best we can: of what we want. Along the PROJECTIVE trail." I don't like at all such cheap use of a word of my own invention. And, secondly, why, if it is you, do you put it "we"? And if it is "we," who is we, and what of olson's work & letters has "we" seen, eh?

It is altogether LOSS, Corman. I have the impression you must be a most skillful operator. Otherwise, how could you keep a radio tent show of verse going, as you have, and, on top of that, get such backing for a magazine as you seem to have pumped up. And that's fine, that's, of use.

On top of that, you have the awareness enough, to go to Creeley to take a body of stuff already in hand, and— and i can tell you I valued that—invite olson to take over 40 pages of your first issue.

Put those two accomplishments together, and you can stand in the light, Corman, you can stand the light. Matter of fact, you can, after a bit, when such action is made evident, stand quite clear, with a coup or two, in the history of this business. You could even look a good deal like a couple of such fine predecessors as Margaret Anderson and Jane Heap, you could. And you could, as they did, earn the patronage of Jim or Jill X and the confidence of—o, say, such writers as one Creeley and one, olson.

But there it is. You think—in a flash—to have something else, that which is not so easily earned, that which you do not have and which cannot so easily be arrogated to yrself.

No, Corman. You have yr limits, too, quite recognizable limits.

Note the shrinkage, and ask yrself—as I could ask anyone—how come? What, other than your own fear of your own lacks, accounts for:

BANG: "am offering you 40 pages 1st no."

    BANG #2:   "won't you be contributing editor"

1st DEMUR   "well, no 4 letter words, &, er, ah, o,
                 not, let us not, we can't afford, it is un-
                 necessary, er, to attack, a.a.a, education.
                 And you do throw names
                 around. . . . ."

1st NEWS of HOW THE WIND BLOWS:

                            "olson (2 poems)"

      & NOW, when his hand is called, LOOK:
"Fuck (4 letter word, exact) everything said by me to date: re mag.
FINE idea of duet (article): let's see it. (Oh, yeah? "article"?)

NO assurances."
                  I repeat: "NO assurances".

                            Look, lad, get off the pot.
                            You want to do a job? Then,
                            stop fucking yrself.

                                          olson

Olson got thirty pages in the first issue of *Origin* ("featuring Charles Olson")
and, on receiving the issue on 27 April 1951, wrote: "the fullest satisfaction i have
ever had from print, lad, the fullest. And i am so damned moved by yr push,
pertinence, accuracy, taste, that it is wholly inadequate to say thanks" (*Olson-
Corman Correspondence,* 1, p. 126).

49

To Rainer Gerhardt (1951)

On the eve of his departure for Mexico, Olson felt it important to communi-
cate with his young ally in Freiburg im Breisgau, Germany. Rainer Gerhardt
had translated "The Praises" for the first issue of his magazine, *fragmente,* and
was working on *Call Me Ishmael,* which he tragically did not live to finish.
With this letter Olson enclosed a copy of a comment by William Carlos
Williams on the recently published "Projective Verse" essay. In a letter of
16 December 1950 (at Storrs) Williams had written that it was "the keystone,

the most admirable piece of thinking about the poem that I have recently, perhaps ever, encountered." *Letter (carbon copy) at Storrs.*

217 Randolph Place NE
Washington 2 DC
January 15, 1951

My dear Gerhardt:

The fullest sort of thanks for yr greetings, and for yr exciting (and excited) letter!

Look: I am leaving tonight for my first vacation in 7 yrs. (On top of that it will be the 1st time I have been out of the States in 22 years!!) My wife and I are moving by bus to New Orleans, and, there, by a Norwegian freighter across the Gulf to Yucatan, specifically, Lerma, just outside Campeche.

SO: let me answer you (say, on EZ, & St John of the Caribbean, ETC) as we go, fr the boat, say, or as we hang, for four days, in what is probably a stink-hole, Vera Cruz. The 22 yrs is the real clue, to my wildness, this day. For, this MOVE, represents, god help me, some sort of a huge passage out of a fixed purpose, to go down, go in, find out, what, to squeeze the stem, the very stem of, my people. It is strange (like a triptych) that, at this point, I am free, feel it is over, that, the rasslin with, the stubbornness to stay, to exhaust, not to take the "out" (not so much the old, and, to me, worn out proposition, "exil," as, the out of geography, which, given my vision, is like the temptations of, yes, the: what I love, out there, the flesh of it. Strikes me as the opposite Puritanism to DhLawrence's or Pound's—and still not the stay home of WCW's

((let me, without vanity, just, as, a transfer to you, as a sign of, the relation, as of, yr purpose, *fragmente 3*, let me enclose to you Bill Williams on the PRO VERSE piece; and to start telling you, how, that distinction there, of form & content, must, I take it (yr trouble with the word "content"), must be a language question. For if Bill, say, & Creeley, and I (who certainly, any of us, are absolutely committed as you are, to the premise that a poem is the man who writes it, that that origin is the single life) do not in any sense find in the separation of form & content anything more than a declaration of methodology, then, I take it, all that stands between you & us on this point must be language, must be, the meaning of "content" when it goes over into German, say. For you have the essential understanding—all, in fact, that I am after—that, a poem IS integral, and is only a coming and going from the man who makes it.

I am peculiarly concerned about this, and want you and me to exhaust it, and soon, simply because if you, reading the PRO VERSE, take the distinction as a separation (instead of a putting together for methodological needs NOW, in the practice of verse), then, surely, you and I must, for your translation of the PRO VERSE piece for frag 3, discover if the difficulty is, at root, language. And solve it, so that that principle, "form is never more than an extension of content," is seen to be a law emerging from the organism of the poet not from outside things.

Well, this is not good enough. Please wait for more from me, when I am on the move. But I am excited today (as I say) and want you to have this, as it comes, hot!

To get back: I feel finished with the frame of my people—that is, as an urgent necessity for me to come to conclusion about it (CALL ME ISHMAEL, surely, was a document of that struggle. And so much of the verse—KINGFISHERS, e.g.). And I go off with an ease & a joy & a hunger which surprises and delights me! (Just to tell you.)

Now I don't want you to be concerned that, this vacation, will interrupt anything, either our going ahead with literary affairs or our going ahead with the possibilities of yr trip here. As of these things,
   (1) continue to write me here until I give you our new address (mail here will be forwarded directly to me)
& (2) as of yr trip, I shall move it ahead by mail anyway (am sending your letter along to Creeley, so that he is posted on yr questions; on top of that I shall let Bill Williams know that you are ready to

make such a trip when and if all of us can arrange enough engagements to make it possible. He is a powerful help.)

(2a: one question—you wrote "ich stehe ab 10. 2. 1950 zur verfü-
gung"—did you mean as of February 10, coming up, you would
be free to come? I ask this, for, it would be my impression that,
such a trip—engagements, etc., wouldn't be arrangeable much
before next autumn. And I should not want you to get yr hopes
up, for any scheduling much before that, certainly not by this
spring (knowing the slowness of all but about three live human
beings in these States!)

At the same time, I don't think you should be too worried about any of
us, so far as war is concerned: I take it both Creeley and I are not army
men. And Bill is setting there, solid, in Rutherford. And these are the
workers who ought, among them, to bring about this much desired
thing: your coming! But it will take time. For it means raising up institutions! (Oh, yes: a motorrad, is, here, where space is so huge, of no use
whatsoever! Bus, my lad, BUS, or PLANE, is, the way, der weg ueber die
steppen!)

It is very fine, how much progress you have already made on the German edition of CALL ME ISHMAEL, and I am enclosing to you air
mail a stripped copy for yourself and whatever publisher seems to you
the right one (or the possible one!).

At the same time I am enclosing a letter legally declaring you my agent
and (yrself or yr wife) my translator, able, as both or either, to make
whatever contract seems to you best. I have notified my publishers here:
HARCOURT, BRACE & Co (incorporating REYNAL & HITCH-
COCK).

I am very happy that you think it can be managed (one good piece of
news came in with yr letter, the news fr GALLIMARD, that the French
edition will be out in either June or September).

Well, I hope that takes care of what is pressing between us as of the moment. I shall write you soon, but please, whenever you are of the mind,
write me, write me. It is so very good to have yr letters, to feel this elec-

trical joining between you, Creeley and myself, and to know that already, perhaps, by the time you read this, lobgesange will be sitting out there, in German, for someone, someone, to read! I am full of pleasure, & do, when you can, let me hear, what, if any comment, you and yr fellow workers have, of it, or anything!

Affectionately,
Charles Olson

Gerhardt was never able to make a trip to North America. The news of his suicide reached Olson in August 1954, whereupon he wrote a memorial poem, "The Death of Europe" (*Collected Poems*, pp. 308–316).

V

In January 1951 Olson and Connie began their vacation in Mexico. Yucatan became a vantage point for seeing what the modern world lacked and what would be needed for a postmodern future. That it has a great deal to do with mythology and the archaic is evidenced in *Mayan Letters* (edited by Robert Creeley from the many letters he received from Mexico) and in the "Human Universe" essay, which was written there.

While in Mexico Olson kept in touch with those he valued at Black Mountain College. He returned to teach full time in July 1951 and began organizing his own Institute of the New Sciences of Man. The years from 1951 through 1953 were vital ones for Olson at BMC. They were the years of *Origin* magazine (*In Cold Hell, In Thicket* was published in March 1953 as the eighth in the series). They were the years when the first volume of the *Maximus Poems* was finished and published.

50

To Robert Wauchope (1951)

From Lerma, Olson wrote to the Middle American Research Institute, Tulane University, for their map titled "Archeological Sites in the Maya Area." He discovered that the director, who sent the map, was the Robert Wauchope whose book *Modern Maya Houses* he owned.   *Letter (carbon copy) at Storrs.*

Lerma March 17
Campeche

My dear Robert Wauchope:
   I struck something the last two days which I thought I would file with you. In fact, won't you tell me if there is any use to you in such information, and if you would like me to keep filing same, if any, when I come on it?

   It is a correction, I think, to what yr map shows for the environs of Seybaplaya, specifically, today. CHUN-CAN. Or so I was told, last night, by natives of Seyba, is the name of a set of ruins I went to, by my nose, yesterday. (I had spotted this pyramid, from the bus to Champoton.)

   If one coordinates yr map to the country, yr map shows CHUN-CAN approximately directly east of the pueblo of Seybaplaya. But the complex of ruins I worked over yesterday (which the natives say is CHUN-CAN) is a good deal distance farther south, is, in fact, as the highway goes, exactly 7 kilometers farther on. (I have just checked yr map, and note a contour marking almost exactly where the ruin is: the marking is easy to see, as it is the only one near the coast.)

   I make a point of this, because, from a first examination, this ruin is of some importance. For example, against the bottom of the pyramid there is a good size hieroglyphic stone (with its worked face in against the hill). And two stones, alike in size, abt 7ft by 3, which look suspiciously like stela (though, if they are such, the faces are in the earth, and I had no crowbar, and was alone). Also sections of columns.

But what is perhaps of more importance is the rest of the complex farther in the country, approximately east by south: 1st, a series of houses, apparently, abt a kilometer and a half fr the pyramid, and (2) a small pyramid another like distance farther in, and all, seemingly, on the same axis.

It suddenly occurs to me: if you show CHUN-CAN, perhaps you
have on file a description of the ruin. If any of this interests you, perhaps you would have somebody copy for me what you have on the
ruin, and I can check all details, and report back.

In any case, this, for what it is worth. (The wagon-road directly in
to the pyramid, leaves the highway precisely at the kilometer sign, 40.)
(And the name CHUN-CAN means, "Trunk of the Sky"—which, indeed, it is, surveying, as it does, from its high sharp top, the whole coast
from Ensenada to Seybaplaya.) (The top is no more than 12ft by 6ft.)

Cordially

51

To Fielding Dawson (1951)

In his *Black Mountain Book,* Fielding Dawson described the great impact Olson
had on him from 1949 until 1953 when he left Black Mountain College to enter the
army. Below are two letters that were not transcribed in the book; both were
written from Mexico. The first is a kind of long-distance directed studies session,
a response to Dawson's asking about Leo Frobenius ("l.f." in the letter). The
second expresses a bit of homesickness for BMC and hints he might want to
return for the summer session. A hint was enough; the students levied one
another for the dollars that would give Olson the necessary minimal stipend.

Letters at Stony Brook.

lerma
april 11

flea:

excuse delay, but, i go away to ruins for long stretches, and when i
am back, there is much of the ordinary businesses to catch up

my knowledge of l.f., is, african genesis, childhood, & the cat. of mudandartmuseyroom, on cave show, circa 1930, so far as stuff here goes, plus small creepings through PAIDEUMA, and, above all, a series of articles in THE NEW ENGLISH WEEKLY, back abt 1930, a resume, by Fox, of l.f.'s "theories", as you call em, (excellent jobs) ((i had same with me at bmc, and they were bound there, & circulated among such as jack the rice, etc., anticipating one leser's (as well, of course, one dawson's) coming!

> only mama giffs
> rosses & koseys, not
>
>   pop
>   Salud!

————————————

                              lerma campeche mex april may 1st
fiddle-de-dee:
    damn nice letter, lad, and, thanks.
                          all news of you, vic, nick, don,
mary, tim, fine—and tell nick, glad, he, too, like me, made it, 4f: FINE,
all round

    am disturbed to hear, the school may, go, away.   sad.   liked, that
bowl, there.

    and you are quite right, the summer, session: Ben, Litz, Siegel any-
way (don't know others, Callahan, etc.). Shld like to make it, back, myself, and will, if, things here don't, keep me, eh?

    and followed you, better than you guessed, maybe, on, the entwin-
ings: "love", at black mt, are, substitutes for, news, eh? ok ok

bad days, here: farmers burn their fields, and, it's, like being under, a
burning, glass

will you please write me again, just, such?
                              yrs,
                                    o

52

To Stuart Z. Perkoff (1951)

Stuart Perkoff was a youth of twenty when Cid Corman published in the second issue of *Origin* two poems that caught Olson's fancy, "The Blind Girl" and "To Be Read on Festival Days" (which begins "The basket is wrapped"). The letter below, probably written 23 July 1951, was Olson's attempt, having just returned from the Yucatan, to get back with some difficulty into the North American scene.   *Letter (carbon copy) at Storrs.*

                                        my wish is to address you from no such
                                        place as i am in, hating the separation.
                                        So, let me put it, where i *was*

                                                            lerma, july
                                                            whatever
                                                            wherever

stuart perkoff:
                        i have just been telling creeley how very moved i was
last night to find you there (origin 2) with us
                                                that those two poems of
yrs belong with us, and are something neither of us, or anyone else, can
visit as you can such another hell
                                        that you move me as the clearest
speaking of such things i have heard in this half century of the false forwarding of like cause
                            that you have extricated yr statement from the
cause without losing any of it, in fact, with a intensing of it which I
hope you will allow me to put in terms of the only other man whom i
can think of as somewhat satisfying (tho, he, was, as you are american
are not, able to speak from the *activity* of an already happened revolution: Alexander Blok
                        It strikes me, that, verse-wise, the BASKET is
beyond The B G,   but still The B G
                                                (((what i would wish otherwise,
say, is, instead of "life's," "her" full turn—or what's full turn, figuring, a
word like "life" has to be restored by just such work as you also are engaged in

or the adjective "holy," and the "nest," because the "holy"
won't modify it exactly, to my ear

              BUT, the "holes in her head"! how
wonderfully you have done that—and how, done, "world" here, is, how
compact and large, how, what "life" and "holy" are not! this is very
beautiful of you, the, "holes"—and the "soft"

                    and so, likewise, the
push, of, the next stanza and the closing line, impeccable!

                      It makes me
very happy, how, that, you get such pain—in fact, verse-wise, i should
also say, i take it, this couplet-stanza of yrs is a very damned fine
methodology for you

              But let me, before I say the other who, comes
into my soul, reading you—just, as determinant—no more—you, making your own, all the way (and i very glad you are here, and hope you
are here as often as there are such things, that, for me, you & Creeley
are the ones i am most glad to run alongside of. . . .

                    that THE BASKET
is one of the very rare ones, that, so far as my knowing goes, it is standing by itself, that here you have done a poem that any man would be
proud of however much he would not be able to do it

                      that there is
nothing in it which disturbs me and so that i would have different one
syllable: that yr tactile power is the sort of fineness only the best poet
has

    for all the other powers: how that adj "uninterested" drops! Or
"hard"

      No, these are lovely things (the no, was, the thinking of, your
line: doesn't matter—yr couplet-stanza, and that windup single, is, a
speech form of great force in your hands

                 (((((I marked this first in a
poem in RESISTANCE, about, a year ago, how, your fineness of ear and
touch makes it possible to reintroduce materials that so many others
have torpedoed, and kept torpedoing, since the days of—in our language, I'd say, Dickens

             that, Dickens least once in a while got across
what you here in two short poems do throughout them

You deserve to be hailed, and I am proud to tell you how rare i think you are. Please go on to make many things. In fact, if you felt like it, I should like very much if you could send me all that you have in print. For you already interest me as the most interesting poet I know now working in these parts.

> Well, to be quiet, to go quiet, and so
> to leave you alone

with the deepest affection
& thanks
Charles Olson

When Perkoff responded to the invitation to send further poems, Olson "turned back" everything, as Olson tells it in the *Olson-Corman Correspondence,* vol. 1, p. 227). Although the younger poet was "bitter" and "fell back before critique" (p. 260), he rallied to publish *The Suicide Room* as Jargon 17 (1956), dedicated it "For Charles Olson," and included the two poems praised in the above letter.

53
To Ben Shahn and W. H. Ferry (1951)

The well-known artist Ben Shahn always had strong connections with the labor movement; one of them was with W. H. ("Ping") Ferry, the director of public relations for the CIO–Political Action Committee. Olson had his own connections, but this time he is using Shahn's, since the funds he is seeking for Black Mountain College would include money to bring Shahn back for more than the one summer session of 1951. The correspondence below gives a sense of the high feeling that existed during those summer weeks. Shahn was, after all, an old friend from the Office of War Information days, and Olson had collaborated with him specifically on the forceful and gracious *Spanish-Speaking Americans in the War* (1943); now they were working together again.

Olson's poem "Glyphs" ("for Alvin, & the Shahns") appeared posthumously in *A Nation of Nothing But Poetry.* Shahn's rejoinder—tempera on paper, titled "A Glyph for Charles"—is included in Mary Emma Harris's *The Arts at Black Mountain College* (1987).

Letter to Shahn and letter (carbon copy)
to W. H. Ferry at Archives of American Art.

thursday

BEN!

   i better get the enclosed (with carbon for you) on without further delay

         (lost yesterday doing a 15 page job—prose—on an idea flashed up in me hot, Tuesday night, and too urgent to let it ride over)

the roster of faculty fr '33 to now Con and I will try to make up and type tonight, and tomorrow

   the point is the place ain't the same, with you all gone—like half the world gone—as tho the moon had ripped off from, the earth

                                      quite a palpable feeling, the loss of yr weight here, yr resistances—all the light headed is too noticeable, eh?

   i do what i can!— had two big sessions   (tho Motherwell—goddamnim—busted up my go last night by scheduling that "delayed" lecture at 9 last night—which pissed me off, that, three ways his changeableness (?) had hit you and me: (1) that he forced me to read my verse two days ahead of Sunday, and thus, not so fresh; (2) then Sunday; and (3) then, balks me from a five hr go I wanted, to push em, on several fronts, several of which you were part of:

                                  am giving it to em, on social action! (assigned the Barr, and other things humming in their ears

I MISSED MOTHERWELL BECAUSE SHERMAN AND A COUPLE OR MORE WANTED TO CONTINUE THE CLASS—and talk abt the value of art in the face of the value of a gang getting together & singing pepsicolahitsthespots!

                okay?

will see to the Katy movements to scale

already saw harrison on the words to abby's present—sez he, that was a *piano* piece!— well, we'll see what we will see: he has set the glyph to you—haven't had chance to hear it, yet do let us hear from you all—cards, anything, so we know, eh?

and anything of any hope out of the ferry & the joe deal, eh?

love to you, bernarda, abby, su and john

> fr us both, and all
> the others, i
> imagine

> charles

> Black Mountain College
> Black Mountain,
> North Carolina,
> August 7, 1951

My dear Ping Ferry:

I am asking Ben Shahn to put this in your hand. It is a month now the two of us have been chewing over some notions our presence together here provoked, about education generally, and, the situation of this college alsowise. (You see, it was a sort of combustion, to be together again, he here for the first time, I coming back direct from Yucatan, to do the summer session job in writing as I had two summers ago, following, then, on a year of a special business, when Albers was Rector, of lecturing here once a month for a week, entraining down, from Washington.) (Some sentence!)

One of the reasons I came back, was, that the Shahns were to be here. On top of that I like to work here, found, three years ago, that the place, the students, and the chance to work with some of the others of the faculty, was a special sort of thing, and was worth more to me than any other educational situation I knew (I had backed the hell out of education when I left Harvard, where I had last had a special appointment from Conant, in 1939).

It's a damned queer place, and I kind of promised Ben, at a faculty meeting ten days ago, that I'd try to state, for him and for Ken Chorley, how I saw it, how I took it that the place was now (as it had been another thing when it was founded, in the first year of the Roosevelt Ad-

ministration), why I, as a writer, was able to get work done here, was
able to say—what I keep saying—that, as of now, the place offers lessons in how American education generally can make another heave,
make an advance by the locking arms of active professionals and regular faculties, anywhere.

You see, when Albers invited me down to do three lectures in October, 1948, it was to be, for me, that one-shot job. And when he asked
me, for his faculty, would I and the wife come and teach the rest of the
year, I said, nothing doing, I wouldn't mix myself with a college community for any dough, much as I damn well needed, always need it,
verse, not being worth more than a buck, a few times a year, eh?

But
why I like Albers is, that, right then & there he was flexible, and said,
"Well, if you won't come live here, will you return next month for a
week, and continue to do such a thing the rest of the year?" And so it
happened, that, as I found out from Robert Payne, later, between Albers
and myself a method of education which has long been the law of Chinese education got applied again, here: that is, that a so-called creative
man stays at his own last in a capital city, doing his work where men
ought to do their work, in the midst of active society, but once a
month, or whatever, they come to such a retired place as a college is
(and this Black Mountain sure is the quintessential retired place, as Ben
can damn well tell you!), and give out with, what they have been doing
in their own trade, so that other men or women who have been working at their own lasts can hear them, can exchange businesses, and what
students there are who are interested, can find out whatever the men or
women have to say, whatever they have to show, of work accomplished
where, as I say, work can be accomplished (which I damn well don't
think is a retired and adolescent place, such as a college is—that is,
no man, I take it, could well, long, do his best work in such an atmo-
sphere). But that fact shouldn't, any longer, deprive education of what it
so very much needs—the active professional man, in the arts and in the
fields of knowledge, who is not an historian (as, basically, all "profes-
sors" are) but is himself actively a maker of "history", eh?

Now what
has been happening here, for several summers, is something like what
happened this summer—for two months, a Shahn, a Katy Litz in

dance (or a Merce Cunningham), a Lou Harrison in music, a Paul Goodman or an Olson in writing, a Harry Callahan in photography, or (had it been possible) an Alexander Gianpietro in pottering, come together and give out together. And the nice thing is that, despite the wearing *closeness* of everything and everybody—the isolation and the common meals, the all-too-aesthetic compression, the gab-gab-gab, the just-too-spoiled-for-their-own-good-students—despite that (and a little *because* of it?), Shahn teaches Olson one hell of a lot about his verse, Katy Litz picks up clues for pushing her own important advance in dance, Harrison makes music for Abby Shahn and others, Bernarda comes to listen to Olson when she can and shoots in shots of perception about the stuff he reads to the students which opens the eyes of sd students and lets them find out how to hear, how to dig the jug out of their own ears and clean the gurry off their senses—and the regular faculty feels a little sad about it all, that is, the more worn down ones do, but those who are still with some pep (and at Black Mountain, at the moment, the good thing is that the faculty is quite young, most of them recent graduates who have moved in to take over the instruction just because the kind of faculty the students want are such men and women as they can only get in the summers, such summers. . . .

WHICH BRINGS US TO THE POINT: isn't it about time somebody got hep to the fact that such a system as these "summer institutes" can be limbered up so that the whole year is a "winter institute" or whatever it was that Albers and I arrived at, that year, when, instead of this dead residence principle—which has kept any men and women of sense the hell away from campuses, American education move out into a more alive approach to its job, by inviting men and women to come for short periods through the college year, in an organized way, so that education as knowledge alone (as "history") be *interlocked* with the arts and the sciences, interlock itself with the active work active men & women are doing?

Now the thing you must say for these students here is that, at least in two cases this summer, because the college couldn't afford to bring all the active people it wanted, these students dug down in their own pockets (or got their hands in the old man's pockets—pockets, smockets, whose got pockets—) and financed the salary of these faculty members! (The College offered their board and room). In other words, another evidence: that the "young", 1951, also sense that something has to be done.

I take it the reason what is happening here, students & faculty, is not at all local—is, in fact, answering a need of the whole society—can be found in this proposition as it got stated in the Black Mountain catalogue two years ago. Let me quote it for you, for it seems to me to declare the shift of the base which education and knowledge generally, even the arts, are beholden to, now—and what all of us can do about it, why Ben and I do come to this outlandish place, why the regular faculty welcome the invasion, why the students want it so badly they finance it, as far as they can, and why educators and foundations generally can afford to turn their minds to the phenomenon. Here it is:

> At the middle of the 20th century, the emphasis—in painting as well as in political theory—is on what happens between things, not on the things in themselves. Today the area of exploration, the premise underlying systematic thinking, is that of function, process, change; of interaction and communication. The universe—including man and his interests—is seen, in microcosm and in macrocosm, as the continuously changing result of the influence that each of its parts exerts upon all the rest of its parts

What happens *between* things—what happens between *men*—what happens between guest faculty, students, regular faculty—and what happens *among* each as the result of each: for i do not think one can overstate—at this point of time, America, 1951—the importance of workers in different fields of the arts and of knowledge working so closely together some of the time of the year that they find out, from each other, the ideas, forms, energies, and the whole series of kinetics and emotions now opening up, out of the quantitative world.

And just because of the dispersions of the quantitative world, small place, whether, for a man and family it is Roosevelt, New Jersey, or for a group such as a college it is Black Mountain, a small place now offers this sort of chance, this sort of experimental locus.

Well, no use making any more abstract definitions. Let me just quickly summarize some of the developments already shaping up for Black Mountain the coming year.

(1): Due to Ben's interest, and his perception that GRAPHICS is a shop core for work in the arts, there is a possibility that one of the fine printers will come here for, perhaps, two weeks and lecture, look over the equipment of the print shop, and give the lads some sense of what projects in printing the world, over there, needs. Already Ben and I have moved them away from too dandy a conception of projects to a little tough business like pamphleteering, how to design, write, print, and distribute such. The advantage of such a shop core would be immense, just because at this precise point—more, even, than any exhibit—the actualities of these kids' social and political world will be brought home to them—they will be reminded of the towns and cities and families from which they come—and which, at the peril of themselves, and the place, they forget, are altogether too apt to forget!

There is also the hope that the faculty will be able to find the funds to restore an instructor in printing—or better, from my point of view anyhow, a full graphics-knowing man. Ben already has a good candidate in mind.

(2): DANCE. My own impression is that, dance, here, has been the most forward of the disciplines, there has been more continuity of a group of professionals (conspicuously, Merce Cunningham and Katherine Litz), and thus a greater thickness in the learning by several talented students. But there is another side to this: dance, like a print shop, has served as a core to what we might call the performing arts: music, of course, writing in that aspect of it which is verse and theatre, and painting as it is three-dimensional design. Again, the small place has helped—and one of the nice things which emerged from my own attempt two summers ago to drive the performing arts closer together by pegging the whole summer's work in writing on two performances at the end of the eight weeks called "Theatre Exercises", was, a thing initiated by the students and regular faculty themselves, a going "Light-Sound-Movement Workshop", tackling problems of invention in the three, and making performances where all dance teaching is done—in the dining hall.

This
dance situation is going to be increased the coming year by making one
of the three collaborating New York professionals—Litz, Cunningham
and Meedie Garth—the regular faculty instructor, with the other two
visiting—granted funds to pay their fares—and both giving demon-
strations and teaching, for what time they can be here.

(3): I should, properly, now join music, but the music situation needs
special words, and before I discuss that, let me just lay home here the
WRITING problem. Here there has been some concentrated push in
the last three years, due somewhat to the fact that I have been here one
of the two academic years and two of the summers. But equally important is, that the place now understands it has to have active writers, and
even tried, at my instigation, to bring WCWilliams here last summer,
and again, this. For what I despair a little at making absolutely clear, is,
that a certain homogeneity of instruction in *all* the arts is possible
today to a degree that I don't think was so possible just a short while
back, here, or in any college. That is, one of the reasons why just what is
happening here does happen—the bringing in of *active* education—is
because a growth of *action* in art itself is noticeable. I would put it—
have put it—that PROJECTION, with all its social consequences, is the
mark of forward art today. And it is one of the best ways we find out
the kinetic secrets of projective art—the very way we do it—is to put
art *in action,* to join the arts *in action,* to break down all stupid walls,
even the wall of art as separate from society!

(Ben can tell you what a
happy business happened amongst four of us guest faculty this summer—
a GLYPH show, initiated by Ben as the consequence of his giving me a
drawing as a trade-last for a poem, and now, because of these two acts,
Litz the dancer has added a number to her repertory, a GLYPH, with set
by Shahn, and my words set to music by Harrison.)

(4): I don't myself know how the place will kick itself along in PAINT-
ING except as it can induce Ben to come here and carry forward what
he has already started. That is, as it is, there is instruction. And there is a
continuing attempt to use lessons of paint and design in theatre. But
here—as unlike dance, music, and writing—there is no such profes-

sional as Ben, and he is needed, badly—not only for that alone, but for the huge reminder he is, that the *myth* of America (which is any of us) is in the *facts* of America (which is much more than any of us as individuals, however sensitive).

The students have asked that, in any "plan", in any attempt to get financing for a "winter institute" of "guest faculty" Ben Shahn be got here, for as much time as he can spare.

((You must surely think, by now, I am trying to sell you the place—like Brooklyn Bridge! And that the whole point is lost: that is, that Black Mt is only an example of what I take it American education needs now, generally, to find out about.

But the truth is, a double one: I want most to pass on to you my own impression of the advantage of such interlocking as I have found here for other colleges; but I am also, actually, hoping that, if all this interests you, that you may have some ideas of where Black Mountain can immediately turn for the sort of financing any real push of this WINTER GUEST FACULTY plan requires.

For example, the (5): MUSIC. Lou Harrison, the present music instructor, tells me that there are four composers who are as close together in their intentions, interests, and ability to work together as, in the dance, Garth, Cunningham and Litz are, and, so far as the other arts go, certainly Ben and I can work together. The four are Henry Cowell, John Cage, Varèse, and himself. Now here is the interesting thing: all four of them know this place, Cage taught at least a summer here, and all four have this dream: that someday, somewhere they get together to experiment on two things—(1) old French & English music and (2), of particular interest to Cage and Varèse, the effect of electronics on music now, both audience & composer. What Harrison would like to do is to manage to bring the four of them together here this winter, for as much time as moneys can make possible.

Now this to me has several gains. First, these composers actually work, separately, in New York, with the above dancers (again, note, separately). On top of that, this place is prepared—has the isolation, & buildings—to offer a lab to the composers for electronic experiment. And another thing: this could be a professional project without necessary reference to Black Mt, but if it took place at Black Mt, it would give the students and the rest of the faculty the kind of forward and wholly active sort of business I am talking about, throughout this now long letter.

Well, here is something that neither the men themselves can finance, nor the College, nor the students! And yet there it sits, as something, as a project of 4 American artists just idling because of no dough!

As, really, the whole project of this letter is, essentially, being held back from real forward push, here, or elsewhere, because of the same thing: no dough.

And yet I ask you, as a knowledgeable man, do you honestly think most of the several other sorts of projects which are getting money go anywhere near as far to attack the problems of education now?

That's my leading question. And I'll leave it at that, thanking you, for hearing me out!

With respect.

54

To the Fulbright Committee (1951)

Olson wrote to Robert Creeley on Thursday, 18 October 1951, that he had the previous Monday "whacked out a Fulbright application—just to give myself a play, a chance, to get the hell out again, next year ... to go Mesopotamia!" (*Olson-Creeley Correspondence*, vol. 8, p. 64).

Letter as quoted in Alcheringa 5 (spring–summer 1973): 11–12.

I have found it increasingly important to push my studies of American civilization back to origin points on this continent and this, in turn, has involved me increasingly in questions and in the development of methods to investigate the origins of civilization generally ... Just as surely as the backward of America led me to the Maya, and to the study of a 'hieroglyphic' language as a valuable core to investigating morphology of culture, so the backward of Western civilization led me to the Caucasus Mountains and to the civilization which first flourished in the Mesopotamian Valley . . . My method has always been to put around any such core the full picture of culture, both where it came from and where it dispersed. And I am particularly interested in the whole region and the plateaus of the old East, the old routes of people's movements . . .

My desire is to go to IRAQ to steep myself, on the ground, in all aspects of SUMERIAN civilization (its apparent origins in the surrounding plateaus of the central valley, the valley-city sites themselves, and the works of them, especially the architecture and the people's cuneiform texts.)

The point of a year of such work at the sites and in collections is a double one: (1), to lock up translations from the clay tablets, conspicuously the poems and myths (these translations and transpositions have been in progress for four years); and (2), to fasten—by the live sense that only the actual ground gives—the text of a book, one half of which is SUMER.

(The other half is the MAYA, and the intent, in putting these two civilizations and especially their arts together, is to try to make clear, by such juxtaposition, the nature of the force of ORIGINS, in the one case at the root of Western Civilization and in the other at the root of American Indian Civilization.

The further intent is that such a study throw a usable light on the present, the premise of such a study of origins being, that the present is such a time, that just now any light which can lead to a redefinition of man is a crucial necessity, that it is necessary if we are to arrive at a fresh ground for a concept of 'humanism.'

It may make my purpose clearer if I mention how Dr. Henri Frankfort found it necessary, in his 'Birth of Civilization in the Near East' (1951), to examine both Toynbee and Spengler's conceptions of how civilizations come into being. My difference, however, is marked. For such a method of juxtaposition as described above cuts across 'classified history' and demands, as these other methods do not, both the substance and the forms of art, and their examination by a man who is a practicing artist himself, a 'professional' in the arts as signs of the culture.)

55

To Henry Murray (1951–1952)

In his diatribe against the academic Melvilleans, composed as a "LETTER FOR MELVILLE 1951 written to be read AWAY FROM the Melville Society's 'One Hundredth Birthday Party' for MOBY-DICK at Williams College, Labor Day Weekend, September 2–4, 1951," Olson "extricated" Henry Murray from the general condemnation, although he wished "the doctor, whom I love" was not going to Williams to mix "in such salad as these caterers will serve!" He sent the verse pamphlet, wet from the Black Mountain College student press, to Murray at the conference: "I hope, beyond all else, you will *enjoy* it" (letter of 31 August 1951 at Storrs). It was hardly likely that Murray could, but there was no remonstrance. Murray alerted Olson that the paper he had delivered at the conference would appear in the December 1951 issue of *The New England Quarterly* with the title "In Nomine Diaboli." Below is Olson's long letter of response, preceded by an announcement of the birth of his daughter Kate on 23 October 1951. *Letters at Storrs.*

monday oct 28

Harry! by God, & by, the USA!

a DAUGHTER,
Kate
7 pound 2 ounces, & ¼
NINETEEN INCHES LONG!
Of course, the hands, & the feet are
PRETTIEST!
called her Kate just, to give her, the straightest—
CHANCE
(seems there couldn't be a poor woman—don't know one—
by such a name: & could be, a ROARER, eh?)

Constance is wonderful:
wldn't have taken any anesthetic but for the doc, who in the last few minutes, decided, to push her: it all took place inside 12 hrs

Both my
girls send you their fondest—can she call you 'uncle?

uncel 'arry?
Anyhow, she's started!

I was slightly confused, at the news. Was standing outside the delivery room, and my confusion was, I figure I'd know how to raise a boy BUT—to raise a woman!

Tell me, who did it,
HOW to do it, will ya?

OK. And let us have all yr news: you are the dadblasted man for not telling what YOU are up to:

and what abt that
idea, of yr coming here, to tell these hyar people SOMETHING, eh?

they
need to hear such as you. Please, if you can figure it.

And my love, in
this extra DIMENSION, eh?

Charles

——————————

Saturday, February 16   52
My dear Harry:

Yr IND came an hour ago, and I have read it, and it breaks my heart. In two ways: that you do know HM, and have told the unhappinesses he was locked in, and they are of such an order, are still so much the fate of several of us—are so, not only in the context you put them in, but so in contexts such as LANGUAGE and such as that CIVIL WAR he saw as well as the INTERNATIONAL CW we are watching—are so so continuingly & wideningly that to put it the way you have, to suggest that an incompatible marriage is an ending of it—this is what I mean, dear large friend, who here, by language, has said so much but has said it in such a way that you make of yourself such companions as these men NOW—Arvin, Chase, Mumford, Stone—the latest published men—and not one of them, not one of them one of the tribe who are, today, batting themselves against THE SAME, or NOT SO DIFFERENT WALL!

Harry. Harry. I write to you in faith—faith I can demonstrate from
your own text here—how rich, & subtle you are in your sense of this
man: this piece under hand proves again what I have always insisted,
that you have, by your own TECHNOLOGY, gone into this man and
his books and have the pieces of his heart in your hand.

But you are also, surely, the one person present there that night
who could, out of other parts of your experience, have known & said in
what way the ACT of Melville is a continuing one, is still AFOOT, is still
the QUARREL, & the FIGHT. For you well know that it is—and leaving
it out, letting the enemy have your good words—have the benison,
even, of your praise—your reference to them—breaks my heart, leaves
my pieces in your hand, too.

Let's, first, get rid of any idea it is I, my work, that is, because it is
unmentioned, essentially of the matter: I would not *fit* in that company,
that picture, and am well left out, simply, that I removed myself, simply,
that I did not say—as you well pointed out, that lunch, 72nd Street, that
spring—and on the train afterwards, made the old mistakes again (even
in the very act of mailing you a copy of EBOLI)—missing, another
chance to slay the same MONSTRESS you show my poor brother disarmed before, eh? It was crazy, the way it happened that afternoon,
Broad Street Station, DIRECTLY on the finger you had on what I HAD
LEFT OUT OF ISH—
                            but *had i left it out?* had I? exactly
in what sense is it that character is assassinated, except, that, the very
act of it is the act of art which rides, as you well state, by imagination
over perception? Exactly. Exactly, but, this then is the struggle, the problem, the one—and it is not local to us of this tribe—it is the huge unre-
stored thing of all the people, of this society, the ACT OF MUTHOS.

You see, Harry, why I take this piece of yours to be of the moment
it is, is, that you are here putting your hand in—as I always found you
putting your hand in— to the very MEAT of the thing, to where we
men LIVE, WORK, HIDE, & DIE.

That is, I think you know me, know me well, know where I, too,
hide. And so I write as straight as I do to you—have never written so

or said many of these things to any one but you. OK. Thus, you were right—in *that* context—to leave me out, to be calmly certain that I have written no MOBY-DICK, and so do not deserve to be talked about when there is my brother there who did write such a book and so told what men of our tribe can say on the subject.

Which gets us to the HEART & PARADOX of my response: I would have you wholly *relentless,* and because you haven't been, here, and because I believe—*want* you to be, wherever & whenever you write on this subject again—I take up this machine this afternoon, and, all crawling with nerves and the collidings of love—for I do love you— do know love, the love you have him speak of, there, that other androgyne

> ((((question: do you know any modern man other than an
> androgyne, who makes sense? who is capable of love—
> *or of power?*
>> e.g., your own pegging of AH as co-
>> pralagnist; your own acquaintance with FDR, probably
>> more than my own look into those boy eyes; and Mao?
>> that is, *before* Peking—*before* power (for power, like all
>> accomplishment outside art, deceives, makes men think
>> they have OVERCOME their own enemy!)

You defer too much, pay too much mind to (1) LITERATURE and (2) RELIGION. I mean that this way, that, your own discipline, PSY-CHOLOGY, is serious enough in its own right to be an ordering offered *without reference to* either (1) or (2)— or, which also bulks large in the present piece, (3) SOCIETY. And it is this *purity* which I would urge on you, here, & anywhere.

> I even can dare to suggest to you the very
methodology which I am as certain as I am that I am more or less alive is IN YOUR OWN HANDS—and would make it unnecessary— impossible—for you to throw a single curve to any other creature.

> It is
DOCUMENTATION, RESEARCH, ANALYSIS, the very methods you use each day which—I ask you, Harry, in all the pain of this moment— why do you *abandon* for some other language, such a language as this speech?

why do you use HM's language at all?

This is a mighty issue, the very issue of the very discipline you practice—in fact, much more: IS the issue of the USE of present knowledge.

Let me put it back on MD, and just as you have here discussed it. You yrself emphasize how thoroughly HM bodies his book by encompassing the TECHNOLOGY of an industry. The question then is: DO YOU THINK IT IS, OR CAN BE, BY LAWS, ANY DIFFERENT TODAY? Do you think I, or you, or any man can do anything else but USE the TECHNOLOGY present to ourselves—

and here I give you the greater nobleness of your profession, the very reason why you or any such MD as you need not for a minute pander to any other present discipline whatsoever:

that PSYCHOLOGY is, if not the only TECHNOLOGY (I am thinking of how useful I have also found ANTHROPOLOGY, and GEOGRAPHY—ANTHRO-ARCHEOLOGY, better), is one of the GOVERNING disciplines of our time—

and is so completely seen & understood as such by us practicing writers that it is hugely, tragically more important than any such union as you there put it—with literary criticism: it is of the body of our own creations, these days, my generation—and I do not mean cheap short stories in the New Yorker using psychiatric or psychoanalytic "materials" direct:

I mean in the CONJURING, of our own images, our own MUTHOS

((cf. to understand my using MUTHOS, the careful discriminations on it & LOGOS in J.A.K. Thomson's THE ART OF LOGOS, as study of Herodotus, LONDON, 1935, pp. 17–19, & footnote))

Look, Harry—god, in your own notes, in all your work, there is a language already in existence—a methodology—for telling us all that you have found out about HM that will make your work of the immense

value it is—I know it is, from the way I have seized it, from under conversations, and from under the words of this present piece—as I seized
it from under the preface of your *Pierre* edition:

   please PLEASE, harry, listen to this young 'un—listen to this boy:
don't, please, think these are LITERARY ravings, or smarts, or anything
but DEVOTION TO DUTY:
                           please merely *tell* what you have found
out—there is no necessity at all to wrap it up in the ordinary packages
of discourse—no need to make any ANY generalizations: the MAP of
Melville's PSYCHE is in your hands to make, and it needs to be made as
quietly and as carefully and as modestly (the modesty got nothing to do
with anything but the scrupulousness with which the continents are
drawn, the soundings are indicated—exactly as disciplined as an Admi-
ralty chart
         as firmly as I ever asked any man, I ask you to present
Melville to us by staying exactly inside your own fine discipline:
                                                        exam-
ples, from the present piece, to show you I am not talking without
case:
         447, starting (and note your own phrase, which begins it—"If it
         were concerned with *Moby-Dick,* the book, rather than with its
         author, I would call *this* my third hypothesis . . .), starting right
         there
                  and down through p. 448, exactly, ending *before*

              All this has been changed, for better and for worse,
              by the moral revolutionaries of our own time, who,
              feeling as Melville felt, but finding the currents of
              sentiment less strongly opposite, spoke out, and
              with their wit, indignation, and logic, reinforced by
              the findings of psychoanalysis, disgraced the stern-
              faced idols of their forebears. One result is this:
              today an incompatible marriage is not a prison-
              house, as it was for Melville, "with wall shoved
              near."

You see, I know too many—I know only one person who doesn't—go
groping through like woods as HM to think—and I think you too must

grant me this—that it is time yet to allow such a "hope"—a "difference"—even with yr phrase "and for worse"—to BULK—to be allowed
by you to bulk as the equal of the very STATE you have so impeccably
poised in the previous page and a half

  this is the subtlety I meant that is of the heart of the paradox your
  presentation in this piece raises:
                            the weighing of the *dimensions* of
  experience: the *weighting*
                          i ask you: isn't this EXACTLY what it is all
about? isn't it exactly what your science gives to men, the advantage of
taking these new tokens and taking them off for themselves to make
what use they can of them—to figure, as Melville had to figure by way
of the Judeo-Christian counters Maria was a creature of, how to find
himself?

  The thing is so dense, now, as then—and what I so value in the passage I have bracketed off as an application of your method, is, that it
  does not do—what you do later—overweigh the Puritanism as single or largest factor in this assassination of love which went on in
  these States.

  I am the more able to talk to you about this that I have been trying,
  by my own methodologies (and the curious thing is how much my
  work in preparation for the PhD in American Civilization exactly
  there Harvard where you are is now flooding back—particularly
  you, Merk, and Ellery) to see what was the full body of the causation
  which, around the very same years, tossed up such like psyches as
  Melville's, Whitman's, Lincoln's
                              what was there in those decades,
  say, 1830-1850—what happened? and you see what I am cautioning
  you against is, that, the JOB OF PRESENTATION ITSELF is now as
  much of the matter as the FACTS—that is, I cannot leave out of the
  explanations the very thing you elsewhere mention: the TECH-
  NOLOGY—I could not, actually, leave out the girls of Lowell &
  Lawrence, any more than one can, bearing on what you have here,
  leave out—AT THE VERY INSTANT OF THE DISCUSSION—that
  story THE TARTARUS OF MAIDS, eh?

Maybe I can put it simply: that any method of discourse other than the full bearing of you or me from inside our own disciplines—without bowing to any other, without even *granting* any other (((that is, who can say the literary method is, today, necessarily the great one it was, say, not with Melville—for he was not at all a perfect writer (one reason why it has been only truculent & American writers like, say, Crane, & myself, who have found him source)—but as it was in that day so long ago which Homer wrote in, eh?

> that any method of statement OTHER THAN the one you use in your own work each day is bound to do wrong to your materials—and to one's self, as a result of the premise that our work is us
> > (((which last is why you do distinguish—above—the book rather than with its author!)))

o, Harry, hew to yrself: pay no compliments to anybody. At the same time, I assure you there is no need to push any evidence you have in your hands one decibel beyond the statement of it you'd make in the company of your own profession:

> do not give yrself to the company of literary critics, or societal professionals, or even let the conclusions about myth—"this branch of the tree of psychology growing in the direction of HM"—get even as extended as Jung permitted his to be:
> > > conclusions, any round
> > > statements, are no longer
> > > ANY OF US's BUSINESS
> > > what is so beautiful

(and men's words, when they come from there, are always beautiful: any man's words, of any profession) is, that we are all workers, & workers in such a time of discontinuity that it behooves each of us to speak no further than the EVIDENCE & the materials: THE TECHNOLOGY, & THE PRODUCTION: allow

OK. I have emptied my mind, pretty much. I want only to give you my own selection of sentences & parts from this piece IND which seem to me (beside that central passage) to mark the DOCUMENTATIVE METHOD I so heart-brokenly recommend to you:

436: "scientific terminology"—any day—will NOT be a "winding-sheet." On the contrary, IS, any day, a LANGUAGE more alive than all that Arvins, Mumfords, Stones, & Chases practice— more than Olsons, in this sense that, we are poor men of a poor time: "the last resources"—mark that word—"of an in-sulted and unendurable existence": ASK any present man anywhere out of the fatness of these States—and even here!—if this isn't ONE OF THE MOST BEAUTIFUL QUOTES THAT ANY MAN HAS DREDGED UP FROM HM—((((note: where is it from, page etc, please?)))

: "the normal man" is all over the place, Harry—ALL OVER, believe me—UNCURED, UNHAPPY, SICK—"l'humanite, c'est l'infirmite"—and to say that is not at all—any more than how valuable an MD has been since all the years before Asclepius—to derogate for one instant your own profession

—it is a moral, & continuing fact, that the normal man AL-WAYS IS

437: not Beethoven—believe me, the practice of music now does not find source at all in Beethoven, YET, the practice of writ-ing now finds huge source in HM—this is CRUCIAL, & a matter of discourse, not taste

(Interpolation: Harry, an Anglo-Catholic sd to me the other day: you are too honest to believe in God!

And the person I sd I thought was NORMAL, sd: "Have a heart, Olson—leave off!"

And so I beg you, please, take the vision, & forget the man, THE PRESSER of these PANTS—the edge of it will wear off, the pants can be worn!)))

437: "WITH THE FIDELITY OF A SCIENTIST"—note note
note, Harry—yr own FAITH—and all I am crying for in this
screed, is, WRITE ABOUT MELVILLE AS MELVILLE
WROTE ABOUT WHALING—with THE FIDELITY OF A
SCIENTIST—let no sentence stand on paper which you
would not let stand in front of your CONFRERES

439: "a potential set of dispositions which may be constellated
in the personality by the occurrence of a certain kind
of situation" BEAUTIFUL—and the more so, that you
also say, "not, let me hasten to say, as an *inherited fixed
image*"
BEAUTIFUL—and the sort of contribution each of us needs:
an EVIDENCE, of the essential mobility, and the necessity of
the act of WILL (I am using Brother Lawrence's 17th Century
distinction of WILL from Understanding)

′′′′′: "An explanation of all this in scientific terms would require all
′′′′′ the space permitted me and more."
′′′′′

AGAIN, Harry; you KNOW: you know yr METHOD—*why
use any other?* why not let that BANQUET listen to you in
your true role, yr TRUE discipline?

was there any reason WHY NOT?

439-40: "very similar to those that Aristotle used . . ."????? is it not
rather, by your own earlier statement, "very similar to
those that HERMAN MELVILLE used in setting forth the
dynamics of his own existence?" FUCK GREEK TRAGEDY,
in the face of MOBY-DICK! fuck Aristotle fuck literary
critics

442: "an anaconda of an old man"

: the PARA, starting, "Capt A . . . sun-god" down to, & thru
"Easter-tide"—but leaving out the Black Mass biz, as, on another plane of vibration

      : (((((a 1000 questionings of the Paradise Lost gig: please write me what evidence there is for this)))))

443: PARA, on Fedallah, thru "Oriental religion" but before "Q T D"—again, another plane of the use of racial or religious figures—I hammer abt these discriminations simply, that, as a scientist, you will know that THE SCIENCE OF MYTHOL-OGY is a professional field as delimitable as any other—and that us practicers of it ACTIVELY are trained, experienced, sensitive

next PARA—beautiful—and the more so that you slug in that wonderful word, "ROUGHLY"

443-444: BASIC, yet, I WOULD TAKE TO BE SO BASIC that you need to assume it all as part of our vocabulary, and DIG IT—assume it as a writer assumes that his reader also has a body of life experience against which the writer can play his own conjectures & his creation, eh?

444 BOTTOM—the double "imago"—"Who is the psychoanalyst?" well, I'm in his presence, his name is HAM, and does it then go right on to let me know what light he can throw on the double presence

o dear, right in these succeeding sentences, you are giving out with what i want and what i know you can give, but GIVE IT ALL—FOREVER give it all, straight, full, and scientific, PLEASE

o, christ, harry: here it is in these following pages, BUT, IT AIN'T, simply, that it is NOT WORKED, not GIVEN, not pushed & pushed & pushed until WE CRY FOR MERCY, the true MERCY

****

I must stop, and take Con to Asheville, to get food. I have written this in one lick. I offer it to you.

I was also to write to you today, at the dictation of the Faculty & Corporation of Black Mountain College in full meeting last night, February 15, 1952, to invite you here whenever it is your pleasure to come to visit and to lecture (if you should, would, everyone wants!) formally for all: to be the guest of the College as long as you can stay (though, the Faculty is so poor, not able to offer you transportation or honorarium). BUT asked me, they did, to be emphatic, at what a desire there is to have you here. And to emphasize to you, that this is not Olson alone, the Olsons, but a formal invitation of the College in assembly to you!

Love,

& let us hear as often as you can!
Charles

P.S. It turns, out, Harry, I have only one hour to get this Asheville trip—so please excuse me if I send this without proofreading, not being able to go over it all.

Murray wrote in reply that he appreciated the spontaneity of Olson's letter and that he was on Olson's side whatever the issues might be. The following year (16 September 1953) Olson wrote inviting Murray again to lecture. But there is no record of a visit to Black Mountain College or much correspondence thereafter.

56

To Frank Moore (1952)

Frank Moore, a young talented composer, came down from New York to visit Ezra Pound and was guided to Olson. There were many get-togethers, but Moore appears in the correspondence mainly as the one who, with his companion Ibby von Thurn, sublet the Olsons' Washington house and looked after their interests when they were away. For instance, from Lerma, Olson makes the following plea (letter of 28 March 1951 in the possession of the recipient):

> frank, lad: now that yr back, please make great effort (by way of Dave Ornstein, 1st, and then, up at Penna and 17th, the Albion) to buy and lay aside for me BULLETIN #28, of the Bureau of American Ethnology: is on Mex and Maya calendars, etc., and is going to be useful to me, most, necessary

... if it's there, ask him to hold, until you report price to me if it is more than 2 bucks ... o, yah—and Bulletin 57, too, if you spot it (this advance is going to require much books, so, please, buy as tho it was yrself!).

The letter below was sent with some urgency from Black Mountain on 26 February 1952. If Moore appears here as a go-*getter,* it should be taken as an indication of Olson's affection and trust.

Letter in the possession of the recipient.

tues   feb 26

frank:

been housed, and pushed out in two weeks two long prose heaves,

(both results of coming back here with political and economic realities on mind)

one called HISTORY, for walt whitman and his unhappinesses (with much attention to one, Brooks Adams)

and other CULTURE, a Wild Stab at Present Shape of Same (much on the SUN!)

fun. Both turning (essentially) on the year 1830 (or decade 30 to 50)

Also following you in on the Bostonians, then, Sam, etc.: please give me more of yr leads on these people, and especially yr judgment on the books most usable—1st sources, of course, most, but anything else

(((TASK! Along those lines, could you make me up a package of my own stuffs just now needed—promised the lads and lasses I'd write you and ask you to ship off to me some several items two weeks ago::

(I) a READING LIST for History 62(?) HARVARD—the West-ward Movement—Frederick J Merk: it is paper bound, thick, pub by Harvard Press, and shld be, I'd judge, in the case under the french windows (probably around abt my Gloucester-American stuff, right hand side)

(II) my notes of Merk's lectures—now this may be a pisser, and if it doesn't come easily to hand, forget it—my last memory of them was in that pile of odd large stuff tucked in at the very right of the right case, under the Rembrandt or whatever that big volume was in flat: they are two (?) wide flat notebooks (with coil spring back, and with Lobeck's physiographic maps tucked in) ((I originally had them with those Brady loose issues, but I think the Brady got moved, without the notebooks, to the bookcase against the kitchen door)

(III) the copies of FOUR PAGES containing (1) Bill's slam at Eliot on Milton (WITH FORCED FINGERS RUDE) and (2) Kitasono's THE SHADOW: they are in that run of little mags in the case backed up to the kitchen doors. (This shld be easy.)

Those are what I remember now. And shall be thankful, suh. Much.

Glad to have yr note in, that you are not leaving Wash. And the good news of all you have yr hand on! Fine. Please tell Ib also to write us one of those letters, eh?

Ourselves, know nothing—await, as decisive, the biz of Iraq (March 15).

Will also write Rufus right now.

Love, and keep at us   O

Olson's application to go to Iraq as a Fulbright fellow was turned down. "I doubted State wld take a risk on me at such outposts of the empire as Istanbul or Tehran, simply, that, in such places, they can't afford more than pink-cheeked servants" (*Olson-Creeley Correspondence*, vol. 9, pp. 71–72).

57

To Merton Sealts (1952)

We here see Olson engaged in confronting head-on the state of Melville scholarship twenty years after he had added his first contribution (his M.A.

thesis) to what was then a very meager amount. By 1952 Melville studies had been taken over by heavyweight academic boxers, and Olson was ready to get in the ring against them. This is the mood, anyway, in which he was tackling a review of the first scholarly edition of *Moby-Dick*. We are granted this picture of Olson at the punching bag because he had one friend in the Melville world to whom he could reveal himself frankly. This was Merton Sealts, who had gone to see him in New York in 1941, a typescript article in hand; Olson had liked him immediately for his modesty and his honesty. Sealts was destined to do what Olson would have wanted to do if he hadn't had to be a poet instead—that is, the full account of Melville's books (Sealt's draft list, which appeared first in *Harvard Library Bulletins* of 1948–1952, developed into *Melville's Reading,* published by the University of Wisconsin Press in 1966). Olson exhibited no jealousy but helped him all he could, a fact confirmed in the total correspondence presented by Sealts in *Pursuing Melville, 1940–1980* (1982, pp. 91–151). *Letter at Storrs.*

Sunday March 7   52

My dear M S:

> After that go to you last night, I read more—& this time read in MD itself! (1st time in a long time, and very heartening: read THE TAIL & then THE FOUNTAIN, and got wholly involved again in this man's knowingnesses, his incredible natural knowingnesses. For surely (as I once horrified Matthiessen over a beer in Clancy's, was it, that bar on Mt Holyoke St, next to the Hayes Bickford, was it, when I sd, Matty, I think I'll do a rewrite—clean up—MD) surely any professional could clean up that prose at all points YET, so what, for what counts—what he gets in there—is something the like of which (I still say, repeating that long spume to you three years ago just about this time) ain't happened since Homer: that absolute familiarity with *sensation* as it really is, that impeccable swiftness of register of the faster-than-light intricacies of *the motion* of experience. I still find it crucial to speak of it as a space-power. For it is objective reality, and its workings, which he is as delicate to as his whale's tale (tail!)—that lovely statement, its power even in its play (in fact, any rewriting is always where the "play" gets playsome, is coy or cute or so avoiding of sexual hardnesses (their "zones," e.g., as against Montaigne's straightness about the same elephant: "and now and then over her band put his truncke into her bosome, and feele her breasts") that he gets to writing fit for the family parlor!

But la! how reality springs up from his hands *as it damn well is!*
The accordioning of it, in & out, the speed, there, the telescoping of time
& of space as any of us are presented to its bearing, the way the human
system buzzes its way through it to its death!

It is an extraordinary
man, this phenomenon, HM, an extraordinary system—and none of us
can rest, in our explanations, short of a continuing examination of the
nature of this *kinetic.* For the closest one can get to an extrapolation of
this literal magic is to recognize the import of motion. And I would
venture to think that a way of understanding why Melville did suddenly
appear, did have this thing unsaid since the Odyssey, is that man had
gone away from that "truth" of the nature of Nature which the Ionian
physicists had not lost and which the non-Euclidean geometers contemporary to Melville made it possible for modern physics to discover
anew: that the minute particles of substances (including any one of us)
is in vigorous & continual motion.

And how precise an instrument for
the recording of this motion on all of the planes on which it asserts itself he was, how spontaneously & completely he was able to express
those interlockings of those planes which make up that sphere which
we then call reality!

One further observation provoked by a footnote
beyond those two chapters I reread: the footnote on *gallow:* that time,
in his hands, historical time, in this instance, gets the same *fluency* (or,
better, to make clear the difference from time-bound men, the same
manuable character that substance has: this is a determinable difference
from others' handling of time, and is of some importance, simply, that
Melville apprehended history proper in this strong image-ish way
(metaphor as not separable from object, but is *another* character of
object—and with no needed reference to spirit, simply, that substance
also exists *because* of its space-time loci, that this location of its motion
is a factor of its motion, a qualitative determinant as well as a positional
& mass determinant

((((i was overwhelmed, e.g., to find these editors putting HM's relation to Nelson in such flat words as, Nelson was "one of Melville's
greatest heroes"!

       How such phrasing destroys the very relevance of Melville, the still insufficiently explored singularity & usefulness of him to any of us—one needs only to turn immediately to Billy B and see how M was trying to cope with Nelson as fix for the situation he wanted so much to give the proper dimensional & kinetic life to—and how he felt bitterly the *loss* in his audience (or the absence, still, 1890, of a comprehension of man in time & space. . . .

> you see, Merton, there *is* this important likeness of HM to Rimbaud, that both of them, in wholly different ways, got exasperated because a reality equivalent to their own pene-tration of reality *had not come into being in their time*

(You will recall how I argued this point—as of the King James Version—in that Western Review piece, David Young, David Old. But I now see it as much more crucial than I then understood: these two men were deeply balked just because they had in themselves manumitted the *inaccurate* estimate of reality man had gone by since the Ionians—due to a loss of a recognition of the absolute tenacity of the space-time context in which all things, including man, are set—and yet, because of the lag of events (it was not until, say, August 1945 that man as a whole was shocked into the recogni-tion), these two men (because any one of us, even a Rimbaud? cer-tainly a Melville, are not possibly ever that sure that they are right, however firm they feel their "intuitions," Melville called his sense of his own exactitudes) were *hindered*

Melville & Rimbaud were made (made themselves) capable of engaging reality *as it is.* And if Melville grabbed on to Nelson as a figure of his "system," then any of us had better gauge that "prehensile" (is his word for what he wishes the whale's tail might have more of, so that, like an elephant it could woo, & pick out the darts thrown into itself—as Nel-son couldn't the splinter which took off his eye) this prehensile neces-sity *seriously, simply*

       _____ modestly (god damn these *insolent* fucking im-posers—users—*vulgarizers* of a man they hold *their jobs by:* my god,

Merton, how can they be so *dishonest* as to *peddle* him whom they owe their feeding of their children to?

(It shocks me to the core, to see the *carelessnesses, the presumptions,* such as these:

take it another way. Just pick up on that word *hero.* How Vincent & Mansfield derogate man's continuing struggle *right now* by speaking so *lightly,* so familiarly, so offhandedly of Melville's involvement with Nelson. For it takes no particular insight to notice that one of the central preoccupations of man today—one of his central necessities—is exactly this problem of *hero:* which is, any time, man's measure of *his own possibilities*—how large is he?

now one of the greatnesses of HM's work is the very way he cleared man in his attack now upon the heroic as a dimension (the

Specksynder is the first created measure of the Dictator

(((curiously enough, the one *major* contribution these men have made (so far as I have yet found) is their evidence of what Goethe contributed to Melville's thinking on exactly this point

(((but there you are—there I am, in facing the problem of reviewing them: they are, essentially, as *ignorant* of what they have done positively here as they are guilty of destructive acts on Nelson: they rush on to *muddy* the Goethe biz by fussing it with De Quincey, Carlyle, Emerson, & a host of other inexactitudes

they do exactly what Melville *undid*

For the very reason why HM stays, is now valuable, is precisely that (and I would again assert it is because he had found out the secret of apprehending reality lost since Miletus—what is now again a common property of all of us, even if not yet taken up and acted by, seen by, experienced by) precisely that Melville cleared the HERO problem of history in the one-plane and romantic sense in which even Goethe was defeated and certainly M outran Emerson & Carlyle, whom they, in these notes, seek and seek to drag HM back to

> for these quotes of V & M from Goethe on his prob-
> lems with Mohammed, Prometheus and the person-
> age he finally settled for, make clear how Goethe had
> to give up an engagement with the major problem,
> on which he shed such fantastic light—see him on
> Demonism, as applied by V & M (*Daemonism,* actu-
> ally) to Ahab's *Sultanism*

Goethe had to give up just because he lacked what Melville had: proof
evident—he settled for Egmont, when M took on both Prometheus *and*
the Prophet

o, this is important stuff, and it teases my mind to wildness, how these
editors *destroy* their own work! detract from even one such discovery

Question #1	—so far as i know it is their own contribution, but wld you be so kind as to inform me if you know if they are in the clear here, or has someone else already laid out this hugely important relevance of Goethe's TRUTH & POETRY to the act of Ahab?

and why it is necessary to gauge them here where they are strongest is,
that this ignorant derogation is what they do to all the work of all the
rest of us who have spent our years on Melville

(exceptions, where they

do the opposite, *exaggerate* such essentially automatic work as Anderson's, or Vincent's own (The Trying-Out):

it's a pisser, to make all this clear—for who would know, except us who
have been inside the job, how much that issues from research is, essentially, automatic, and is made out to be more only for the deception of
fools:

> yet it must be made clear, for such men batten, and take power,
> have positions, even become influences (((Vincent, e.g., is actu-
> ally molding young people's sense of literature due to his editing
> of Compton's Encyclopedia:

(((((((and the most shocking

prostitution to the State stands exposed in his table of American
Literature in that important set:

he has the gall to expunge the
name of Ezra
Pound, and his works, from the list. And it obviously must be because Pound is charged as traitor!

Imagine: in the face of the
Bollingen, and the whole struggle, this little man is in a position
to *remove* from the public record in the dark the work of such a
man—

and this is the same man who is (on the other side of his
street) constituting himself the chief agent for the circulation
now of Herman Melville

Surely there must be a connection. And
it comes too damned clear: the Melville whom Vincent (and
Mansfield, to the degree of his accompliceship) peddle is a
scrubbed and school-boy "Classic"

is a man so subtracted from
his *nature* & his *act* that one has finally to see their representation of him as as *dishonest* an act as the omission of the
name of Pound from the encyclopedia

God, Sealts, I beg you to follow me here. It is the immorality of the politics & economics of our time walking unseen right in the midst of
something very close to both of us: HERMAN MELVILLE

I beg you to, simply, that all of us must find out how to *clean up our*
own house

I am bewildered. I sat down today to outline to you what I then
thought might be the most useful thing of all to haul out of the labor of
examining this book. I thought I would offer to you for yr fine correction
something like this—even call the review:

SOME FIRST PRINCIPLES
TOWARD THE PROBLEMS OF THE EDITING OF THE WORK OF
HERMAN MELVILLE
For I believe one could lay down some canons such as Greg & Pollard
have brought to Shakespeare emendation—could set up some ordered
thinking to offset the lack of it behind this edition. And thus be of some
use to the community—perhaps get it so clear that others would have a

gauge to do their own work by, at least so that others could peg—as Leyda pegged Vincent's Collected Poems—work in the larger & more difficult area of annotation to such a work as MD

But the ignorance & carelessness & disorder which makes the ill proportions of this edition is only the outside of the corruption on the inside—of these matters of *high sin* which Vincent's career is only one example of

Yet I fall back in despair. Who is ready to see how *crucial* it is that Melville's work be left in its own "life"? who of any of us is yet ready to gauge the *import* of this man's heave? If I, after 20 years of preoccupation with him, still find each day a little entrance into the depth of his act—a new thing more blinding to me than the day I read Benito Cereno (it happened to be the first, by some accident of it being to hand one afternoon I was not well and had a chance to read something)

I don't know. Two weeks ago I finished a long go called CULTURE, in which this point—of how seriously do any of us take the work of a book (by comparison, say, to those obvious acts of history—like the Bomb, or Adolf Hitler—we are all convinced are important)—was put out there.

But when I am confronted with the *uncleanness* of thinking, feeling, self-taking—of even the scholarship—in such work as this edition, I am bewildered as to how to expose it, how to carry out what I am sure is the moral imperative of any worker in any field: to be responsible to the public for the conduct of the other workers in that field:::

that is why I beg you to follow me. For who but us who are inside *know* what is being done here?

And Question #2: how can we together arrive at any determination of action to keep our house clean by exposing those who dirty Melville?

I have this other nuisance, that fools like Chase have let Vincent's review of Leyda in the Times lead them to make as though it was a sort of contest, the Melville work, between the "healthy" non-intellectuals and the "wild" intellectuals—have played right into a canny politician like

Vincent's hands by so doing. For Vincent grows fat on the notion that it is a contest, that there is some "virtue" in his work, some "correction," that he is on the side of the sane, the realists, that—somehow— anything other than *historical facts* distort Melville,

when the truth of the matter is—by the proof of this edition—that there is more essential distortion going on—*actual distortion of facts*

by (a) the muddying
of them due to mis-
leading inclusions &
exclusions, by patently
false emphases

O, i am overwhelmed at some of these: let me just throw in one for you to examine (which hurts me no end, as you'll be able to see: look at 617-18, where "Virtue, if a pauper, is stopped at all frontiers" is footnoted by all the "Truth" quotes from Shakespeare & the "Mosses"! God, imagine, Virtue & Truth made as tho they were syn- onymous! God, Sealts, how can one find any way to excuse or ex- plain such dirtiness *of mind*—that such *stupidity* should be puddling in the affairs of a man of Melville's *mind*

It comes to this: that *scholarship* itself is what these men sap. And that is all there is of a "contest": that in one house—the house of the examina- tion of Herman Melville—there are *corrupt workers.* They cannot, any longer, have this "game," that they are pious, and the other workers, are impious.

Q#3
Let me ask you the same help I asked Leyda: because you are much more current to the work than I, can you tell me of any one I should add to yrself, Leyda, Miss Wright, Hayford, Murray (as psychologist) as they who have done clean work because they have stayed inside the recognizable limits of *research* & of its announcement, its presenta- tion

You see, the *hinge,* it turns out, on which the whole thing does hinge, is this thing you & I in particular are experts in: *sources*

And if I do do those PRINCIPLES of EDITING, I shall have to make clear
in what way the presentation of the sources has to be *governed*

(it is not
a personal matter: the problem is as definable & delimitable as emenda-
tions, say:

> yr CHECK-LIST is exactly *an act of mind* precisely because it (1)
> presents the known facts; (2) recognizes that those are only the
> known facts, that others obviously also existed which have disap-
> peared or have not yet been recovered; and (3) leaves those facts as
> facts, and does not claim to analyze Melville's use of them

> LEYDA, likewise, on a level where historical fact is most self-evident
> (where any public would be aware of the limits simply because they
> too all have a personal life—(((this is more important than its obvi-
> ousness seems to suggest, when you think of yr problem & mine,
> say, with *sources* as books—only *some* of the public are experienced
> of books, and how men use them: you see, what Vincent trades on—
> and is not decent enough to *proportionately* make clear (he will tuck
> in a phrase, but, a phrase won't do—in fact, *another* analysis called
> for, is to take apart the two places where he & Mansfield, in their
> Intro, advance a "theory of art"! (CF., top to middle of p. xvi;
> & the same thing turned over, last para of Intro, pp. xxxii-iii

> leyda leaves the historical facts as they are now known, as he has
> been able to make them known

neither you nor Leyda have at any point, so far as I can see, allowed yr
work to "spread," to make featherings of itself, to swell at all: you have
looked upon the issue of yr labors as the evidence of the labor. And thus
you have done no other man any slightest wrong, have—if you have found
corrections of others necessary—let that correction sit inside the facts as
you have righted them:

these are the silences which breed honor
and dignity between men, which breed alertness, which *justify* scholarship,
which make it *a thing of life*

((it is *not* courtesies, or acknowledgements,
or thanks, though these, like all gestures,

are pleasures which fellow-labor can allow
itself, and does, generously, when the labor
has been itself *thorough*))

My impression is that the work of men like Heflin, & Gilman—like
Hayford's on the Dana letters—stays in place (though I should think it
is going to be necessary, due to several pretensions, that one mark, as a
distinction, the *difference* in the *scope* of the projects:

> that is, to set out to do a Checklist like yrs (I am an expert on the *di-
> mension* of that effort!) or to set out to do a LOG like Jay's, and to do
> it in the same simplicity & clarity that Heflin or Gilman disclose two
> ships Melville sailed on, takes *much more power* than what these two
> men did, however much any of us respect the accomplishment

The measure of this is a man Vincent gives altogether too much to: Anderson. Exactly because Anderson swells his work out of all proportion
to its value is why I refused it as a reader for the Harvard Press (and was
supported, by god, by Dumas Malone & Murdock, who understood, as
scholars, what water was here, what water, & vanity, had not been
squeezed out

> ((again, a counter:
>
> > > do you recall Scudder's job years ago
> > > on M's use of Spenser in the Encantadas?
> >
> > > > > > > my re-
> > collection is, that that job was as straight a job—
> > almost a touchstone—as one can ask of source-
> > discovery

> Q#4   ((((*please check me on this*))))

It does keep coming back to this *source* rub. And I better try to think it
through right now. My quarrel is right here at the hinge—and I can
give you the evidence of what a sizable quarrel it is by pointing out how
all measurement of critique by they who think they are "healthy" rests
on their own pretensions or extensions of their *source-scholarship*

Ok. Let's tackle Vincent. Now it was evident to all of us that M's use
of whaling, travel, and sea books was bibliotechtical! Some of us—to

get the feel of it—had back-tracked him (I need only point out how
Weaver had been so led away by the Pacific literature that he let some
of the shape of his book go with it.

  And I remember myself reading for a long time in Ellis, say, and in
  such modern anthropologists as Linton, & other publications of the
  Bishop museum
Yet that Vincent set himself to do the thing *exhaustively* (note that this
premise is what lies behind Leyda, or yrself) on what he now jocularly
keeps calling the "fish documents"—

                    ((((is this HM's phrase?
                    and can you, out of yr head,   Q#5
                    spot it for me?))))
that he did what, essentially, is a parallel job to what Anderson did with
the "Pacific"—

                (this is something which represented a dimension of
task, and a value somewhere—shall we say—in between such articles as
Heflin's, and such scope-full attacks as yrs and Leyda?)

Ok. The hierarchy is not important, but it is one way of reining in the
pretensions which follow

                (they seem, the pretensions, to grow by direct ratio
                to how "literary" the scholarship is, how close in
                to the text of Melville's work the research has to
                reach!
                    tho, here, again, note *Scudder*, or yrself, in that
revealing job on THE CHIMNEY—& was it you did the job on "THE
TARTARUSES"?
                        Q#6

Look, Merton: just because this is the heart of the problem I feel myself re-
luctant to spell it out, simply, that I am still *in course* on the reading of these
250 pages where from one note to the next the unclarities on Vincent's part
of what is the *fit*
                ((by god, maybe you could help me: I never could
                    afford to buy The Trying-Out: do you know anyone
   Q#7   who would have an extra copy they'd either give or
                    lend me while I do this job?))))

what is the *fit* use of any of our knowledge of M's sources in the annotation on any given passage

> (god, any of us, that ever set one foot in a gradu-
> ate school—at least before the days of PhDs in
> American Civilization!—were expected to know
> > (I) *the laws of evidence*
> > & (II) *the laws of the imagination*
> neither of these are either known or beheld to
> by this little monster of patriotism & ignorance,
> this creature of pejorocracy

Q#8   (((what in hell did he get his PhD in, could you tell me?))

Christ. I am thinking of Kittredge's superb book on Chaucer, as a
measure—on exactly this little prick's pretensions—of how to do
sources at the same time that you do not *intrude* on the writer's own act
of passage *from* the sources to his own created thing

There are two gauges which I would have—to do the right job—to
bring to bear:
  (A) on the scholarship proper—to expose it—compare it to Kit-
      tredge on Chaucer—surely, after that book, any book on any
      writer—even an American!—has to be as good or better,
& (B) another time, as furthest measure of *all* Melville work, the schol-
      arship of Victor Berard on THE ODYSSEY

((((why such men as V have to belittle *critique* is because they can't do
it, but what is not observed is, that they can't do it simply because *they
haven't done their own work!*

THIS IS WHAT I SAY WE HAVE TO ASSERT—HAVE TO KEEP
POINTING OUT—HAVE (you, me, Leyda, Hayford (((what
does he do now, anyway—Q#9)) any one of us who has done
his work) WE HAVE TO EXPOSE THESE MEN JUST WHERE
THEY ARE EXPOSED, but where only we who are inside can show
that they haven't:

$64 Question
have we any moral right to leave it to any one else—
any reviewer—any editor—to anyone but ourselves
to MAKE THESE THINGS CLEAR?

I'm going to shut up. If you have got this far, do see it all as working
my way through talking to you this day. I should be most aided if you
give me answers to the questions spotted throut. But please: don't let
any of this (except the reading) be a burden. Only what it provokes
you to say. Don't feel it calls for an answer in its own terms: these are
my headaches, and the only reason I toss them around with you is my
respect for you.

OK.   Much left unsaid!   Loce, Loson
Olson

Olson's review of the Luther Mansfield–Howard Vincent *Moby-Dick*, along with
Ronald Mason's *The Spirit Above the Dust* and Lawrance Thompson's *Melville's
Quarrel with God*, appeared in two parts in the *New Republic*, 8 September 1952
and 15 September 1952, under the title "Materials and Weights of Herman
Melville" (see *Collected Prose*, pp. 113–119).

58

To Merce Cunningham (1952)

This is the only known letter from Olson to the renowned dancer Merce
Cunningham, who had just arrived at Black Mountain College for the summer.
Later in the summer, however, there was a poem, "Merce of Egypt," which was
Olson's response to a dance performance (*Collected Poems*, pp. 269–271).
Letter (carbon copy) at Storrs.

May 15   52

My dear Mr Cunningham:
    (It was like the time I dreamt:

> of rhythm is image
> of image is knowing
> of knowing there is
> a construct

last night, seeing *transformation* for the first time, my eye brushed you there in the air in 3 to the 3rd power and saw out of its corner your first italicised sentence, but it didn't see it, for i had a bad headache and was not reading

          at which point i took an aspirin and lay down and it was in the dark that i sd what i thot you sd, to myself:

                 dance
                 is an action AND a thing

                    I thought i wld send it to you,
                    this morning, when i woke up
                       Charles Olson

59

To Connie Olson (1952)

After the Black Mountain College summer session in July and August of 1952, Olson and Connie were happy to retake possession of their Washington house. Olson decided not to return to BMC for the fall semester, but by late October, Connie, with one-year-old Kate, had gone back to the college to resume her post as registrar. She had private reasons. Olson had felt compelled to visit Frances Boldereff in Brooklyn again. That he did not want his involvement with Boldereff to end his relationship with Connie is clear from the mass of letters written during the six-week separation. Connie received long letters practically every day, full of intense introspection fueled by a reading of Jung and Fenichel, full of dream analysis, and full of loving recollections. There never was a midlife crisis so energetically conducted and so thoroughly written out! The letter below, midway through, records a dark afternoon of the soul.

Letter at Storrs.

                        Sat (2) *Nov 15th*
You know who is acting like a very shit towards me? Maryan Richman. I cld knock her puss in. Right from the start the two of them were not content (as all others are) to take it I meant it, you wanted to be at

BMC for Kate, & I had to get away from there to get back to work in my own house & on base.

Richman came to me when Leach & Hamada were here, & sez, flat, "Anything wrong between Con & you?" And something abt, "If so, we wld be very disappointed in both of you." Imagine! And last night, by god if pinch-ass herself doesn't even not even welcome me at the door of the Sitwell reading—no indication she'd even have let me in! I intended, anyway, to go through Beatrice Rudis (who had told me of the reading, at Pietro's opening). And did. But jees-zus!

I shall cut her dead. I thought she stunk (was only putting up with me because it was Leach & Hamada) the night at their house. But last night her face was like something of Daumier's!

What an axe she'll soon be. The two of them, anyway, must think they are taking on the morals of this town as well as its *culture!* They kill me, how *old* they are, how fast they are—gone

> (I suppose I make so much of them:
> (1) that they were in on that terrible time for you;
> (2) that that reading at the Inst. was a *very* big thing for me;
> & (3) their long attempt to treat us as though we were on some same floor of life as they is one of those things

which—ONE OF MY *SEVERAL* FLY-PAPERS!—where I learn so much by continuing to permit my bewilderment to exist.

This latter point is, somehow, *important*—is a characteristic of me which lies along that complex you are dealing with when you speak of my sentimentalities & superstitions—that I also cling to *any* "kindness" (shall I call it?

> My sight is plenty *hard*. And fast. But I do allow almost anything to "run on," you might say.

> I think I have said before I imagine it may have to do with the fact my life as a child ran-on so—that *nothing*, really, interrupted, came into, that drift of—what?—17 solid

years? (Maybe one reason why Wesleyan, *to this day,* gives me a sickness, is, that, right there, fall 1928, the dream was broken: I *had* to deal with others. And actually, didn't know *how* to *begin!*

And so, two things: (1), I was Wheel House, used the only thing I knew, da brains—picked up *those* marbles; & (2), why that *convulsion* of those other marbles in that barber shop looking down at that girl got so built up

Maybe, even, why sexuality, as you keep telling me, has remained so long some illusion of (1) *how to deal with others,* instead of by the mind's flashings; and (2) how to recapture the state of an *only child* in a relatively comfortable, relatively peaceful *house*　(I say relatively, simply, that that thing which hit my father— 1920—from then on did shift somewhat the life

He never lost that look of hurt & trouble & set of his jaw to pay-em-back, from then on, even when he put on a front, & tried to be what they used to say about him, happy-go-lucky Charlie O (Do you think my inordinate compassion for him over this thing might be a source of my peculiar "soft-ness" towards him & of my long exaggeration of males? That is, granting that the psychopathology had already been laid down (as outlined in letter to you yesterday), is it possible this event, & its consequences to him, were so decidedly

the only outside event of my life for so very long that it fastened on me both (1) an exaggerated sense of event (I suddenly think of Read Lewis' astonishment I took his firing of me as such a *drama*—I remember him pleading with me not to take it as so critical, or a *judgment* of me, that it goes on every day all over this city, he said!); and (2) to increase an

Oedipean tendence, possibly, to give a sort of feminine care to *anyone's* troubles! especially, a male's? (The imagery of *Stocking-Cap* suddenly comes in to my mind—the fires, & their guardianship; as well as the fact that Nick obviously thought that was the finest thing I ever did—& Payne!)

I go back to that biz, of 17; and faced with others for the 1st time; and how only two ways seemed available: (1) to "show 'em," by prizes, positions, etc, which got done; & (2) sexuality—which *didn't*. (And the latter prized, both, I suppose, because it didn't, & because, somehow, to this day, I would imagine the sexual was an illusion of a return to the womb of 4 Norman Avenue, Worcester, MASS

> (Another distinction of our life to-gether was that the sexual never did get *any* of this comfort or peace to it—why, actually, you never were "domestic" to me, never need have feared that thing. I mean, at Bottom. My confusions, may have confused the *surface* of my response, made me say things, or do things, which hurt, here. But *inside,* no.

And sexually—jesus: how damned *clear* it stands—how I never *huddled* with you, how there never was a night it wasn't you, clear, & me, *clear*—sharp—& *close,* not for comfort or for peace, but for the *life of it*

I'm sure, darling, this was & is *decisive:* made it all as *essential* to me as you say my calm destruction of evil gods was to you.

What another break-through! For doesn't it exactly throw light on what this other thing is I have whored after? Isn't it that false sexuality which got stuck in me then, Wesleyan, 17, as the warmth & "protection" of my *family*(!)—& why both (1) the men get crossed over with my fa-ther, the women with my mother, the *sensations* of both with my child-hood

& (2) why, as you have charged (at least on my mother), I have stayed *sentimen-*

tal over them, been unable either to deliver them back to themselves (as you said you found it possible with both yr father & mother) or deliver myself free & standing clear from them?—Why my vision of life has stayed, in spite of my mind & of our love, a sort of mush?

This does make *absolute* sense, doesn't it?

God, it does take *time,* doesn't it! I mean *right now.* I have the feeling there just ain't enough hours in the day to get the work done fast enough to keep up with the breaking-through! Real crazy. Never felt so thick—& *right.* Never took such pride in *language* as in all these completely *artless* letters. Don't know where it leads. Feel really *in* where I believe. Yet feel so *simple!* So *uninteresting* to anybody but you and me. And *frightened* of the issue (not actually, but just don't want any of these sights ever to be turned aside, soured, lost or distorted again)

—*Maybe, even,* the fright is that I'll have to *give up* that other sexuality! Maybe that's the *real struggle.* I kind of wonder if it ain't! And that I don't want to!

—Not really. But (1) it's a whopping excision (if I am right, it's all those 17 years *as I have hugged them* plus *all adventurism!*

And (2)—which is the thing I *really* am dealing with right now—*when* does one have enough of it—or how does one handle life so that one has it, if the craving comes up?

This latter sounds very damn *weak* & dirty. Damn cheap. But I let it stand, simply, that

(1) I *do* have to know

& (2) I owe it to you to state my temptations—my yellownesses—as well as my triumphs

And—also sounds also *indulgent.*

This last half page gets me in the pit of the pit! God, Con—(1) to have to see yrself—to "weigh" one's soul; & (2) to do what has to be done right!—*to have to question one's courage!* It is courage which makes one essentially forever *sure* of one's self, isn't it? able to make use of one's self—also to be *straight,* with any other person, *others* (that class I have stayed as ignorant of as I have stayed ignorant of my unconscious). I really need to find out so many lessons in *how to live.* I sure left them out, in my "education"!

> There is so much that I now know is shit that I am scared to lose because I don't yet know what (1) the shit really is and (2) what one has if one throws it out.

I suppose Jung would say I am on the brink of individuation—and want to turn back! that I don't want to lose what has *warmed* me (again, that image of fires!) oh, Con, Con—this feels like the thing *joined* and I feel too weak to make it

just sit here looking myself in the eye, and asking that eye, "Have you got it, Bo? And how does one declare it?"

It is too much. Do I have to give up what it seems to me I had too little of to *know* that I am right to give it up—that sexuality? Is this the risk on which a life is gained?

And the terrible sense there is not anyone or anything who can help you—that, here, you are *alone,* that *you, yourself, have to decide!*

The other thing is: how did I get here? what could I have done different so that I might not have had to come here? Or is there always this place somewhere, no matter? (This last strikes me as undoubtedly true, and makes me feel a little better—in fact, takes off our backs, maybe, that remark of mine which cut you down, so—that my whole life was in error.)

Maybe what I have to find out right this instant is, that all lives are error until one has made the act of courage to truly take one's own up & wield it?

but what in god's name does that mean? what *do* I have to do, right now? what *is it* I have to give up? what do I have to do? what is required of me?

I am honestly unclear. I feel, actually, I have to do what I have been doing since Election Day—that that is what I have to do. But why did I have this sense of crisis, the last two pages? (It's just gone off. I ate a bean sandwich!)

Now I don't question my strength at all. (What was this thing? God, it was *strong!* I honestly felt like *praying,* asking God's help! I did feel literally *too weak to make my life!*

How about that?

What you have just read was a live recording of a man right up *against* it! Damndest thing ever!!! Equally crazy, that it seems to have passed—that I feel I made it. Or at least, don't feel *defeated,* anyway. Feel there is hope.

(Do you think it was just hunger?!!?)

Craziest sensation I *ever had.*

It is also crazy I feel right now—25 minutes by the clock later—jim-dandy! terrific

(The crisis was 5:30)

Must have been hunger. It couldn't go, just like that, without my doing anything but eat 3 open bean sandwiches while I continued to get it down for you. But there it was—right spang in front of me.

And I feel—FINE!

Write me a special separate letter all about this, if you think there is anything in it as it came at you reading it—or if you have any suggestions (other than St Elizabeth's!)

Sweet, I feel fine
—*full* of *courage*
—& *life*

Olson,
the Pep Boy!

No, seriously, thanks
for being there

Charles

60

To Carl Jung (1952)

Olson had not much liked Carl Jung when he was introduced to him briefly at Harvard in September 1936. Picking up *Psychology and Religion* ("my 1st reading of Jung"), he decided that "Mr Jung is, as I always hunched, a lazy fraud" (letter to Frances Boldereff of 6 July 1950 at Storrs). It was when his marriage was beginning to break up that Olson turned seriously to Jung's theories of personality. He read Jung's work intensely during the period from October through December 1952. The personal rewards Olson received from that reading are reflected in the awed tones with which he addressed an invitation to Jung to lead the Black Mountain Institute of the New Sciences of Man.

Letter (carbon copy) at Storrs.

217 Randolph Place NE
Washington 2. D/C USA
Sunday, December 7, 1952

My dear & honoured Carl Jung:

This is a formal invitation to ask you to come to the States and be the Director of an eight weeks Institute of the New Sciences of Man to be held at Black Mountain College, in North Carolina, from February 7 to April 8th this coming new year. My own hope also is that you will feel able to give some, or eight lectures during the session.

The Institute is my own dream, but I have talked to Hugh Chisholm of the Bollingen, and he gives me the assurance that if you will give me any least chance that you will let us fly you Air Suisse, and take total care of you while here, that all that you will require, and that your wife might greatly and properly expect, will be provided for. In fact, the moment I have your answer, if it is at all affirmative, I shall go see Paul Mellon at Upperville and seek to make all arrangements to your satisfaction.

I emphasize this, because I imagine you have to think first of your ease and health. And I am aware that what I am asking, at this date of your work and life, may seem extreme. Yet, great doctor, for you, again, at this time, to make another trip to the United States is as fit as your work has been, as proper a further act of it as all the books I should want to tell you I, for one, would wish that you would still write, as full of total admiration (more than for any living man) as I am for those you have written.

Let me put it this way. If you do not come, I shall do the job myself. But though I am a poet, and my wife claims that you only have allevi- ated the grinning god more than I have (for her, at least), yet, I assure you, that though I am 40, I am poor poor substitute for what will be, are, your acts, work, books, for such an examination of the work of men of your order (since Dorpfeld at Olympia) that this Institute is conceived to present. My conception of it is to turn the attention of a year of like Institutes for these eight weeks on to archeology & mythol- ogy, on the bio- and geo- disciplines, on psychology and literature. And I do not know a single living man but yourself who can properly turn all who will be at the Institute to the problems ahead of the areas of knowing and happening which this group of sciences surely comes to grips with.

Pardon me. I am writing this fast, as it comes, simply, sir, that I am so anxious that you do give the least hope that you might accept our in- vitation that I am forgetting everything but asking you, from my heart, to consider it. If you will tell me that we might start to negotiate your coming—that the idea attracts you, that if things were perfect, you might consider it—then I can say more, details, all the smaller things. But my point tonight, is merely to do it: to ask you, with complete de- sire & respect, would you even think of it?

I speak, by the way, for the Faculty of Black Mountain, as original director of this Institute, former Guggenheim Fellow, and present grantee of the Wenner-Gren Foundation (for work on Mayan hiero- glyphic writing). And the project I offer you has been talked over, as I say, with Bollingen people, as well, earlier, with the Rockefeller Foundation, in addition to my own foundations. Do consider it, and if you can give me a gleam of hope, I shall write more, and go fur- ther.

With the deepest respect and complete admiration,

"Thank you for your most refreshing and encouraging letter," Jung replied on 16 December 1952. "Unfortunately, I happen to be in a pretty low condi- tion as to my health . . . I have to be proud and content to be able to walk from my room to my library, or to climb the stairs once a day" (letter at

Storrs). Olson wrote again to ask Jung if he could suggest a substitute, and one of his closest assistants, Marie-Louise von Franz, came to Black Mountain for the institute.

61
To Edgar Anderson (1953)

Carl Sauer brought Edgar Anderson's work to Olson's attention in a letter of 17 November 1949, suggesting that Olson get an offprint of an article Anderson wrote with C. R. Stonor, "Maize Among the Hill Peoples of Assam" (from the *Annals of the Missouri Botanical Gardens* for September 1949). Olson did and in a letter of 10 June 1952 broached Anderson with hypotheses about the role of maize in ancient Yucatan. Anderson's response led Olson to invite him to the Institute of the New Sciences of Man. *Letter (carbon copy) at Storrs.*

January 24, 1953

My dear Anderson:

  just do keep that barely qualified YES on the fire! just do—don't let it not even yet do anything but grow warmer!

                              this is just a note to tell you how delighted we are that you do give us hope (i was sitting here five minutes ago watching a cardinal hen on the small tree out my window, and found myself asking Anderson what—if the landscape was such a transported thing—about birds?

                         I tell you: yr emphases on *cultivated* (man's interference) and on *migration* (man's shifting about) are just exactly the precisions of the new learning which I would give my eye tooth (even tho it is long gone from my mouth!) to swap some of my knowledge of the early epics and their migrations, them as interferences, with

  Give Black Mt the chance to have you here March 16-28, with Hawkes, Braidwood possibly, and above all (I say it too) C.O.S. I *will* pin him down!

Even if it's for a day, come! Give us every chance to fold it in with your Guggenheim commitments: let us shuttle you there if necessary.

I'll be back on soon. But do, as I say, get warmer! And above all, remember this: it is just where your mind now is, just in those quiet pastures, that we would have you address us from!

Cordially

Charles Olson

Olson could, in the end, "pin down" neither Christopher Hawkes, Carl Sauer, nor Anderson; however, Robert J. Braidwood, author of *Prehistoric Men,* was persuaded to lecture at the institute.

62

To Worcester Classical High School (1953)

In *Classic Myths,* the Worcester Classical High School Yearbook for 1928, Olson's entry reads: "Gifted with a charming personality, a sterling character and a keen mind, Charles has easily assumed the leadership of our class. A model student, he has guided successfully the Student Council and the Debating Assembly, where he has made a host of friends." *Letter (carbon copy) at Storrs.*

March 24, 1953

To: the Principal & the Faculty of
Classical High School,
Worcester, Mass.:

I write to you as President of the Class of 1928, to try to start something for June of this year which I cannot, myself, manage. It will be 25 years since that Class graduated, and my feeling is that the School (just because it was such a school, and a high school at that, not at all any college—that the education Classical then offered was still so superior) Classical was such that it would honor us, and Worcester, to notice it anew now.

I don't know that a "reunion" is necessarily what is called for at all (such things have been so cheapened by the colleges, etc.), though it might well be that my fellows of that year might well like to look at each other, and, again, at Richardson's building (I am so long out of Worcester I just take it for granted that you are still where you were!).

I also can't see that the present graduating class, or the rest of the students, would be anything but bored by a lot of 40 year old people to stare at. Yet it would give us great pleasure, I dare say, to see the present Faculty, and such (if there are any) who taught there when we were there. Some coming together of us, and you people of the Faculty, might be a via of making the point it strikes me this 25 year date might be made to signify: some sounding, like a gong, of what the local is when one is a "citizen" of a city and went, then, to such a superb school. (I speak, perhaps, for myself—or ought to—that what I got there, from Shaughnessy, Howe, Arey, Post, Porter, Fenner, Miss Peirce, conspicuously Brennen, Miss Pierce, my last Latin teacher (?), from "the Duke" in French & baseball, etc., etc.)

Anyway, there it is, to try to get it started. (I myself might not even be able to be at anything, may well be where I am supposed to be by that time, Guatemala—enclosed flyer will indicate my own present concerns.) But that doesn't at all matter. I take it my old post only requires the pressing of the button.

Which brings up this point, that you of the present High School, conceivably, may not want to have any bother with such old matters. In which case, please think of this letter as only going to you as the exchange box between myself and my class. I suggest, for example, that the Secretary of that Class, Dorothy O'Toole, may still be in Worcester, and known to you by her married name (she married a member of the Class, Dunegan, was it?). Or Connie Williams, who was so active. Or Brent Rafter. Or Farrell, who became a priest. Or Doyle, who was an officer. Or Allen Eaton, who was so much my "rival." Or such from the West Side as several who may now be bank officers, or officials of companies.—Or, for that matter, such men around '28 as Higgins, who went to Amherst, Miller (who is back in Worcester): such an honoring of Classical & Worcester as I am suggesting might well include a cluster of the "Classical High" of those years—to mark an education was the superior of the colleges some of us then went to!

Let this, then, be my speech, in hopes you, or such others I have mentioned, might be interested. In any case, my respect to the School.

63

To Jonathan Williams (1953)

The correspondence between Olson and Jonathan Williams is mainly made up of practical letters concerning details of publication, for Williams, a student at Black Mountain College (later a poet in his own right and a publisher of many titles in the Jargon series), was first and foremost the publisher of the *Maximus* poems. The initial launching was the most unlikely sort of set up: Williams went from BMC into the U.S. Army, posted to Stuttgart, Germany. It was there he found a printing house, and it is to him there that Olson addresses the letters below. These letters have been chosen to exhibit the circumstances in which *The Maximus Poems 1–10* came into being. *Letters at Buffalo.*

JOHNathan

              it should uv happened

                     & did!

                          U jus hold yr
                          'orses

IT's
a vol. all by itself—and still coming

               (why i hasten this to keep you on

all one piece:

        THE MAXIMUS POEMS
            1 - 9 (to make a guess
        or
        First Maximus Poems

Am going like. . . . Get everything ready to shoot—And I'll be in on you (promise!) Keep cool. Very excited. All's BETTER than could have hoped for

& best to Rainer

> (& yure idea of brush & yure own suits me
> *April 8*

---

sat apr 11

jonathan, publisher, strasbourg:

> get this *wide* enough
>> (by type *small* enuf?)

to give me that *long* line of mine going all the way across the page without

>> being hooked back (like
>> so,
>> PLEASE!

(it was a damned pleasure, once, there I C H, to have that sense that the breathing has its way

Am all fired out, just becoz, that you were going to do this, has revealed to me what I am abt in these

> maxies

Am in the process of gathering the thing together into a book mss to ship off to you (air mail, through PM, N.Y., right?)

>> and "1" suddenly

reveals itself as INVOCATION, classic beginning!

>> Very damned pleased

>> (The HEADS—

running or otherwise—well, I guess it better be

>> LETTER 2
>>> 3
>>> etc.—

tho I shall introduce whatever variant strikes me at the time of writing

> to freshen the openings

In any case, what we are embarked on is more than I'd guessed—and am very damned grateful already!

a note of a sunday with the callacanthus
out again (the golden fury seen
through those red candles,
and not at all a dead
car, even though it hasn't moved
as what pushes out buds
has

     not
deadwood (as Grady's

and, beyond, the grove of little
dogwood

        but by the heavy red flowers (their smell
will be heavy) the large dogwood,
back of the stone stairs,
glares

                o

PS The mss of the book shld be off
to you in a couple of days—the trouble is,
more of them keep coming, and interrupt my
making copy for you! Which is fine, but
delaying!

---

                tuesday, april 21
Jonathan:
      Final mss. all done two days ago, but the first "letters" (now
that the others are added . . . all the way to #10) bugged me, to have
them right.
      Today I broke it, I believe. So mailing shld be close on top
of this one.
      Excuse the delay. But it's actually due to this damned fine
thing, that the book (that you wanted to do it) has created the whole
biz, brought this Max biz to a head, and ahead.
                I am obliged—
                  am-O

One thing: hope to God the *point* of the type is
small, no more than 10 pt. For the width of the
lines will require small pt, I shld think. —It
worries me!

———————————

jonathan: (THURS—APRIL 29th? 2 PM

just this second FINISHED—and to make up for all lost time, will
drive to Asheville to get this posted air mail, the best, and fastest way to
you   OK

it was a wrestle, more damn bugs. Plus the fact that it was shooting
out more Maxies all the time—14, are now done, in first drafts,
that is
            but where I here stop—10—is the RIGHT PLACE, for your go,
no question

(1) One damned thing: tho I had carbons, when i thot i had it set
    for you, 10 days ago, in order to rewrite all fresh, I abandoned
    carbons. THEREFORE: please, when you get me PROOFS, if
    possible, send the copy with 'em

(2) *Spacing:* this has been mostly the problem of the rewrite, and
    please, have yr printer follow my spacings (that is, the right & left
    ones) specifically as they are here laid down
                                as of the spacings
    vertically, he shld keep a *proportional* leading to what i have—
    but here the problem is different, simply because a typewriter
    doesn't have that exactitude
                            (for example, my own machine
    broke down, and this one I have had to use has too great a dou-
    ble space, and too little a single. So yr printer shld feel his way
    proportionally with his own sense of leading

(3) The width of page (i'll take yr word you can get these lines in as
    they run here—they are pissingly long, some of them

(4) also, let me repeat, favor a small point type (10 pt as abt it)

Well, excuse these fussinesses. But I'm exhausted fr this push, and damned anxious to have a pure printing from it!

The best of luck—and the best of design. It's a happy thing, and I thank you for involving me in it—it has sure raised up a biznesss!

Ok. Quickly, & love, O

PS The damn *e* on this machine! I have marked in margin in brackets any obscurities fr the *e*, but alert your printer, please.

God damned good luck! It's a pisser (close, tricky, etc.—all my best. Just gave it a last reading!

C

64

To Paul Blackburn (1953)

In George Butterick's *A Guide to the Maximus Poems of Charles Olson* we are told that Paul Blackburn, in his "formative stage" as a poet, came upon Olson's work in *Origin* magazine and wrote letters to "probe" Olson about "the way to come at a poem" (*Guide*, p. 101). Olson's letter below responds to one such probe about the influence of Pound's verse. This was a challenge close to Olson's heart: to defend his open verse as distinct from that of his predecessors. He is in the midst of a sequence of *Maximus* poems and immediately brings the issue, and Blackburn himself, into a draft of what would become "Letter 15." Olson enclosed the draft in the letter, commenting on it in a postscript. Four days later he rewrote it, incorporating wording from the postscript itself (see *Maximus Poems*, pp. 71–75). *Letter at San Diego.*

May 4 or sum

My dear P B:

I just don't know abt this biz of "sounding" like EP. And it strikes me funny, just now when I have sent off (last week) the mss of 1-

10 of the Max Poems. For here, surely, is something so close in (and the difference, too) to the C's, that, I dare say the critique will (whatever there is) damn me by them.

        The kicker, for me, is, I take it I did as I do long before I ever read the master (1st caught him, in Hemingway's copy of Personae, living in Hem's swim-house, KW, 1945)—not, of course, that the reading is so much of a sign, I figuring anyway that advances of men go up into the air, and settle, anywhere, without that conscious experience reading, and meeting, or whatever . . . that smell, etc.

    The answer wld seem to be—and it'd be mine, is the one i assume i make without even thinking of it: that what Grandpa did goes way beyond any "original" (for which read "personal") achievement.

                          (You'll see a thing soon I wrote in sort of answer to WCW's thing in 7 Arts on "Can anything come after the iambic pentameter?". And in sd go I take back the idea that I advanced in the Pro Verse gig (you probably know it, *Poetry NY,* fall, 1951, I think it was—no, '50, must have been), that it was the trochee Ez made the heave by

Think, now, it is something much less obviously technical. And thus is a founding, of which any present signs of derivation (such as I seem charged with) only look so, because the present is such a narrow eye view.

    (I say it that way, not out of any pinch, simply, that how it comes out, seems to me so much the way i am (((yr own analysis of how i do it, miles of something, you say, and then, at the end, thrust, thrust, thrust))), that I'm no longer bugged by coincidental resemblance, the copyright, etc., not seeming to me to be any more than,

                          reality, as we now have it, have had it since ep was a pup, too—and if i didn't dislike Mr James Joyce so, i'd counter anyone, even the O M, with James' leer at WBY stepping over his prone form in the alley alongside the Abbey, "It's just too bad, Boss, you was born too young to be influenced by me!"

    What amused me more—and seems to me to put the crying-up in its place ((as both old genius & old aestheticism))—is, what Creeley told me, that the English peg C's and my work as beating the same bushes WCW was, 25 yrs ago!

This is closer home, simply, that (as a guy sd, the only night I ever was with Bill, "Now, Olson, I know who your father is!"

In other words, the virtues of the fathers are the vices of the sons. Or something. Nuts: if the pa's were as good as these (I must have grabbed my paternity out of the air

(((the same air)))

The hazard, anyhow.

Ok. And as of Caedmon, please, you tell 'em. I got plenty to keep me busy, and so, if they do have to have it done there, please ask them to give me a wide swatch of time in which to do their recording. But however it is done, here, or there, I'm all for it—and do damn well acknowledge your pushing it. In fact, just because it is your idea, wld prefer to have it in yr hands, instead of my coming into one of those paper relationships (publishing has gone all to hell just because the only personal relations left in the commercial field are between male editors & lay writers (female)

((((male to male, the editors
want to be writers themselves:
and you can't fuck that way!))))

(Like, by the way, yr title, there, Divers: PROENSA. And am looking for same. Still don't have your picture.

As of yr economics, was saying two nights ago, abt how Robt Duncan types mss for graduate students Berkeley (and Eng Dept, at that!) to pay Bern Porter for publishing his books! and Mary Barnard (the Vancouver virgin with an extreme maxilla whom EP taught to write saphics) did Carl Van Doren's indexing—also Oliver Wendell Holmes Jr's letters! (I can teach for one year—and within days of the end of a year, have traumas the like of which. . . .

it seems to be each man's poison

OK. Back to work. And thanks

O

PS:

    you see (yes, enclosed, done, since writing above letter—and still in process)

        how difficult can one get! how tortuous:

                          (even yr point abt olson's verse as being vocal)

                      to prevent the reader is crucially the means of the beauty of such a practice—to reach the response i take it is called for

        That is,

                there is never any purposeful prevention. Au contraire. The preventions are—it wld be my experience—exactly the way reality does interrupt herself, cross-cut, go below anything explicit, even of the other senses than the verbal

                         (exactly the way a poem does write itself:

when you talk of digestion first, i hear exactly the aesthetic seems to me to have exposed itself

              not, for god's sake, that i think i have proved, or can, that one can take language (which is itself an extrication) and make it a rail on which anyone else will ride (as in a Pullman, with that sense the advertisements are right about, that, you are being taken care of, in fact, if you take a compartment, your whole damn family, especially, the kids!)

I call it prevention, "safety-prevention", say. But of course it is actually enabling. Or I wldn't be able to stare my puss in the mirror. Enabling a reader to come up at it from those places where (I swear!) response does lie (not at all in the head, in the receiving of a package all done up, projected, after, digestion

what i lose, i wish i might not: that universality, what?

but i wld rather catch by envergure, i think the word is spelled (how do you have it? olson, you write too much around a subject

                            I don't even know that one of the heaves isn't, to question that a poem is a subject (as you know, i take it it is exactly the opposite, is, an object

And as
such I don't (for the life of me!) see how it can be any less difficult (and
blessed) than. . . .

so the end is where the thrust—that, if one has the illusion that one has
made a form out of, that present going, then, one is gone, and, ought to,
just there where one has come to a stop, crow

why you are right it all is meant to be heard, is, that, from where i work,
language is sound, not eyes, ears are what it is
                                               rhapsodia: to bang on
the ears of sd listener until he lets you sew him up

and talking (singing)

(if the object is an object)

goes about a bit

                                O

65

To Bernard Kneiger (1953)

Bernard Kneiger, one of the students of modern literature who actually read the
first issue of *Origin* when it came out, asked for an explanation of the Oregon
reference in "I, Maximus of Gloucester, to You." The poet answered.

Letter at Storrs.

                                June 15
My dear Bernard Kneiger:
                        I feel very badly, I have been so slow, to
thank you for yr original letter—and now, again, for the buck for 2
This
        I am apt to get on a run (like any fish). And I do drop everything,
for that time. So please excuse me. (In fact this time, it was, I think,

worth it: 29 Maximus "letters" are now done—you wld, i think, know
#1, was the opener of Origin 1?

Of course! Yr original question was,
why Oregon! wasn't it?

And since it recurs again in letter 10 (abt James
Conant asking Oregon, to send its brightest!), I gather it is some
fix in me of, how John Chapman's apples do rot, despite, the beauty
of, the land! (If you know that coast, fr, say, the Columbia south
to Crescent City, Cal., you'll imagine why, to me, Oregon, is so beautiful

((Crazy thing was, too,
that just there I got the best chowder (chow-dah!) I ever did eat—real
newengland chow-DA H

And Port Awful

And a-Bandon: shipwreck

coast

(even the people, seem to have come there, fr
wrecks—English, & New English, vessels

It may interest you that "The Maximus Poems, 1-10", is now in proofs—
in Stuttgart! And to be published sometime this summer. By a Jonathan
Williams, Publisher, Stuttgart!

But I weep that I am left with the mss of
11-29 (they only got written as a result of the propulsion of doing 5-10
for, that book

(My regret is, that the scope, & intent, of the POEM, will
not be seen in one swipe—as it wld if, I take it, all 29 were thrown at sd
poor reader in a piece

For it goes away fr Gloucester just abt 11 (to
come back, every so often, like
we do, eh?

Maybe Oregon has more import than I yet know. Writing to
you like this, it occurs to me that I may have thrown out some
filament there in #1 . . .

that the intent was more known

to me than I yet know . . .

I guess so: Tyre, to Port Orford,
say.

I think so. For though the "West" (in our sense) is for another time—I don't feel free to load this poem with any more
extensions of the material than, say, Ay-ron Burr—the States
as a measure of men's misses,

is my story, yes?

It is a question of how far you can stretch an elastic: starting with
Glow-s-ter, there is a limit westward that I can take this baby (however
much eastward Max himself leaves me, free

((tho that's a limit, too,
come to think of it: I am already suffering fr a time-wall, in him

It is
not, however, substantive (as the space West already is denied me). Tyre
is "civilization" (again, as we use the phrase

And a whole wealth of
material natural to me lies back of that Max.

In fact, thank you. Saying
these things instructs me. I shld suspect that the next long one will have
these two axes:

substantively, not Gloucester, but—say—St Joe (some
fix off there—maybe more, Amarillo

& time-wise: back, Cro-Magnon (or better, the earliest
poems of men, The Destruction of the City of Ur, say

and forward? what we don't even know.

Yes, that shld
about be the two legs the thing can stand on—bestrid, not the ocean,
but man (his generosity

like his eyes saucers!

It fires me. But here I am
sunk in this other, with no end in sight! For I have the feeling, to exhaust what Max # 1 contains, will take me a year (years?

The weakness
of it (or the engagement!) is, mnemonics (here I am the stem; there, it
wld not be me, it wld be (of course, me, but not at all so personal, quite
otherwise, exactly any man as, classic-wise, it used to be for a poet to
keep himself the hell out ((classic forms—now so reactionary, to my
mind—will have to yield again that virtu: that each line shall live as
stars appear each night, the movement of them the same, the place of
them, different, with the season (no weather mattering, except, that we
don't see them, which, is superficial

It must be very difficult. But I am
hungry to be at it.

> Thank you. And let me hear
> fr you again. Cordially,
> Charles Olson

Olson wrote the next day: "came up with full conception of long poem to follow
Max (in letter to Bernard Kneiger)" (notebook 36 at Storrs).

66

To Ronald Mason (1953)

One of that peculiarly English breed of civil servant–literary critic, Ronald
Mason wrote to Olson after reading the review in the *New Republic* ("The
Materials and Weights of Herman Melville") in which Olson indicated that he
admired Mason's study of Melville, *The Spirit Above the Dust* (1951). The scene
was set for a vigorous correspondence between two radically different minds.
The carbuncle of the crown was Olson's eight-page, single-spaced outpouring
on American literature for the British ear, followed in the same mail by a five-
page, single-spaced explanation of what he had written, followed by a further
postscript of three pages. A more measured follow-up is presented below.

Letter at Storrs.

Mon Jly 13/53

My dear Mason: Yr 2nd letter in yesterday. And I am terribly pleased
you were not knocked completely off by what you call my screed. For I
felt it must be too much for anyone—even a man who loved Melville! I
shld regret to lose the sympathy of yr attention to the common problem as I do so harshly, if seriously, express it.

You will notice that prose
is a beast I rassle with. And as my wife sd last night, I have never made
my peace with it—always butt it, and do it the hard way.

I cld imagine—
the way I am interesting myself in the traditional these days—that I
might soon settle for a draw with prose (or a tie, as we say in baseball,
and that you cricket-men must have a like word for). But my reason for
seeming so recalcitrant, and headstrong about prose, is a more important matter than my present conceits about it. And it occurred to me
that I ought to pose it to you, that you might be interested in the form
problem as I am engaged with it, especially after that imprimatur &
dixit I gave the rest of us writing-amoricans in that scroll to you two
weeks ago.

The quarrel is with discourse—and thus, up to a certain,
but extreme, point, with traditional syntax. Because it is not possible to
say everything at once is no reason, to my mind, to lose the advantage
of this pressure (or compression) which speech is when it wants to be:
that it rushes into the mouth to crowd out to someone else what it is is
pressing in the heart & mind to be said.

It has been very heartening
for me to learn, in the past two years, how much music—which, like language, has this duration-in-time problem implicit in itself as medium—
how much a composer like Pierre Boulez is also engaged with what I
might call the maintaining of the perpendicular of the first, and all succeeding, instants in the face of the tendence of all discourse and composition to—because of time—go out flat and horizontally.

That is, the
1st instant is that all-at-once drive I spoke of. But what is equally important to form in writing is that this crowding—and I don't think I am
"volcanic", or am being solely personal in this analysis—this crowding
is the act of language, and so is the constant of all the instants which follow the 1st, all the way to the end of the communication.

At least one
can say this (allowing that I am leaving out a great deal of the self-
generative that language is, after the 1st instant—that is, that one
word does lead to another. (Or, as, after a reading of three of my own
poems with three of Thomas', here the other night, the 3rd poet sd
abt Thomas, "one damn word after an-udder!") One can say that
progression is now interesting not that it is moving toward a climax
or an end (what one might fairly call the law of traditional form, in
prose and verse), but that it is *also* moving without allowable loss
from and *by* each succeeding instant of itself. Force, we have damn
well learned from 100 years of non-Euclidean geometry plus the superb physicists, is as much from, as towards, itself. And "field," in itself, is—nest is—as the eggs. (The last image is, of course, resting on
that magnificent notion, that the law of gravitation and of the magnetic field are one.)

You will imagine that I am much too conservative to wreck either
syntax or the narrative. I abhor liberalism, for its carelessnesses (defin-
ing a liberal as one who overestimates *both* the individual *&* society). I
have no feeling for the "experimental period" (Whitman through Joyce,
say—to pick the best, and not the constructivists, or bohemians—*note
bene:* I have plenty of feeling for Whitman, Joyce, the Imagists, etc.; I
mean, *because* of their work, it is possible now to engage the essential
questions of form, not to, any longer, continue to *epater la surface!*)

I am persuaded that both syntax and narrative are being refounded
in an order of space-time which shows up the old ordering of discourse
as necessarily thin—thin of time and of logic, of an arbitrary system of
presentation which, because it was arbitrary, forced a great deal of reality into statement, where it dies, simply, that life is not the statement of
itself but—itself.
You see, I don't think that the act of language, in
either prose or verse, is statement. Nor do I think that the limits of language are the "meaning" of its words (that meaning, which is palpably
"intellectual," forces an intellectual construct on to the use of words.
Note: the error here is again correctable by recent mathematics—the
sum is greater than the whole of the parts because the factor of the rele-
vance of the parts to each other creates an organism of which the "life"

of it is more important than any "whole" that it is. (I proposed this co-nundrum, the other night, to the 3rd poet mentioned above: "It is not it. It is these that it is."(!))

>((At which point painting, as now done, is as illuminating to our art as music is. I cannot urge you too strongly to ac-quaint yrself, so far as you can, with a bunch of NY painters who are known to the Boston painter Jack Levine as the "Space-Cadets"!
>
>The one of them all whom I wld place with Boulez is Franz Kline. But Philip Guston and Esteban Vicente are delicate workers. And I have a hunch that William de Kooning—whom I know least—is just now advancing on the narrative question as (I believe) in writing only Robt Creeley is (with myself, if you will excuse the completeness, running behind!)
>
>For these painters, in utter ignorance of Melville, are—as Vicente recently sd—"painting space." And in the most cu-rious & perplexing of ways, space *is* this time-component I keep speaking of as the "instant" or the "perpendicular" which has so changed progression in writing.

I was about to write down Boulez's *l'ordre seriale,* that phrase of his to cover composition we know as the 12-tone scale, when I looked up pro-gression in the dictionary and found this as its mathematical meaning: "a discrete series that has a first *but no last* element. . . . ."!!!

and the rest of the definition is in point: "esp. one in which any intermediate element is related by *a uniform law* to the other elements."

(*note:* that "uniform law" is what I'd imagine is the "syntax" and "narrative" we are seeking, and why I do ask permission to call myself a conservative & classicalist!)

I think we are only beginning to find out something abt the Law. But signs of it peep out. E.g., the trochee, say, as against the iamb, to get the force of the 1st instant in—and keep it in. (2) the circular, or field, as the compositional law. (3) the parts achieving the coherence, not the whole, and doing it by obedience to their particularism, by the obedience of the writer to their particulars, not to his appropriation of them or to any Socratic context of their Ideal form. And (4) *attention* rather than analogy, as the source of humanism.

As of the latter, my wife read me, last night, *Adonais*. (Note: it is a wonderful chiasma of our correspondence, Mason, that I, just now, am back-tracking *your* literature!) And I was very moved by the cleanness & clarity of the great old compositional attack in this poem. As, say, I have been, for 20 years, by Chaucer's Troilus & Cressida.

In other words, there is no *aggression* in all that I am saying. In fact, to us who are in the thicket, these happy ones (Shelley, Chaucer, Thomas—up to age 30!) are like in Paradise. And we wave to them, over the dearth, with wonderful brotherhood—we who are without—as Vicente did put it—portrait, landscape, & narrative!

We who paint space, write dream, or compose magnetic tape!

(I find that the saddest ones—the ones least engaged, no matter
their genius (Thomas, or my friend the composer Stefan Wolpe)—
are the "humanists", the ones who can't get away from subject-
matter.

It is they who think reality is desolation. Imagine! that a reality like ours shld be taken so!

They can't get away from
the models when I am sure there never was a time when pattern-
makers could be so busy!

Their humanness is unemployed! And so
they sit, like Richard, and tell sad tales!

One cld write an Adonais,
for them!)

So please, whenever I seem dense, stupid, wilful (and I am, in prose, because I don't yet know how it fits to the Law—the "knots" in it, like you say—do allow me this charity, that (1) verse is my business, but (2) that language, including prose, is where one does try to find out how to make form out of it!

I do still debate & debate Ford Madox Ford's formulation (what, 1908?) that verse must be at least as well written as prose. (True)

And Swinburne's dictum, that anything which can be equally well said in prose should not be said in verse. (True)

For just the margin, of prose & verse, is, by the very good fact of both of them (that they both exist, for our use), is, I am sure, where the accomplishment of a space-time discourse does lie.

Well, to thank you for yr letters—and to let you have what's on my mind these days.

And whenever you can, let me have letters from you. For it is a great pleasure.

And I equally hope I may get over to see you, one day. For two years we have been here, having our first baby, a daughter, and enabling ourselves to beat this frightful economy of the States. And I imagine we'll turn back to Guatemala and the Yucatan (where we came from, 2 yrs ago) before we do any other adventuring. But it wld be terribly pleasant to be in England again: I was there once, in 1928! Imagine, that long ago!

Fondly,

Charles Olson

I shall send this 1st class mail. But *please,* so long as you can, do answer me *air mail.* It closes the gap.

In a letter to Robert Creeley the next day, Olson referred to having a "fine sense of forwardness" because of Mason's invitation to the "17th century house of his 15 miles out of London . . . And I sd to him, probably not. But the feeling, suddenly, of, yes, Guatemala, Mallorca, and why not England, too—very damn free. Haven't had a like sense since a long time, when I used to just go!" (letter at Stanford, 14 July 1953). The correspondence with Mason, however, faded by the end of the year. No visit transpired.

67

To Frederick Merk (1953)

One of the most valuable courses Olson attended while enrolled in the American Civilization program at Harvard University was Professor Frederick

Merk's "The Westward Movement." Olson's only "who's who" entry, that in Stanley Kunitz's *Twentieth Century Authors: First Supplement,* names Merk as one of the "chief intellectual disciplinarians" of his formative years. He wrote Merk to that effect on 28 July 1945 (retaining a copy in his notebook) and again on 5 February 1952: "For you conceive history from a ground I do not know anyone else to offer. . . . It is a humus which no amount of ideas or theories or the too heavy traffic of facts is permitted, by you, to take out of the soil. . . . You restore that sort of thickness to whatever events you set down" (carbon copy at Storrs). The following letter, full of specific matters relevant to the ongoing *Maximus* poems, was the result of Olson's borrowing from Duke University Library a copy of Frances Rose-Troup's *John White, the Patriarch of Dorchester and the Founder of Massachusetts* (1930). "Letter 23" was drafted soon after this, and includes the following lines (*Maximus Poems,* p. 104):

> What we have here—and literally in my own front yard, as I sd to Merk, asking him what delving, into "fishermans ffield" recent historians . . . not telling him it was a poem I was interested in, aware I'd scare him off, *muthologos* has lost such ground since Pindar.

Letter (carbon copy) at Storrs.

Black Mt. NC Sept 10 1953

My dear Professor Merk:

Again I have the distinct pleasure to write to you. This time, it is to ask you if you can advise me about the state of knowledge about what is, in fact, the very ground I was raised on: Fishermen's Field, Cape Ann.

I am engaged in a work which pivots from that field, and wish to saturate myself on all the history of it which is now known. And I wonder if you will be good enough to spare me some of your time to say whether recent scholarship has attacked some of the questions I shall pose below. Or—if all this is now something you do not especially keep your eye on—if you can direct me to some man who is, now, peculiarly involved in such researches. (I am thinking, for example, of a F. X. Moloney, who, 20 years ago, did an honors thesis on the fur trade in New England. Is he still active in such work? Or are some of the Canadians who were inspired by Biggar still going in, at this point?)

With the libraries available to me here in the South, I am weakest just in the latest work—that is, from 1930 to the present.

Well, to the specific areas, and their "time":

(1), *the "Dorchester Company"*: the latest usable work I have found is
that done, and published before 1930, by Mrs Frances Rose-Troup,
on the "Early Settlements," on "Roger Conant," and on "John
White."

question #1: do you know, or can you direct me to one who
            might know, if any further work beyond hers has
            been done on:
   (a) John White
   (b) Roger Conant
   (c) on the changing of the "Dorchester Co.", through what she
       calls the "New England, or London, Co." (of Cradock, and
       other London Merchants), to the "Mass. Bay Co." (with
       Winthrop, Saltonstall, Dudley entering the picture)
   (d) on the very decisive economic question of what was the divi-
       sion between the "Joint Stock" of the Old Adventurers (of the
       Dorchester and the London Cos.) and the "Common Stock"
       of the New Planters (Winthrop, etc.) ((1630-1637))
 & (e) on, precisely, what part the beaver in the streams along
       the coast south from Cape Ann, especially between the
       Charles and the Saugus, played in the shifts from Cape Ann
       to Salem, and, most noticeably, in the shift to the Boston
       area—
            here, the Gorges Grant, Oldham, at Nantasket, Cra-
            dock's part in the London Co. and both Oldham and
            Cradock's story after 1630, are of interest to me.

In other words, to summarize (1), *the economic history of the planting of
Massachusetts north of Plymouth 1622-1637.*
(2), *the Fisheries* of the North Atlantic *before* Boston, that is:
   (a) do you know if anyone has done anything like Mrs. Rose-
       Troup's very valuable research into the Weymouth (England)
       Port Book? into such other ports as Bristol? Plymouth? Or into
       such French ports as St Malo? Or even the Spanish records?
            I am aware of Lounsbury and Innis's work
            on the Newfoundland fisheries. But Innis's

only in magazines: do you happen to know
if he carried his work into book form? Or is
still working? (H. A. Innis)

But the slant of this which is vital to me is how it points straight at
Cape Ann—why it was that White and the Dorchester men did take just
the fishing in Massachusetts Bay as the soundest economic ground for a
plantation? Has anyone, to your knowledge, dug this thing specifically,
since around 1930?

((*Note:* Some of the above sounds a little bit as though I was doing
the unpardonable thing—the Innis question, e.g.—, asking you to do
my own research! But I beg you to understand, that my specificness is
only so that you (or anyone else you might want to point these questions at) may see the precise area, and period, of my necessities. And
actually, as we well know, a great deal of work in progress may not at
all be known as in progress except to some specialist in exactly these
matters. All I wish to ask is, who are the men, so that I may reach
them myself.

(3), and last: what I might call *the "maverick" settlements of Mass.,* that
is, has anyone chosen to wonder about, and then seek to see in one
piece, the several individual or "irregular" Particulars, Planters, Traders,
who were spread out between Plymouth and Cape Ann?

I am thinking,
of course, of Oldham, Lyford, and Conant at Nantasket before Lyford &
Conant came to Cape Ann; of Morton; of Maverick himself, and Black-
stone, at Charlestown; and, of course, of the funny crowd—200 of
them, someone reports—at Fishermen's Field itself!

It is a curious phe-
nomenon, these traders in fur, gun-sellers, and fishermen-farmers, simply that they got ground out by the bigger & religious plantations to the
north and south, and then in the middle of them. And I rather imagine
that some one of your own students may well have tackled the possible
research here. If any has, I should be tremendously aided to know.

That, then, is about it. And I beg you not at all to think of this as an
exaction on you. Or in any way a burden. As you well know, you are the

pivot of my respect for history. And if I turn to you again, it is just because it is a joy to register, once more, my deepest respect.

And any-
thing you can give me back—or direct someone else, if there is someone who happens also to have come into this time with a distinct
economic, rather than religious attention—shall be exceedingly
helpful.

As I say, I have put it thus specifically, not to point any of the
pieces at you, but to suggest the sort of saturation that *my own front
yard*—literally, that field was where I grew, our house being on "Stage
Fort Avenue," Gloucester!—bred in me.

Cordially, and affectionately—
with all thanks,

Charles Olson

68

To Robert Duncan (1953)

Olson had spent a brief time with Robert Duncan in Berkeley in 1947. Until the
letter presented below was written (which is of special interest because it became
the basis for Olson's essay "Against Wisdom As Such," published in the first issue
of *Black Mountain Review*), their correspondence had been concerned mainly
with the broadside that the Black Mountain College printers wanted to make of
Duncan's "The Song of the Borderguard." Then, almost out of the blue, came a
letter from Duncan on receiving *Maximus Poems 1–10*. He felt that Olson's
writings were like those "friends coming from far quarters" that Confucius
considered to be one of three civilized pleasures. "What more central love,"
Duncan wrote, "than the disturbance and trembling awakend by each new song,
the calling up of one's own spirit in answer, the still center in the excitement that
comes as the poems are comprehended. . . . What more central love than the
comradeship in devotion to the art?" But, Duncan cautions, in words that Olson
picks up on in his reply, "it is not central yet, it is still coming into view, another
devotion. The wisdom we seek. The counsels of the language. The purpose, the
effort—is part of the wisdom" (letter at Storrs).

The other Duncan writing that Olson mentions in the letter below is "Pages
from a Notebook" in the *Artist's View*, no. 5 (July 1953), where we find (p. 3): "It
finally dawnd. It was a painful lesson. To give up greatness when one was not

capable of it . . . I shall live out my life in this small world, with my imaginary
genius . . . I am a poet, self-declared, manque."   *Letter at Buffalo.*

black mt collitch   Monday, dec 21st

RD: the greatest. You'll know. Or how cld you, that your own, is, plus one,
what has come in—and on both of the bks. So you can guess.

But—and
how to say this—that it is you, both that sd it, and had it, to say—this is
very damn important to me, having (since that Milton, there, Circle)
had what you have, by god, awarded me, in that bracket, that,—well, reverse it: since '47, it has been *your* technical achievement compared to
my often very damned often inadequacy . . .

So: to have you say these
things gives me *the* sense of having done the job, the sense of that comradeship, that central love

Look: it's now three days since yr letter
came. And that I waited this long (haven't even read yr own thing enclosed) may be sign of what food & water . . . and how i had to do
nothing but savor it, falling back into that: enjoyment. Christ! That's
walking up to a man, and giving him what damn little he gets, eh?

OK. Just foolish to try to say it.

Now: wld you, without at all feeling jumped, let me publish it, as
it stands, as a review? For it does have its own damn form, as it
stands. And is so beautiful (I'm sure, for another, as well as myself),
that, if you wld let it stand as a review of Max, I shld be damn greatly
spoken of.

The place: the first issue of what looks as tho it will be
called The Black Mt Quarterly is just these days beginning to be made
up. With Creeley as editor. And it is there that I'd like to place this
thing, if you will permit.

And leave it as signed, R. D. And leave it as it
opens, near-far Mister Olson

(So far I've sent Creeley one thing, also
a review, under pseudonym, called "The Name Is Smith,"—the name is

Hines, actually—but it's a thing on John Smith, as of this new book on him by Brad S.

I plan to send Creeley one of the Maxes fr the 2nd set, one i like, called "On First Looking Out of Juan de la Cosa's Eyes." And may I urge you to send him all the verse you think the highest of (as WCW sd, when he 1st put me in touch with Creeley, when he was then, Littleton NH, proposing to do the magazine it now looks as tho he may actually get into print. His address: Divers Press, Banalbufar, Mallorca, Spain.

Question, on letter: is the ideogram "young birds learning flying in the wing" or in the wind?????

And might i change that bracket to read "(that he has such technical achievement compared to my often inadequacy)"—this one change I think formalizes the whole matter, the only change necessary to do it.

And if you want to make sure you'd pass on it for public place, I'll send you a copy. But do let me urge you that, as it stands, it is perfect. No man cld have himself sd so finely—and richly.

Very damn wonderful to have you
breach
Nothing,
like it
o
let me know
Olson

the beauty is, not that anything is curable
but that it
continues

why we have it, on all these religious
ginks, is
that what you can do with it
—and it is enough, god damn well ENUF, is
compose it
—that it is
composed

(later)

As for the wisdom isn't there—"yet," i read it you are saying, in
Maximus

that it is (1) friends, (2) the effort—you call this "part of the
wisdom"

but i take it confucius sez the 3rd is no more than perspective,
the 3rd that is every where and every thing

Which wld be enuf, for me,
if that cld be got in

That is, (tonight reading jung-wilhelm's golden
flour, and protesting—there—j's having to be the White Knight—why i
had it, in pencil, away with curing, art
does not heal, medicine does, art
composes. And that's good
enough

and, last, reading yr "Artist's View":

u see, i don't
at all take it you are as balanced as those sentences up to the IT
downed
on u. NOR
manqué.

neither.

That that's the trouble with wisdom. It isn't a measure. And thus has to go, from language (not knowing abt art)

Doesn't
it honestly—to be flat—come to, to love? that all springs up, there?
And that what springs up is *energy*, with which to do anything, think
(which is to be wise), cut wood (& i mean for no other reason than to
keep warm), push something, ahead, make it different, etc., anything,
all

that all the vocabulary—the words you seek to make gnomic
by doublet—are valid enuf as reductive (that is, that they do analyze
validly the worlds love opens one's eyes to,

that *light* is reductive, and
that . . .

but here i do go off, or must explain i think the classic order of
water, fire, light has to be changed, that light was before electronics.
And we are after. And so fire . . .

Sound

is fire. As
love is.
     That is, *all*
is reductive except
fire. (Heat, to get rid of any paradox in the statement—U see, i think
thinking is analytical, and has to be severely single statement on single
statement because thinking is that way. Writing, isn't. But writing is not
thinking. Writing is not reductive. Writing is
what love is (and again, to keep off aphorism, love is the heat which
so reveals energies in and beyond us that, like the act of writing you
testify to, things we did not intend to happen—and we then, need
light, to reduce what has been found out . . . why you say you do
study what you have done as text. But the revision, is the next
writing

    One thing Jung got a hold of (but because he does not know form he
knows nothing, only astrology, or some such description as Dr Rhine's)
is, what is opposite to, the reductive: the *synchronistic*
                        This seems to
me extremely useful, as a fact, say, of the writing of a, poem—that the
most compelling fact abt sd act is, isn't it?, that it is simultaneous—
that this is its homogeneity which tells us when it is done, that does
bring in what comes in, that it is time (rhythm is time, no? "flow" i
think *rhein*, the root, means "to flow," that "measure" is only late,
Alexandrian, when the pedants . . .
                    but i (again) don't want to leave it
at that word "time", i want to try to convince you of what you have
proved to me in poems, that yr own experience in a poem is ordered by
a seizure (Frobenius' *Ergriffen*) not so much in time (Poe's Poetic Principle) or by time (metric, measure) but of a characteristic *of* time which
is most profound (and still most unattended to, that it is time, in this
sense—and in all those other senses of the synchronous, how another
person, how an image is forever in that moment impressed upon all
men thereafter "absent thee from felicity", say . . .
                 This fact that time
is a concrete continuum which the poet alone—i insist—alone prac-
tices the bending of

why this art is, than

no other
that only also love is,
simultaneous
that this is why we invoke
And why—if we were ulti-
mate (& i believe we are, when we do bend to the law: the law is,

/whatever is born or done this moment of time, has the qualities of
this moment
of time/

But you will not mind, having in mind two things: (1) that i am stuck with
such particularism; and (2) have had the conviction, from things you have
done, that they have had this moment of time—and so i do not think it is
the same thing that you also have to trouble yrself abt how it is to become
a child; or that you care to complete your pretensions with yr wit

I want only to urge that those are measures. And that a poem is not
wise, even if it is—that any wisdom also is solely a quality of the moment of time of that poem in which there are wisdoms. There are obviously seizures which have nothing to do with wisdom at all. And they
are very beautiful.

I guess i don't even believe it's beauty—that how Bill has it (in To A
Dog Injured in the Street) that he and René Char believe in the power
of beauty/to right all wrongs . . .
that this is partial, "social," wisdom

It is time (love) is difficult, Mister
Beardsley

(Why you say the aesthete, will have a hell of a time with, what you
have unselected—why you say yrself you have found out stuff you'd
throw away, turns out later . . .

How to get it all in (which is, i suppose, an olsonism! like you have
picked it, "go sing"

I'm so foolish. A song is heat (not light—light, yes, but not the *state* of a poem: the state is the fever of (and it is not fever-ish, is very cool, is—the eyes are—how did they get that way?

"He who controls
rhythm
controls"

This wld seem to me to be the
END

Otherwise we are involved in
ourselves (which is demonstrably
not so very interesting, no
matter
who

     I think when you exercise your (faculties, it is in yr letter; fa-
     cilities at large, you are altogether separate and more than
     even the way it means, to make
     love

     I pick out the para.: "Here I am, at last . . . at last."

Well, haven't any idea what hour it is, but the cocks across the gulley at the farm are crowing as steadily as minutes. And I must quit and have more blue cheese, before
turning in

                    yrs,

                      c.

(last, next day)

        i think wisdom, like style, is the man—that it is not ex-
tricable as any sort of a statement, even (and here is the catch) though there be "wisdom," that is, that life can be shown to yield "truths."

                                    But
truths are as mortal as the life in any of us, which we cannot, for sure, heave (as Cordelia couldn't) her heart into her mouth.

I take it only
sectaries can deal with wisdom as tho it were thus disposable. And even
they, then (and i don't think it is at all persecution which makes them
secret, but it is), symbols which they then make use of. And symbols as
signs (example, the *I Ching*).

In other words, I fall back again on a
difference which I take it the poet at least is crucially involved in: that
he is not free to be any sect, that there are no symbols to him, there are
only his composed forms (and each one is the issue of the time of the
moment of its creation), he cannot traffick in any other sign than his
one, his self, this man. Otherwise God does rush in, and overwhelms
art, turns it into, like that, the other great force, religion (in the exact
sense of the religious experience).

It was thinking abt an early eastern Westerner, Apollonius of Tyana,
which led me to sit down to write this additional note to you. That insistence of his, that there is always "the moment that suits wisdom best
to give death battle." It is in this sense of something which is carried like
a gun—like a man's own life—which I mean as what seems to me important, these days (when the wisdom of the East and the unwisdom of
the West are like looked-for dispensations, by the Right, and the right
Right), that it is important to assert that wisdom is that same thing as
the skin of one of us, which we lose only when we choose to, not pour
out, as of any, moment

> ((I don't know enuf Anglo-Saxon to say, but if the noun
> "wise" (AS. *wīse*) is the root of the adj. (AS. *wīs*), then
> by the noun one is back at the sort of force I suggest the
> whole concept of wisdom properly rests on: "Way of
> being or acting" ex.: on this wise))

VI

The years of change were 1954 to 1957. The Washington house was no longer available to the Olsons. The Olsons were no longer— after fits and starts of breaking up—a couple. Olson was made rector of Black Mountain College, but it was a last-ditch battle against the college's decline. These were heroic years for those who remained: Robert Creeley for a time, Robert Duncan for a time, Wesley Huss till the end. BMC closed officially in October 1956. Olson then spent six months alone at Black Mountain with his new wife and son, winding up the affairs of the college.

The *Black Mountain Review,* in seven issues edited by Robert Creeley, endured as a binnacle during this period.

69

To Irving Layton (1954)

Olson wrote to Creeley on 8 January 1954: "good chance I may make it to Canada, for that break, Layton has kept coming back to: letter in this week saying, McGill, and Sir GW, and maybe a little cash to defray however the hell you get up there!" (letter at Stanford). Clearly Olson was looking forward to being in Montreal to meet the young Canadian poet who had brashly announced that he was going to do a rebuttal of "Projective Verse" (*Olson-Corman Correspondence,* vol. 2, p. 71). The polemic did not materialize, but Olson had been so impressed by Layton's precocious verse that he phoned to see if he would come to teach at Black Mountain. Layton was listed on the masthead of the *Black Mountain Review,* but he was never able to cross the U.S. border. And the proposed visit by Olson to Montreal fizzled out by the end of March. (See Tim Hunter's " 'The North American States': Charles Olson's Letters to Irving Layton" in *Line,* no. 13 [1989], pp. 123–52, for the full story.)

Letters at Concordia.

Black Mt
Jan 21/54

My dear Layton:

Thank you for both yr letters. It is damned moving, how you have it there, that, the Canadian, is between the English and the American. And of course just what you wish EP or Bill wldn't do, is where I like them—that is, I like them, for letting it show, just as much as showing: Pull down, thy/panities,   oh—britches.

And I wld argue one as clearly on as yrself, to come with us. Without patriotism, and solely because speech has gone ahead of any of us (english canadian american australian indian, who: Kitasono plus men i'm sure neither of us know of)—

which certainly means reality, is, out-running us, no?

Avison (abt Pro Verse) sd, Olson's—or any man's programme—is his own. Not quite. And for this reality reason: that the thing does run, alongside each of us. And can be—I'd say, has to be—grabbed hold of.

I'm sure that what you are objecting to, in Bill say, and wanting (form as climax) has been disturbed and shifted by the dying, and now death of, dimensions.

You will know how much Creeley and myself do still work with that idea, that form is never more than an extension of content. And I just, today, had to send off a recommendation for Merce Cunningham, the dancer. Don't know whether you know him, or his work, but the immediate point is, that, he says it flatly, as of his own biz: the meaning of movement is inherent in its own nature.

It is these flatnesses—in the sense of no distances—which lie at the root of any of these "Americans" practice. And I myself track em to the obvious change in reality, begun by the non-Euclidean geometers a hundred years ago: that the round isn't only out there, it's in, to.

By the way, there is a distinguished Canadian geometer whom I have learned much from. At Toronto. Christ, what is his name. Did a wonderful book on polytopes.   Shit. Lost it, at the moment. Take a look at it, if you're interested (one lovely story in it abt an Armenian rug merchant in Hartford, Conn.,—whose models I know!—and how he came to make those models: dreamt em!

(The Geometer's name begins with C, I believe (not unlike Comstock or Grierson)—christ, what is it

Any-
how, just to get word over to you. And tell you how pleased I am that you are with us, in #1, of the BMQ. Figure we can all help Bob turn this one into the damned best anywhere.

Yes: COXETER!! a great guy
Yes: do take a look at his book. Wonderful.
In fact, if he has anything like it out recently—or it itself—I'd like to review it for the *Quart.*

Oh, YEAH; as of the shit in Bill's pants, or EP's—how you had it— messiness: I once sent this one, to Bill:

these days

        whatever you have to say,
leave the roots on.
Let them dangle.

And the dirt.

        Just to make sure
        where they come from

I think it was. It's the idea,
anyway

And I shld so much like to come up there. Do you & Dudek need a lot
of advance notice, to arrange something which might cover my travel?
Give me some idea how much time I'd have to let you have ahead. For
that will be the only difficulty now: otherwise, I wld jump off. And
come. Bang. I now toy with some time in March—middle, say. But let
me know how it all sits there. If you do need warning. And what wld be
good.

        Back on, shortly. And please
        keep letting me hear fr you
                O

costs (this is the pisser—too old to bum;
& not much for traveling with others!)

———————————

[letterhead]
BLACK MOUNTAIN COLLEGE   BLACK MOUNTAIN N.C.

        hot off yr letter

Layton
      God damn it. I'm sore. And just becoz I'd set my heart on this
thing.
   Look: fer chris sake (1) do you have to give it up so easily? & (2) why
didn't you damn well let me know at any time previous that (a) it was a

Lit Society, & (b) that you were having such other guests as Campbell, Auden & the shit Viereck? (How much do *they* cost????)

I stress this latter simply that (1) if you broached the thing to me in the first place, and it had this formalness to it, you ought (a) to have let me know that, instead of going on the assumption it was personal alone & (b) so long as the Society did manage to have V,A, & C, what kind of a fight *are you putting up* so that at *this late date* you dump me

(1) when I was scheduling the thing, & making all plans for a month around it

& (2) when, by god, if you mean what you say abt us Americans (EP WCW & CO, say, not to speak of Creeley etc) *how come* you find the *till empty* just now??? how come the money got spent on Auden (Eng)
    Campbell (Eng)
    Viereck (*Eng?*

By god, Layton. Come on. Come up to it. Or don't, for Christ sake, dangle somebody like me 5 months or more, without

(1) telling all

& (2) dumping as late & gaily as this——Sore. And want you to make it still come off.

On yr honor
    & for cause

Christ

Olson

Layton subsequently explained that it was Louis Dudek at McGill who had put the kibosh on what was to have been a joint invitation. Olson wrote back 8 April 1954 (letter at Concordia): "sorry I screamed. But at least you do know I was set on it, and hugely disappointed. And still am."

70

To the Department of Public Instruction (1954)

Olson was appointed rector of Black Mountain College in March 1954, and his first administrative job was to persuade the federal bureaucracy that veterans

enrolling at BMC should qualify for financial aid under the congressional act
known as the GI Bill. *Letter (carbon copy) at Raleigh.*

May 21, 1954

Mr. Gilmore W. Johnson
State Supervisor,
Veterans Education & Training
The Dept. of Public Instruction
Raleigh, North Carolina

Dear Mr. Johnson:
  The Faculty of this college has given considerable consideration to
your letter of May 6th and has been in consultation with others to find
out how to proceed so that it may have the advantages it believes it has
a right to under U.S. Public Law 550.

  Your letter reports a "decision" of the Veterans Education Committee of this State. But we are so far unable to see that that "decision" either (1) states or (2) was made under that section of Public
Law 550 on which Black Mountain College based her formal and
written application—required by the law—in our letter to you
April 6th.

  So far as we can see neither (1) the materials before your Committee were those we asked the forms for (and which you yourself
said were necessary, in your letter of April 15th); nor (2) that the
Committee was, in fact, considering our application under that section of the Law we specifically have requested to be approved
under—Section 254.

  We understand that you say that it is the "present policy" of the
Committee to apply accreditation requirements, but as we read the Law
these are the requirements under Section 253, under which you turned
us down a year ago. Our application April 6th specifically asks for approval under Section 254, which section says specifically "Approval of
Non-Accredited Courses."

And we beg to call to the Committee's further attention that the Section says nothing whatsoever about "vocational" versus "collegiate" courses—a distinction your letter applies—but says simply "educational institution": which Black Mountain College most exactly and legally is.

The situation, then, as we see it, is that until you have sent us the forms asked for in our formal application—which, you say, are required; and until the Committee has acted on them and on us as individual instructors offering specific courses of instruction—which we have offered over a history of 20 years as a college in business, the Department of Public Instruction has not applied Section 254 of Public Law 550 to us.

We very much wish the Committee had done this. For it is now better than a year that we have been held up from accepting students under that Law, in spite of the fact that under the previous Veterans Education Law (the so-called "G.I.Bill") we were so approved. We want only the chance to have the chance to enroll those veterans of the whole United States who might want and gain from the individual instructors and unique sort of courses a College founded as Black Mountain was can give.

Our question is this: is there any will at all in the Department of Public Instruction, as reflected in the action of the Veterans Education Committee throughout the past year, to give us this chance, even when—so far as we can see—the U.S. Law includes a section which specifically covers and applies to both veterans and institutions just that chance?

It should be obvious that this College is most anxious to work this thing out with and through your Committee: we have been trying to, for over a year. Some of the Faculty, for example, wanted me to ask you if the second paragraph of your letter of May 6th, in which you say "except when these courses or the institution", indicates that there is a policy of "accrediting" individual courses pursued by the Dept. of Public Instruction? If so, if that is a *modus* in our instance?

The majority, however, take it that the paragraph rests on the clause, the "present policy"—and, as I said above, that that policy actually is an application of Section 253 instead of Section 254.

It would seem to us to come to this: if there is any chance that the Committee would review that "policy", will you be good enough to send us the forms asked in our formal application of April 6th so that the Committee might, for the first time, actually consider our application for approval as we are given to understand Section 254 of Public Law 550 requires.

If not, and your letter of May 6th does constitute the ultimate action of the Veterans Education Committee, we see no course open to us but to appeal the whole matter directly to the Federal authorities responsible for the full discharge of the Law.

So let us hear from you at the earliest possible moment. And believe us, both the invitation to yourself to repeat your visit, and to Dr Hillman to repeat his, stand: it was a pleasure to have you and your family here.

Cordially yours,

Charles Olson, Rector
Black Mt College

71

To Gerald van de Wiele (1954)

Great care was taken with the (few) students who applied to Black Mountain College in its later years. None was appreciated more than the recipient of this letter, who later evoked from Olson one of his finest poems, "Variations done for Gerald Van De Wiele," undoubtedly because of the young artist's loyalty, which he expressed to Martin Duberman in an interview: "I don't believe I ever in my life felt that I belonged any place as much as I felt I belonged to that school. I loved that place" (*Black Mountain,* p. 407).   *Letter (carbon copy) at Raleigh.*

Office of the Rector
August 30, 1954

Mr. Jerry van de Wiele
5628 South Lake Park
Chicago 37, Illinois

My dear Jerry van de Wiele:

Just a letter to tell you how pleased I am that you are coming. Fiore and I have gone over your application and both because of our impression of it and of you from your visits here, we want you to know that we are admitting you without waiting for letters from your references. These letters have gone out and I believe you have already received a letter from Elizabeth Baker on the money business. Those matters anyway will be settled with the treasurer after your admission has been approved.

Keep in touch, and we'll see you round about September 20.

Cordially yours,

Charles Olson, Rector

P.S. In dealing with the V. A. you will probably be asked to state one field or course of study. It can be either painting or writing according to your choice, and either way you will be able to get instruction in both.

72

To William Carlos Williams (1954)

In a letter of 29 April 1951, Olson told Robert Creeley that he had just written a short note to "Papa Bill," having heard about his stroke: "always such a pleasure to write to him, yet, i do it no more than once a year: funny, that, but, seems to be the way it comes out, and (like with cagli), doesn't seem to subtract fr movement of, affection between same" (*Olson-Creeley Correspondence*, vol. 6, p. 24). That short note and Olson's "annual" letters for 1952–1953 are missing, but we have the letters from late 1954 in which Olson, trying a last-ditch attempt to put Black Mountain College in a viable position, is recruiting Williams, or his name at least, to the colors.

First and second letters at Yale; third letter (carbon copy) at Storrs.

[letterhead]
Black Mountain College   Black Mountain, N.C.

November, 1954

My dear Bill:

The formal part is this. The Faculty here asks me (small as we are, we are that, call it so, a painter, a composer, an actor, a weaver, a potter, and three writers, one of whom teaches such languages as Provencal, Mallorcin, Catalan—one Robt Hellman—and another of the writers edits the *Black Mt Review*—from Mallorca, Mr Robt Creeley, than whom etc.—and both the mag and him you know

all right. These all—and count me in as desirous, so very desirous too, that:::::

will you, William Carlos Williams please consent to accept our joint invitation to constitute, with Albert Einstein, physicist, William De Kooning, painter, and Norbert Wiener, mathematician, the first four members of a new Advisory Council for this collidge?????

What it means is this: that, without necessarily putting your life on the line for a college, but out of your knowledge of the literary push here, would you let us have your name to identify us to the world at large as a group of men who, at least in the writing biz, would seem to you competent to give the young an education in how to begin?
                    In other words,
what we would like to assemble, based on you four, is a carefully picked group of men whom we respect—and who respect us—to see if we can thus do what promotion and publicity damn well isn't what we care about: give the world a sense that real men know enough about what goes on in this isolate desolate somewhat busy place, so that the young will get here and get what we got to offer
                    I dare say you should also
want to know if this involves you in any fuss. None, so far as I can see, at all. We would simply join your name to these, and carry as a pennant to the world, to say, here's a damn little boat wants to keep moving, because it thinks it does this education thing clean. And puts writin, paintin, weavin, musicin, actin, potterin at the center of how one might

then want to find out something: knowledge would then be the cat
some man or girl swings, not, the, reverse

What we god damn well need is just a little money to go on (haven't
paid ourselves since January last, yet, in that time, have added the Black
Mt Review, now include the Divers Press, Jargon Press under the wing,
and have added Creeley and Hellman to the Faculty, as well as a new
young weaver (23 yrs old), a new potter (Blunk, from Japan, coming, age
28), and, with spring, shall have (we hope) Martin Sprengling, age 80!
from the Oriental Institute, Chicago, to give us the word on the alphabet etc, as such things arose in the Middle East, 3500 BC to 1500 BC. It's
that sort of a rumpus you'd be lending your name to.

                              And no touches
on you: all from us out to da world. Which we want to let know about
us.

    WELL: please, if you possibly can. It would honor us.

                                        (PS: as
you have damn well done same by me in those letters on Max to Wms,
which, hereby, I tell you were a shot in this arm! Muchas gratias. And
god bless you for telling me!

                        LOVE,
                              Olson

[letterhead]
Black Mountain College   Black Mountain, N.C.

                              Friday Dec 3/54
BillBillBill:
    Great. And thanks, from all of us: the honor, Mister Lovely Man, is
Black Mountain College's.

                    Lawdamercy: the Beloit Whitman is in here,
and that Jewelled Prize of yours is such another as the Work in Progress
(of which I imagine it is a part?

                    I did the craziest thing with it. Have
been reading such things as round & about 1500—William Cornish,
a guy named Heath whose first name didn't come down. And Skelton.

And happened to set yours—this new one—right on top of Skelton's
two or three to two or three Mrs. (Wentworth, etc.

You oughta hear
yrself in that context! It's real gone, all out, wild: even yr Anthony &
Cleopatra gets that *ring* of, the call of, like you mean it, the, luffers as
poets (the "Ivy Crown"?) also: "fair Isyphill"

And still the craziest, to
me is how that three-line

> We are only mortal
> but being mortal
> can defy our fate

the way you have
placed it there, doesn't at all be . . . oh, of course, it's the "doubts" does
it! Beautiful

OK. Just to tell you. And the thorns. And the children. And the last
three lines doing just that. (By the way, that biz of yrs, that the will,
shall be once more, a garden is

well. Uh-huh.

You are blessing life all over the place—people (and now this place,
for which I am personally moved, as well as these others are, I can tell
you:

we will be mounting an appeal shortly, and from the dough won't
you and Flossie take off, fly down here, I meet you at the Asheville-
Hendersonville airport, and you come stay here awhile, just to get away,
and do anything you damn well please?

If you can, it could be a "vacation," like they say, in the "mountains."

Well, try.

Ok. Love,

C Olson

———————————

Tuesday Dec 21

BILL: the word I don't hear in all this is QUANTITY—and it's the only
one which makes sense to me. That is, you know how far I had got,

back when you reprinted that Pro Verse gig: that it was the syllable and the line. Well, lately, I've been trying to see it more exactly, and in the last two months, batting out a book on how it is now by way of looking at how it was suddenly circum 1602 when, so far as I can see, Campion soundly up and sounded a blast against rime and meter (meeter he spelled it). I was led into this by pleasure in Shakesp. own late verse, lines here and there like

wheat rye barley vetches oats and pease

very flat, very much bigger than those sounding lines makes blank verse such a damn bore (even when it is absent thee from felicity awhile etc)

now why i don't think foot means anything is that it can only mean that which one does with sd foot listening, say, to jazz: tap tap tap. Yah. Just keeping the beat. In other words has nothing to do with the *a-ccent* of words.
The accent of words now, at least, would seem to be essentially only a rise and fall of ict-us, and thus about the same level of the art as breath—that is, those sorts of stoppings, which phrases, or consonants ending one word and beginning another, involve the voicing in. But the third force of prosody (calling accent & breath 1 & 2) would seem to me the prime: how long it takes to get the letters, syllables and words out. It's that slowness they used to talk about as of English. God bless its slowness. What's wrong with slowness? Actually my own impression is English-American says a hell of a lot, and says it fast enough, slow as it is. It even dances on the tongue, doesn't have to be all those sibilants etc—or whatever it was used to be thought to be the virtues of the "larned" tongues. Bah. If this tongue we use is vulgar, like they say, let's make the most of it.

In other words, if I can't get beyond quantity as the true, then I'm still talking about syllables, and the line. That is, the only token I know for ending sd line is the sense that the music of quantity has spent itself for that phrase of time, with whatever play (what I think you mean by relatively stable foot) of some certain repetitions (accent & breath, and parallels of quantity) have occurred in that time-space

So I guess I'd
put it that the relatively stable thing is not the foot but the line—a relatively stable line

And what I think is behind my damn great pleasure in your own
later verse is those *dimeters* you got there (especially in *Work in
Progress*, where I think it's working like a steam engine

But aren't they lines, not feet???? that is, isn't their true force because
they are broken out like that, and represent quantities of the articula-
tion rather than any patterns??? (that is, patterns of symmetry such as
feet, in the old sense—da*da*, da*da*, da*da*—were?

The advantage of quantity is it puts it right back in the mouth: how
one gets the letters enunciated. And all that glot of consonants, and
what moo those vowels do accomplish, the sweet things. It's dentals,
labials, thoraces, or whatever those linguistic bastards call all those
parts of speech, one might call them, just to cross em up: hard palette,
soft palate, whatever!
And gets that biz of how we do, despite common
pronunciations—all that accent is anyway, isn't it? that one will say
labratory, another, the bloody Englishman, will say laBORatory—how
we do differ, in getting the words out of our mouths. How great: that
we do. There's, the play I count on. The people say the sherffs office, all
one fast syllable

Ok. Just to get this off, as a beginning. Been all day

The carbon copy at Storrs breaks off at this point. Olson may have gone on to
mention the appeal he had just written: "To All Those Who Care For Black
Mountain College." Presumably he sent a copy to Williams, as he did to others.

73

To Vincent Ferrini (1954)

Olson knew he had "drubbed" Vincent Ferrini mercilessly in "Letter 5" of *The
Maximus Poems*. While his Gloucester friends rallied for a fight, Vincent "held."

But it was not easy. The line in the poem that "hurt deeply for its tart freshness" was: "There is no place we can meet." Ferrini thought it had "the finality of the irreversible" (*Maps*, no. 4, "A Frame," p. 51). Cid Corman has described the tenseness of driving Olson up to Gloucester on 12 September 1954 to effect a reconciliation:

> We arrived just after noon and Vin came to the door. Charles crawled out, straightened up, strode to Vin, took him at once aside and in to a separate wing of the house, embracing him and asking for a drink. They joined us half an hour later in the extra-rented part of the soon-to-be-condemned house that was used as a sitting room. Larry Eigner had been alerted to Olson's coming and his father duly delivered him. Olson took a seat opposite Larry, in his wheelchair by the fireplace. Vin was seated on the rug beside Charles. The big man read a little, upon request, from his poetry and asked if there were any questions. Larry, spasmodically trying to frame his words (and C.O. frankly unnerved by the task of trying to cope with the garbled sounds), came out with, finally, as repeated by someone else in the audience, "Why did you attack Vinc in your poem?" Olson flushed and the room was exceptionally quiet as he began to work out a reply, naturally in terms of the larger thesis involved and not as a personal attack. It wasn't quite coming off. At which point, unexpectedly, his wife, Con, who had been visiting in a nearby North Shore town, entered—to his transparent relief and joy. I never saw so large a man move so fast as he eagerly embraced her, and the scene ended there (*The Gist of Origin*, pp. xxviii–xxix).

In the Arriving was written, as Ferrini put it in the above-quoted memoir (p. 52), while he "was hot with the sting of Letter 5 . . . in the white heat of rebuttal"; but it turned out to be "a 32 page love poem to him, his 'brother poet.' " There was, however, at least one remonstrance: "love does not / judge / he / is / too busy / making / anew." The letter below is Olson's response to *In the Arriving*.

Letter at Storrs.

friday dec 54/

BY GOD VINCE
    this is a gentle remonstrance   And moves me to the core. (Wild-wildwild is the color of my true love's place   And sweetsweetsweet is the silence of true)thought   you

                              give me such a thing back (the slap
of the hand

missing) that:

     listen, right off the bat, having just this
minute put it down after the sweep of the first—and I, today, silly
with a cold, and obviously not in the best shape ((having just previous
looking

    at Jonah/coming out of/the mouth of/a
    Big Snake // and a Big Snake coiled
    around the good/ tree (and whether apples
    or a fleece-(ing, JAY- son, who
    married fair Ipsypiel, oopshy-peal, oooo

           (you see?

so (I'll be back—forever?—to this text ((and why not, why shouldn't
we, like we said, one wharf, two doors down from Florence Evans and
Florence Cunning-no-ham, one night, late, not so long ago, why shldn't
we, you & me forever, swap

      camotes? eh? let's/let's carry on this collo-
quy until the lights either come on or go out, what do you say?

      And no candles. no. Electric-
LIGHTS. Yes sir. Three sheep full.

     Yessirs.

      whhottoyah yah say
by god what an idea, that the very remonstrance (the moon's MON-
STRANCE (monster eucharist)

     the very monstrance you here offer me (gen-
tly, gentle

   MOO-
n—oh goddess excellently bright, be with us,

       hey FERRINI!

         it's
wonderful—to write letters—in PRINT!

I'll quiet down. Or try to. For I do want to pick up on one passage
immediately, which sends me, pure, as yours, and all the way out,
gone, real:

how you have it, as though Mason Andrews was reporting, that

the Gudrun
hasn't been seen by any passing
stranger, gull
or heard by any sea town wharf
for 2 years

and we here wait
           for news
another scanning from the window of
Connolly's short stories

& who shall deny or condemn
the pitch of any voice
or the meat of his meaning

it is not one tongue
that speaks for this country
we talk so much about

no one knows
what the other does
or is changed
by how he works
         change—
           Sable

it's this
Gudrun, of
course, sends
me: you sub-
tile fell-
ow

  (may i
maybe steal
it?

   That is, if
I didn't have
a cold today I
bet i'd ride out
on such a vess-

hell

     But the other
thing is i think this
whole passage, & this

"it is not one tongue
that speaks for this
cunt-

ry, no one

of course.   and you'd know i
wouldn't.

Yah.   Great.   And THANKS.   Look: i shall be back, i bet! It is
that damned question: how does one? (And I don't think you know
that the epigraph the maximus will carry when done, is this:

      All my life I've heard
      one makes many

How is it
done?

Crazy. Real crazy!

Charles

74
To Raymond Souster (1955)

Olson was not to meet Raymond Souster until his visit to Toronto in April 1960, but somehow, by the time of this letter, he had already warmed to this young ambitious Canadian poet enough to send him poems for four issues of the mimeographed *Contact* magazine, and to read Souster's *For What Time Slays* (1955) with some care. He evidently thought him worth a good talking to.

Letter at Lakehead.

Black Mt   Oct 8/55

My dear Raymond/
                Thank you for *What Time Slays*/Wld like to sit
down and go over each of em

As you know I have a strong sympathy for what you have been doing. And so I want to speak out to you

It comes to this question of what society is (I told a girl here in her dream that 7 is the society of woman but 8 is woman). What this new volume declares is, that you must get on to 8, which is 4, which is 1 (to reverse Maria Prophetissa, or the Jewess, or the Copt, or Isis, or the sister of Moses, or Anti-Mary Magdalen, etc), in fact to make a point of Paracelsus:
                that 4 has the power of 1, only it has more power

You will forgive me if I say there is not a personal poem here (and I don't mean person as personality). I mean Souster the man, like the rest of us, with much coming at him, coming from him, the which is more complex than even any verbal component can declare (no matter how very fine that component)

That is, you must catch all these falling things like as tho you were a kid outside the Leafs park who tried to grab that ball your Pa poled over sd fence into the Bay—as tho that kid was willing to go into the water (is, in fact, as water, you, Souster, or any of us, all fingers, like water, trying to close—trying to close over that long ball

And you ain't doing that, man. You is Yonge Street. Exactly what you despise. You is staying pavement (instead of the crack in it). You is linoleum.

Now I see that what you sought was a sympathetic magic. But I would urge you that here is a fallacy of another century (a century still hanging in this one): the comparative. (Note, Ray, the number of occasions and subjects which are generalized as a street is. Or a newspaper.

I come back to society. You shld study with some constancy your own line

    Or more simply too much pity to waste on the
    people of this earth.

        It just ain't true. Number 1: no man has enough. #2: it ain't pity anyhow anybody wants (check DHL on Whitman, and how (for any of us to whom polis: Whitman, me, you, say) how DHL carries the knife good on exactly what shit love is in same. (But his care, note, to distinguish the OPEN ROAD from LOVE:

#3—and here is where I carry the knife: the pity, sir, is home.

Thus man i come in hard. And don't mind me. I wld be straight with you, like they say. I have believed in what you swept up. Now you must make a broom (the Blind make the best brooms, they say.

Do nothing but disentangle the split seconds (the water drops) of one R S. Forget sd old ladies with no pennies, sd lays, sd self, sd bed, sd poets, sd arts and society, sd whatever—even the sparrows or the squirrels.

SD RS alone. WOW

Society is no more than what is outside. Thus there is no more generalizing possible (sex crime sentimentality) as of the hoomins, than as of how nature happens to you—which is surely not as a tabloid falls down in the street. That is, I am begging you to pay attention to how small and exact your own experience is.

And no matter how the counters of protest have been of use for some time when you were Yonge, they are for any one of us soon not at all the equal of (that is, the protest forever, but the *experience* is quicker

It's this *quickness.* . . .

No relative or comparative or complementarism—no description will equal it.

There is a sourness you are not heir to. Or why would you have— why not make a success, eh? why not have that ticker tape Miss Scott?

At which point one can talk of the verbal component, the art of verse.

You deserve it: you owe it to your

Language is to be as thick as water, to be as hopeless.

Then, if it can't catch, you can measure the displacement (you can put a boat in)

You admire too many men—not to practice. The bourgeois are a bore. They are not interesting. No poet can make them interesting— even by slaying them. They are dead before you lift them into your subject. All numbers, dispersed numbers.

The thousand pieces of your littered mind is true and not at all true: that is, at any given instant (verbal instant) there is only 1/ Mind you: 1. Or a choice between 1 or 2. Positively: you are binary not millennial. (The millennial is solely the *massa confusa* of experience as it is distracted, of the swelling of the mother turtle in us: to be overcome.

My point is to urge you to close, to come in, to deal with the double. Why I say broom. Why I urge, blind.

Words are blind. Let em be. Light won't come from opening the fingers. The fingers want to close.

OK. Hell, but believe me. I wish no more than what you do.

How are you? What's new? Miss CONTACT, I can tell you. Was a loss. Was a thing   (KPA Taylor, by god, summers in the Monte Vista Hotel here in town—and we never see him!! And this Gael Turnbull, what of him? Is he Toronto too? Write me a letter of yrself. And poems of same.

Affectionately,

Olson

75

To Larry Eigner (1956)

"Maybe the most of the trip was coming on EIGNER in Ferrini's house," Olson wrote to Robert Creeley (letter of 30 September 1954 at Stanford), just after his visit to Gloucester. "What a beautiful thing! The eyes the most. And this wild whirling body, frothing at the mouth, listened to for the things come out of that head! So direct and witty and delightful." These two "north of Boston" poets maintained a cordial although not close relationship. The reference to "arbitrary etymologies" has not been tracked down; it may be in a letter from Duncan to Eigner. *Letter at Berkeley.*

[letterhead]
BLACK MOUNTAIN COLLEGE   BLACK MOUNTAIN, N.C.

June 20

Larry—

Thanks for the delight of yr card—please write more often, & don't mind that I am slow (this place occupies what time I have beyond my "studies". . . .

What that Duncan means by arbitrary etymologies is a part of his department of misinformation =s "invention". Note that he includes it along with puns—& *note!* with projective verse!

He means etymologies *one makes up!* Wow! You will imagine how I don't figure that one, being, as you sd (Gloucester) a hound for meaning!

Comes any word I go the other way, and what's most needed right now is an *Indo-European* Dictionary—*roots*, so one can feel that far back along the line of the word to its first users—what they meant, in *inventing* it, not any one of us at the most free-wheeling drag-race time in man's gasses
                    —I'll not only let you know if we actually hold this session (we *have* to have a guaranteed income to cover costs this time, or no operation) but both Dunk's work & my own is going toward publication
          (I have promised Cid I'll have ready what now seems best to be a sort of précis of it for his culminating Origin 20

Please send me any new poems
                              And write
                                        Love,
                                                  Olson

76

To Edward Marshall (1956)

A month before Black Mountain College was to close, Olson was planning a metamorphosis, a spreading of energy: Robert Duncan and Wesley Huss would do theater in San Francisco; Robert Creeley would continue the *Black Mountain Review* from New Mexico, and Jonathan Williams would be the official publisher; and here Olson is soliciting Edward Marshall's interest in editing a newsletter. Marshall was a young poet from the Gloucester area, whose "Leave the Word Alone," published in the *Black Mountain Review,* had impressed Olson very much.   *Letter at Buffalo.*

August 20, 1956

My dear Ed:

As a part of the re-conception of this place now in progress, wld you take on to edit a new small sheet which at least Duncan and I are pledged to supply material for?

The idea is this: that a fast, essentially a press form, of printed matter to get ideas & books out and circulating forcefully (a sort of constant Boston Commons) as, say, some title such as BLACK MT NOTES

VALUES (?)

(anything better you think of, great) . . . *reviews,* as notices (e.g., right this minute I have come to know the new national weekly of the "Conservatives", the *National Review:* I shld like to have a say on it now it's on my mind; or last week picked up (thru John Wieners) this "Ishmael Complex" in article in *Commonweal* on the book on Melville called *Ishmael:* I am asking the publishers to send me it for review

statements, as principles discovered: Duncan has grabbed on to this notion of *the peripatetic nature of learning* at this stage in these States, and wld have his 2 paragraphs of what he calls *condensare* on that, quoting John Adams "I will rouse up my mind and fix my attention" and Giedion on the maximum interplay of moveable parts

sentences (one fr a letter of Mike Rumaker on why he writes, e.g. comes to mind

Now my sense is, your mind is, and yr sense of the polemic now called for, etc.:

we have this new printer here, John Grady (formerly publisher of the Eastport Journal); I believe I cld get the money set aside fr the college for stamps, cost of paper; we have mailing lists

I should price it at 15¢ an issue say small 4 or 6 pages—letter sheet broadside conceivably; and issue it irregularly—whenever you felt you had a clean body of quick sharp material which deserved to be called to other's attention

The *bias* wld be: (1) *education,* as peripatetic (Duncan?)
                    (2) *politics* as value not junk (who?
                    (3) *learning* as constelled today best via mytho-archeo-bio-geo- (my kick, and I dig stuff for you

(4) *religion* (yourself
(5) literature & art, but *only* as force in Culture not
"art" (aesthetics) except when fit (?Creeley?

You cld be where you are, or anywhere you are, and merely gather the stuff, paste it up, in other words be "The Editor, Edward Marshall", and ship it to Grady here at the print shop to issue; and I can try to see if we cld also get you some small stipend for doing it (at least yr stamps and paper etc cld be covered)

Now: this is only one piece of a series of pieces to make a set of this new set-up of the place. And only if I can get them all in shape, and backed, can I say SET.

So please regard this as breaking it to you, to see how it first sits with you—if you'd be interested. Write me back, and I'll then take it another hitch.

Then, if all pieces prove possible (say, by two weeks) I can let you know for sure.

Meanwhile start figuring abt it, and make any suggestions: point is, to make it small fast cheap firm sharp—and like a news release or broadside, in format (even maybe a newspaper pulp???

Ok / just to give you the juice

Yrs,

Olson

Marshall's response from New York City on 30 August 1956 was: "Wonderful idea! . . . I shall call my broadside Cross-Town Muses" (letter at Storrs).

77
To Ruth Witt-Diamant (1957)

Robert Duncan was the organizer of Olson's two-week visit to the Poetry Center of San Francisco State in February 1957 to present "The Special View of History," among other things. Ruth Witt-Diamant, head of the English department, was his hostess, as she was for many other visiting poets. Back at Black Mountain, Olson wrote a thank-you note. *Letter at Berkeley.*

[letterhead]
The Black Mountain Review

April 1/57
My dear Ruth: Forgive me I am so slow to thank you, but it has been nothing but real estate trial fire couplings natives etc since back. Bloody thick. Maybe yesterday made final deal—or something close to it. So. . . .

Pt is, you mustn't also mind kickbacks (James wrote me you phoned him, upset at something abt our stay: if my tongue in any way hurt you my tongue also can tell you straight you sure carried us, and with me really in a sweat and with the damn weather the same: look, the next time. And please: give us a chance to entertain you. Come here. Or we'll be where you are. Jean and Stephen likewise (Chas Peter in levis and a top shirt J gave him carried his visit into this scene, and he swaggers!

Also, the recording has come in, and I shall get Jonathan to take me out to a place tonight where we can hear it (the poems done at the station don't sound so hot: actually the College tape (even if I sound like Wm Carlos—or Ginsberg—anyway Paterson—what I once called Bill's Jersey dum-smoke voice) makes it the most of anything yet done

The whole trip still stays upstairs, and hasn't come down into me, simply that I can't, until Black Mountain is now over. But maybe that is the trip: it gave me a good bite of the world again—the apple—and I want it. I want the original sin. This place (like all Utopia) is full of soap—like that old riddle, an Old Maid and a Nun in the Bath

In other words, this is just over the fence, or across the hall, and let's keep on

Fondly, & for mine   —Charles

Olson was invited for a return visit by Witt-Diamant in December 1957, but had to refuse: "a very hard decision . . . I hated so to give up the chance to come" (letter at Berkeley).

78

To Robin Blaser (1957)

This is the first letter of an interesting correspondence with the poet-philosopher Robin Blaser, which will be published in a complete edition.

Letter in possession of the recipient.

Black Mountain
May 3, 1957

My dear Robin Blaser:

You couldn't have timed your generous and gracious letter more. I've been sunk in the debris of the property of the College—I mean, in the process of selling it, and meeting a suit against the College by some of its own for wicked reasons—alone with the event, and with the fruitlessness of money and property after the will has departed (not my own will, for one reason I stay doing it is to realize assets to continue at least those parts of its program which are afoot and make sense to me, that is, the men who are doing it do: Robt his plays, Creeley the magazine, Jonathan the publishing, and—if I cld mount them—the "Institutes" in what I do believe is a New Learning—

((date 1875 I'd take to be something like 1300, and not, say, 1429 which was the Renaissance, and the change of 1875 was on an order to establish premises which go out the back door of Athens at 500 and probably the change is only, as I remember once preaching in "Gate & Center", the 2nd Heave!

What I started to say was, yr letter came just as I was wrapping up the sale of the rest of the property, and I had no will for it after this trial two weeks ago, it all had become too long and too late, interminable, even the climax was a 5th Act when it shld have been a 3rd! ((5 Form, which I respect in Chaucer's Troilus, but no time thereafter, all "Beethoven", even Wm Shaxpere!

And you equate breath with texture, and I am made again, I have lifted since, going abt the tedious details of selling old automobiles desks etc

That you say texture gives me more light on Pro Verse than I have ever had, I do believe. Suddenly I comprehend much of "space" as a principle of order (a new principle I shld think, thinking at the moment of Melville on the tail of the whale, which has struck is as the purest Non-Euclidean act in writing yet ((but what is the 85th Canto????

                o yes, of course, the restoration of the internal object into that space (that is, Melville's whale's tail is the 1st time external object got treated fr a position of space as no longer only external—that "perspective" we were deluded in after Giotto; but Pound's Sagetrieb is word as object capable of its own gravitation *because* it is understood that man is a space which is the root of physical space and therefore. . . .

Man is shafted by, & thus is more interesting than—sap, that each year the trees do. One does not cancel one with the other. It is merely—la difference, vive la difference.

And Dante: for two springs now I have come back to him on words, shaggy combed out glossy etc. (Used them past December in a piece on Shakespeare's last plays, for the BMR). But his count, his sense of the power of 3, say, of asymmetry:

                what I wanted to say to you is (and I have not, in the debris of my days still, had a chance to read yr poem), hold fast to yr power over old form, let you only be busted out of it like the door of a safe when some nitroglycerine you may not even yet know has been applied to the crack in yr door, blows you open

        For yr poem, pay death's and those earlier four I saw in a magazine (an angel, songs, death, the Virgin Mary???)

                these masterpieces of what you will understand if I call old form, are too important for you to lose in any welter:

                        until that welter say has blown you up, broken yr door off

                          I say it under the sign of quaternity:

                look, Robin, 3 *and* 4. We need 4 badly, all of us. It is form in life. We have to go like feathered daggers propelled as automatic Colt

revolvers into the place between form and form in life, and a characteristic of post-1875 is that (1) we have to have what we want but (2) there
is no end to what we need. I protest any patriotism of any "New form."
It is a bore unless it is as wide as a whale's tail. Or, sagetrieb is!

Ok. Just
to pour it out to you, in my gratification you have found anything in
Max or PV to stir you yrself up as you go.

I jump with yr identifying breath with texture. It gives me all I ever
wanted to protest that stupid oral verse, and voice! Shit. It is not sound,
sound, like all the other powers, are eternal, and one participates in it,
like form, the moment one attacks *a* form.

And the problem, anyway, is reality and language, *any* use of it—*a* use
of it, not just a poem. Lord! If we wrote a poem except both (a) to write
a poem *and* (b) because we can't help to, and breathe!

Wow. I sure say breath, like testing whether a person is alive, on a mirror, does it show—I mean not the mirror, it is now opaque, there is fog
on it, this girl does breathe! Ain't it the greatest?

Esau's hand, as well as Jacob's, as well as: hair on it, or not, but that the
word or not the word in that moment—"space"—is right. C'est n'est
pas le mot juste, c'est le mot shaggy ou glossy, le polysyllable ou le
monosyllable. Or as Fearless Fosdick will not lose his head to la gullo-
tine because les americains possede l'honeur. L'honeur!
        That she be there, in
all
    her
        splendeure!

Ya. Great. Gracie! M. Blaser

Love, O

Please keep in touch—and all power to you in whatever
Olson

1 8 7 5

Even 1300 had still the formal and spiritual unhinged fr the physical, due, I suppose, to the validity of Xty. Xty (ecstasy) was still valid, Augustine had not yet spent what Giotto was the other evidence of, that East-West was One Eye still. Or again. Yet that there was a division of powers, the form and the content were in some imagined struggle, an agony. Instead of as I take it we start a-new fr zero, like some plane, each time we take off. Our agon.

1429 was merely a dialectic to support the increasing vulgarity of space—which was still object-ridden, the geography of Ptolemy lasted until the Americans chopped up everything in a Bessemer process.

Greekism. Or Egyptianism (better Xty be taken like the lousy Tarot cards of Alouette-Etoialla than to bother with Hebraism: it's being dished out backwards these days if you know the Bulletin of the American Schools of Oriental Research, each issue of which—Albright and such, his boys—exposes the Mesopotamian behind the Hebrew thing until one doesn't even have Semitism, one has Sumerian source: "I weep, *fountain* of Jazer"

> When there were no depths
> I was born, when there were no sources
> of the fountains of the sea
> (sd Maximus)

Mosesism is best taken as fr Egypt, fr Ahknaton.

As Hindooism is better seen to be fr the same division of the East-West Monocular as the other one, Moses, who produced the half-truth monotheism

All of these typologies of our thought are Renaissance-ridden: they divide up what is indivisible (by principle of quaternity) and then are on our back as a dialectic as burdensome as Hegel. Just because it is formal and spiritual we are more intimidated than we are by metaphysics at this point of time. So we stay ridden.

I am saying much went out the backhouse cut-outs, the moon-
shapes and hearts, come 1 8 7 5

Landscape; and stereoscopic vision, "monkeys apes and men in
which overlapping images permit three-dimensional perception at a
short distance—e.g., at hand's length"

> At hand's length I now grapple
> to confine
> the overlapping flaking
> of the core, no waves
> I am left with the fine edge
> of my amulet fingered
> in my pocket, if I shaved
> any longer I'd try
> the neolithic razor
> on my hair, the sea
> is postcard
> of my fountain
>   (he continued)

Geography is landscape, man's interference 1 8 7 5 thereafter, but of
course his interference is exactly as old as an eolith, sd first eolith used
by Homos Prometheos to get at a delicacy, a baboon's brains.

Thereafter man made dumps. And got cereals, and several other
things, including history. His. Hers. And more interesting than the latest two sorts of razors, one for her legs now that she is all male and
one for his now that he better hide his face. She is barkey. He wears
glasses.

Two big changes, c. 1 8 7 5

> Out of the dry sea,
> Dr. Moon. And tears
> now that the fountain,
> o Jazer: raise up your breaths,
> monkeys. Let us look on
> the windshield, the mirage

of the sun, the rain-slick
petrol-ridden

    Diesel-dewed
    is my rain-slip,
    dark is my glass-
    es, I'm following
    a truck

I am full, to overbearing
I play pocket-pool
with sources whose edge
cuts my finger
              Look Jazer:

    it weeps

For the finished poem "*'I weep, fountain of Jazer,'*" see *Collected Poems*, pp. 419–420.

79

To Michael Rumaker (1957)

Michael Rumaker seems to have been the person with whom Olson was most able to discuss dreams and the unconscious. On 28 January 1957, writing to Rumaker in San Francisco (where he had gone after graduation from Black Mountain College), Olson responded to a dream poem Rumaker had sent by enclosing the newly finished "The Librarian" as a counterexample: "any success there," he says, "is whatever transposition it does succeed in." The dream has to be changed by the act of writing, to get "reanimated in another form than the dream-form (the hardest form, I suppose, to force writing to undo, and recreate its own)." Rumaker responded to this by writing an essay, "The Use of the Unconscious in Writing," which was published by John Wieners in *Measure,* no. 2 (forwarded to him by Olson, as indicated in the letter below). The essay prompted Olson to turn to "the pro."—as he calls Carl Jung—and in this reply he incorporates two quotations from Jung's "Archetype of the Collective Unconscious," in *The Integration of the Personality* (pp. 89–90), which he owned.   *Letter at Storrs.*

Mike (Sun May 19/57

I turned back to the pro. (thinking of yr piece—also wrote John suggesting he use Sec. I in his #2, as ex. of true magick)

& found Jung being precise on our point, I take it: "The symbolic process is an experience in the image and of the image"

Also, he continues (& it is another statement of what you have so firmly put, that beauty, like the sacred, is dangerous:
"CURVAS PELLI-
GROSAS" was the title of a movie playing in Campeachy one night—with a bim filled with curves sticking out of the flyer on the CINE SELEM
      "The process, in its unfolding, reveals an enantiodromal arrangement like that in the text of the I-ging (I-ching?), and so presents a rhythm of destruction and creation, of error and truth, of loss and gain, of depth and height."

If you should run into anything in any of your reading on the "archetypes of transformation" I should be particularly helped to know it. For all that you and I are talking about it swings, I am sure, here—
      not the personified archetypes (the more familiar—my anima, yr old wise man, the shadow ((which I least understand!), but these archetypes of THE PROCESS!
That's where
story (action!
          image (lights!
CAMERA
love
O

PS: a propos the 1st quote above, in other words I take it he is saying the process is symbolic (good enough, no need to argue—transfer of force "a throwing together") but the material of the process is image. Which is what, as you know, I have always felt had to be insisted upon.

VII

Olson rented rooms in 28 Fort Square, Gloucester, in August 1957. He still had to return to Black Mountain one more time to deal with loose ends, but the move back home to Gloucester was accomplished. He and Betty would raise their son, Charles Peter, in the fishing town of Olson's own boyhood.

Then there was the history of Gloucester to absorb him. And the *Maximus* poems, now of epic proportions. By the time he looked up, it was 1963. He had been in hibernation for six years.

80

To Vincent Ferrini (1957)

The *Maximus* poems began in May 1950 as letters from Olson in Washington to Vincent Ferrini in Gloucester. By the first week of August 1957, Olson, his wife, Betty, and their son, Charles Peter, had become residents of Gloucester. Even though Ferrini was now less than a mile away, Olson wanted to restart the serial poem with what is obviously a letter. The text below was titled "MAXIMUS, Part II"; it was published posthumously, in *Olson,* no. 6 (fall 1976) pp. 61–62. It is presented here as an unsent letter of about 9 August 1957.   *Letter at Storrs.*

I return to the city and my first thought, Ferrini, is of you who for so long has been my body here and I a shadow coming in like gulls

Now that I am back

We are on the Fort, have the upper floor of Lorenzo Scola's house, over-looking the Harbor. As soon as we have a chair to sit on, etc.

It's the light (like she sd). Or that the sky is full of noise and variable, the harbor is big enough to be the size of the sky, the nights are not dead of sleep Birdseye is going all night they are taking out pogeys (actually black backs and shad) at the Fish Pier draggers are putting out any hour trying to get a load of trash in the Bay or to the west-ward. Sam sd yesterday they are trying to force fishing to stay alive here. Eddie Frigata (28, here 10 years and skipper of the Golden Eagle, in at Cape Ann Fisheries with 130,000 red fish) says the best years were '41 to 47, and he come in '48! Or Randy Lafond says (when I ask about his father, and we sit on the last of three wharves, two gone where I first went to sea in the Riggs, gill-netting), we didn't prosper

The future, Ferrini. Tourists, I hear the fishermen bellyache. Or just one big marina—for what lawyer Burke called in the City Council meeting this week the outboard motor cowboys

I laugh, from my height, and decide to tell you stories, Ferrini, so long as you will listen to me. I'm going to start them today, and I'll send them to you as they get done, just one right after another, to amuse you. Maybe by Christmas—

You see, I take it there are only two forms of mind about how it is human beings live on the earth. They either do, or they build nine chains to the moon

              (as that devil in pants Fuller called his book, whose very name Fuller—full a——

Geodesic.Horshit. O my geOmorphic sOul, Vinc: I citizen of the Cut now standing for election from the Fort just to see that the way of the mighty does not here prevail—the mighty mice (the boy downstairs tells me the one thing kids can spell in the pre-school— it's all pre-school—is, Mickey Mouse, Mickey Mouse Fuller the Builder of the Frostline, the Deep Freeze men, the Awk line, the Goofed

they are apparently winning Gloucester? Of course you know I don't think they got a chance, Gloucester's got reason: I want to go to England very soon to get the information to show how this city was in the mind of John White even without his knowing what she was, as a place to go fishing from. She is still a place to go fishing from. She is still le beauport. She is a form of mind.

81

To Betty Olson (1957)

Charles and Betty Olson were rarely absent from each other; when they were, their kind of togetherness did not beget long letters. The letters below come from the time of Olson's final trip to Black Mountain after he had just settled his family at 28 Fort Square, Gloucester. He wrote the first from Black Mountain on 2 October 1957; the second, special delivery from Frederick, Maryland, post-marked 5 October 1957, on his way home. *Letters at Storrs.*

Wed nite

My love—Trying to use the steam yr call gave me to get all paper work
done before I throw myself on to the last job of all—da books

So I'll get this check off, and pray god the next job—da books—gets
done during the night, and morning, and I leave this place of much &
little

Have an order of bean sprout & port cooling on the icebox (whc I hope
i sold to Pick for 20 cash, for gas on rd—gas i sd i did not rhyme i am
not a rhymer—well, I have read mr Thomas Campion

(what yr note-
book etc drove out of my mind was my careful reading of Thomas
Campion!

(and think I'm not sure mr C is such a howler as I thot, but
I can't read or trust my reading here—OK

free-
wheeling. Please light
a candle for me that it will be, and above all KEEP THE HOME FIRES
BURNING!

Mine are, love, yr hombre—and I mean man man!
I mean man

little ole charlie

———————————

[letterhead]
The Francis Scott Key Hotel, Frederick, Maryland

Sat night

Sweet one—

Made another 250 today, but it was rougher on me. Had fun though
by going most of the way new roads, via Appomattox Court House,
being pinched for crossing a solid white line ($16.25), and arriving here
for the Frederick Fair!—at which I saw two kinds of "Thrill" shows:—&
both of 'em this unbelievable new Junk America, one the grandstand
show turning cars over, piling into them in "death" & "killer" leaps, and
the other the dirtiest "girlie" show I ever did see—something Kansas
City right in the middle of the street of whores (or over Burnham's

Field in Gloucester) wldn't have countenanced. Wow. One's gotta stay off the streets! (I saw two, the other was straight burlesk, & had a stripper was a pleasure—much more down to earth, like the saying goes, than the hootch at "Port Said"! I walked out on the "Egyptian" dancer here tonight, who was billed to do a "gardenia" dance as a hootchy-kootchy!)

Am pretty beat but will let the hour I wake up tomorrow decide, whether to push on to Stony Point (it's another 7-8 hr shove going any fresh way, and it turns out to be the way to do it for me, such a pleasure to see new things) or dawdle along

So far it holds up, just to be coming to you gives it drive. But does it take time, the goddamn 1000 miles! Maybe even if I do get to Stony Pt tomorrow I better kick Monday away. Will see.

Am shovin along

Love, love—Charles

PS: I think I'll strike for Stony Pt anyway, catching Gettysburg, on the way, and going as far as I can stand it.—Yrs.

[back of envelope]

Sun morn:

Bad weather / heavy rain / whc means won't go Stony Pt today but half way Hellman's. So possibly Tuesday home—Wednesday probably for sure.

82

To Philip Whalen (1957)

Philip Whalen was one of the poets Olson met in San Francisco in February 1957. After receiving the second issue of *Evergreen Review,* the San Francisco edition, Olson wrote to Whalen: "I was in Maine last week with my daughter visiting Robert Hellman, and sure enuf it was your poems, and Bill Everson's, which he picked up on out of ER also. . . . if I was sure I cld write any more (after the past six months of nuthin) I wld want to do a piece called THE ARETE OF PHILIP WHALEN" (letter of 13 September 1957 at Reed). Before the end of the year Olson would write in this spirit, a poem, "The Company of Men," with the dedication "for Phil Whalen for Christmas 1957" (*Collected Poems*, pp. 423–424).

Letter at Reed.

Sunday Nov 17/57 "cld rain says Abe
Weatherwise"

My dear Phil:

isn't the seriality of all occasion (proceeding fr the consequent toward the primordial

"unbegotten & imperishable"

—than which whitehead principle I do not know anyone who hath caught on to what sd Christ seems to have figured out in

his bean (sometime between 4 AD, say, allowing he probably was a prodigy . . . talk abt Rimbaud, this other Bird was daid at 30, and had sure done some thinking before that date 30 AD ((even if one is led to suppose (by test of experience) that all his inventions of his image—last supper, the kiss, the crux, the descent, & the resurrect—came in a rush, probably all that week, and why he did retire into the garden and pray like mad, as well give over a bit on the sd crux asking God to come to his aid:

I mean, that the God of Nature (the Creator) isn't that big WoolyBooger who let it all fall out of his hair way back there (like yr lad Hoyle says, a Universe which began is a dodge for leaving there all the unanswerables, much better we assume a steady-state one) but the one sd christ invoked with some freshness (it must have been what he was hammering at the Teachers there at age 12 or thereabouts)

a God of man ("unmingled but undivided"), one who caught on a bit to what it was for sd creature to make it

(I figure Dostoevsky put it the most when he sd if Christ was proven not to be the Truth he'd stick with him)

(Can you tell me, fr yr studies in Tantric yoga etc, any evidence that, *previous* to *date* Xst, any man had so definitely replaced *myth* by *history?* that the acts of the life of the individual?)

I was taking you seriously, in yr letter, that you are bugged abt puttin work together. And nothing I have seen (except Dr Wms) changes my mind that all this biz of story poem novel is like easel painting: we don't know that. What we do know is what we do. I take it the poems of yrs I've seen, or anything out of yr mouth, or on paper, *hangs together.* That strikes me as enuf to make books or whatever. Put em together. OK, sd ma-HAT (hey ma look no brains), shuts up

    Am very laid open the last 137 hours and no good for this world (even missed the Great Gloucester Fire the night before last highest building Main St tho I guess Dr Bill once more has done fire up

                                             am way
back there where as boy i got hung up (what i mean the Donner Party   poor Reed making it down the Humboldt, not poor at all— found (at Sutter Fort Museum, in 1947) his map of his camp fires how he did get over thanks to daughter girl coming out to him on her pony with his hunting rifle after he'd been exiled ahead of the train for killing the wagonhand in anger at some mistake all the Company figuring he was a goner
                (do you know a paperback called The Buffalo Box??
                a beauty of the country by some journalist as hepped as
                myself on the Donners

the way a single *plane* will slip out of that above sd geometry of a special nature and extend itself like the celestial equator or the elliptic and go on freewheeling for the rest of a man's life (or does it? does he curve it back in? I'm just finding that one out, maybe
                              anyway, to investigate
such possibilities by doing same. It seems THE TASK (what did Cowper mean can you tell me do you read the classics? like you do Stein. And can help me

I damn well trust you (wow: please don't find that anything but a help

I guess I take it all the planes which slip out—or ain't brought to the
skin (that's another bale of fish): don't get out to the smooth 360 or—
what's more exacting—such protuberance as, around the earth's middle, causes sd precession of the equipnozes

(bedazzled anew that those
Indians had a Platonic Great Year themselves, and that at Copan on a
scientific anniversary they computed when *all* the stars and spheres
which were then as they were overhead day and night HAD PREVI-
OUSLY BEEN in exactly the same fix:

and it come out 456,862,359 or
something ANTE

I mean some such as the diffrunce the Continent
does do to the MIND and so to the attentions?

OH Whalen you is
such an Armorican I desire you poke right straight out—accumulating—and what novel? what poem? knows who knows what the
SERIAL is?

Oh yah if you won't mind let me get off my mouth the present sense
of what this means: the word is EOPITC (EOPTIC) god damn it
EPOTIC

not lyric (Dr Wms, a year ago this spring, when, for only time,
I'm in his house—with Hellman—"After all olson you are a lyric poet"
keeryst

NO.   and then there is drama and epic, right (doesn't it go
like that, and legit—in verse—that all 7 kinds of muses ((I can't for the
life of me figure that the two History and Astronomy are anything but
the two studies of man guidance vocational guidance as the Grks saw it
for correctly doing the 7 kinds

well, if there is a word to go for form
like American for the sd declared diffrunce, it's—dictum—epotic

Anyhow it gets me thru, at the moment. Rhabdos, the man sd, was
the root of rhapsody, not sewing song together but beating it out

Ok. Love, and by christmas
olson

83

To Allen Ginsberg (1958)

In January 1957, just before leaving for Tangiers, Allen Ginsberg dropped a line to Olson at Black Mountain College, inviting him to New York and making complimentary remarks about the recently published *Maximus 11–22* (what Olson calls "Max II"—"I" being *Maximus 1–10*). Olson responded on 19 January 1957 (letter at Columbia):

> So you'll also know how much balm it is to have you say you thot Max II
> something. Wow. I even judge you prefer it to I (?) In any case, that you pick
> it out, and right now, gives me go ahead. (You see the English—and Am.
> counterparts—give it the dish because, I take it, there's so much "history"
> in it. Shit. Don't they know I'm writin' saga (ha ha ha
>   (isn't it also true
> that you & K are biting into sd saga ((sounds like a sanskrit word, don't
> it?—that is, dimension not masks? and cld I urge you guys to grab hold of
> figures you take literally—and take yurselves likewise????

He also seemed to be worried about their trip: "THE STRUGGLE IS—(isn't it?)—NOT TO SLIP OFF INTO SPACE—OF ANY KIND."

Contact was resumed when Ginsberg returned and Olson was living in Gloucester. The main subject of the letters below (of 11 November and 3 December) is poetry itself. Asked in a 1971 interview about Olson's influence on him, Ginsberg said: "Oh, yeah, sure, I knew him well—I carried his coffin to the grave! Heavyweight influence, yes" (*Allen Verbatim*, p. 162).　　　*Letters at Columbia.*

> Nov 11
> 28 Fort Sq
> Gloucester

My dear Allen Ginsberg

Was in the City long enough last week to leave a message with Ronnie? (*Robbie?*) at the Cedar—hoping to fish you out, so we could sit down at a table, & eat

A great desire to see you, of all

Figure now to be back there quickly, to do just that. Some great hunger to talk directly about *the poem*, persuaded you care that way, &

set to any one of them with such sense of scope (& not necessarily sd
subject you bite off: this is for a Classical poet like Gary of consequence.
Strikes me we romantics (thou & I) want the thing to tremble otherwise (or wheres, like, be-
                              low, la-
                         bas sort of thing?
                                        Probably all this lazi-
ness at not being able to do any such thing. Not doing it.
                                        "Hunger," like
the lady boss sd, of the salesmen—for customers.
                                   I sure did write you
(before you went Algiers) damn delighted to have you warm to Max II
(still yrs, the *only* word on same! And I myself of small faith in it (except for the *La Cosa,* thinking the rest "tells" too much, & too little, by
getting wrongly subjective.
                         But then that edge of self-love & sentimen-
tality. . . . you awake me by standing so fully on the true mirror verge

    It was Phil who gave me, SF, at yr direction, *Xbalba*—& you there
at night, & back in the States, very much size to both the placing & the
question. I have the hunch you have some doubt just now about standing exactly on yr own troubledness (?
                              Presumptious. And excuse. Not
even the desire to take a shot in the dark.
                              A strong conviction the next
12th month will show about three of us are arrested—hung
                         "Not prophetic" (like the old buck
                         for which read one-horn Bill,
                         even with saddle sores) sayeth.
                                        Simply
by god I do distrust *any* power position. And verse & painting (&
music, *except* Boulez—conspicuously the exception, the rest) stuck
on power.

    Craving for something so *open* it hangs like the whole fucking
universe itself, in itself—trillions or whatever, who cares. At least my
dreams so instruct me. And without benefit of any authority. Or
reference—proper noun at all (Yes—*one*

Flower / though just
flowers right now have become too goddamned glib. The flower Glib

(I am having a terrible time trying to review Bill's PAT V—for Evergreen. Feel lousy, that it should be some younger person who is coming-
on to him, rather than I who (despite all statements by others) never
seem to have picked up on him as much—love the man, that's all (as I
gather you, too, no?

OK. Just to get over the fence
With love—
O

[On back of envelope]
Or (precisely on the form-of-the-poem biz) a better differentiation
than Classical-Romantic (which will do perhaps for the personality
difference) wld seem to be Classical-Gothic.
That is, I more & more
discover (e.g. say the "house" in the poem—& the dory/schooner:
"wood") that the *Maximus* thing winds down & out, & from, some
such older, & later, disposition than the Classical (Bach, & Holderlin,
say, being men I value more than—Goethe)

I dare say I am suggesting the form-struggle right now—for a poem
which will stay as open as, & be there as firmly—is some such clash as I
propose we are enlisted in (?)
Dharma is the *wooden* stage (-platform) plataformia, isn't it,
the railroad carriage you-I traveled in

My dear Allen:
One wants the soul lifted up. Back in business. Fair enough. No
longer does the death of children, with one fire escape, rouse the situation. (The corruption of event has been overtaken by the suppuration
of every thing & person.) And yr leap (practically a private one, so far
as I can see) into an alternative system makes very great *radical* sense
to me. That is, I'm not aware you place it on fellahin, and those ground
cries & pains you hover over to gather like a host body are the cries of

the undamned. And unblessed. Not a group of raiders, or displacers. It's good enough. (I don't know that I know which section of Howl was III, but it was the Moloch passage which struck me, when I read it last— last summer in Maine, Little Cranberry, to two artists (one writer one painter) at breakfast, to show 'em.)

I myself am interested in moving steadily ahead out of the miserable school fire—turning the subjective (screwing it) in, until there the traces (of the Energy) are the objective. And are not even "known" in the sense of the knowing power. Only the loving power, like the Unknowing Man sd etc. (It sounds misty, even as I say it—but then, that's just it, one does not want to break through the Cloud *until one does*, fire all the arrows, radical and dry, one wants into it, from below, until, one would go through.

Something like this, for today. (I leave out all my own feelings and thoughts on the hysterical, only because I so agree with you—without countenancing the word—that I don't know what to say other than what you do: many thanks for the quote of the boy in the asylum crying to them all, Come off it.

Love,
Olson

84

To Gael Turnbull (1958)

The late 1950s were fallow years, perhaps generally, and certainly for Olson—a fact he had to face up to when challenged to tell the poet and publisher Gael Turnbull visiting from England what of interest was going on.

Letter at Columbia.

28 Fort Sq
Gloucester Nov 12/58

My dear Gael Turnbull:
   Very great to hear fr you. Had wanted myself to write you a year gone now, at least when I heard you had polio, to wish you well, and rid

of it, and was happy to learn (as I believe it is true?) you dumped it all out of your system? Pray so

I went ahead, with White Rabbit Press, with the O'Ryan, and now that I have the whole back I am suggesting they issue a 2nd edition of 1-10 (you had persuaded me the even numbers were best!

Felt very badly at missing you, when I heard (in NYC last week) that you had come thru there—one of my lads overheard you say you didn't know if your work was so well known in the States (to Ginsberg) and he up to you and sez, Sir, I and others very well do know it (if you recall). I believe it was yr Icelandic poems I had thrust at that fellow (am I right, Icelandic? were those ever got together as a book?

Please (now you are here) keep me on. Feel myself hungry to move. So maybe we'll cross. At least in two years these years wow. Where might we be? I shld think sure to meet. (Gloucester doesn't keep me, as I thought it might. Perhaps I was for settling. Or something. And was a fool of my own bourgeoisness. I don't. Hungry. Etc. I still wld like to own a room (barn was preference) on ground my own here—where I cld leave everything behind. And git. To come back, if. Etc. That's abt what I was after. Plus to work the vein more directly. Which petered out fast. Rather I shld have come to England, as I then planned, I'm sure. That wld have given me a lift. And now the money is gone, perhaps!

I'm left, funny. Don't know myself. Have altogether other ways of feeling anything. Activity all somewhere else—and so puzzlingly displaced (for me) that I don't do very much. Or don't know how to. Tho suddenly, when something does come up, or is set to, I am in and on it much more (and less) to a satisfaction. (I dare say this is most familiar, in human history. But as you'd know just there is where I have no information. Perhaps I shld read novels, for years!)

The wild thing abt yr putting Capts Courageous and G together, is of course that the book, with Synge (via whom I wrote my first play, at 18, on sd same subject Gloucester) was the companion of childhood. So the movie, when it came, by god there I was in the back of the North

Shore—and the only time I ever saw fishermen at the movies, they
themselves all in the back rows turning to each other with gruff critical
observations abt the blunders (sea blunders) in the film. The most! The
film—and the factors. Crazy. But never cld see how to make a poem out
of it (after EEcummings, for all, ended that one, in his wonderful poem
to Sally Rand. . . . you know,

> she does, what the movies can't do, I
> mean, move

I dare say Allen put you on, but don't miss calling on Philip Whalen,
now that you are there in the Northwest: c/o Judge Richard Anderson,
County Courthouse, Newport, Oregon. It's on the coast highway
south fr Portland. —Oh yes, and a delightful old friend may by
chance be in Takoma: Wilmot Ragsdale (father in book). This just in
case you were idling in Takoma. Not sure he isn't solidly now in N.Y.
(Cancel: silly)

And what abt Gary Snyder? Isn't he somewhere there too??? (Very
wonderful poems of his shooting out these days.
                                                          Also Mike McClure,
in San Francisco, whom you are sure to meet, I guess (as well as all
there)—do dig John Wieners out of whatever hole he's in. For some
poems of his this summer were really on, in a French way which lighted
up his natural sensational Irish powers so the plums stayed on trees, instead of falling off and rotting all over the ground (no matter what fine
grass I thought that made, the next season, anyway!

You come to the States at what strikes me as a wonderful date: a
whole crop of first rate poems being written. And those same (as I had
occasion to say to Ginsberg) cutting right through between too much
smartness (incredible gifts, but not enough difficulty) and of course the
usual "poetry" loose all over the place.

Also, when you have seen Dunk, wld love to hear fr you abt him: he
hasn't written me anything of his work in 9 months, and miss knowing
what he's up to (always, of course, believing in his star—or candlelight,
as he prefers, I think, to picture himself, like the Hermit in the Tarot
cards

And the States as well themselves: what a terrible society. And the strain so thin (as Lawrence once sd abt the people, the strings over-tuned, wasn't it?

Utterly boring, but ghastly—which shifts it, no? Result: all the live ones going full tilt, what?

But the division (at least to an old Henry James-Melville (Supplement of Battlepieces) man or plain New Englander: hard to give up the dream, of, the, Republic!

Or something. Anyhow, yellowbirds along those Wyoming highways in early morning. Plus those hills (Bozeman Road) on which Indians left cavalry men cut up in little pieces, as a sign that, these brown hills were OURS! No end to *that* poem. But who the hell cares, any more, to write it, the future leaves so little interest in anything but our will ("His Will is our peace," etc

In other words, greetings. And do keep me on. Enjoy the picture of you going about in your car everywhere. Let me do it by your proxy. And maybe I'll think of others to look in on (oh yes, when you are ready to go to Carmel Highlands, let me know. By the way, it is medical practice you are after, isn't it? Come to think of it, how do we know maybe just Carmel wants doctors. In any case I have a friend there who is an internal medicine man. And good I think. Of whom we might in-quire, if that happens to be yr intention.

Yrs,

O

Charles Olson

85

To Elaine Feinstein (1959)

The "Letter to Elaine Feinstein," published in *Collected Prose* (pp. 250–252), is a letter of 27 April 1959. The next day Olson wrote an addendum, perhaps not sent, to the well-known British poet.   *Letter at Storrs.*

April 28/59

Dear E. B. F.:

I shorted you yesterday on Image. By taking that swing at society I was meaning to underrate the dependence on "contemporary" image as as limiting as a small understanding of speech rhythm. "Society" is as sentimental as "Nature" (or Classical mythology—Keats) if treated by subjective grab of it, and losing the complex (nexus) of its energic happening. One does berate the present mob thus, but hope is now interesting somewhere else than in progress. We have substituted epater le monde for the old poet maudit. It's fashion . . . c'est le meme chose.

I suppose I ducked, on Image, just that it ain't possible to split it from sd "speech" one is throwing. (An example is Robt Creeley. He is like a new part to the tale of the Emperor and his new clothes, in which the Emperor is the one who isn't fooled: he knows it's himself who is wearing speech so the image is naked.)

I come from the other side, to come up on it. As I wrote you, I put the local hard in, on Image, as I had the common, on speech rhythms; and sd, Muse over Psyche, thus extending same as speech extends genetically (here psychology as there archeology, but so dreary is psychology as taken by the moderns one doesn't get the strength out of the word as the other. Nor will a "science of mythology" equal the investigation, because the old truth—that the poet is a muthologos—doth stand. By Muse over Psyche I mean that position of form most strictly from content.

(You will be aware that one is constantly shifting 90 degrees and cutting cross-section in any of these doubles—why an enantiomorph makes such sense as the picture. Otherwise one doesn't get the vital: the dimension is always thus *n,* and saved. But statement has trouble here mathematics don't.

Burroughs, I notice, is marvelously after the libidinal, and does exactly the opposite of Creeley: he makes his own body into a literal corpus (text), a precise physiology to the t of the bottom of his foot for a fix. Burroughs wants a post-libidinal like Creeley wants a post-speech. It's terrific, both these drives. Clean.

I would revive the old sense of a precise plurality of "forms" (zzz). Dose Muses. I'm sure each man has one as firm a shape as a locality. Forget the proper nouns of same Muses. Remember only their mother. They have nothing, I'm sure, to do with literary forms. They are, in our gab, archetypes.

Thus the psyche, and them, bound, vertically, and shot from the "side" (by habit or choice, Burroughs or Creeley, as instances) comes Morphe. Genes to speech, morphs to me and you, and yr chains, senors, will drop off, comes the strawberries mit cream.

Yrs, over, the, waters,

O

86

To John Wieners (1959)

After their first meeting, which took place in the middle of a hurricane 11 September 1954 in Boston, the poet John Wieners could do nothing but follow Olson to Black Mountain, feeling, as he later put it, "ordained." The postcard below, addressed to Wieners in San Francisco, is available to us (whereas other correspondence is not) because it was not sent. *Postcard at Storrs.*

June 26 /59

Jawn!
    Of the Charles you know
why don't you write the poem?
   It will instruct me (!)
  We *lead* one another.

Love,
C

I *am* there. For the poles
to remain erect.
        There are *many* things to
be *said.*   There are *no* walls.

(Saw Robin last night who sez you are headed East! ?)

87

To David Ignatow (1960)

David Ignatow was asked to edit a special section of "Political Poetry" for the October 1960 issue of *Chelsea,* and he invited Olson to contribute. Olson responded immediately (the "59" date on the letter should be 1960). After finishing the wide-ranging letter, Olson suggested it might itself make a good contribution, but the hint was not taken up. *Letter at San Diego.*

28 Fort Sq Gloucester MASS January 5 59

Dear David Ignatow:

Surely will. Glad to hear fr you again—and for one of yr crazy "specials"!

Right off the top, don't quite get what you propose as "political", especially as of the history of English poesy, like
and/or that you are talking abt the drop, since the '30's, of the social subject—like the old "Left" (as far as anarchism—of which we still have, like, David Wieck's *Resistance* etc, Goodman—or recently that fellow out on Long Island who was the best writer INTRO produced (???

I lead to you, simply that both Duncan and myself, say, have been for years doing nothing but poems almost of—in his case, *polity,* in my own, *polis* (the Maximus, now coming out as Volume 3 in March etc)

And Ginsberg, like—altogether political no? in such as Death to Van Gogh's Ear—or much of the "protest" of the Beat persons is political, no?

Just for my own stimulations wld you write me back—with examples, like (I have been myself a "politician", and like I say have spent 10 years already on the Maximus poem, and see no end to it yet, like; the *conception* & the *creation* of a *society* is the act of *politics,* is it not?

No 2: I see no reason not to think that exactly the "political" is what is (a) conspicuously corrupt as in present existence (both scale-wise: bipartisanism; world-wise: universalism etc, and (b) that as a point d'appui for man or for the poet the political is defunct

        3: the restoration of that "vision" (that man lives among public fact as among private fact, and that either is solely a face of the double of the real) is conspicuous and crucially demanded

and 4: that the poet now, as much as any Dante, or Homer (who was a "flower" of the last "polis"—unless you count Bach, who was the purest sign of the local when it was "round") that the POET NOW is MORE POLITICAL in the root sense than has been true in English at all

OK. The other thing I wanted to urge on you is to get Robt Duncan in—his address is Stinson Beach, Calif: he has a Pindar ode which has been published but has a rollcall of Presidents, and includes Whitmanesque vergings, which would seem to me just what you want

Also invite Robt Creeley? Address: San Geronimo Miramar,
                             Patalul, Such.
                             Guatemala, C.A.
Also a crazy one (just finished a piece on the "local") Ed Dorn:
        501 Camino Sin Nombre, Santa Fe, NM

notes of observation & thought via yr letter:

A.   much of the present subjective poetry is "*political*" in the striking
      Beat / McClure /Whalen   (a "strike" in fact)
                                      to get at an *anthropos* at all, on
       HOMO ANTHROPOS   which to conceive *any* excuse
                                        for *any* existence of *any public*
                                        fact of any order

B.   the science or art of *government* (the old base meaning—Aristotle/
      Plato, like, begs now the prior question, that any *organization* of
      any thing is questionable
          ("the will to a system is a lack of integrity" Nietzsche)

thus Duncan's investigation of *polity:* the stress moves from government to *state:* what "state", for "man"? the "body" politic?

SOMA SOCIOPOS

(the "Companions": socius =s "companion" love-kin   the "company" of the imagination (neither *sexual* NOR social ((—Burroughs' sex-without (POST)-libido; society-without (POST)-libido))

C.   *Polis:* my point would be "it" is broken up BROKEN UP (like the "Host" is busted all over the place. Broken down all the way AS MUCH *OUT* AS *IN:* no conception of the unit POLIS *at all.* Thus begin anew ON *ALL* FRONTS including (like!) the SOUL

MAXIMUS—man, *AND* cosmos

You see what you've done! Wow I didn't know myself any of this— like! (Are you not a PRINTER? as such, and EDITING now to my knowledge these TWO special issues—didn't I offer you the post at Black Mt, and you had to refuse because you are a printer?—don't you yourself disclose one of the OLD UNIONS of the writer and the word? Wow   crazy   "local"

Ok   Not to come on like too much   I solely take it there are guide lines in the area   PLUS *much work* being done   (perhaps what you mean by 25 years of the metaphysical and the subjective is only the *falling* of us out of any previous formulation due

(1) to the loss of hope; and (2a) the "death" of law (17th century) by police power taking over, moving in, insurance companies, skip tracers, any of these nits which invade the individual—like—legitimately? Ha ha (The She-Briareus, Massachusetts)

and (2b) the *rational* stupidity of the contract-social ((musique-
concrete, e.g. knocking *that* in
the face

Positively: (1) dreams, or, the rerecognition of the volcano the "Self" is
when left to itself (staying put as Ego
and (2) the return-in of the cosmos: the knocking over of the idea
that society is only an image and
way of knowing of a construct
WHICH IT ISN'T capable of being
((like Creeley says, "the social fix
which sexuality (any) has to involve" is the limit there (*IS* AS
THINGS ARE); thus the present attack on the Family and 2, on
Woman (as Mother etc (also the
"rise" of the homosexual (?)

THE RE-BASE of the political is—or strikes me altogether as—RE-
BIRTH of the conception of MAN and of COSMOS; only by that width
and down-drive can the "creation" of society be reimagined; thus
politics—which is literally only the *conduct* of same by *the governing* of
same (far wider than state or government proper—including the police
power)—only has "character" after AFTER (PROTO-ANAGOGIC
McClure cries legitimately) the character is restored, of Man and Cosmos ("Confucianism" isn't good enough: equity is not honesty but
aequus = imago equal to, the "picture")

Michael McClure
2329 Fillmore Street
San Francisco (most important to ask him
direct your question—the political
as well Philip Whalen
1713 Buchanan Street San Francisco

Let me hear from you again
Olson

My dear David Ignatow:
the *enclosed* got written as an answer to yr letter

I shall still submit a poem, but it might also fit your purpose to use the enclosed per se? (My own experience is that such "forms" coming via the occasion carry a drive into discourse that the older formalisms (of paragraph etc) don't

 in any case you will therefore sound how much yr request has carried me!

Best, and let me hear fr you again
Olson

In any case *please keep*
letter for me if you will
be so kind

No poem was written for the "political" issue of *Chelsea* or for a subsequent issue on William Carlos Williams. In a letter to Ignatow of 26 April 1962 Olson pleaded: "I find it difficult to conceive that a poet is any subject for a poem any more than poetry is." He asks for a copy of the issue of *Chelsea* on politics: "I never did see it, and wld like to" (letter at San Diego). It was duly sent, but no further correspondence ensued.

88

To Michael McClure (1960)

The poet Michael McClure had been trying out poems on Olson for several years. The one he sent in late 1959 (manuscript at Storrs) begins "COURAGE COURAGE" and contains the line, "I am a Beast a Bulk in the Black Lilly of space. Oh courage." *Photocopy of letter supplied by the recipient.*

Jan 25/60

My dear Michael
 Forgive me I've been so slow: I wrote a whole damn letter to you on the poem and the poetics when they came in before Xmas and it got

lost in the shuffle thereafter, and since, I have kept going without turning back:

or I never cld decide whether I was right to question the
"lily" in yr "black lily"

that is you speak some truths of the soul, and
such truths have to be exact or we do wrong, and my desire was
solely to check that one through, feeling you were talking right on
the target

also running alongside (thru myth) so many lines you
seem to me on, that I carry on a double line with you sometimes
daily

(quoted you by the way straight on as of proto-anagogic in piece
sent off recently to a new NY magazine, but no word out of the editor
so assume doom the dope

love to yrs, and hope all holds on—wow,
please keep it coming to me, and when I
find out to be more fluent, or stop for
what I heard you call yr chores (you do
in the morning) I'll be back:

bad time, anyway, month of January: come
out of solstice like molasses—and too
bright

love,   O

89

To Gordon Cairnie (1960)

Gordon Cairnie's Grolier Bookshop, just off Harvard Yard, was of such use to
poets of all shapes and sizes that it should not be thought that Olson was not
part of the traffic and appreciation.   *Letter at Harvard.*

Feb 18

My dear Gordon Cairnie:
    Many thanks for yr card (& do keep the old check: here's a new
one

—while I think of it, the $9 did include that copy of the magazine "The 50's" (black) which had an article on "The writings (or Work) of Robert Creeley"; it wasn't in the package when we got home; cld it have slipped out back on to the table? If you still have it, wld appreciate reading about our common friend!

Very sorry to hear you weren't able to get *PV* direct from Leroi Jones; he's very decent, & sharp, and something must have gone wrong
(he's *had* a hell of a winter

try him again, & when I write I'll mention it to him
402 West 20th
NYC 11
Keep me posted! And see you again soon.
Charles Olson

Try me on Jung's *AION*
if you have it—or when you do

PS   one new thing we're abt to burst:
(1) *New American Poetry, 1945–1960*   big part in
edited by Donald Allen, Grove Press (hardcovers) April
&   (2) *The Maximus Poems,* complete, to date, in one big vol.
which includes 17 new ones!
Jargon-Corinth books N.Y.
also (3) "Collected" GROVE later (this year?)

90

To Donald Allen (1960)

In the spring 1958 issue of *Evergreen Review* editor Donald Allen had printed Olson's "The Lordly and Isolate Satyrs"—and put a photograph of motorcyclists on the cover. It was Olson's most conspicuous publication to that date. Olson greeted it with a letter to Allen on 19 April 1958: "Did anyone tell you how it is to be put out there by another man who has covered you like your own skin?"

(letter at Storrs). In 1960 Allen planned an even greater launch for Olson, giving him the prominent first place in the anthology *The New American Poetry, 1945–1960*. Olson responds to this in the first letter below, postmarked 7 May 1960.   *Letters at Storrs.*

Saturday May whatever *1960*

My dear Don:

That is the coolest and nicest introduction, and betokens the total page by page work of the Anthology from cover to cover. It just came in in today's mail (instead of yrself, whom I have expected for days!), and seems to me the lightest *interesting* damn book imaginable—isn't it? I shld think anyone wld have a ball; and the play of the persons via the poetics at the end, plus the biographies is like tesserae. wow.

Also, the divisions, because of the delicacy and exactness with which you have stated them first, and then let them go free in the text, seem to me to work all in favor of this moving table & ceiling of the present (I hadn't myself seen even such things as Creeley's Orts, or of course Denise! and McClure's wrestlings with his own position in the world! and have been having a ball reading here alone in the house with the sun out, and Duncan in Boston, whom I shld have called etc, and taken today to see Wieners, etc, and it is like a free day—wow

The Toronto trip was especially meaningful for me, and the reading worked—I always have that trouble that I wish to do it by composition then and there, and this time it did. Got a tape of the whole thing by CBC, and they promise me a copy: ought to be the record volume Jonathan has been asking for, if he still wants to do it. Also was on TV! and, shopping the next day for something for Bet on Bloor St, by god if the clerk doesn't say that another clerk saw me and wants to meet me lawdy, altogether over, into, the TWENTIETH CENTURY. Mark that Mark Allen! (The "Smith" poem went like a dream; also read the earlier one on him, Letter something or other, including his own poem; and by god—going on abt recent Hungarian proofs that he wasn't lying, who turns out to be an intellectual father to the young in T but Laura Striker's brother, Karl Polanyi! Dig that

Ok. Hope you can come soon. Days go on now funny—that is, the work sort of seems already off onto new tracks (the trouble with economics) and I footloose and real crazy for anything new!

Congratulations altogether, and let me hear the whole progress of the world's receptions!

> (Tell Grove any Toronto shipping or promotion of any of the doings is all to the good: and the center is THE ISAACS GALLERY
>> 736 Bay Street
>> Toronto 5. . . . like copies of
>
> Ishmael etc
> Evergreens
>
>> the new Anthology
>
> & I was interviewed & appeared (picture & all) in the T *Star* or something!

Love fr us all: CP still sorts his cards like
the World's Deck!

> Chas

───────────────

> Thurs June 9/60

Dear Don:
don't mind any silence—enjoying the lull before the economic storm or something

and only found out last week that you weren't coming: went over to get the address for you for forwarding as promised and bang she told me. Very sorry and you must be most unhappy, no? Myself was hoping I'd land something grand, for the summer like, and make it up to you by inviting you to visit us wherever like Vermont haha or Dalhousie say (as tho one cld pick those things out of the air after having stayed put in the frogpond all these years yah!

she says she'll return yr deposit if it is rented (minus some sheets maybe she sd she never bought before) and we all keep our eyes on the sign to see if it disappears! (one thing you may comfort yrself on missing is Vera Andrus! apparently she had her hooks ready, fancying herself as she does as a writer and art critic and was all aglow at the thot of your being there beside her for everything! la

    have been floating in new places back and around, and it's been a recapitulation of all done and now undone—very useful business, but a little wan simply that its future is so pale (by the way the pay on the anth came like Jack to the Pulpit or the Lady Slipper to the Dancing Floor and because it was yr check and not some publisher felt like robbing Don to pay Charles but may the bread like on the water like float back in Pond Lilies—for ever!

    we all had a sad party at Vincent's quietly drinking wine the afternoon I found out you weren't going to be the 3rd Member of Murderers Row like they call it so fondly in Baseball here! Vinc and Gerrit and Harry and I happenstance came together there at Vincent's and he was in the finest form I ever saw him due directly to your Anth (glowre) which he had bought the day before and read the night before and like a little man held his broken heart in his throat and talked it all out to me: very damn great. So you see the book also does its corporal works of mercy as well as fame!

Love, and soon,

Charles

My dear Don: The lady says she will be sending you a check this week. The place has been rented and she claims she has been waiting for the new customer to pay the full rent I suppose.

    All's well, still going along down to the end as tho I were free to work my street as tho the empyrean was mine. Great feeling anyway—even tore off with Bet and CP to Castine, of all places, on a speculation: I've gone so far now into Gloucesterism that I suddenly had an idea I might pick up a Lane painting down there which I cld interest a collector in & make enough bucks to get me across to September! But instead found the place sat on by the shrewdest character I've met, among the Lane collectors—a Burton Burton Dustin & Osborn man, very attractive contemporary American success fellow—you know the breed.—Also thereby got to see Bill Snow's Spruce Head for the 1st time (knowing it through him for 32 years!

In other words breached down east (for the 1st time) and it was fine for me.

Love fr us all and keep us on
Charles

Don Allen went on to publish *The Distances* (1960) and *Human Universe* (1965) as an editor for Grove Press and then started his own press in San Francisco, publishing *Proprioception* and *Causal Mythology* during Olson's lifetime, and later *Additional Prose* (1974), *The Post Office* (1975), and *Muthologos* (1979). "But don't forget," Olson wrote to Allen in a retrospective moment, "you and I discovered at the Diner where I now eat more and more we are SIBS" (letter of 4 November 1967 at Storrs).

91

To Kenneth McRobbie (1960)

Kenneth McRobbie, a young British poet living in Toronto, helped Raymond Souster organize Olson's reading at the Isaacs Gallery on 30 April 1960. The following day the three men went for a hike on Toronto Island, an event remembered by Olson in "A Day's Work, For Toronto," seven short poems enclosed with the letter below (see *Collected Poems*, pp. 510–513). Clearly, what is uppermost in Olson's mind, at least at the beginning of this letter, is whether or not he will get back the shirt and tie he left in his Toronto hotel (he didn't).

Letter at Manitoba.

Thurs June 9/60

Best to Ray—
tell him!

Dear Ken

like, enclosed? and may it etc. and it doth remind me of how very
much I did enjoy

        (also please let me know back by pc or something
        that you rec'd it simply etc

also tears tears no shirtee   que???? Ford—Hotel robbers in the house-
hold dept—who among them cld have had a husband as big as or a
neck tie as long as the bastards: please turn the constabulary loose

    I thot you were enuf of a European to know why I had called you so
pronto: that night was the only chance one ever had of getting suits sil-
ver hair brushes etc etc back when I was traveling in little known Loire
and Cote D'azur platzes Wiesbaden before the 2nd World War—before
Hitler that is—the Hotel Rose etc: and floating after having eaten a hole
bole of fruit in Lucerne under the on the shadow in the water of Mont
Blanc or was it SwesterSchluss was

or MidsummerNacht's Traum in Wiessland

                              ou afterdark concerts in Am-
sterdamm

        la the romantic years

                        or the blond in Koln I didn't have
sense enuf to! etc

        yr own trip lifts up all the airs of the world in my hairs

it wasn't Gloucester there which means anything to Gl here (except
that the preacher First a man named Richard Blindman was with
some of his flock fr Monmouthsire—and lord if you cld find his letters home from here dates inclusive 1642–1650 IMAGINE! Lord, is
there a calendar in England anywhere (or in the city of Gloucester my
god) of such letters home from the American immigrants of such
date????????? right smack in the years of the CIVIL GUERR OF OLDE
ENGLONDE. . . . . ?

he later I believe was a pastor in Bristol

no it is Weymouth (Dorchester) which was the covey
from which Gloucester MASS flew out—from Rev John White's Rec-
tory no less Saint no Trinity Parish ((I have a picture of his church and
it's a lovely small Gothic square and strong and warm and he was: was
most concerned abt the poor the years of the 16th had left England
with, on the dole and roads:

what wld be the most if you and Gen were wandering
there wld be what of that movement to Cape Ann they called it does
show in the local record (hoping England, and the West Country had
had some new digging and scholarship since the Great Lady FRANCES
ROSE-TROUP

she the Lady did reveal that she cldn't read (from mold) the crucial
page in WEYMOUTH PORT BOOK

873

873
EIGHT SEVEN THREE

that's it   Consignments to "George Way and Co"
                                        "Richard Bushrod & Co" etc

(these were
the glovers etc merchants of Weymouth and of Dorchester who were
putting out (in hopes etc) to get this place GLOUCESTER MASSA-
CHUSETTS started

CAPE ANN

or NEW ENGLAND

wld
be their words for it if any:

names of vessels are

voyage of discovery ship unknown (?) 1623

1624: 1st   *Fellowship* 35 tons
season

1625 Fellowship & *Pilgrime* 140 tons (a "ship" proper??? 3 masts etc
square rigged

1626 Fellowship Pilgrime and the *AMYTIE* 30 tons carrying 6 cattle

         ok just to supply you; and if you did poke around there
(Historical Commission of Dorchester???? *Weymouth* any such thing in
England as local powerful Records keepers???? of the great past
when?????

and sd Port Book:

look, or

if it wld dig you too!

Love & happy trip   Charles

92

To Anselm Hollo (1960)

Anselm Hollo's first book of poems, *Tumbleweed* (1968), had as its dedication:

'no end to troubles' he sd
gave me heart.

The quotation is taken from Olson's letter below.   *Letter at Stony Brook.*

My dear Anselm Hollo:

    Thank you for your poems, and I read those in *Satis* too, and you
won't mind, for there is no end to troubles, I can tell you, I simply have

the feeling I'd not be equal to the compliment you pay me, by address-ing me at all, if I didn't say: I believe you have the desire, and that can take you all the way, but you are not saying what you must have to say, you are letting brightness speak for you, and bright things attract your eye when it is yrself and yr specially chosen things which all of us have stamped on us there inside, which isn't getting in

OK? and fair—not loaded or pointing at you at all? It's very great to learn you are there, and that too there is Mead, and *Satis* (and Shayer of course I have known before, and corresponded with: do you also come out of that group? or are you from your own quarter, in, to them?

Please let me hear from you, and actually to acknowledge as well the pleasure it was to go to the POST OFFICE to get that crazy *registered* and sit down on the steps and read you

Best, and over—for more,
Charles Olson

28 Fort Sq Gloucester
Mass. October 21, 1960

93

To Gilbert Sorrentino (1961)

As editor of *Neon,* Gilbert Sorrentino elicited poems from Olson in 1958 and 1960. When he became poetry editor for *Kulchur* in 1961, he contacted Olson again, for reviews as well as poems, as the letter below indicates. Sorrentino had also contributed to *Yugen,* which he sent to Olson presumably on publication; so that we can date Olson's response at about 2 March 1961. Olson is amused by Sorrentino's onslaught there on Robert Lowell's *Life Studies* and W. D. Snod-grass's *Heart's Needle* (the latter "picking up the one thing that Williams does which no one but Williams can use. The private man in his backyard, etc." *Yugen* 7 [1961], p. 7). Olson also refers to Sorrentino's "Some Notes Toward a Paper on Prosody," in the same issue of *Yugen,* where Chaucer is mentioned in juxtaposi-tion with African-American blues, and where the question is asked: "WHAT IS THE CONSTANT against which we play our variations? Do we need it to create a viable measure? I don't know" (p. 36). *Letter at Delaware.*

my dear gilbert

the constant is vision

that's why you can say Negro
blues: literally the blues is the constant I got the blues who ain't

and—like—it was only yesterday I was reading that wild man chaucer
(looking for what I know the eagle sd to him Geoffrey you got the met-
rics man but you all ain't got all that soft art you all wan't Geoffrey
that's why I'm takin you up here and Geoffrey turns to the Eagle and
says hanging down there under him, "You wldn't shit me, wld you,
Eagle?"

   crazy how you come on man

and like I'm pleased to be in the
company you keep me in —woof

yrs here chas

Dug very much yr clarification, none "follows" sd private man in his garden etc/And quotes & thots on yr review of Snod & Nod

The Talmud
sez this is the time of the war of Gog & Magog.

Also: as of KULCH, &
revues, prefer not now to involve myself in doing THRONES, & please
let the idea of giving you notes simmer. Also will ask others—like asked
Lansing (here) if he (in reading Pound's *Impact*) had anything to say to
send it to you. But (turn abt) he sd Wld Sorrentino like a review of such
recent bks on *Gnosticism* as Jonas? & a couple of more, & I sd, Try him.
OK? So don't expect me in on yr dead line—unless you poke back at
me some *other* idea (?   OK?

94
To Alfred Mansfield Brooks (1961)

On a visit to Gloucester in June 1947 Olson met Alfred Mansfield Brooks, director
of the Cape Ann Historical Association, and immediately thereafter purchased

John J. Babson's *History of the Town of Gloucester*. This was a formative moment in the process by which the *Maximus* poems became an epic of Gloucester. Maps played a large part in all this; maps are the subject of the one available letter (dated only tentatively April 1961) written to a local historian Olson greatly admired.   *Letter (draft) at Storrs.*

Wednesday

My dear AMB:

There were 4, of the 1851 Map, but the worst was so bad I hope you won't mind that I took the 3rd. In which, with yr approval, I wld like to use the bottom roll of the bad one to repair the 1st map, which is excellent in color & condition, & with a bottom roll will give the Society an exceptionally good one. And a better than fair 2nd.

I also did the other part of our "bargain"—placed my copy of the 1872 Map in the Museum, & took the Museum copy. Which does give the Museum as good a copy as may be, of that Map. But so much better is it, with yr permission I will use it until I familiarize myself with the map (new to me).

In other words our "swap" stays. Only for a little while, if you don't mind, I'll use my own, restoring the Museum copy, & then soon place mine permanently with you. OK?

95
To Harry Levin (1962)

Harry Levin was a junior fellow at Harvard, living in Eliot House, which was next door to Olson's residence, Winthrop House. They saw a good deal of each other, and the obvious fondness translated into some crucial assistance on Levin's part, for he had contacts at Reynal & Hitchcock and can be said to have paved the way for the publication there of *Call Me Ishmael* (1947). The surviving correspondence is of a practical nature, where good fellowship is simply assumed. The note printed below, therefore, reflects a most unusual circumstance. Olson had accepted an invitation to do a poetry reading at Harvard on 14 February 1962, and he was apprehensive. Professor Levin recalls the occasion (personal communication, 18 May 1987):

> I had just slipped into the audience while Monroe Engel was making the introduction, but had sat down in front because of my hearing problem. When Charlie rose, he seemed unduly nervous and hard put to begin. After one or two moments of hemming and hawing and a few false starts, he addressed me directly and said: "Harry, could you be excused?" I was not very quick on the uptake, and he had to repeat his request before I understood and left. I am told that he gradually recovered his aplomb and built up to a rousing performance.
>
> I'm not sure that even now I fully understand. Though he murmured something vaguely paranoidal when he first saw my wife afterwards, I don't see how he could have sensed any strong hostility to his poetry on my part, since I had been a supporting member of the committee that had warmly invited him. Rather, I suspect that he was motivated by an extremely complicated set of memories and reactions against Harvard, which he hadn't seen for many years—and which I may have personified for the moment, as the sole survivor whose presence touched closely upon his own experience in this place, such as it may have been. At all events, when we met at the Engels' for cocktails afterward, he was confused and apologetic, but warm as ever. We parted as the old friends we had been, and I received this note from him next day.

Letter in possession of the recipient.

My dear Harry

I continue to regret that anything like that should have happened. You & Ilyena were so generous to me afterwards & I pray you will continue to be, even inside your own minds, and believe that I was under some duress which only could explain it.

Love

Charles

The tape recording of the reading, available in the Lamont Poetry Room at Harvard, reveals nothing of this drama. Neither does the thank-you letter Olson wrote to his hosts, Brenda and Monroe Engel, after returning to Gloucester, which speaks of "the delightful party and dinner, and the pleasure it was for Bet and I to stay in your house and have our night and day on the town." Or perhaps there is an oblique mention at the end of the letter when he says: "What was wrong with our snow storm? Nothing at all except that one big chunk of coal maybe" (letter of 21 February 1962 at Harvard).

96

To Hank Chapin (1962)

Hank Chapin wrote to interest Olson in a new magazine that was eventually called *Blue Grass,* but it seems, by this reply of Olson's, to have had a provisional title associated with Thoreau's *Walden.* Chapin included the last three paragraphs of this letter in the first issue.   *Letter at Buffalo.*

28 Fort Square
    Gloucester

                           Apr 25th

Dear Hank Chapin:
               Just at the moment sort of hooked around
on things but very much welcome yr letter and wish you wld come
back at me again for something for yr magazine

    in fact yr title caused me to read that Walden Two (which seemed to
me to obstruct yr title, in the sense that any such vulgar appropriation
as Skinner's does just that—fouls the nest of future use ((too much of
that going on altogether, the diluting shitting-up etc of value-words

    but of course all such actually leads to further invention—and I be-
lieve you might pursue that, even calling it Thoreau! Anything to move
it. (Also thought of a previous magazine Albuquerque—did you know
of it—*Landscape?*)

    My own present sense anyway is that society like personal (social
personal) are both bent so they are broken by the re-emergence of
public-private force now carrying all of us forward. (Whether sd as
axiomatically—or dogmatically as that the point makes itself I don't
know: I am persuaded behaviour has got most anyone muddled, and
even if it looms larger, it doesn't matter at all, and falls off the moment
a man takes action. Does anything which formally counts. Function is a
sick dog.

    Problem wld seem to me to address yrself to states now current
altogether on other side of misery and destruction prevalent in system.

What the young know is the price today is huge, and already are clear that institutions are dinosaurs and sanctions are pitiful gasps and procedures all gone dead in their mouths and minds. The task wld seem to be to get the new things sorted and straight for all to have some idea of paths or procedures to follow (other than abandonment and suicide). Guerilla and soft.

Ok. Not to preach. To record recent experiences. Verse is only interesting as revolutionary (not self-expression); and essays, unless they are also likewise potential—devoted to the arbitrary—are not going to get us on.

Many thanks, and please: again. Yrs
Charles Olson

In other words, come back at me—& please use anything of mine you choose, for epigraph aim etc.

97

To Florence Williams (1963)

Receiving a book on William Carlos Williams as a gift in early December 1964 reminded Olson that he had never been able to send to Williams's wife, Flossie, the condolences he meant to have offered on the poet's death in March 1963. He belatedly typed a short note (carbon copy at Storrs, undated), explaining that he had written three long letters at the time, but "nothing seemed the same as his life." Of the two unsent letters extant, the earlier draft especially has the torque of trying and failing to be equal to the life. It can be dated 6 March 1963.

Letter at Storrs.

28 Fort Square Gloucester
Massachusetts

My dear Mrs. Williams, Bill was a hero and I'm sure went directly last Monday to Leif the Lucky's Isles of the Blest. As you know (and it was one of the reasons I have never adequately had my say about him in the

public print) he was more a father/brother to me than at all the Literary
Man, and the crankiness or buckyness (on my part anyway) had to do
with that difference, that it was much more as though I was "living with
him" (though obviously not at all, and especially I wldn't want you to
misunderstand that—I mean that from the very first moment I ever
read The American Grain I was in "conflict" with that man because I
not simply believed in him but would swear

                           "swear" that he was talking about
and was doing (did—*everything* that he did) "counted"; and at the
same time I wanted him to be "right" (like you know one so effected
does do etc:

        matter of fact I *did* once actually have a good "say" about
him, and he never knew it because I never did send the letter, but it was
to Louis Martz, whom you will remember did that piece on him, the
Road to Paterson, and in it I mistook Martz's mention of the Bishop
Pelagius for Pelasgius, and went on for 14 pages on how Bill "needed"
(that's what I mean, "improving" on the man!) to add that whole thing
to that rear he gave himself as an American *for* etc;

    or I also wanted to tell you that when I read "Against the Weather"
(remember? in the 2nd Twice A Year?) one was able, for the *first time*—I
don't believe until *Bill* spoke *belief* any of us cld respect believing. . . .
even if to this day I haven't read and don't know what he was talking so
much about St John of the Cross

    In other words ignorance, and stupidity and a host of lost things
(maybe)—lost matters, of exchange and what else?—but I loved him,
and never didn't think *everything* he did and said and was and wasn't
wasn't of the prime importance, and I wish very much that you in particular would hear me say this as if it might be some kind of consola-
tion, in your loss (as well as please tell your two sons, whom I have never
met—I believe I *saw* the doctor-son through the door of the office the
only time I was in your house, not too many years ago:

                               it meant a lot
for me to have the chance to tell *you* that day (in the restaurant, when
Bill and Hellman were talking acrost from us) what I thought of Bill's

stories (even if I didn't persuade you, or Bill, that day, in the house earlier, in my defense of what I had said about him in the Mayan Letters:

I loved him, more than any other man whom I've had to deal with—loved him more, I mean, in that way that I do mean was how it is when a man *is* a hero—proposes to be a hero (I believe Bill did have an utterly unusual sense of this function and its use, and for other men

(thus—again nothing I cld ever say to him but it is such a pleasure to say to you—the way he copyrighted the Autobiography in both our names, is one of those things I still live with as though, well, it's, *nobody* but *nobody* ever did *any such thing,* don't you think????

He was something and I hope very much you will take care of yourself and forever and if there ever *should* be any possible littlest thing I might conceivably do I would be very happy if you would ask me or let me know (I've always felt that somehow or somewhere that you didn't trust me—and for that matter that Bill didn't either, and I don't mean that piously at all, I mean let me simply say it, *to you*—to "shrive" myself, if that's what it is, and why not?,
                                        the tension, that that great man was alive, that everything he stood for and did was right there on the end of a telephone, and that you were there and I might call (as I did that last time, from the hotel in New York
                                        well, please please take this as words spoken to you with the hope that in some way they may relieve your own experience of the loss of him. I know like I say for sure where he is and there isn't anybody who is going to have to do with the fact that human beings some time once got to this shore who aren't going to have to do with Bill Williams—because he cared and paid attention to that fact, in a way no one else did, and made himself, by that difference, into Bill Williams.—(That again is the same point, about the fact that he was a hero, and certainly he made the point himself, I should think, in his taking the advice of Valery Larbaud as a prescription, but I'm not aware (even right now as I say this to you) that the import of what that amounts to—amounted to—is in evidence by,

publicly anyway, all that he wrote (and did publicly)—hasn't even
begun to be imagined. (Is this possible? In any case he lies in the
ground to me like the very spirit of what I have felt all week since I
learned that he had died, and wanted to say to you in particular, that
his death only moves the whole thing over to this place—that what it
was, and will be, that Bill Williams took the thought that I am speaking
of, and that that thought is of such an order, and he was of that order,
that there is not any telling yet of what it means, and what it will mean,
and where it will go, to change Change.

All my wishes for yourself
and hopes that life will continue to
seem as good,   with love for him to you
whom I felt loved him,

Charles Olson.

98

To George Bowering (1963)

The poem by George Bowering that prompted Olson's response in the letter
below was sent to him in typescript from Vancouver prior to the "famous poetry
clambake" (Bowering's phrase) at the University of British Columbia the summer
of 1963:

rime of our time

Here is Angela's
hair on the side of
my face; love as

clean and soft as
it is immediate
to me. Two heads

on a pillow faces to-
gether eyes closed or
open in the dark.

Time is on our side
now no trick to
scrutinize but behind

us days. Accumulating
sounds we make in
our sleep, our dreams

of one another seen.

Bowering had also asked about Olson's Ph.D., and here gets his answer.

Letter at Storrs.

28 Fort Square Gloucester
Massachusetts
March 7th LXIII

My dear Mr Bowering

I like the poem very much. It is very true, & close to beauty. In fact it seems only "sounds" which keeps it short of the latter, and for the life of me I can't see what else you would have said, having proposed to say what you do say, after time & the point of the accumulating "sounds."

I think I know what does occur with the word: that it is, like nothing else in the poem, an occurrence imagined on a statisgraph. That is, you are both asleep, and thus comes between the loveliness of your other statements (as your own senses) such as Angela's hair on the side of your face, and your two heads—and the conceptual, that this is "love" and how it is, and (for me) the "hit" of the poem, that time is now on your side (here is the key word-wise to a choice which "sounds" isn't) and *no trick to scrutinize*—lovely. It's only that "sounds." And there isn't, I'd imagine, anything more to do about it. That is, this is this poem.

But it caused me to wonder if you know Donne's poem of sitting by a lady on a bank, and their bodies touching—knees, I think, is the "contact" (like they say). At least Donne seems the one who(m), in such discourse—or at least that "physical" problem you seem to me to get into with "sounds" (between the two worlds)—Donne here has been the boldest, and when "right," looks like Heaven itself.

Anyway, thank you—and I even hear the appositeness of your title, even if at first it seemed large, and modern.

"behind us days"—& it may be the "but"—yes, I believe it is: the "but" seems the only lazy moment (again, to *me*) in the choice of the words (that is, doesn't even "connect" rhyme-wise with anything else?? floats loose?? which is not true of any of the other prepositions (are they?) like the "nice" *or*

OK. Certainly that wasn't your question—but you "asked" for it! Regards please to Kearns, whom I enjoyed so much meeting in Toronto a year ago—a damn pleasure to see him stand out from all the poetry goons, or poetry "beats"—or for that matter (but these I never "mind" so much) the "poetry" citizens, the ones who come out at least to hear a reading—or at least to look at the traveling monkey. Tell him I talked mostly to him (as he probably knows) over the "ring" of persons clustering in the sad cleared "dining-room" (Toronto two-something houses yuk)

Now as to your question: I laughed like hell when I saw that summer catalogue "PhD" (thought it was Creeley's joke—and fair enough: that is I sure was a creature in course long time, and did complete "requirements" for same (luckily by studying Chaucer with Robinson; and the History of the Westward Movement with Merk (great "Canada" man: introduced Simpson's fur papers, & taught himself a most discrete prose to write papers on the Oregon triangle question: the Master of Pemmican he ought to be known as when the ages have done with the present).

But when it came to the degree—and I was "offered" it one day years later on the steps of Harvard's library, by Murdoch in Merk's presence—and this will tell you—for Call Me Ishmael (that is, as the "acceptable" dissertation—not bad, Harvard *University*)—I sd, bumptiously and with stupid impossible confidence, no.

So that's the story. With one further fact, to make the answer complete: the course of study was not "Man" but—again "credit" Harvard—the first degrees in "American Civilization," that is the idea being to take the thing as a unit—law economics as well as the more obvious culture or "comparative" businesses—and allow persons to claim some competence.

It didn't turn out (in the cases of the other two "original" candidates—John Finch & Daniel Aaron—you may know the latter's book on the "Progressive" mind in the U.S.—or now, I see, on "Communism" or something in the literature of the '30's (or 40's—or 50's)—and it obviously was the first spread of that filthy virus humanistics (the virus *before* the Asiatic flu creativity) but there we are: where wld we be if it weren't that they can now leave us alone?

Best, & please tell Creeley hello (as well for that matter Davey—*and* Wah (do I have him right?)

Yrs,   Charles Olson

Referring to this letter in the *Minutes of the Charles Olson Society,* no. 2 (June 1993), pp. 5–6, George Bowering remembers how struck he was, "as countless others must have been, by this major American poet's great generosity to young nobodies. . . . Olson shows here some of that good quick close reading we liked him for."

99

To Wesley Huss (1963)

In *Black Mountain,* Martin Duberman tells us that Wesley Huss was a descendant of Jan Hus, "the absolute essence of Protestantism" (p. 339). He was a mainstay of Black Mountain College (not only in drama but in administration) from his appointment in 1950 until the college closed, "the day," as Olson put it, "Wes Huss & I stopped her on a dime, October 11 th, 1956" (letter at Wesleyan). Huss went on to do theater in San Francisco, where this impulsively retrospective letter reached him.   *Letter at Storrs.*

28 Fort Square
March 18th 1963

Dear Wes: Simply to "record" to you (on the 1st piece of paper near to hand) that the way you handled the business of B Mt, looked after its finances etc., as well as—and that Indian fr the other side of the Valley was a part too of the "genius" of the place; and now that it has become "historic" (actually the "great" Black Mt—the one I suppose you & I that day taking that boat ride etc like a couple of sailors looking for cunt (what two sailors) did (didn't we?) give "chance" to? OK. Not to pat *us* on the back but we *were* paying attention, in the way some of the things were done, to something which etc—& I wanted no neglect of that "running" of the place etc.

Hope all goes well

best to Bea & the boys—

Squiddle (was it

must now be already

a sailor!

Yrs,   Charles

VIII

Olson accepted a 1963 summer school job at the University of British Columbia, where Warren Tallman and Robert Creeley had for a year been preparing the way for not only Olson but also Philip Whalen, Robert Duncan, Allen Ginsberg, Denise Levertov, and a host of student poets.

The news that Olson was actually teaching again reached Albert Cook, the new chair of the English department at the State University of New York, Buffalo, who persuaded Olson on the telephone to come for a semester. Olson, although he occasionally may have denied it, entered enthusiastically into Buffalo academic life and stayed, in the end, for two years, resident for the first seven months in Wyoming, New York.

100

To Robert Kelly (1963)

From the time he received the first issue of *trobar* in 1960, Olson recognized the young editor Robert Kelly as a co-worker in the field. He was instrumental in getting Kelly a summer teaching job at Buffalo in 1964. Kelly gave Olson a standing invitation to read at Bard College, Annandale-on-Hudson, although Olson apparently never made it there. Much of their correspondence is concerned with poems and practical matters of publication; the letter below (conjectured as sent in early November 1963) begins with Olson's appreciation of a Kelly poem (one apparently unpublished).   *Letter at Buffalo.*

My dear Robt: Many thanks for that delightful poem (though I think I do miss any connection to our conversation, which you seem to imply, and my knowledge of the Phaedrus is sadly long and not new enough to catch the reference—but this has nothing to do, either of the above, to the strength of the Phaedrus occurring there, and, in fact, that total poem, especially that tanker nosing herself on that river to etc via that Plimsoll line (lordy isn't that a hit you have made, stinging as the image shld and has stayed and stayed and will never leave me as having occurred.—Hope that all goes well, and even if I didn't make it it is an enormous comfort to know now where Annandale is, where I might find you and Joby if the world turned upside down (-like). We are happily ensconced, and if only I cld found or succeed in creating an Institute of Poetry like one of these Greek masters around here named it— I tried to get the idiots (of the Niagara Review) to levy Sitney before he went to Europe—Sitney writes beautifully, and doesn't know it yet (?), in any case is ready for work, and they had their chance: equally other young men of this preparation and calibre appear, and if there were a patron on the scene—we are left alone now with only the University and the Church (with the State become what I suppose it properly always shld be simply the mirror or servant of the people it has to use for itself, gourmandizer) and tho Buffalo is a marvelous opportunity because it lags as an American city as Canada does as a non-American matter (there is a difference there, and the difference is on the side of just such things as an Institute of Poetry *here*) I am waiting for any

chance to get denominated a way which would make it possible to—
actually there is one funny development, and this fellow Cook, who
brought me here and from whom you will have heard, I'm sure, is obviously on to that part of it: next year they will have 50 teaching fellows
on their staff, and these persons, or a bunch among them, are wonderful material—50 imagine (30 this year and maybe 15 of them of whom
5 say are real (3 of them edit the two new magazines, another is the
Manager of one and 1 of these 4 has been of real value to me

                                            I talked
(as of your housing) the other night, when Hugh Kenner was here, and
Carol Cook says that faculty houses, because they go away in the summer, are available and some are very near the place of work. So that
might take care of it?

Am anxiously awaiting *Matter* not at all out of vanity but quite the
other way around—and hope you will put your own best poem since
those of this spring in there

Love to you both—and though I don't get a chance to use it (I share the
Chanel 5 eau de cologne) the Weil vial (vile! pun I mean!!!!! Joby!!!!!!

Wish (literally) I was there   Yrs, Charles

101

To Timothy Leary (1963)

Olson had, through Allen Ginsberg, been included in Timothy Leary's early
psilocybin sessions in Cambridge during December 1960, but he had done no
further experimenting with hallucinogenic drugs, nor had the inclination. The
letter below shows him distancing himself from certain unsavory developments
he had heard about in the LSD movement, which he also spoke of at his
Gratwick Highlands talk on 16 November 1963 (transcribed in *Muthologos*, vol.
1, pp. 20–62). The letter is in response to one of Timothy Leary's dated 19
November 1963.   *Letter at Storrs.*

timmy timmy timmy
   no question you can keep your head etc but ifif u don't stop being
cheap abt what is truly aspirin etc in your struggle to bring the message
to Manzanitas or wherever it was—
                                 it ain't five nights ago I was talking
abt what you might do to Plato if you were that Botanist who made
world search for the Soviets and knocked taxonomy on its ass forever
(as I heard you one night in Harvard's halls state action as a form of
mind ((instead of all this latest fucking jive abt meta whatever
                                          result,
now I see this packet of material in today from
                             ZERO EMERSON
PLACE (do i have it right?) i have to revise my belief in you at least
to repeat Sam Rosenberg's old corn ((he's the fellow by the way that
proved that Othello was written by those five-mile an hour waters
which are called the Bosphorus)) about the best intellectual offerings
in the East and the West are served in Sadie's Brake and Eat on Rt 40 at
Wichita as the best the House offers, beans and brown bread, as the
Blue Plate Special for Today
                      Or like I was also saying it ain't a Salt
March youse going to lead to the waters of the world but a Consciousness Mush it now begins to sound like
                       God damn it, Coach like

102

To Eric Havelock (1963)

Eric Havelock's *Preface to Plato* (1963) was interpreted by Olson as a confirmation
of his practice of teaching archaic mythology as an essential aspect of what he
termed "the post-modern." He wrote a review of the book for the first issue of
Niagara Frontier Review. The letter below, in an envelope addressed to Havelock
as chairman of the classics department at Yale, was probably not sent because
Olson had decided instead to work for an official invitation for Havelock to visit
Buffalo. This visit occurred on 10 December 1964.   *Letter at Storrs.*

Thanksgiving

My dear Eric Havelock,

This is a fan letter. I have just done a notice of parts—mostly of the footnotes to one chapter—of your *Preface*. And I am surrounded here by this new young breed of Americans, the trained classical men, of whom two have put me into your debt, by introducing me to your work, Charles Doria, and Charles Boer. But also there are these flying pieces like P. Adams Sitney, who is young Parry's friend, and Notopoulos' student. It is a pleasure to acknowledge the existence of this fountain-head.

My immediate reason for writing is simply to spend a flashed sense, on this morning, of a rarity you appear to me to have, of a political character which must be being re-born, that no such complex in the person (as against the obvious long history of the political in the other obvious sense) has been—or is still—present, except in such a case as yrself (with no exaggeration intended, but to pluck—as it used to be that flower of honor, as was in Hot-spur (as though from Texas!

In any case to speak to that side of you, and greet it as the day goes; and wish you altogether well in every endeavor.

Yours,

Charles Olson
(Wyoming,
New York)

103

To Ralph Maud (1963)

When the private University of Buffalo became the State University of New York in 1963, the signing of a loyalty oath called the Feinberg Certificate became a condition of employment for all faculty. Ralph Maud and Harry Keyishian (the "Harry" mentioned in Olson's letter below) were two of those who, as a protest, refused to sign. The U.S. Supreme Court eventually struck down the requirement; meanwhile, it was an issue that plagued academic life at Buffalo and elicited the following reaction from Olson on 10 December 1963. The Feinberg crisis is dealt with at length in the *Minutes of the Charles Olson Society,* no. 13 (February 1996) where Olson's letter is presented in facsimile (pp. 17–19). Never sent, the letter remained in his papers as one of the poet's focused statements about his political position.   *Draft letter at Storrs.*

My dear Ralph, I am somewhat vexed by attitudes you may or may not have been expressing yesterday. Attitudes—and expectations, that is, that I, because I am I, and also am a poet, say, can be depended upon to act, even to lead possibly, at least to join solidarity of objection or fight to and against the Loyalty Oath, if that's what it is which is being required, under the Feinberg Law of New York State, of the faculty of the University of Buffalo.—Or that I do misinterpret your last remark that I would act individually when the signing of such a paper came to my attention or for my signature, that I wasn't ready right then and there to join in the steps to object or defeat the requirement, along with others equally involved, including yourself and say Harry who also asked me an hour later as I was going to my car to go home and he was on his way to the meeting if I wasn't going to it. (It isn't true, what he read recently, and he may have shown you the same article by Pete Seeger, on Woody Guthrie, that I was, when Seeger first met me, the leader of the Teacher's Union at Harvard at that time. Actually the leader was F. O. Matthiessen, and the creation of the Union followed from the firing, by the Economics Department of Harvard, of Walsh and Sweezey, an early AAUP case? I was much more involved in an earlier AAUP case, in fact the 1st real one, the firing at Rollins College of John Rice by the President then of Rollins, a journalist, former editor of Outlook, Holt; for it was due to that firing that Black Mountain College was born.)

I mention any of this, or other things I don't mention, to register my own long involvement in such matters (which I guess you do know, or sense, and is why you might expect and ask of me some part in these new proceedings), and I'm writing simply that I am so bothered (again) by the fact that (again) one should have to face anew such question as that a State like New York proposes a signature on an oath that I am not now or you ain't a Communist or whatever the phrasing is, as a part of employment in this State University: as I said to you instantly I did think the instance of the University of California had finally disposed of this stupid testing of men employed to teach. And I would the more readily go into the older action *required* if I didn't actually find this more of the reason why Buffalo at this stage is a drag (why did this University lose Manny Farber or whatever his name was, and the magazine Philosophy and Phenomenological Review go away from here when this University became a State University, to the sister State of Pennsylvania and be now published, and he employed, at the University of Pennsylvania?

That is, I *like* Buffalo because she is late in so many matters, and am proud to have had any part in founding the *Niagara Frontier Review* because by its very name it denotes the freshness possibly of this condition: Lakers, and Canalers at this date; and that at the same time the drag is the Republican back-country I (as you pointed out, with also I thought attitude) live in, that leadership in this area also is drag, in that it also shows old Tycoon habits of mind, and might appear to be capable of McCarthyism at date 15 years *after.*

I have no idea—yet. I have been here almost to a t 90 days. I care very much for that time, and for both Buffalo and the Republican back-country. I care more: I believe that Toronto and Rochester, say, in fact Seneca country generally (as well as the Neutrals of the mouth of Buffalo Creek, and the chemical companies therein and about, lying along the Niagara larger River) than, in a sense, I do Kinzua, or Washington, or those prior constituent pieces (which led Matthiessen to dive out the Manger Hotel window Boston when if I recall it right the Supreme Court did at that moment of time appear to give the Harry Bridges case the back of its hand—and Matty at the same, as well as coming to write about Dreiser, was the Chairman of the Harry Bridges Committee nationally—and had been active as of American literature in Czechoslovakia.)

I have been a person to stay at home; and possibly even so much so that I am "out"; and the more puzzled that such questions as Communism as a test of Loyalty (Americanism it must be which then is tested, yes?) loyalty to the United States? or to the State of New York?????

one doesn't any longer (with one's friends running for the next to the highest offices in the land, from the now gathering larger State than New York) quite know where these matters of membership or citizenship are

That
is, what has bugged me *seriously* already abt employment as Visiting
Professor or Lecturer here is the assumption of Personnel and Payroll
that one *has to* accept all sorts of insurance health tax etc etc in order
to receive a *lesser* amount of salary than that offered when invited to
accept a post in any institution today apparently across this already
heavily socialized nation.

What *are* you butting in bringing to bear on me this late application of
(which) loyalty—not you, but the Administration I assume or Albany
itself (where clearly my checks and number as retirable and all that
stuff is I assume coming from, like they say: what is the point of Presidential politics a rich and once glorious leader of the nation like New
York State—home of refugee Presidential nominees or prospective ones
since Willkie and now Nixon, and I and his wise Irish political adviser
once urged Claude Pepper, if he were going to succeed to get the *Democratic* nomination, he too ought to get into New York instead of being
from a fly State like Florida?

I honestly am only turning over in my own mind anything relevant to
this thing which you happen to have been the first one to bring to my
attention and in the midst of my mind being on altogether different
things, especially altogether different (or not so different) *politics.*

It comes to that: how political are you? and how are you political?—Or
are you economic, and personal—like your enemies are? I'm not sure a
first act of the new Niagara Frontier isn't exactly to declare a difference
from the prior slavery, to shed instantly any behaviour in terms of the
using of the State of New York—any more than I any longer think an
American in any real sense uses the United States of America (and that
clearly includes those Enemies, if they are so, who are behind the im-
posing of a loyalty test:
what have you people who have lived here been
doing while the Feinberg Law slept on your books??????
This is where I
respond and agitate (irritate myself, and your own sleeping dogs): how
active politically have you all been if suddenly this law thrust its dirty
face in front of your economic and personal nose??????

I don't then
find myself much minded—and think it is liberalism—to run up on
this drift when politics is so much better attended to than those who either use or haven't yet got out from behind protecting themselves from
bad laws

Intellectually, I find it hard to see that you people are active—
and not emergency ridden.

But then I better cool it. Like I say I have been home a long time, and
find that I am out more these days than I ever was. So please consider
that I am expressing myself to you; and will continue to act to the best
of my ability, primarily

Yrs over the silly fields, Charles

as of the matter, I find it entirely critical that politics today be entirely thought out; and that I don't believe economics is a parallel or
complementary term. In fact, that the social is economic and that the
political is ethical; and that education, so far as I can see, is as Plato
was clear it was, the crucial preparation of the citizen for political life.
With one now critical reversal of him, and of all educators of the present, including the State of New York in the instance, and the administrators, as well thus as the teachers like yourself: that solely poetry—
and I mean a poetry not to be confused with the poetic—is the means
of same

ok? will you therefore sign here?   yrs, Charles Olson

104

To LeRoi Jones (1964)

After 1959, when Totem Press published *Projective Verse* in a pleasing pamphlet
form, Olson came to rely on LeRoi Jones as "the only light fast runner in the
business (I mean as publisher . . .)" (letter of around 25 August 1962 at Simon-
Fraser). He sent Jones all the avant-garde "Proprioception" pieces for publication in *Kulchur*, *Yugen*, and *Floating Bear*. Because he valued him so highly as

a writer and a teacher, Olson procured for Jones a summer job at Buffalo in 1964. But he was already fearful of the direction the race question was pushing his friend. The letter below seems to be from early 1964, since it is a response to Jones's *Blues People* (1963), which we know Olson was reading in December 1963, and a *Midstream* magazine article, also published in 1963, titled "What Does Nonviolence Mean?" (reprinted in Jones's *Home*). "There is a war going on now in the United States," Jones begins the article, and refers to the "spurious" liberalism of reformers such as Olson's beloved FDR (p. 133): "most of the socio-economic policies of Roosevelt's New Deal were not meant to change the society, but to strengthen the one that existed. Roosevelt, in this sense, like a man who when fire breaks out in his apartment immediately builds a stove around it, gave a flexibility to the American ruling class that could not have survived without" (p. 136). He fears an "actual bloodletting" as in South Africa: "there are very few white men in this country who are doing anything to prevent this" (p. 154). Later, on the platform at Berkeley (Jones refused to come to the Poetry Conference), Olson declared himself "the ultimate paleface . . . stuck with the very thing that's claimed" (*Muthologos* 1, pp. 111, 133).

Olson never had to address LeRoi Jones as Amiri Baraka, because with that change of name, a Newark Wall cut off all previous friends in the white world. The following letter is Olson's forlorn attempt to prevent that break.

Letter at Simon Fraser.

My dear LeRoi:
    Use a world so large.

No man could possibly ever represent other human beings except where power were his absolutely and if then he ruled with decency he effected others' lives (I don't see where or how that is any longer true except symbolically and that seems only interesting—if the person turns out to be decent, reasonably—psychically, not at all politically: all politics has been either adjustment or the oldest place of it, the leading to war because the domestic economy so demands conquest or exten-sion of any neighboring different persons.

Because of size one is talking in signs and symbols unless one in-cludes only one's own doings—the personal therefore turns about and becomes both the arbitrary and the politics (?)

Ok. Simply thoughts on your own position (speaking for the Negro, and being struck all over the place, both in Blues People and in the Midstream piece, on how much you speak of as Negro has been only my own experience likewise—so I am solely persuaded that your position that the Negro solely ought to act as an end and change of what is manifestly no good is in fact any man's who wishes to have had a life in society which was more legitimate. So that the thing comes out has the Negro any particular thing to give any more than any one else who likewise has lived in this society? Which again brings us back to why not but doesn't it altogether come out if sd person does have—unless the power is arbitrary?

I think therefore that the color thing is only an issue of numbers—and in fact that the power of the Negro is in fact the power of numbers of non-Whites now, in so many words and places anyway—that this weight in the scale is real, and the only dreadful corollary is the one you seem not to keep alive, that Soviets and Chinese and Mexicans and Negroes and Whites will all wear watches. Maybe in fact I do think you use history (in these two instances of the Blues book and the Midstream article—as against for example the angry Tokenism thing earlier, or your piece in a recent Kulchir ((along with Joello and Dorn and Spellman etc)) *as it was* almost to whip up your own interest or entrance into contemporary political action (?)

——while in fact the participation can be real enough without signs and symbols:

I don't for a minute think the White Man you describe isn't the same filthy bastard I know who is completely unable to live either, and is easily as dangerous as you describe him; and in fact the Negro you describe is in fact also the retained brother—retention brother—of this other fellow. But that the violence so engendered is not as interesting as the world-wide violence and shit and that why in fact should the Negro be any specialist in redeeming that fact???????

Ok Not at all to argue. Solely to try to get in there where in fact I feel completely free too and want to get back to you with, love, Charles

105

To Mac Hammond (1964)

The poet Mac Hammond, a former student of Roman Jakobson's at Harvard, was now on the faculty at Buffalo. He loaned Olson a copy of a monograph that Jakobson wrote with Morris Halle, *Fundamentals of Language* (1956), and two of his own papers, "Poetic Syntax" and "The Metonymic Poem." Olson responded with a first letter on 15 January 1964 and then with this letter, written the following month. *Letter at Buffalo.*

February 16

My dear Mac Hammond:

Feel so much I better return this to you (having lost that path when I was on it, or—rather—getting removed from it as if picked up by a helicopter, and still not put down yet on the place

. . . having sd that, & believing the matter is not at all *not* much I do still wish to get on with, may I again instead ask you to continue the loan of both the Metonymy piece, & the (two in one) Jakobson pamphlet?

will you, without hindrance to yrself?

(The matters, as you'd well know, are so much on the board I have even found Jakobson over in quite another place I have got to in resembling the same course, on paroemiac meter)

I hope all goes well with you, and that you won't feel it strange at all that a person might seem to take so long over something—?

Yours with great thanks

Charles

(By the way what was *the other* mad thing I ran into *also* happened, & was presented at your Warsaw Conference? Quite apparently different & I came on it in some other connection way off these present courses??)

How is life—& these Buffalo matters?

Do let me hear from you, even I still am a
social badger, will you?

106

To Edward Van Aelstyn (1964)

In April 1963, Edward Van Aelstyn, a graduate student in English at the University
of Oregon, was appointed editor of the *Northwest Review*. Previously a quiet
house journal, the *Review* began to include left-wing libertarian articles and
avant-garde poetry. The fall 1963 issue included poetry by Philip Whalen and
Charles Bukowski, collages by Jess, an interview with Fidel Castro, and, most
provocative of all because of the title, a translation of Antonin Artaud's "To Have
Done with the Judgment of God." Artaud became an election issue: "Is God
Dung?" asked a leaflet issued by a slate of candidates for the Oregon legislature.
The president of the university, held responsible for the offensive material, turned
on Van Aelstyn and dispersed the contents of the next issue, which was being
printed. Olson, who was to have been included in that issue, wrote the following
testimonial, joining others who were trying to prevent the censorship.

Letter at Simon Fraser.

To Whom etc
via Van Aelstyn
Editor

Anyone: *Example 1*   During World War II Ben Shahn & I did a pamphlet together for the U.S. Govt. It was *before* I was Foreign Nationality
Director of the Democratic National Committee, & was then the same
for the Office of War Information.—Mr Rockefeller (the present New
York governor then Coordinator of Inter American Affairs) agreed to
print this booklet (with photographs edited by Shahn) to spread it
throughout Latin America—though its title was "Spanish Speaking
Americans and the War" & was directly addressed to a very unpleasant
fact: that at Bataan an enormous number of the dead had been from one
anti-Aircraft battalion from two small towns in New Mexico, therefore
almost all "Spanish" names therefore almost a resentment throughout etc

OK. A fine photograph in *black* emphasis from the Life photographer
—— ?Brown (cf mast-head) so interested me I wrote a poem

       Bataan
          Shahn
             etc
     & *black* women lean

& Shahn went home to New Jersey & came back with this poem set in
the New Mexico sky over sd woman visiting tomb in cemetery etc.

Thereon enter the "Don't Hurt *Everybody* Man"—Phileo Nash
(since himself almost governor of Wisconsin etc): who told Rockefeller
"black" would insult the Spanish Speaking American of the
Southwest—& of course South America!

Example 2:   current issue of what *must* seem sister & rival magazine to
NORTHWEST REVIEW:
                       current issue of Poetry Northwest with
pale 3 birds by Mark Tobey & pale pale poetry within; but point is front
page alone tells all—*color* tells us

Ex. 3:   the *jump* of N.R. to 1st place—& sole place—as *only* College or
University magazine having extricated itself from *paleness* & happened
under
present editorship
             —*jump* Jip *jump*   leave Alice & Jerry be   No
harm will come to them   All the Phileo Nashes go on
                          Meanwhile
any loss of a magazine *which* breaks through is REAL LOSS

  Testimonial
                Charles Olson

March 7 1964

Extracts from this letter appeared in a mimeographed pamphlet, "Comments on
NWR," along with similar quotations from Don Allen and several poets including
Michael McClure, Clayton Eshleman, Robert Kelly, Jonathan Williams, and Gary

Snyder. Olson wrote to Van Aelstyn again on 15 April 1964 from Buffalo, hoping that he was "still in power": "I can assure you the composure of those who conduct education anywhere gets worse and worse" (letter at Simon Fraser). Pejorocracy ended the brief radical era at the *Northwest Review,* but soon the same editors were announcing a new magazine, *Coyote's Journal,* which had two contributions from Olson, in the next turbulent decade.

IX

There came a personal tragedy. Olson's beloved wife, Betty, was killed in an automobile accident at the end of March 1964. Olson could do nothing for a month. Creeley visited on 24 April. Jack Clarke came for a job interview at the university on 1 May. Then there was apparently a complete breakdown, and Olson was in the hospital during May. He had recovered by 1 June, and only then do we see him begin again with something like the previous attention to correspondence.

In a radical departure from custom, in the summer of 1965 Olson moved into the world of international poetry readings, accepting invitations to gatherings at Spoleto, Berkeley, and Bled. These dislocations interrupted correspondence, which picked up only when Olson fled Buffalo for Gloucester in September 1965, three weeks after the new term had started.

107

To Robert Creeley and Vincent Ferrini (1964)

On 28 March 1964 Betty Olson was killed when the car she was driving alone slid on icy pavement near their house in Wyoming, New York. As this letter to Robert Creeley shows, Olson was still distraught a month later. Writing to Vincent Ferrini three days afterward, Olson has a different mien. Some kind of turning point has been reached.   *First letter at Stanford; second letter at Storrs.*

My dear Robert,

You mustn't by any means mind at all but this place has now in fact become my island—and if there is any point at all for my being here it is an even more drastic extension of the conditions under which we were here this year. In fact if I can stay here at all, and have my son's life with me—and with Kate's now more included—I shall have to rent the other house myself, if I can, that is—and Mrs Hooker sticks to her resolution of two weeks ago, to keep it for herself, and not, as she had planned, to give it away to that damned University

But I am in the worst situation right at the moment, and the drasticness I am voicing to you is the utter discovery that my strength now has to be marshalled like mad: I have been here this week alone with Charles Peter—and it turns out it is utterly impossible without *staff*! Who in turn, it equally turns out (after the experience of having Rosemary here), if they are in the same house with me, leave me dangerously impossible and completely exhausted. Only Charles Peter in fact works for me—and he of course can't be alone with me, needs a much more and different life. I must therefore if I think of staying here at all keep the other house for such people—if there is such, and I can even find them. Or even tolerate that!

Crazy. But these are very crucial questions. And they are just now all on the board. So please altogether don't mind that I can't welcome you—and will have to go ahead right now as though all possibilities were open to myself alone.—One of the reasons you haven't heard

from me at all is the unbelievable combination of events which has
continued to happen even in the last 24 hours—and I honestly not only
have no way of knowing what the next couple of days may portend but
in addition can see no answers to the future until Charles Peter has
finished school here (in 3 more weeks)

So please hear this, and do accept it as the best possible response I
can make to you now.—Will write soon, or as soon as these matters do
permit.

> Yours and with love to you
> and to Bobbie—and please
> write me back, immediately

> Charles

Wyoming Monday
June 1st

> Wyoming New York   Wednesday
> June 3rd 1964

Vince

Having a ball, actually—at the moment—living alone here in the
house, grounds and village and eating out each night in Warsaw with
Charles Peter (Let the girl who was here go home to California to see
her mother. Find these young 20 yr oldish women—like so many if not
all the men likewise—so made up of brilliance and incredible dislo-
cated parts . . . I come almost to believe that if the Greeks and Romans
characterize our intellectual inheritance we need now antidoteishly
anyway a dose of Sparta-Lacedaemonian rigidity (example, the Spar-
tans had naked girls in their athletic contests! These women don't need
fucking so much—even if they are good at it—as athletic exercises (best
looking woman I have seen yet—a queen—was remarkably shooting
arrows in Buffalo many months ago—with legs on her like an Italian
movie queen (as well as features identical to Sophia Loren—all those
movie queens came out of whoring for American, and probably German soldiers, in WWII(?

Just to get love and word to you, and hope you are making your way through present troubles. So am I! (May even add Kate to our team here for the last 2 weeks;

Expect now to come to Gloucester (at least to bring Chas Peter for a visit with his aunt and cousins) after he finishes here two weeks from Friday (the 19th)

Love, and please write

Charles

108

To Richard Sassoon (1964)

Richard Sassoon, a summer school student at the University of British Columbia in Vancouver in 1963, had sent quotations from Merleau-Ponty's newly published *Phenomenology of Perception,* and Olson included some of them in his talk at Gratwick Highlands in November 1963 (*Muthologos* 1, pp. 55–59). This letter is postmarked 7 October 1964; it was sent to Sassoon at "Berkeley, California," but was returned, stamped "insufficient address."   *Letter at Storrs.*

My dear Richard Sassoon,

Hope you are fortunate, and well, and very much obliged to you (again) for that enormous sheet, on which you offered me quotes a year ago, from Merleau-Ponty. Which today again (I have not yet advanced beyond them!) I found my wife's copy; and used, again. Too much, how inimitable I do find his going beyond Whitehead in analysing literally how it is (for any one of us: that is, it is like Buddha *had* a *sensible* disciple!

Please write (on the chance that our correspondence may ((the question is *only* my own continuity)) revive.—I spent the summer (two months actually only) at home in my 2nd floor half-floor 3 rooms by myself, and unhappily (apparently, as it feels now) have been trying to be *here* again (for on promise a year—on contract 3 abominable years!)

Hope you are like I say on and please write (I remember especially writing you—in the 3rd week of March?—about your novel and that ego or subjective-presentation problem,

                                    and am impelled (suddenly thinking of it, and not at all why I write you) how beautifully Merleau-Ponty (God indeed if there were One of this order—which there isn't: there *is* no "human" God Rest His Soul) does exclusively in those words say action feeling and will are no more than ways to posit an object

It wld break my heart. My dear Sassoon,

                                         yours,

                                            Charles Olson

    address:

            Box 139
            Crosby P.O.
            SUNYAB
            Main Street Buffalo
            New York

109

To Suzie Cardone (1964)

Olson wrote in "The Songs of Maximus" of his father forgetting to wind the clock on the thirtieth day of the month

                    as I don't want to remember
            the rent.

Olson in Buffalo had to pay rent for 28 Fort Square by mail, and he too some-times forgot.   *Letter in possession of Paul Cardone.*

Dear Suzie:

    Was very dumb & didn't get this off to you so you had it on the 1st (excuse, please; it was simply oversight—and *not* excitement over the Election! In fact the probable reason is that the 1st came on a weekend—& you know how funny I find weekends!

Hope all goes altogether for you and Pauli and the kids altogether. Miss you all—and that goes for our neighbors, and our friends around on the beach side. Please give them all my fondest memories and greetings, will you?

Charles Peter seems very much better in school this year, his aunt reports to me; I on the contrary *am not*, in fact *don't like school*, and wish I was home with you all.

Love to yourself and to
the others,

Charles Olson

Monday November 2, 1964,
enclosing rent for November
$34 (with credit of $3
from two Am Express Travelers
checks sent for October rent)

110

To Harvey Brown (1964)

A "wandering scion of a wealthy Shaker Heights industrial family" (as Tom Clark puts it in his biography, *Charles Olson,* p. 315), Harvey Brown had an instinct for finding the center of the action. By the time of this first letter he had become a regular attender at Olson's seminars and the editor and financial angel of *Niagara Frontier Review.* In addition to the *Review,* Frontier Press would within the next year publish poems by Ed Sanders in a volume titled *Peace Eye,* and Edward Dorn's novel *The Rites of Passage.* Brown also wanted to reprint important neglected volumes from the past and sought Olson's advice on titles. *Letter at Buffalo.*

My dear Harv— Got you, on that one. Agree entirely Brooks Adams' book *shld be* Frontier Press—as I originally proposed. (Tell Fred. And the reason I flashed it to him, & that way was in fact a *criticism* of the poeticism I felt so much was breaking-out; and I sought to retrieve the announced *plan,* that that seminar, this year, was to be be-grounded in *American* ("world") history. And in reviewing *The Vinland Map and the Carpini Relation* for Andrew's new magazine, I had been made multiply aware again of the paleolithic value of that one Cro-mag man (from Quincy, or *Braintree*, Massachusetts. *Plus his* own-made *MAPS* (plan the most *perfect* photo-repro *with color* of them, when you get to the *re-edition.*) Even maybe get a *picture*— maybe even there is a great *oil* of Brooks' *Face*—and head. Wow: the Adams' Family Trust, Quincy. For the *COVER:* BROOKS ADAMS   THE *NEW* EMPIRE (!

Ok. & thanks for Ed's letter (retained). And have no other course than go straight ahead everything you propose, or all which has been (except that one, of Ezra's translation, was it) I think is all to the good
(and as soon as I can—or maybe Jack can help (he has recently read some Harvard Muslim Ayrab on Al Araby)—I'll find out where & how to get a translation (done?) of the Meccan revelations
Also I hope
to be in touch with that dope Cyrus Gordon again soon, and will see whether he'll give you a light fast stitch-up of *latest* Linear *A* matters. (Or *successes,* I hope.
Equally, consider *Xerox* editions: that *holograph* of Alice In the Underground *is* publication in the *immediate* future
Or look—wow—Prynne just sent me, as a gift, Chadwick's "The Mycenaean Greek Vocabulary". It isn't even a book. It ought to be—& you're the man to make it one. John Chadwick, Cambridge (It is in the German periodical *Glotta* XLI Band 1963 Heft 3/4)
fascicles: you'd
WIN hands down!
Love to Polly & to the newest member
of the human race,   Yours
Charles
Olson

(Monday November 9th)
Brown published *The New Empire* in 1967, with a preface by Olson.

111

To Harry Martin (1965)

Since he was a fellow resident of Gloucester, the correspondence that Harry Martin received was often in the form of notes, such as this one of 21 June 1960, written when Olson cashed a check that Martin had given him:

Like the Man of Eld I always assume the next day is going to be different— la (like the Wandering Jew he never knows etc   Was dreaming somebody wld suddenly ascend or descend & figure that I was worth a fortune. Or at least a lecture. So you see it always turns out that those who are your friends etc In other words just what you did did it.

Other letters, such as those below, of 8 and 15 January 1965, tended to be continuations of conversations.   *Letters at Storrs.*

[letterhead]
The Tavern   Gloucester, Massachusetts

Harry,
    God is the Father. That is, it is a matter of belief. But if you shift your understanding of your experience there is this fact that is common to men.—What, because he is Christ, doesn't get heard is that he does most say "My Father" 's house kingdom forgiveness etc. I'm pretty sure this also is confirmable, that it is, for each man who does believe, his own Father. Which isn't that literal one we have our life by, but in effect there seems no way the two figures don't mean Father. That, at least, is why I came myself to believe in the (so-called) Lord's Prayer—and my own experience also argues that His Kingdom, and Power, and Glory—just those abstract (or as you feel them rhetorical) phrases equally can be attested as party—as the figure one's own father to Father: one's own realm or place, "power"—in the sense actually of a route for our own personal forces, and that there is a qualitative difference to achievement from the process or materials of it——

All right. I woke up wanting at least to write to you on the matter.

Love,

Charles

Friday January 8th 1965

_____

[letterhead]

The Tavern   Gloucester, Massachusetts

My dear Harry,

Simply not to return you the subject—actually sitting here wanting to write to you anyway, to thank you for your letter, and most, I suppose, for making it known to me (again, maybe, though I don't know that I did know it was St. Augustine who did say that utterly exact fact: what attracts me actually in writing you the Epistle of Charles in the first place to Harry is that I wasn't at all "asking"—or in fact, which is even more exciting, "teaching" (that is, "preaching") but myself feeling so strongly that, as I had said, that that disk, which they had hung on us, the Lord's Prayer—which one might have imagined was or could be a gorget equal to the occasion. I should imagine, though I have no text for it—and certainly probably Augustine may never have referred to it, but the excitement to me is that, in my own experience, and not so long ago, and not at all far from where I am writing this letter to you, the words, not "asking" anything, in that sense you buck at, as indeed I always have for almost identical reasons to your own buck, spelled out every piece, wildly enough, of what belief had come—and that certainly is only what all the matter is about: I was only walking turning both bigger toes toward each other, and muttering to myself

Love, anyway

—and pro-Catholica without any of their load on it, my dear and beloved Friend (to write largely as an Epistle ought—it being a possible thing that the days, years before Augustine and with no problem that Anti-Christ Fish is ending, co-evally with First Fish, necessarily; and that Water-Carrier is who is lapping Earth's shore—time's a-comin'

Don't ask

Love,

O.

from Gloucester to
Magnolia (Ravenswood, Hesperus
Avenue just the other side of
the Coastguard
Station

112
To Edward Dorn (1965)

Writing of LeRoi Jones's *Blues People* in 1964, poet Edward Dorn doubted "that
a white american could feel a part of this book or these people in any *easy* sense"
(*Views*, p. 76). At the end of the review he was moved to say, "Happen what may,
the spirit of this book and its author cannot fail" (p. 78). Dorn was just about to
travel to Buffalo to teach summer school alongside Jones in jobs arranged by
Olson, who saw them there for one evening before he retreated to Gloucester. In
the letter below, Olson is writing to an Edward Dorn who, because of Buffalo,
has undoubtedly become close to Jones in the way a tough, loving elder brother
might. Dorn as brother and Olson as godfather were saddened at Jones's move,
after Malcolm X's death in February 1965, into black politics. Olson begins with
a reference to a "difficult" letter that he had written to Jones at the time of crisis
(it is apparently letter 104 of this volume).   *Letter at Storrs.*

[letterhead]
University Manor Motel
3612 Main Street   Buffalo, New York 14226

Friday March 19th 1965

Ed: Balling me out. Ok. For the said letter *was* enough to ROUND MY
YEAR, and for sd letter altogether was and still is first word I had—
except for Leroi's quadruple talk that night in the kitchen Wyoming—

on what had seemed a "difficult" letter to write.—I have no "judge-
ment", and I gather you don't either, on what he is now in, for himself.
But if I go by language alone—and I never did know any place I both
trusted my judgment, and also wavered, was on it. And on it I can't help
but feel he has gone over to nerves, and because of the same thing you
talk about, his sd mind, I understand that switch yet believe he hadn't
need to, now, or any time thereafter, in fact that he is like they say agi-
tated more than involved, in any sense which strikes me as part and
parcel to what he has got has done and is party to. Which still seems to
me the place any of those of us are who are like with it if possible
too.—I follow, that it is color (and thought he said that enough and for
good in inscribing Blues to the first two Negroes I ever knew). That
seemed everything I knew myself when, joining kindergarten, for some
reason a girl about Kelly's color was sent to show me the toilet; and
competently did, so far as I remember taking me to the boys' part (but
here my memory wavers, as of another instance, when 9 when my father took me to Plymouth—for sd 300th anniversary of the Pilgrims'
Landing—and like a good Catholic boy I sought to attend Mass, and we
did find a church near the Plymouth Cordage Company (which my father wanted to visit) and I did go in, while he was next door, and they
did ring bells on the altar at what seemed to me the proper preparation
for the raising of the Wine and Wafer—yet, to this day I don't know if it
wasn't a Protestant-Episcopal place).

I just have the sense a heroism appropriate to the boat we're all in ((and
Lord your Sea is so large)) is just what Leroi—*because he is a Negro*—
was the "hero" of, simply by being literally a writer *without that adjective.*
I in fact wrote a long poem the day Kennedy won addressed to Leroi
who seemed then and seems now the "key" to that very sort of politics
which goes way ahead of these obviously transposed events of the sd
present—100 years late ((even to quote that time-serving white bastard
from the Southwest)). But there one goes off the basket, and I am grateful to you for telling me how bad you feel. I wasn't as close to Leroi but
he was this sort of fellow for me. And I'd give anything if I thought I
could reach him with the idea herein groped. But I can't feel sure, and
because he didn't answer that letter I feel of course a proper white
square.

I'm enclosing the one I had mentioned (I read it to the people, with John present, and he said—he is always willing to help anyone—he thought I should send it. Even if he didn't think it was as interesting etc. And as I told you I thought I had "pulled it" off—even if something there around that "west of" is in fact too literal to Hector's own "history", that still seems what I am pushing, and will. OK. Anyway, to have you see it.

Also, please use that "like a fold-out" one I sent you last summer (for Wild Dog, as you suggest. That wld be great with me, as I haven't any more *West* poems, and don't like to be out of it this long. (Had a mad visit here—in this motel—from Drummond Hadley and wifely as he calls her—wifey too—and he had new snowshoes just bought at Abercrombie and Fitch, and there was clear sharp snow across the street, and if he didn't get me on them to try them and I walked right up and down humps construction had left: it was as easy as moccasins, and very like them in the lightness of sense of walking. Have you any impression of Hadley's poems? He has seemed to me since I saw a single image—doubled—in a poem at Vancouver a new sensibility; and his nutty syntax, which he is a bear to maintain, makes it. (?)

Very delighted to learn you are all making it to England, and wish the report were true that I was also to be there. But fact is time has gone very slow for me, and I need to haul up, and though one way would be to travel—that is, if I get the means ((I ain't saving nothing of this huge salary because I am spending it all eating sleeping and moseying around, and anyway it is so much I don't like that much—I mean I do, but I don't know how to put it away (why?

I keep thinking I *will* go somewhere; and if I do I cld come see you at least (via Ireland like)   And also have a recent desire to see Greece. But it will only any of it happen if I get all dragging stuff caught up. And being around here doesn't help: I invent things which make things worse!

Love to you all and cut out a big piece of it for Helene (whose letter in the issue inscribed to Bet I did find and read). Charles Peter's being raised by Bet's sister Jean in Gloucester; and I've seen him three or four times this year, and he seems very much better having boys to live with, plus Kathy, and to go to the same school with ((we all went, including Kate, to his Baptism! at Thanksgiving; and then, at Christmas, I busted, on his First Communion (at our Lady of the Voyage) where for the first time I attended a Mass in English and walked out.—Kate gets to be quite a chick, 13 going on 14, and most of the problems are her education: she wants out of Friends (in Philadelphia) but her mother, as well as I, fight this etc.—Creeley was here, with Bobbie, appearing with Robert Graves (who was swell) and Snodgrass (who also is something: the post-Teen Cub Scout Poet—wow: healthy, and—successful—opinion). Creeley looking younger handsomer and better dressed than ever—smooth, *tight* (and going, I'd still think—as I had at Vancouver—thru a won-drous close squeeze, the like of which only he will make.—John fortu-nately is here and it has made this silly return to do the term of this promise at least to Cook to put in a year (I felt it wasn't any harm for me to stay with it at present) but if John hadn't been here I'm sure I'd have come to grief. He is a comfort like the Irish say, and besides his poems wow me. I'll cut this, and please come back to me.

I'm obliged to you for giving Davie the haircut and close shave but he does seem finally simply a new one of the old kind, with a care & a cau-tion sitting where a prick ought to, or a bean. (I read his last chapter in the Pound book—stuffed into my hand by Andrew Crozier. And I couldn't tell which way he was taking either Ezra or myself.) Actually *still* Prynne's mind interests me most (of the sd English—though I must say, working this seminar here, one comes on some very attractive comparable attentions to Prynne among like historiographers or tech-nologists (methodologists?) as Prynne seems intellectually to be (?)—Christopher Hawkes, say, as an *early* example: if you have any way to see *Antiquity* read Hawkes' *present* prose in a screaming piece against the British govt. & museum on their failure to publish sufficient reports on the *Sutton Hoo Burial Boat!*

Love and all best to you all

(Tell me your plans—
& schedule

Yrs

Charles

Hector-body,
my Cow to the left my Cow to the right:

> Goddess—

shield Ajax
    or the Knossian
who is compared to Enyalios

> crossed in Helladic to

Troy
      now moves on east from
west of Albany

> got home again,

> Wednesday
> January 20th
> 1965

113

To Mary Shore and Vincent Ferrini (1965)

Olson was invited to Gian Carlo Menotti's "Festival of the Two Worlds," 26 June–2 July 1965, in Spoleto, Italy, where many poets gathered. He was the guest of his old friend Caresse Crosby in her castle near Rome. From there he traveled to Bled, Yugoslavia, for an International P.E.N. meeting. In these letters to his closest Gloucester friends, we get Olson's reaction to being on the one poetry junket of his life. *Letters at Storrs.*

[letterhead]
Grand Hotel Toplice, Bled, Jugoslavia

Sat July 10th

Mary! From Wop-land, to Slovenia. (so far—and *unless* I revolt, that will be about *all*, on this shot, for I am *supposed* to be in San Francisco within abt a week! Hurry Hurry.

Crazy scenes: Spoleto last week (very hot, and hot, and good—here, for something called Internat'l P.E.N.(!) : kalt, and Germanish tourists, and *English* very English, very German— ROME delicious hot, and good—but I *may* (to get out of here, have to fly to London (via Regersflug, over the border nearby, Austria) in order to return to Rome—where I left my baggage—& warm clothes.

Love and greetings, and keep the home fires burning; *maybe* I will fly right *home* (That's how much *minded* I am for *this* scene!

Charles

[letterhead]
Grand Hotel Toplice, Bled, Jugoslavia

Saturday night
July 10th

Vincent—Vin-scent, properly you shld have had a letter from your own family's olde country—but I was *run* fr. Spoleto to Rome, and vis-

vice-

versa (including Roccocinibolda, Caresse Crosby's Castle—*365* rooms, literally, and flying the flag of the Citizens of the World above it like the *only* Renaissance I have seen (in Italy—the poets of Europe are *all* 'umanismo—and you can imagine how I do! (Only *Neruda* sounded like etc—and of course le grande master, EZRA POUND, whom I read in front of, and in homage to, at the Teatro Caio Melissa, Spoleto (here the scene was different—Arthur Miller!

Love, and over

Charles

114

To Suzanne Mowat (1965)

Twenty-year-old Suzanne Mowat, who had come to the Berkeley Poetry Con- ference by car from Vancouver, was the person whom Olson palled around with during those hectic days, the last two weeks of July 1965. On 12 August, back in her own room in her parents' house in Vancouver, she wrote a five-page long-hand letter, which reads in part as follows:

Hello Charles;

Sometime you will certainly be going home to Gloucester, and when you do I hope it pleases you that I am in a letter to you. God knows what this letter-to-be will be ABOUT, but I feel like writing to you, wherever you are. (Perhaps at this very moment having, finally, dinner with the Sister in San Rafael!) I feel like *TALKING* to you—I'm so *bored* with writing—I can never do it fast enough. . . . I am under a hair dryer. I am wearing a dark red denim shift, very short and loose, which I wore my last night in magic young girl Paris, the night before I left for London and Alice Donovan from FAT HILL ILLINOIS left for Loudres on a promise to her mother, to fill the wine bottles she had emptied around Europe, many many of them in a huge string bag on her back, she wore Lederhosen, to fill them with *Holy Water* to take as gifts to her friends and relatives in Fat Hill, USA. And we met two painters and in a wild whirl of taxis and waving and laughing we were separated by accident/lust/circumstance, and I still have this, her shift, and she owes me about $50. And I'll never see her again, though we write and promise it to one another.   Now it is later. In the meantime two friends from London came to visit and now it is 3:30. There seems little reason to go to bed. Just as I sat down at the beginning of this letter, they played on the radio the "Loving Spoonful," singing my magic song:

> Believe in the magic of a young girl's soul;
> Believe in the magic of rock and roll;
> Believe in the magic that will set you free

etc. It made me *nostalgic* of all things,—for all the things that San Francisco was to me. And all the people it was to me. Wasn't our "good-bye" AWFUL? So abrupt. But perhaps that was the best way; is there a best way? It was, anyway, the way it happened. I didn't sleep that night except for about an hour at dawn, wrapped up in my good white coat, on an old mattress, in the most incredibly depressing room, ALONE in that vast house . . . and wondering what I felt about GOING HOME. How strange to leave the city I had always wanted to be in, the city I had felt GOOD in, I mean REALLY GOOD . . . To go with you (and John?) was certainly *appealing*, to say the least. But do you understand at all that *by all that you offered* you made it impossible for me? I mean it would have been *SO EASY.* And I have had things *made* easy for me all my life. . . . Don't laugh at me, please. I have no sense of humour about myself tonight. No poems need writing about me; I'm just walking around. Should I mail this *garbage*—I mean, are you interested enough in me to accept *this*, or does this rambling get you angry? What are your reactions? These are not questions to be *answered*, but simply my attempt at *seeing* you, in Gloucester, reading a letter from me. Will you answer?

Olson answered, though not at such great length. His letters, or notes, of 21 August, 9 September, 30 September, 20 October, 2 November, 9 November, and 10 December 1965 appear below. *Letters at Storrs.*

Suzanne   You are it. To walk in here last night (Friday Aug 20) & find all yourself—& see you in the line as I never fail; if you don't write me at least as therein constantly—& if you think I threw everything at you I don't think we have yet begun:

You are *the*

special

one,

him who says so, &

in love,

Chas

Friday Sept 9th!

My darling Suzanne,

Going back to Buffalo tomorrow but happily enough feel reasonably certain I shall actually something or other & want you therefore to continue to write me here—

Actually, been in Maine also, & having a wonderful time here on my own Main Street

Love   love every word
you have sent me

& until things settle down (? that is I mean maybe they won't?? horrible thought: it wld be like chasing around with *you*) you mustn't expect more than this from me (except if I walk in here some night—I suddenly seem to be leaving my "flat" (tenement, actually, & real slum I should imagine to anyone (including my ex-wife I

found out this weekend to my horror) open, the door somebody tells
me tonight *wide open*—all right you are just as I found you & please
keep telling me, your

own

Charles

---

28 Fort Sq

Suzanne: Why don't you ask your own friend *McClure*? (In any case
February's no good for me) *And John*?? *together*   (Actually the idea of
asking Pound is a beautiful one—& *I'd* do it *1st*, if I were you. But I
very much expect WINTER wld keep him home—& then ask Mike, &
John (I'd love to come but I want to try to go far far away this winter
myself.

Love—& quickly—   Charles

I have a new way of measuring things—like just now not going to

But—

etc—& of course since you refused to marry me: it goes I've just got
loving spoonfuls for my self

Love

O

What is WRONG with you, any how?

Where are your letters?

Please let me hear what's new up & etc:

you *know* how *busy* I am,

love,

O

My dear muffit   it is a pleasure to hear from you—& to *see* you (I'll
keep it for a little while just to look at those legs (the nose isn't that
good!)

And you have (besides those legs) the egotism of a man: wow
Mow what a combination (I honestly can't see

          how Mow

                  you can be

anything except

      what you damn well are

              going to be

  It's a pleasure

       to *expect*

            love

              O

  & for coming there
every *June*   what a lovely
thought—or if I were ever that far or I mean that way
with it!

            Come back—or come *here*!
              Soon
                C

Hey Mow, that's a doll of a picture—And who can't see the eyes for the nose? Marvelous to have ya in this house again. (Miss you.) Doing all right. Maybe the only drag like is it's taking too much time

           And Ed

(the Sanders, now running the Spoonfuls a long 40th on a new record—you know *his* group—featuring Maximus from Dogtown #One (that is 41 on the Hit Per-rade—& they're (the Fugs) going to England for a *spring* tour—and have asked me to join them (as, I suppose, vocalist (?

  Anyway you see while you sleep—

        OK. Hope you are like happy.
And I mean that (the other I know you are,

         Really missing
       Your own Very self,

          Charles

There were about ten more exchanges of letters in a similar jocular vein up to October 1968. The two correspondents never did get together again.

115

To Albert Glover (1965)

Glover was a graduate student at Buffalo. He worked with George Butterick on the Olson *Bibliography* and *Archaeologist of Morning*. His dissertation was published as *Letters for Origin*. The following letter, probably of 7 October 1965, was published in the third issue of *Magazine of Further Studies*.

Letter at Storrs.

Al,
      Imagine: simply to be an animal.
Imagine, that that is all we are. Life-wise,
that is. The doe has no more eyes
than we do. Or the fly
fly differently
than us. To go around this corner
is to place Death
in its wise. We are not plants planets or
do we sleep
hereafter. Rest. Or wither
in that sense weeds
do—turn back into
seeds. We both move,
as an animal
do. And our procreation
is choice (that difference,
possibly, chastity,
care. But solely within
life-time. Not after, not for any
after, not for any reason,
or reach, other than
life's) Death's province is
death, a definable animal
nothing: Cause or occasion of loss of life;
Cessation or privation, as of function, existence, capacity
for development, etc; extinction. René
Char, and William Carlos Williams on
René Char's trauma, that, that is

what happens. So be it, so many animal
bones. Charnel-house. Thrown over, in a pile
all solemn bones we lie, in death. Dead. Unmotived,
no farther revealed (that is, by ourselves)
unable to take breath, look out of our eyes,
call over the near fence, plan to go to Swamps-
cott,

        can transcend anything there is or men have
done, watching out the window the dumb
beady eyes
of a sparrow (birds are not animals
in the sense of pattern, including
geese, and that their calls, are
territorial) animals
experience
death————————————

                            Love,

                              O

116

To John Clarke (1965)

When Olson left Buffalo abruptly in the third week of his third year, John Clarke was the one faculty member who could take over his mythology seminar. Olson's letters of advice from 10 to 28 October 1965 on how best to conduct the seminar were collected into a fascicle titled *Pleistocene Man.*   *Letter as published there.*

           Don't read this as a letter: read it as though I were
                 —as in fact etc—*Paleolithic!*

Jack—
   It's almost like poetry. In fact it *is* poetry, Pleistocene, in that simplest *alphabetic* sense, that you can learn the language of being alive—
in that most elementary way which is so easily taken for granted (or

used as though it were only elementary)—that with which you are most familiar—as though you were learning to read and to write for the first time. It has that turn around an impossible corner of what is so much it that a modo is the last matter one might think is one—that it is there, outside, literally, and can be observed—Venice Observed as well as Venice Destroyed, For All of Us.

        (I judge I'm trying again to urge you to sterilize it as knowledge; or in fact to plead some advantage, as against knowledge—in fact, as against the very advantages of mythology, that *her* stones and poems are creations, and that those—*that*— *technology* of Pleistocene—literally (again) that *ice*, and just what you say Sauer is riddling, why Yuma, and Folsom, people would have NOTHING TO DO WITH *LOUSY* mesolithic curds sherds dried dogshit Man. And their new weapons and dogs. I should think so.

        But

equally you yourself *AVOID* puns (domesticity: i.e., Lew Welch as poetry) and "history" (Anthropology—or (by the Rule above, this is *not* mythology. It is the preparation (of Man) for live, there isn't any such *Multiple* as those 1000 faces of literally Joseph Campbell: put in front of *yourself* Zimmer (that idiot JC's own teacher)'s *India*. For dogmatics. Literally. For *Composition*. For exact etymologies & to the best of his abilities, recoveries—the same recoveries Buddha used the Upanishad to give himself a sense of the usefulness of the Rig Veda, probably. That is *note* how *objectionable* Coomaraswamy—aestheticist—is, every time Campbell in his greasy White Man lousy lazy shitness, has legged something from a fucking "Indian."

    I'm, like, recommending, urging on you, that the hard-stuff here— that if you begin with pencil, & paper, & eraser, & duplication & & & put out in front

        expose an intransitive verb: I mean that the million billion specifics of Pleistocene as so many facts from 1) an environment & 2) of a man both fresh in an impossible way to man at this date—700 years after the birth of Dante

        and including such marvelous advances or genetic conditions

        advances of present-day Liberals
        do-gooders as William Boyd

and such an out & out Fascist
as Artemus Gates—
                              (my own experience still is
there isn't any other Halicarnassus—or whatever City it was Heraclitus
came from & put down so as example of how also *he* became the *1st*
loser by
analogy   pissed-off excellent man who he well is (what was his native
town?

                    Pictures
                get someone to duplicate
            all objects *to scale*
          get blood-types *all* across—&
      with ribbons on maps for
      migrations (of surviving blood tests
                among Esquimaux as well as
                Indian-types—

                              you were asking for *Survivals*
(wow Sauer please note—no actually—get his, & a woman's 4th
grade *Geography* called Man in *America*

                              (starts with California nut-
grinders
            the job is quieter, and sweeter, and no performance, and an
entrance like into the Trophonian cave or the pretty—*beautiful*—nun
with the big hands gazing like Garbo at Pope Paul   how come *she* entered the Church?

    Take it all around the *school* side. Honestly, not the *big advanced last*
graduate seminar: Henry Lesnick for example Wow Or Charles
(Brover) Or for example John Wieners and John Temple: Come in
every day with new sweets, & all covered on top with those sprinkled
colored infinitely *small* sweet-pepper tops on top
                              In fact look: plan it
for the year. The pay-off, if you bend them to these *childish* attentions
& things (like *reverse* Speculative & Applied) Winter Apples—&
Mirror
        will be *position*

                  like bus trips to a Museum never before
accomplished or lying out like Cezanne's 2 men & 2 women or the

brookside the Cop chased us to or Constance Chatterley noticed the
collar-color red on Mellors's body when she realizes how white his
body is
>   or that undisturbed dust on the floor at *Les Eyzies*
>   any of
those crazy supermarket displays the Earth itself—& single man
>   the Reindeer bone
>   carved with a
>   *Waterfall*

You: check a U. of Chicago Press Book Catalogue for that *Anthropology*
I (or II) "Human Origins" *Earliest* Xerox-publishing known to me
(1948?): in it is the *geographer* whose thesis on how the *ends* of all continents are the *Earliest* people because they were *pushed* out, & *South*
(! — or to the *Islands* or by-passed like Alexander did Halicarnassus etc

117

To Ralph Maud (1965)

Ralph Maud, having moved from Buffalo to Simon Fraser University near Vancouver, British Columbia, sent a postcard depicting Tsimshian Indian artifacts.
This was Olson's response.   *Letter in possession of the recipient.*

>   Wednesday October 13th
Dear Ralph,
    Delighted to hear from you, & to have the Tsimshian stone "clubs,"
they call them! You may recall I used Richard Payne Knight's *The Worship of Priapus* as the *sole* text of sd seminar previous fall. These are excellent objects, and I am happy to know of them. Some years ago, at
Portland, there was an extraordinary exhibit—the catalogue is worth
looking up, it was their Museum, & the date I'd think would be 1948
almost—a general collection of Northwest Indian, and you probably do
know the masks in the New York Historical—the one on 86th street—
Natural History
>   in any case, talking the other night of the *delay* of all
Northwest people—& that would seem to go from Crescent City north,

& only Oscar Heizelman, of Portland, who presented himself to me
again after one of those afternoon gigs Berkeley—& is now a *Hopi* Indian. Sole exception to rule, that Northwest Coast & Province people
are *delayed*, humanly
                              But my point is how *dazzling* and by the law of
inversion how equally late (they say "recent") the art of the Tsimshian
etc—any of the mouths or reaches of the salmon rivers, the Norwest *Indians* were. (Gary Snyder & Co. take notice—plus all my girl friends,
Vancouver!!

—(2 So keep me on. Hope your pondiferous position ought to give
you a sense of "light," & that your wife is happier: she deserves to be. I hear
of course from Al Glover & the rest of the gang. As you'd know I started
Pleistocene (and was, in fact, *after* Berkeley, finding the poetry seminar this
year much more a possibility for myself—had great plans) but I couldn't
face *another year* away from home, & have taken leave. Which Al, Cook
that is, as usual, was extraordinarily able in giving, & arranging, for me.

I owe you, by the way, a great deal, for the "idea" you had, to dig me,
on the Maximus poems, that steady run last June. It "occupied" me, & I
hadn't realized how much I did need just that. And as you know, & saw
(not the *best* instances of, but *at least* that first lecture—& that last
seminar—were possible, probably, because of the "method" your caus-
ing me to gloss myself produced.

Best all, & to your wife & boy, & the Vancouverites (they are sorts of
stones too,
                                                    Charles

118

To Andrew Crozier (1965)

On 25 May 1965, as he was winding up his teaching at Buffalo, Olson read
Andrew Crozier's graduate seminar paper and commented: "No trouble actually
allowing you an A on this: let's do more Sumerian-*Gothic* next round!"
(manuscript at Simon Fraser). Crozier had refused to deal with Greek mythology
and had turned to H. R. Ellis Davidson's *Gods and Myths of Northern Europe*

(1964) as more attuned to his temperament. Thus fixed in Olson's mind as Eddic, Crozier, when he started *Wivenhoe Park Review* in Essex on returning to England from Buffalo, received from Olson a series of pieces on Northern mythology, beginning with a review of *The Vinland Map*, enclosed with this letter of 18 October 1965.   *Letter at Simon Fraser.*

                    Monday   28 Fort Square Gloucester Massachusetts
Andrew
      With great pleasure sending this to you immediately
                                                  But please will
send two or maybe three—and one of them sort of a large 'scrip
                                                       scribal
"map" (a Maximus *poem* occupying several pages

      Very happy to hear from you, & delighted that you have begun
this magazine   (Temple, by the way, yesterday, sent me wonderful
gripe poem on Eastward inclines dealing with Cambridgeshire
FENS (dig?
            Wld make very much sense for your OPENER

      ALSO:
            what abt *asking* for *newer*—or using *MRS* Xpher HAWKESES
FATHINGHAM MAN or whatever?—so even the EDUCATED get A
SENSE how WE ARE RESTORING *ISLANDS* AND *MARS'ES FIELD*
(end of even gerund not to speak of end of METONOMY) ALL OVER
THE NEW—AND OLD—& excluding ASIA (because she is a Renais-
sance DRAG (CHINA et al MAO'S EAST WIND BULLSHIT
                              Love,
                                O

119

To Albert Cook (1965)

Of Olson's final days at Buffalo, Albert Cook in "I Remember Olson" (in the Olson issue of *boundary 2*) paints a rather dismal picture:

Holding forth to Carol and sometimes myself through afternoon break-
fasts in our kitchen, about his life and the cosmic vision, subdued in the
spring months after Bet's crash-death;

Expatiating on the love-life sly and heartbroken over a bad Chinese meal
across from campus;

Holding forth on the swings of meter after admitting me on invitation past the
"Keep out this means you" sign tacked to his second-floor room door in the
motel across from campus of his last year, half his worldly stuff of the moment
in the wrecked, often breaking car on the lot downstairs, his telephone wrapped
in several thicknesses of shirt and shut in the flimsy dresser drawer . . .

The fall 1965 semester had barely begun, but Olson had to flee. His letter of
resignation was written at the Buffalo airport, a portion on a Mohawk Airlines
boarding pass, and was dated 23 September 1965 (now at Storrs).

My dear Al—It's silly for me to try, I'm worn out from trying, I've been in
that damned Motel, and now in this Airport since Tuesday trying to figure
out what to do But the truth of the matter is I haven't been one hour
happy or well—except literally while working—since I left home.
     I hope you will therefore hear me, that the only possible conceivable
thing I can do seems to be to stay at home—and because I'm doing this at
what must to you and anyone else seem an unconscionable date, I must
take anything which follows. But I also want directly to acknowledge to
you how much I hope you will accept this as the very best I can do and at
the earliest I could.

As a superb department chairman and understanding friend, Cook made
Olson's departure all right with the university. Although in fact he never
returned, Olson was happy not to have the door closed shut. The letter below
records one occasion on which he regrets not having the income the position at
Buffalo would have guaranteed.   *Letter at Storrs.*

                                        Thursday December 2nd
My dear Al,
     Can you actually tell me then where I am *now* on the salary ques-
tion? That is, as I read Allan Sapp's you enclosed to me (as of November
23rd) it was some remarkable possibility (of a *sick leave* expiring but *re-
establishable "for a period of an additional five months"(!)!* With yours of
Nov. 30 just in (acknowledging my wire) this moment I *judge* my OK to
you on your wire has therefore *removed* that "*re-establishment*"(?

I am *not* holding a hand out, and my impression also is that you must yourself have (in putting my leave to College of Arts & Sciences) given me some whopping advantage already (? ?

In any case simply that my own present living & future possibility has suddenly taken on this further aspect, can you *personally* inform me what *more*(!) salary—and I mean of course actually only by virtue of *the machinery* itself (that is I am clearly getting gravy as is!) But do (when you have a moment) drop me a line on where, *in this term of money alone*, now be. *OK?*

Love to Carol & yourself
& the boys,
Charles

Had a *lovely* day Thanksgiving with Charles Peter, and his cousins, and Jean (and her husband, to the degree that he *can* actually appear to enjoy anything!) The 4 of the now grown cousins—13, 11, 10 & 10 Charles Peter—danced for us, And it was

Whiskey A Go-Go

all over: there *is* an unbelievable dance revolution in this belted stuff. I swear it has already topped the sex argument, the *Fish*, I mean, the Monkey, the hip thing (developing out of the Twist) I can't catch the double name at the moment

like Huckle-Buckle

—beautiful movements *all* use

(in formalness like minuet—or polka) & thus each person on the floor (I'm thinking of that club in San Francisco the night we all celebrated the binding & therefore publishing of Human Universe) is themselves like a professional trained dancer—

go with it, let go
& how utterly they *therefore*

—because they have these forms—take care of, & have feeling towards each other on the floor.

It is almost a dream how this particular develop-

ment has come on (out of the Beatles, & actually in the last year & a half)

Also the last *two days only*—and the reason why suddenly I have *money* on my mind!—been *thrown* into the City's life (I *think* tonight

I shall "resign")—it all started when I saw Hagstrom's crane destroying *another* of the Middle Street houses—a *beautiful* Neo-Classical—
marvelous columns—Solomon Davis, 1840. I wrote three "Letters to
the Editor" (two poems actually, one *a* poem the other a *scream.*
And the Times will print them tomorrow I hear—(all three). But
the sudden upshot was (yesterday) that the Historical Association—
which *was* about to have Hagstrom

        his son was a Princeton football star two years ago!
smash the servants' quarters of their *own* precious fucking "90 Middle".
Which I have celebrated in verse. And by god (having written & just
posted—or sent by *cab,* actually—to the paper & feeling I wished to be
straight with my friend here the architect who also, unknown to me
until yesterday, is the Chairman of the Historical Society's *Finance Committee!*) if he didn't ask me if I'd like to buy the Servants' Quarters—1st
time they have ever suggested anyone make an offer! (dating from 1783
at least according to my own scholarship)

           So overnight, &
this morning bright & early there I was *at the bank* seeing what kind of
an offer, & what mortgage etc—

        dig *that,* for a,
development!

      So *rush* the information asked for(!)

              Actually I *don't*
think they'll even entertain an offer even if I cld make one (turns out
the *price* isn't the sticker—its the *condition* of the poor shell—& god
knows the *only reason* wld be to hold a line of *argument* at least

            (I *am* after all
             somewhat of an *inverted-*
             Socrates! is it not possibly so?)
which—if the *Times does publish tomorrow* (they were *originally* going
to, *today,* so you see what a press(!) or pressure it has been—and *hardly*
my universal, (again: I do *throw* down Soc's raison of his death that he
'twere a *citoyen du monde*) such a local involvement (brand new, in fact,
& very much thank you Mr Cook due to my financial power—or status
at least at the moment . . . !!!!

              Love & *over*
              Charles

Love /
                is

well—didn't you *say* what it was, una noche?

                        Yr most admiring (*former*) servant—
                        happily when or as under *such* circumstance

(Many thanks altogether once again for
swinging the bucket.)

                                Your old *Admirer*
                                        Charles

120

To the *Gloucester Daily Times* (1965)

In sending to Robert Creeley a clipping of this "letter to the editor," Olson wrote: "It certainly looks as though I'm looking for trouble. But you can see I have some allies, eh?" (letter of 6 December 1965 at Stanford). One of his allies was Paul Kenyon, editor of the *Gloucester Daily Times,* who gave Olson's letters prominence in the paper. This "Scream" was published on 3 December 1965 in facsimile typescript, with an accompanying photograph.

                        Letter in the Gloucester Daily Times.

A *Scream* to the Editor:

Moan the loss, another
house
is gone

                Bemoan the present
which assumes
its taste, bemoan the easiness
of smashing anything

Moan Solomon Davis'
house, gone
for the YMCA, to build another

of its cheap benevolent places
bankers raise money for,

and who loan money for new houses: each destruction doubles
our loss and doubles bankers' gain when four columns

    Bemoan a people who spend
    beyond themselves, to flourish
  and to further themselves

as well made the Solomon Davis house itself
was such George Washington
could well have been inaugurated
from its second floor

    and now it is destroyed because 70 years ago
Gloucester already could build the Y, and Patillo's
equally ugly brick front and building

    (between them the Davis house, then 50 years old,
    was stifled squeezed in no light on one side a Patch
    of soil like a hen-yard toward Patillo's

    houses live or else why
  is *one room* in 90 Middle Street worth
  $100,000 to the Metropolitan Art Museum?

  If taste is capital of this order had not
  Cape Ann Historical Scientific and Literary Society
  or Cape Ann Historical Association—

  if John Babson the historian *founded* both
  the abovementioned society *and* the Sawyer Free Library
  —and was a banker too, and wrote, with two others, the
    principal history
of Massachusetts banking to his time,

how many ways can value be
allowed to be careless with, and Hagstrom
destroy? how many more before this obvious
dullness shall cease?

oh city of mediocrity and cheap ambition destroying
its own shoulders its own back greedy present persons

stood upon, stop this renewing without reviewing
loss loss loss no gains oh not moan stop stop stop this

       total loss of surface and of mass,
          putting bank parking places with flowers, spaces dead so dead
      in even the sun one does not even know one passes by them
Now the capitals of Solomon Davis' house
now the second floor behind the black grill work
now the windows which reached too,

now the question who if anyone was living in it
now the vigor of the narrow and fine clapboards on the back
now that flatness right up against the street,

        one is in despair, they talk and put flowers up
      on poles high enough so no one can water them,
and nobody
objects
      when houses which have held and given light
      a century, in some cases two centuries,
               and their flowers
    aren't even there in one month

             —the Electric Company's
lights are there, every night, to destroy the color of color
in human faces—Main Street is as sick at night as Middle

Street is getting banker-good in sun light—a swimming pool
is now promised where Solomon Davis sat beside the Dale House
& looked with some chagrin at Sawyer's not as tasteful house
across the way,
        I'm sick
      of caring, sick of watching
      what, known or unknown, *was* the
        ways of life . . I have no
        vested interest even in this which
        makes life.
            Moan nothing. Hate hate hate

I hate those who take away
and do not have as good to
offer. I hate them. I hate the carelessness

For $25,000 I do not think anyone
should ever have let the YMCA take down Solomon Davis'
house, for any purpose of the YMCA

Peter Anastas has collected Olson's missives to the newspaper, seventeen in all, into a volume, *Maximus to Gloucester* (1992). In a note to the above letter, Anastas writes: "The site was used as an outdoor basketball court until the original Y was torn down" (p. 90).

121

To Betty Smith (1965)

This letter is in response to a social invitation from Peter Smith and his wife, who owned a well-known reprint publishing house in Gloucester. It was returned to Olson, as per his request on the back of the envelope, postmarked 8 December 1965.   *Letter at Storrs.*

My dear Betty Smith
      That really is very gracious of you. Actually I am pretty crusty, and I *was* mean in swinging like that, and the *hope* is, I suppose, to see if one cld *arouse* everyone! And of course one only ends up with probably—or quite clearly—most if not exactly everyone thinking I too am personal about it. I'm not, and I *cannot* stop seeking (one actually in fact has *about* given up the expectation that *anywhere*, within the bounds of the exact geographical limits of specifically the United States of America—and there is *no exception* to this, *nature* even being abused—and now *overtly*, human nature having been so squandered, within these boundaries that *every* human being who isn't ready today to change, and utterly, and immediately—and it is *known* how to do that, just what it takes, & costs, and it is *delightful* in fact, all *any* kids practically (not that *I* will give them any "room" I don't mean. Or any of the present allowances they are receiving. None of that. That isn't what I mean.

      It's goodness, actually, of any kind (other than as *he* said who called Judas he who betrayed "*the Best*"—and it was in fact a still most interesting if (again) like everything else we have had our lying saliva on, spoiled . . . the quote is from Measure (in the sense fair measure—or *foul*, if that were the exchange for fair or foul Measure.

It is disgusting—and I hope you will hear me speak with honor, for I can *prove* that the Americans actually (again, actually—it seems only the word to acquire, or offer, equal demand) the Americans, who have made themselves, their land and the world, for they *are* still conquerors, offensive, and it will be worse, they alone *also* have—not the same *ones*, that's I'd now assume is why one hates and fights, even if it was one's *mother* like they used to say, the other way about, that he'd sell his mother or something

> again I am thinking of Christ's requirement (and in which gospel is it?), I come to offer swords, cut off your wife children husband own . . .

not at all please to hear me quote like scripture I *think* in fact—or know things are so bad even Christianity has lost by abuse of its text the very thing I wld *swallow* each thing in Gloucester which is *good* I mean *able* skill at fixing an oil stove a man today 81 who comes to my door and did *not* say one word out of his mouth which didn't drop in to my ear like the sweet poison of original creation—

> it *is* nature and God

and man—and there isn't any other thing at all which is true or interesting except these three conditions—all of which have been played with and now not even any longer can *that* even be said because even this monster ourselves the Americans have fixed that up: they *now* have actually only two fake conditions themselves. Only two: acculturation, and an-aesthetics (anaesthesia, literally

> aisthētēs one who perceives
> anaesthetics *not* feeling

they will themselves blast like a blastophore or they will be *blasted* from the earth—and please, Mr & Mrs Smith, hear only that my disgust is so free I don't even feel it, my feeling is so enlisted in what *already*, and can and certainly will remove the debris no matter how successful, and *pretty* and powerful and all the world *fooled* the debris shall show itself.

That *is* what is so altogether exactly what is going on *wherever* you *look* or walk or simply try to go out & buy the necessities in Gloucester and I suppose *right now* for the very reason that *the universal has* become now the *end* of any more tolerance of any least allowance: Gloucester is a figure of the "steel" of a "feather" which as you know doesn't even have—I mean a feather doesn't—an edge.

Thank you, I think there is *such* future even exactly *anything* done or proposed can't even be allowed unless it is expensive, the best possible, and I mean *technically* (technical-ly) and *economically*

I don't

mean at *saving* anything, actually the other way about

Oh yes the *epigraph* to what I had sent the Times I have with no connection found this statement in the Paradise: it is made to the poet by the woman who is taking him part of the way in the direction of his chance to see the face of God or at least the possible effulgence of light instead of course any such impossible direct sight of the face

> no change a worthy one
> unless what he takes up contains in it,
> at least as six does four, what he puts down
> (tercet 20 of part 5)

Charles Olson

PS   I am, as you might know, only comparatively recently *back* from the enormous wastage, if some gain, of being away from Gloucester now more than two years, and you must excuse me as I have had to ask all practically but my sister-in-law if I am not free, at present, to go out except under my own steam. Perhaps though—and I shld enjoy it—I might surprise myself as well as you people and call up suddenly and ask to see you! It isn't so long since at least we spoke. Your husband I haven't seen for a very long time. In fact if your husband will fill in the enclosed check in the right amount I will have accomplished what I told Herb & Theresa Kenny Friday night last at their house I wanted: to own the complete diary of that Salem fellow who used to come to Gloucester at the time so often he found her so, I understand, much more to his taste—it was before & perhaps somewhat also a few years' visits after 1800. I forget his name. He was a doctor, and I *think* he is the fellow who bought that quite remarkable library of an English scientist which was part of salvage when the ship carrying it fetched up somewhere about the coast, around or near Salem—or Beverly. Maybe I have that not right.

[back of envelope]
Note added Tuesday:

Cuteness has descended upon the world like wrist-watches—the sister of cheapness. Which is production, which is male, for when *men* do not do their work—or selling replaces labor, arousing appetite instead of renewing goods—all goods & acts become or are allowed to be easy, easily acquired (credit) & deliberately easily destroying. No woman can respect this—or any man, either.

Final note (I hope!): if your husband has a Xerox machine I shld be *very* obliged if you wld return me copy of this—inc. *this envelope*!

122

To Henry Rago (1966)

The pages of *Poetry* were hospitable to Olson's poetry on several occasions. The editor, Henry Rago, made the friendly gesture of sending to Olson a copy of *Poetry* for March 1965, which included a memorial Rago had written on the death of T. S. Eliot. The following is Olson's response.   *Letter at Indiana.*

My dear Henry Rago:
    I dislike (as much as Eliot) private mythology. (Even if I wldn't have known the phrase, except by his use of it, and equally of course would hardly seem, or have anything like the thought or grounds for which he speaks it. Though I very well do exactly agree with his application of it, and in irritation, to Rilke.

It is so valuable—and *fairly*, and *specially*, can I, I do think, say it! He is so right—and so many poets, especially in a time in which they are led, with rings in their nose from Freud to dig for trifles.

I am obliged to you for it. Curiously, due to the fact it was addressed to the Tavern, I only received, & have read it, today. (I can also say this: your memorial is the first time I have had the feeling of his loss—and as you would know Gloucester does have its place in his life, rather, I think, surprisingly, or unnoticed by a good many of people. I have the impression actually the garden (the rose-garden, so much in the Family Reunion—and Ash-Wednesday of course if I remember correctly—is, like that proposal of Bill Wms to Flossie, stuck here. Have you ever heard of any such idea? A lovely incident took place at the house—I *think* it must have been the woman herself by which I know it (not from her directly though)—on Eliot's last trip. He asked to go up in the attic, and there, unknown to her were all her dress-maker's forms, over the years—and her grandchildren, supposedly, had got in there & re-dressed each of them with abandoned corsets they also found under the eaves. Whatever revery Eliot intended (if that was it) was driven out & down-stairs in his laughter at what he'd run into—instead.

His wife by the way was here recently, I saw in the paper, talking to the new librarian (the first time, the paper, says, it has been a man). So I suppose the family does know—or she does—or could it be solely generally, as from that section of *Four Quartets*?

Curiously (also)—and with no connection to *him* at all—my friend Ferrini's wife, I believe, did her M. Ed. on Eliot here. I've not seen it—but again it does raise that matter I ask you about, if that "garden" was here, or is this news?

> Greetings—& very obliged to you for
> sending me the memorial: it is
> very precious to me,

> Charles
> Olson

Sunday January 30th (1966)

123

To Bruce Loder (1966)

In January 1966 Bruce Loder, looking for the right graduate school, wrote to Olson for advice. "I don't honestly know," was the reply (letter of 7 February 1966 at Northwestern), "except to turn right to the *nearest* one of them—like in fact you wld, for a library or a bookstore . . . & *EXPLOIT* IT: get its *SERVICES*." He mentions the Free University being started by the *Work* magazine group in Detroit and says he would be happy to help with Cambridge University through Jeremy Prynne, or the State University of New York at Buffalo through William Sylvester. Loder then asked about preparatory reading and got the following answer. *Letter at Stony Brook.*

Excuse please any delay in getting back to you: there is *one* Berard in English, *Did Homer live?* translated by Brian Rhys, New York 1931 E. P. Dutton & Co. Inc which summarizes the story of Berard's researches from 1888 (through December 1929

Eliade—and Kerenyi—are useful *informationally* but my own experience is they are *best* (as so many like men to them are) appearing under the auspices of the "Eranos" yearly meetings (from the late 30s on) You can find selections from all these men in a series published by the Bollingen Foundation. Campbell I do believe is misleading altogether & throughout (his usefulness only exists in his having edited Zimmer's papers in "Art & Symbols of Indian Life" or some title like that—also I think Bollingen)

on the caves now *Hallam Movius*'s work in the last 10–15 years

Frontier Press Buffalo ought to have *New Empire* out in a new edition in a few weeks

My *memory* of Mathews' *Wakondah* was the relative clearness of it as a current report *then* of Indian life: he had, had he not, been the son of an Indian agent at the Pawnee reservation?

I *have* the Hymes, but haven't yet read it.

Write me further, and I shall try to answer you.

Somewhat hurriedly, Charles

Olson   Sunday   February 27th

1966   28 Fort Square Gloucester

Massachusetts

124

To Lawrence Ferlinghetti (1966)

Lawrence Ferlinghetti, the well-known poet and proprietor of City Lights Books in San Francisco, was at the Spoleto Conference in June 1965, and presumably it was there that the possibility of a reissue of Olson's *Call Me Ishmael* was broached.

Letter at Berkeley.

Dear Ferl—

Love to have you do it. Wonderful! Glad to join your Yacht Club's "flags"

So: let's go. One thing only—& I *think* Don has done it or was *going to* get letter into my hand to sign, but *we* must—to save *both* of us 50%—at least me 50% with that fucking Harcourt Brace (as was). They turned the book down (as mss., originally) but then *acquired* it when they bought out Reynal. *Since*—the bastards—they've been taking etc.

Now: a letter to them?

(Anyway check with Allen—& *goodspeed*

Yrs

Captain Over-Soul

March 10th

LXVI

PS   How goes it? I *bet*. Keep in touch—Alumnus! (of Spoleto: Barbara (Guest) also lonely, asks to come see me this month.—Crazy scene, that was: actual "college"! No?

—OK. Yrs

Spumoni! Gatta-pone.

From London on 27 February 1967 Olson telegraphed Ferlinghetti his pleasure at seeing the published volume "for the first time in the hands of Mr Tom Maschler three minutes ago": "The point is to tell you that the cover is unbelievably marvellous . . . and the back cover as writ by I assume Lawrence Ferlinghetti is a pleasure to myself" (letter at Berkeley).

125

To John L. Sweeney (1966)

Jack Sweeney, as curator of the poetry collection at Harvard, recorded Olson's reading there on 14 February 1962 and demonstrated afterward an interest in New England nautical matters, including James B. Connolly, the author of *The Book of the Gloucester Fishermen* (1927) and other source books for the *Maximus* poems. Samuel Eliot Morison ("Cousin Sam") had sent Olson an offprint of his recent article "The Dry Salvages and the Thacher Shipwreck," *American Neptune* (October 1965), which prompted Olson to write the letter below, sent on St. Patrick's Day (17 March 1966) in recognition of Sweeney's Irish background.

Letter at Harvard.

28 Fort Square   Gloucester
Massachusetts

My dear Jack,
    I don't suppose you possibly cld have missed seeing—in fact things *said* in it *about Connolly anyway*, & Eliot, and his brother's, talking with Connolly, sound as though you might have yourself been a source

but "Cousin

Sam"   (and I always have, & still do, believe Frances Rose-Troup
        was more than correct, in her charge—1930, "Foreword," p.v,
        to her *John White*, G. P. Putnam's Sons, N.Y. & London—that
        Professor S. E. Morison had in fact—in his *Builders of the*

Bay Colony, same year, Houghton Mifflin, Boston & New York—had her manuscript *twice* before that, &—as she writes there, in her "Foreword"—"was thus enabled to print certain hitherto unpublished items which I had obtained by laborious research." If for no other reason than: (1) "Cousin Sam"'s a book maker; and (2) Cousin Sam doth run as he writes,

but my point immediately is to call to your attention (just on a very odd chance it might not have come to you) that fellow's piece (in a current, or recent, *American Neptune*) on the "Dry Salvages and the Thacher Shipwreck." It's loaded on "Tom," and does have that *interesting* statement that, as young yachtsman here, Tom & his brother Henry had talked to Connolly: I had not remembered that the letter you showed me (from Eliot, when Bet & Vincent Ferrini and I were in your office February 14th, 1962) had said that (as relevant to Eliot's declared interest—which I so much share—in Connolly's value or *usableness* certainly as a writer of the period of the climax of Gloucester fishermen, and her fisheries.

By the way, I have continued to pursue the matter of Connolly's "papers" at Colby, and as soon as spring is farther advanced, intend to shoot up there, and have a look. (The fellow who is in charge of the Library—a Professor—indicates there are a good pile of mss, some unpublished, and I'd hate to miss anything which by any chance was as good as stuff he published.)

Wld you by any chance enjoy accompanying me? It's not a bad run, even if my car—a Chevrolet station-wagon 1956—shldn't be trusted. But I know a good old fashion hotel in Augusta, at least.

Many thanks anyway for your note on getting to Phil Weld for that piece here on the destruction of *good* property!

Yrs, St Patrick's Day
& bedamned to him,

Charles

126

To Albert Glover (1966)

In this 3 April 1966 letter, Albert Glover is addressed by his then nickname. Glover's letter to Olson had referred to several of the texts Olson had prof-fered in seminars, especially Alfred North Whitehead's *Process and Reality,* and G. S. Kirk's edition of Heraclitus's *Cosmic Fragments.* In mentioning "P'town 'sprinkles,' " Olson is remembering his previous comments on a poem by Glover about Provincetown, Massachusetts. So here we have another letter continuing a conversation.   *Letter at Storrs.*

My dear Mike:

    Been approaching for days to write you (to answer your letter) but machinery (of the plant—industrial (Niagara Falls, U.S.) keeps on— with lights on etc—and colored smoke and *fumes*)

                                                                  OK. So at least,

(1) *Feinstein* letter *is* "Poetics" II (hope you count that in. *In fact* "split" (mentioned by you—or now part of *curriculum* University of Essex as "Sociology of Literature"!—Herder, Taine, Adorno (!) Charles Olson!!) *is* still on (between "Part" I (Projective Verse Part I & Part "II" (Projec-tive Verse Part II, *left out* by Dr. Wms in his Autobiography)

    That is—1959(?) date Feinstein letter (or 1958?) anyway, *same* split (also *now* continuing). *Add* in fact, to Feinstein (as "pair") review Chicago Review "Zen" Number "Equal That Is To the Real Itself"— *there's* your
                         "physics" *PLUS* atomism (which is solely
                                 geometry: Riemann, after
                                          Gauss, after
                                 Lobachewsky & Bolyai *they 1823* (after—
                 by *5 years solely*—Johnnie Keats (Dec 1817

Problem still is
to
make *The Two Worlds*

"give up" their
possibility

    (I *shall* yet check passage you mention, of W'h, but in any case he
possibly *alone* of men after—or *ever* saw the
simplest & *oldest*, that etc)

There *is* in fact no
division as you
in saying what you are seeking—& I pushed at you in note on P'town
"*sprinkles*" was saying:
                    science is simply ½ of scio- of what anyhow
(etc) or proportion is 1/13th to say 1
                         Grebe's 'g' is $\pi/4$ 1.12888
                        (Inventor of *Styrene*)
proportional dimensions for solids then are in the ratio of two, three,
and four. *Period*

Proportion in fact is *probably* the "missing" only—& is, at this date, worth
all attention (*Measurement*
                the *rest* is well in hand
                        Again, *solely* White-
head seems to have gone for it by both going for the fence (like you sd, *all*
the cards) fence *and*
                discovered something
                      equally well-known also.
by)
   discovering

    OK for moment. Hope this meets you
             (don't be bothered by bi-p. Either a *typo*(!) or in context)
                    di is
              the business
                    O

                  April 3
                  MDCCCCLXVI

Added note.

Don't *please* get misled into any such idea as Heisenberg's that one can change the word fire in Fragment 30 of Heraclitus' Fragments to energy. This is a modern cant, scientificism anyway (meaning actually solely what gets the work done)—and like so much of that vocabulary, useful as it may be (once turned into mathematical symbols, & then yielding engineerable results—engines' work(s)) it abrupts & destroys nature as *we* are her "engines".

I don't even say this—as I believe you'd know, and grant—to hug any humanism for present man, I care only for efficacies which I know *words* have in themselves—when they are right (careful, exact, equal to what it is they are "standing for"—in a very different if associable to the languages, say, of mathematics, and of music (possible also *paint*, though here the visual has some of the same danger of *externalizing* at another cost as science has, with its extensors—hands beyond hands, arms etc eyes all extra length extra powerful extra extra (in *my stove* ex-perience 3XXX or XLXLXL!
or XXLL
XXXLL?!!)

Colors certainly	*fire*
& *these* can be brought	definitely
as *paint* into	—& as such: read the *Master One Step Removed*
"painting"	(the Ephesian)

". . . But that he knew that the world exclu-sively as such, composed of all reality, is eter-nal, he makes clear by these words:

(Fragment 30 is	This (world-) order (the same ? for all) did
Clement of Alexandria	none of gods or men make, but it always
talking, *Stromateis*	was and is and shall be: an everliving fire,
V, 104, 1)	kindling in measures and going out in
	measures."

That then is it and though I might as Heisenberg (have in fact as you'd well know been thought of either as *only* energy or at least only a pusher for same!) an *active* state of knowledge lies & lives more in

Heraclitus' *transformative condition of* substance he therein calls
"   ": first into *sea* (think of that!) then into earth (this
doesn't give us so much trouble—but *then* what *is* Heisenberg going
to call what's now known to soften the asthenosphere so that *currents*
alone suck & spew ocean bottom *different than* gravity-force), and then
(to continue from Fragment *31*) the reverse: earth into sea, sea into fire,
fire into its ever kindling ever dwindling measure? *world-order itself
having existence?*

One is then in a presence more interesting than simply at least what the *word* energy too immediately

—unless as an East-
ern Catholic you'd have the experience, say, of *the Mass* to qualify
Ergon(!) (I *tease* my *Roman* Catholic "family" or better my compadres!
with *that* one, lazy religionists, ready to serve in the Vietnam of the
Transubstantiation with no questions asked!)

Thus fire, sea and earth are the three main world-masses, of which
fire (presumably—I am quoting G. S. Kirk's summary on Fragments
30, 31, 36 (& 76D), 90, 64, 65 (& 66D), 16—it is his parenthesis—
presumably that (meaning "fire") *composing the sky and the heavenly
bodies*—wow I mean Heisenberg! *mirar*, Heisenberg, *mirar*!

We have these three main *world-masses*, then: the sea the earth & fire
& fire *presumably* is
the sky & the heavenly bodies
(*ta meteura*):
fire then (Kirk continues) is the *originative one,* & "steers" all things
(Fragment 64): is *Helmsman.* (Kirk stresses—as of Frr. 65 and 16—that
they may well, even if of uncertain meaning, re-emphasize *the regularity* and *directive capacity* of fire.

In other words, I suppose, I am urging on you to keep a "counter" as
demonstrably (no?) useful *as is*—as fire and not changed over to fit (in
a fit of modern man's fit!) words he's used successfully so far (like, say,
energy).—The question in fact—& Heisenberg may or may *not,* by
now, be practising it—is such a *reversal* as (if Kirk is right) Heraclitus
does—of *course* he does—offer: that cosmological operations flow back
through the masses, maintaining themselves, equally, *because of the*

preservation of the measures. This is going—or is now to 'be the "strug-gle": the full "argument" of & on the irreversible. (You'd know of course where I as an Ismaeli Muslim stand on that one!)

I want then to end on what in fact Kirk earlier has in so many words called the world-order itself, why, in fact, he is at such p ains—& his edition of the *Cosmic Fragments* (if you are turning to the ' 'study" of Heraclitus will save you immense labor)—to question Clem(ent's—or previous translations of—or the validification of the Fragme nt 30, on the point "(world-) order"—& he's right:

> the *other* big que stion (beside irreversibility) *is* the meaning of *Kosmos*
>
> Cosmos

—Anyway Kirk, in summarizing this group of Frr. (whic h he calls GROUP 10) defines parenthetically the world-order itsel f as (*i.e. the element of arrangement in the perceptible* cosmos)

Very elegant.

ok.

Hope I offer you something fo r like Holy Week!

Yrs

Charles Ol son, R. C.

Passover Eve
MDCCCCLXVI

Einstein's world is homogeneous like Euclid's—& I shld *imagine* Heisenberg's E is E's—& those rigidities—*Inedible Ea ster Eggs*—are what etc we have no Reason any Longer to Worry Ab out; or Worry.

127

To Robert Hogg (1966)

The poet Robert Hogg was one of Olson's students at the Vancouver summer school in 1963 who followed him to Buffalo. In April 1966, still at Buffalo, he sent

Olson sheet 2 of *Physiographic Diagram: Atlantic Ocean,* edited by Bruce C. Heezen and Marie Tharp for the Geological Society of America.

> *Photocopy of letter supplied by the recipient.*

My dear Bob that's
something: It was *yesterday* curiously—and never a day sooner I
thought to myself I ought actually to have that South Atlantic part of it
so here just now marched up my old Letter Carrier—now Parcel Post-
man whistling and I thinking, from the steps, it isn't my neighbor men
who get into fish work or building construction are not happy that way

like Gerry Van de Wiele could
whistle Black Mountain up & down & made her hills I never climbed
already over & I out into one night helped by Tokay more
all the air literally
walking   Now Abyssal Hills and fitting
                                     Marginal Escarpments over Ocean's
                                     (Basin Floor so Georges Northern
                                     Edge ties to
                                              off Cape Joly   narrow
Shelf and Terceira (sinks (in later Time the rind
(& music's whyn e: my neighbor
just comes home from Odonnell-Usen—Taste o' the Sea employee—
and, before he I hear him speak Magnavox big Colored Television in
this Waiting Room a house Supreme Court of the U.S.-A u-s 194seven
decides Capitol Records in Capitol Transit's street-cars as earlier Syracuse Jehovah Witnesses' noise is allowed!
                          I'm gone to
                          Morocco's
                          Southern Edge   North
of the South Atlan tic   Georges Northeast Peak stuck
                      to Fuerteventura!
                                     Love &
                                         physiographic
                                            thanks,
                                                 O

April 12

128

To Frank Davey (1966)

As founding editor of the Canadian journal of literary opinion *Open Letter,* Frank Davey published in the third issue, April 1966, a contribution from Ted Whittaker that posed Wallace Stevens against William Carlos Williams and Olson, ending with a quotation from Stevens: "The great poems of heaven and hell have been written and the great poem of earth remains to be written" (p. 24). Whittaker adds that *Paterson* is "the best rebuttal of that statement" yet offered. On 6 May 1966 Olson wrote the following response as a letter to the editor but apparently decided not to send it.   *Letter at Storrs.*

Open Letter 3
              I don't of course believe at all what Stevens proposes,
that the poems of heaven and of hell, have been written and it is the
poem of Earth which now is ours to write. His error is
                        essentially the same one Milton's
                    was, that
9 days & nights from Earth & still the 10th
before Tartaros is reached is
Hell: Dante
knows better—and St. Thomas Aquinas
As well as
Giotto—or St.
Francis—And Heaven
doesn't go away so
easily or
is so easily put by as
accomplished. I
welcome something Ted Whittaker
is looking for, for *himself* in finding
Wm Carlos Wms so
useful.—It is only
        that *value*
mustn't be medley'd in
uses, personal as well as the conspicuous social
medl'ying going on just still now . . .

                                             I solely wanted to
keep the 'orb
     Orb
out of Whittaker's own
     need—or at least to make sure
he has it right,
if he wants it—And *when* he does

                                   Yrs

                                        Charles Olson

May 6

129

To Ed Sanders (1966)

Someone Olson once referred to as "Ra himself," Ed Sanders came into Olson's
life with amazing hip energy and solid knowledge of the classics (including some
Egyptian). Olson was happy to publish a *Maximus* poem in the inaugural issue
of *Fuck You: A Magazine of the Arts,* Sanders's outrageous journal, and also to
write a formal introduction to the Frontier Press edition of Sanders's poems,
Peace Eye (1965).

   In May 1966 Olson was expecting Sanders to visit Gloucester, but there was
the court case—the Peace Eye Bookshop in Manhattan had been raided and
Sanders charged with obscenity. He was busy with his defense (the ACLU helped
and he was eventually successful). Not only that, he had created a rock group
called "The Fugs" and was touring as its lead singer. The group had by this time
put out an album, which included a song, referred to in the letter below, that was
based on Olson's "Maximus from Dogtown—I." Charles Peter Olson improvised
a dance performance to go with this song at his birthday party on 12 May 1966.
The letter is dated by this event.   *Letter at Stony Brook.*

Fair Fug where art thou (or Norseman or Angle or Jute?
                                        And no news
either of the hearing—or upshot?
                              I *did* by the way hear most attrac-
tively the *songe*:

my son & his cousins *danced* it as a present for me on his birthday.

Do let me hear at least the news of the case—for history of course is now being made!

Yr true Polyphile,

you *plūsculus.*

130

To Jeremy Prynne (1966)

There are a hundred letters 1961–1969 in the Storrs archive from Jeremy Prynne fellow of Gonville and Caius College, Cambridge; an equal number were posted from Gloucester across the Atlantic. These were working letters, and the sample below is typical. Prynne was able to use his proximity to libraries and his ease in them to provide Olson with quick answers to questions that would otherwise have required Olson to leave Gloucester for whole days on research trips to Harvard or elsewhere. In a letter to Ralph Maud on 25 November 1965, Olson expressed his appreciation of Prynne's resourcefulness and generosity, describing him as "my *Mercury,* in the world. Golden hat, and sandal shoon, and in his hand pussley" (letter in the possession of the recipient). *Letter at Storrs.*

May 14th

Dear Jeremy,

Don't please mind that you have had no acknowledgment to all you have sent me, yr own poems & letter, and the several pamphlets—& book (that is, the Kirk Cosmic Fragments also came, in this time.)

Truth is, a combination of my own worsening nerves *&* publishing pressures (proofs etc) have kept me from enjoying, or feeling at all free literally to live at all, that my springs of life & attention—& indeed any sense of poetry itself, or other pursuit of knowledge than the surprising pleasure of the local subject(!)—did you, by the way, ever receive that funny, almost querulous(?) request, as of a William Stephens, Stepney—& his great ship the *Royal Merchant* (600 tuns? 400?)?

All's well really—though very scoured & dour—& to hear fr you fr all quarters is a joy,

Charles

131

To Edward Dorn (1966)

Ed Dorn and Charles Olson were filmed at Berkeley the day after Olson's reading at the poetry conference of 1965. Their camaraderie is visible in that footage (see the transcription "Reading at Berkeley—The Next Day" in *Minutes of the Charles Olson Society,* no. 3, pp. 6–14). It goes back to Dorn's student days at Black Mountain College—he was one of the few who actually graduated during Olson's term as rector. Born in Illinois and of a "gunslinger" temperament, Dorn immediately became for Olson a representative of the American frontier spirit. In January 1955 Olson wrote, as his teacher, "A Bibliography on America for Ed Dorn." The letter below is, in effect, an inquiry a decade later into where that proposed reading list has taken them both. *Letter at Storrs.*

Ed (*Sunday* 29th May
   Got yr *Thursday* letter enroute London *Saturday—yesterday morning* (That's all right!
                As you pick up on this Far West stuff let me in, if you wld, on anything which seems to you to shove anything *new* there—I don't mean so much on say the *material* (though that too wld be welcome, if it were in fact interesting
   (—like Jerome Fried, excellent text editor New Directions, had Creeley asking me wasn't it *Jim Clyman* was 1st in to Yellowstone, & did my insistence of using Jim Bridger need change! Lovely: of *course* I refused (& happily shortly thereafter read Chas Peter's Mountain Man—& hadn't in fact run into that wonderful story of Bridger when 1st out there building a coracle out of bull hide and branches one morning to go find the outlet of the Bear much to Jim Fitzpatrick concern he should, by himself

and turned up 5 weeks later raving about the huge salt ocean the
thing did end up in—(Salt Lake!

What I meant was any *turn* in sense of thought or method—such as
has happened as of Eastern U.S. History

                     just so I *ain't* silly back there if
there *is* any re-sharpening of Spring fields or any real inventions of
nous

    (Ex: is Henry Nash Smith's book anything more than what Merk
taught him, say?

                I've never had my hands on it.

Also, do you know Sauer's Camino Real? Blaser, by the way, has asked
me to review S's new The Earliest Spanish Main—(did I tell you
this?)—on basis of *Wivenhoe stuff!* Lord, I aren't *that* interested in
Columbo—but Sauer, I do say—And at same time am *scared* to "review" him! He's like the Library itself!

Also his or their *Landscape* that mag Sante Fe? Albuquerque.

(Wretched, that they have now called that Lake's flooding Window Row
Vuga & Rainbow Bridge Etc—Lake *Powell*)

My *own* hunch is the best advance epistemologically has not been
in the West (not that we need it!) except with a couple of notable
exceptions—or at least one! but is oceanic research: the ocean
bottom.

How abt Parkman: *Oregon Trail?* And does DeVoto's Year *1846* stand
up?

                       Yrs, in flight or trying to get the
                       ship back into water,

                                Chas.

                       Sunday dreary Family Day (John here
                       over in his "House"—Fine,
                       & probably already has written you.

132

To Tom Raworth (1966)

Tom Raworth, the poet, then working for Goliard Press, Fairhazel Gardens, London, supervised the publication of Olson's small volume *'West'*, dated July 1966 in the colophon. The introductory note by Olson reads:

> I've been absorbed by the subject of America all my life. One piece of it has been what the enclosed hopes, in that sense, to set down. Actually as in fact it was reading and playing it out as a child in redoubts we imagined trenches and trees on the foot of Fisher's Hill we were sure had been a part of earlier Indian wars the books of James Altschuler—and I am now convinced there are indeed only "three" American stories—that which was 1st, the one Cowpens actualized (the "line" which the Proclamation of 1763 made the Appalachian Ridge)—and then the West. So I *have* here a much larger story than would appear.

When Olson sent the original note for Raworth via Ed Dorn, it included a final sentence: "It ought to be added that these are the first seven or eight parts, of which more are intended" (letter at Storrs). With the letter below, Olson returns proofs of the book and requests the sentence be deleted, which it was.   *Letter at Storrs.*

28 Fort Square
Gloucester, Massachusetts

My dear Tom:

I *had* forgotten that America like all places which don't know how to work as a living *love* holidays—and have so *many* of them that they are always breaking the moon—and the Year's—stride. (There are obviously two ways twa corbies to have a holiday) So *this* one was Decoration Day as it once was called with some meaning, in the South, starting with *1863* (as few recognize, except for say Gettysburg & Antietam—or *there* called Sharpsburg—most of the Dead of the American Civil War, a *frightful* War still by all War Measure, died on Southern territory, both sides. And so it was Southern Women who did take, as early as 1863, to putting flowers on the innumerable mounds—like in fact 'chuck holes or prairie-dogs nests, the countryside was so covered between the rivers running to the sea. . . .

if you ever come to this house, although I *believe* my wife *did* throw it out, I *had* believe it or not in the backroom here one piece of a chevaux-de-frise some soldier had whittled out, to make himself some sort of a "stand" right in front of his eyes (and I dare say, the stick was so small if so sharp, solely if some Southern soldier *had*, while the Boy in Blue were sleepin, wiggled into it in the mess & darkness of the Wilderness battlefield

but the kicker is I *found* that stick—picked it up in not even a dense place—in position and as was that night 1 fucking hundred years nearly later. Dig that for like Decoration.

So my *point* is I got delayed a little by several—I do except John Wieners with whom I pleasantly sat here at the table with nothing of consequence occurring one whole night—pointless visitors, of such relaxing weekends, I mean for the likes of them, sad fraternize-ing chicks & their cockalorums not even waking up in the middle of the night nor jumping from their beam with daylight to peck corn or feather a few—like—20 times in the henyard during the like day.

So the enclosed which I hope is tight as a drum-head is now yours—

& I only have one request to make: please excise that short last para-graph in the prose note I typed & sent Ed last week (for the page *opp.* copyright page): I *think* now the single paragraph itself, ending as it does in "more here than wld appear" (I believe) says enough—& the other does have that danger of debouching the poor reader's *will* before he even has a chance to be effected.

Yrs & please keep me on: I judge you & Barry Hall have, with Ed last Thursday, settled all *Clouds* inc. that one who simply because he was so named seems practically the symbol of the whole fucking she-bang,

> Yrs & sobre as a Crow, & with only Vicks (Vapor-
> Rub, in case it *isn't* sold in England) up my nose,
> Olson

Tuesday May 31

[back of envelope]

Thursday. Delayed again, & therefore send this on, to you so that like mirrors on the plain I signal
to you—

O

133

To Constance Bunker (1966)

Connie was married in September 1959 to George Bunker, whom Tom Clark, in his biography *Charles Olson,* describes as "an independently wealthy Philadelphia art teacher" (p. 275). Olson reported it to Ed Dorn: "Kate now Katherine Mary Bunker, to my dismay" (letter of 29 November 1959 at Storrs). The draft letter of 10 June 1966 below is one indication of Olson's wish to continue the responsibilities of parenthood.   *Letter (draft) at Storrs.*

Dear Con

I *do* have $1000 in savings which I did set aside—as you had requested, Con—to help pay Kate's education this coming fall. That is, it *is* there, and can be drafted as a lump sum by you & George whenever you "call" it. It's been there and drawing interest @, I believe, something about 4½% for a good part of the year. Or I'll leave it, and you can figure on it for whatever time you need it—and its use would abet and effect any decision you both want to make over her education.

I *have*, in fact, and with absolutely *no* result—not one penny yet!— "declared" an Educational Fund (for my children!)—the $1000 actually is all I have, & *that* is but strictly Kate's—for any income from sale of say manuscripts or collection—magazines etc—in this house. *Maybe* that will—or might!—eventually mean something. It just hasn't yet. OK.

I say that in case it might have any bearing on your and George's decision at present.

I hesitated to say it earlier—or in fact don't want now to have it throw any special weight—simply that I assume we all know there is now probably seven years ahead of considerably greater costs.

I shall be good for as much as I can in fact raise each year—and if I should fall into anything I shall be quick to let you and George know. My difficulty has been that the year has not got me as far as I had to, in fact, go; and that, therefore, exactly how things are going to be for any such extended period ahead as, say, those years now which will so much matter to Kate, I haven't yet been able to lay out.

I say this solely that I did not want to mislead either you or George into exactly how much and how steadily I can provide, but I do believe 3 things can be assured:

(1) that—and it *ought* to be possible on the best or better schools (and, to look forward, colleges too) than the poorer—we *should* be able to get *some* reductions in costs (??

(2) that though I *don't* see that any "success" in any money sense is going to come my way, and that any help I may be to either Kate's or Charles Peter's lives in any *useful* sense, can only come later, if it does— in fact even, that would seem true in any educational savings probably (—maybe! God knows, where there is room, these days!

But I shall—& I hope you both will take this as earnest of how much I do think Kate has already gained from her education, as well that I shall contribute all I can as constantly as I can so that your own best judgments on what will be best for her are not hampered by money.

OK? I am aware it doesn't say in so many dollars etc or guarantee what is so much now the question—the *several* years right now ahead—but *please*, both of you, cut me in

And I'll do as much as what *does* look as though it ain't going to be any great pickings—unhappily the old kind of income but with *some* chance of (though this is when the devil of *promising* anything of solid amount over a dependable series of years hangs me up, and has—or you'd have both heard from me earlier) some or occasional patronage

OK—

& please I *shld* be very obliged if either of you can or care to give me your response to this attempt to promise something;

as well that you direct me—or correct me—if any of the things I try or think can be done to meet Kate's own requests of me or do suggest (those I would I should think clear with you & George anyway—& in turn would very much appreciate either of you asking of me) shouldn't fit your own best judgments.

> Yours, & *hope* all does go ahead so that she *does* come out, in this *very* crazy time for I should think anyone, in school or out, as best we all can make it the best
> (and *hope* I can give Kate some pleasure—and fun—in the time she is going to have now before, as I judge, you all go to Maine
> Charles

134

To Joyce Benson (1966)

"I met Olson, by mail, in 1966," writes Joyce Benson in "First Round of Letters," *boundary 2* (fall 1973–winter 1974), a presentation of some of Olson's responses to poems she had sent him. The first was a short letter dated 23 May. The second (below) was sent in an envelope postmarked 15 June 1966; it is long and affectionate, obviously a response to what he felt as potential in the person as well as in the poems. This was followed the next day by an impetuous request that Ms. Benson buy *The Maximus Poems* and identify his place on the map of Gloucester.

Letters at Storrs.

28 Fort Square

(hope you can read this: I'm hurried—my groceries are outside)

My dear Joyce Benson,

    I've not delayed   it was only just this minute walking in the door and I had left your letter & poems on the kitchen stove that I saw—at least I can give you my impression, & it *is* one of those marvelous matters which suddenly *seem* at least to me so true there is something in "Laws" Laws (in Plato's sense, I guess) more in fact than that whole of the mind there also of yours

    Anyway, it *is* the organic itself not simply the difference of biochemistry which no longer lets the life in. In fact the stiffer—or the *softer* but then one is talking altogether—again, or *maybe* even for the 1st time—our selves now, a humanism may never in fact have been before like ground corn gristed I mean by a wheel

    What in effect it seemed the two poems you sent were was too easy—& your own lightenings which are deliciously, & sharply (quickly) verbal then get *away* with too much—it all flows all over & your mind's not feelings any more (you're smart & not oppressed & dragged & loving & you're sane (and *inaccurate* by the way—*all* too easy, references
                Heraclitus for example Miss Dickinson.

    Anyway I don't *at all* mean to hammer it   it's that *any* biology or for that matter all Darwinian is as fatal as Marx Freud Einstein—and *only* because altogether our selves have happened or stuck at or it stuck somehow

    OK. And *cheers*: just write it out. You find out, eh? OK. Wow. Let me hear from you.
                       Yrs,
                       Charles Olson

June 14

    In fact like that the Earth herself is *inorganic* and I was thinking that fire is, literally itself: that why Fragment 30 (is it?) in which Heraclitus—& Kirk here is very useful in getting it shredded down to what in fact (in fact it's Clement of Alexandria, to whom the quote is owed) the ever-living fire quickening and going out in measures (as against say Mme Curie & rad-i-um: I'm saying the object (inorganic in that sense, and radium & X etc rays are process made knowledgeable: fire is only (isn't it—except if you do what that Buddhist man did this week, burn yourself up in it—*only observable*

We are the subjective, & the advantage of yielding no life to process in fact only *our own action itself* then is H's ever quickening ever dwindling in measures or however he does have is always the same—only active

I guess I'm pushing to you the inorganic and the active as the best— & I mean that absolutely *aristo*: that one fucking trouble in all mindedness (those I slammed at by listing earlier) modern mindedness is as Spengler sd the disease of the end of Fish is epistemology the 6th science—or the subjective wheel

I'm really just giving you the gospel acc. to Hesiod: *Genet*, that *before* (that wld be in the state of the "World" before like created things— these are the Muses *telling* him—*Urania* like one of them too—& whatever *Kleios* means) *before*, there was heat or the End of the World— *muspilli* Muspelsheim in Norse (and a Bavarian poem called *Muspilli* of the 9th century)—and there was wetness—Nebel (of course clouds) but Niflesheim (again) in Norse—that wld be then process, & the only other thing was in fact hunger: *Ginnunga Gap* a big mouth eating practically without in fact anything like to eat. So: the 4 *genets* are what came into being literally or bee-d (like pee'd) are

Xaw	
"Earth"	(& this is the
—GE (I think)	"order"
Tartarōs	chronologically
& Love	acc. to the
lusimeles	Muses

Love which makes the limbs all-fire

And this is it, that's Creation! Wow: objectism in my book all spelled out!

I love it of course as (though what you say you know, or have say like
the *Distances*—well: look (if you can get a hold of the *2nd* I think it is
or maybe the 3rd *Psychedelic Review* (Leary the Kook's magazine: there I
threw all this into one big crash-pole of poem all solid Hesiod. Also
look at a review of Eric Havelock's book 1963, Preface to Plato in—it's
notes in fact simply calling attention of people to the fact he's busted
through that big hang-up of Reason ratio against Art poets (Plato's Republic's a tract an educational blast to get the fuck the poets out of society's training—& get encyclopedic knowledge which is real (wow—
like at *this* end of the string! It's in *The Niagara Frontier Review* Issue #1,
1964 (in fact then you'll see what I look like also only I cld show you a
better picture!—I mean literally, taken by the same guy & I'm like danc-
ing (like look Ma *all* limbs!

OK. Hope the *hell* you can read this. If
not ask me to—return it & I'll record it on tape! Look: it's the Mythological (Cosmological which I'm saying every rock and paleo wind direction in Devonian sand is worth every utter previous image (or
thought) because feeling—which is *all* (& here I am swiping straight on
the "philosophy of *organism*" Imagine the *grab* that Whitehead made)
that again in fact—& it is Heraclitus by the Lord Christ who's words—
all is *rhein* all does do that—that's why the goddamn organic filth steals
now altogether & genetic high is crap as against the World both Before
& like *After* Love, & do come on

Yrs

Charles O

Get by the way The Maximus Poems: I live actually on the dot exactly of the i in Point in Fort Point on the cover.—I never noticed it
until this moment and it felt like news, to tell you. Also, I was raised in
a house which is the ear on the g of Stage (Fort) on the back cover, of
same. So i g,

Yrs

O

who lives who's lived i g
—& played, once, the Boig in Pehr Gynt: & is of course BIG (they
measured me in a bet apparently at the gas station yesterday: 6′7+ &
turning the Tables at 250 lb. OVER   WOW

I *can* in fact send you this.
For I *just* found the added note—I mean, on the "reed," so that I am
playing to you, to *your* requirement: I can tell you it this way—: "de reg-
lement des senses (?) le abaissement, c'est necessaire (de niveau mentale
pour participation mystique!" *a very low threshold to disorder*

Thursday, June 16th XLVI
for the affectiones—(daemones
(Spinoza's *affectiones substantiae*)

There were more letters. Joyce Benson came to Gloucester; Olson visited her on
a trip to Oxford, Ohio. In a letter of 17 November 1967 (letter at Storrs) he
addressed her as his "angel of aid and human touch": "the *one* person in all this
world literally who speaks to *me* so I can feel at least that it is myself who is
addressed."

135

To Walter Lowenfels (1966)

In the 1960s Walter Lowenfels returned to the world of poetry after a period of
many years entirely devoted to Communist Party activities. On 28 July 1966
Olson received from him an invitation, which had gone out to numerous poets,
to contribute to an anthology to be called *Where Is Vietnam? American Poets Respond*. Olson shot back the following brief reply. The anthology was published in
September 1966 as a Doubleday Anchor Original; the list of famous contributors
opposed to the war did not include Olson or Michael McClure.

Letter at Washington University.

Oh *that* I don't believe I have *anything* to add to   But I *can* put you
on—in case you might not have by some unhappy chance known of:
the *most* & wld I also say only distinguished poem on same, Michael
McClure's *POISONED WHEAT*? It *is* superb—& was privately printed
as a pamphlet—a year ago (his address is 264 Downey   San Francisco

Equally of course—so far as our policy is expressed—McNamara's full
speech to the American Publishers abt 2 months ago?

I dare say you also know that editorial in the New Republic recently called *The War President?* It seems to be one of the few instances of an attempt at the facts.

136
To Bill Berkson (1966)

Olson never had occasion to write to Frank O'Hara, but on his sudden accidental death he wrote the following note to O'Hara's close friend Bill Berkson. The address to which the letter was sent was no longer in use, and the letter was returned. A later testimonial for O'Hara, solicited by Berkson for *Homage to Frank O'Hara,* was written and dated 26 April 1969. Never sent, it was discovered by George Butterick, who made it available for the *Homage.* In the testimonial, Olson recalls "quietly walking" with O'Hara in 1964 "around the dead streets of Buffalo": "The next morning I tried to reach him but he was all day at the Museum and in a Chinese restaurant with his host, and that was the end. Except that I believe it was Frank who was chiefly responsible that I was invited to read at Spoleto, the following summer—and himself didn't go" (p. 178).

Letter at Storrs.

My dear Bill Berkson   I just feel so much the loss of Frank I wish you would also tell John and whoever else of his friends this might reach (actually I never knew Larry Rivers so if you would or it would have any meaning say so too. It is such a loss simply that he was so much (as John is and, for me to literally learn of you all last summer enables me in fact to ask you to tell Maxine and who else anyone for whom he was *personally*: this I only knew once, when he read in Buffalo in 1964 & we clomb the streets looking for some party we also could have gone to. I can't for the life of me shake the horror, and the anger that death is also those filthy killings of people who simply are out (I don't in fact know more of how Frank was hurt, only the reports. In any case the thing he and so many of you stand for is in fact, & will be seen to be the track literally of two say tracks only which this time in a person like him he *so* made clear—oh Lord I hate the fact that he will not continue to be a master

Love & forgiveness to write to you as Company head solely though to ask you as well
to speak for me hoping you will as well let
this be as it is to yourself,

Charles (Olson

August 10th 1966

137

To Pamela Millward (1966)

Pamela Millward's *The Route of the Phoebe Snow* was published by Coyote in 1966.
Some of the poems Olson would have seen in *Wild Dog*. The Olson poem
discussed in this letter is "Maximus, in Gloucester Sunday, LXV" in *Poetry* (July
1966) and in *The Maximus Poems,* pp. 449–450. Millward had mentioned the lines

Now date August 1965 returning
Gloucester from as far out in the world as my own
wages draw me, and bitter
police cars turn my corner, no one in the world
close to me, alone in my home . . .

Letter at Washington University.

My dear Pamela—Damn nice, to be worried about. And much obliged for
the tea, wch I shall try to use. I wash dishes—or not I, *someone* happens to,
like my sister in law or my *daughter* did 3 months ago—once a year!

I'm *so* convinced now after 2½ years that it is hopeless to expect myself
to be able to do anything *well*, in *this* world, that I am now considering
putting myself under some Yoga or such in some ashram—where at
least (I opine) sleep & food *might* come for me!

PS
    And *don't* please find that shingle (or *shake* poem, in Poetry sad:
I *still* think the *poetry* of it is of a 'nother sort, that is, that the *mode*

(of sadness, or, flatly, loneliness, actually eaten up by it) is "sung-against" (?

        Anyway, was (as companion—"*On Cressy's Beach,*" in centennial issue of Tuftonian) *"felt"*—intended, simply to, like, *name* my *few*—& a *quarternity*—? no? *friends* ("companions")

What *is* the Rte of the PHOEBE SNOW" like
knowing of course the BOX-CARS
love
O

Wednesday Aug 24 (66)

138

To Alan and Diane Marlowe (1966)

The poet Diane Di Prima and her husband, Alan Marlowe, visited Gloucester on 20 August 1966. In a letter ten days later Olson expresses his appreciation.

Letter at Buffalo.

    Simply to tell you things here still but that the visit by you both was for me a very special matter: I *am* an American, & exactly the way you each are of the same "blood" & "breathing-exercises" I am or wld be, this puts me on,   Love O

PS: & thank you for mail so far. *If* as Diane did mention you *cld* come by both Sir John Woodroffe's *Serpent-Power* and Evans-Wentz *Tibetan Yoga* I do have the money to pay for such!

The following day, 31 August 1966, Olson wrote a note (at Storrs) to Alan Marlowe as proprietor of Poets Press suggesting "Idea, for a, book": Sacred North American Texts: (& Places).

139

To Zoe Brown (1966)

Zoe Brown and her husband, William Brown, the novelist, were prompt to ask to transcribe and publish Olson's Berkeley reading of 23 July 1965. Within three months they had sent him sample pages they had produced from the tapes at the language laboratory of the University of California. Olson backed the project and helped with a couple of details, but it is evident, from this and other letters to the Browns, that Olson did not sit down and examine the transcription before its publication. *Reading at Berkeley* (1966) had Olson's approval but not his attention. (See the revised version in *Muthologos* 1, pp. 97–156.)

Letter at Columbia.

Zoe!

Don't please *mind* my idiotic delay in getting back to you on the "broadcast"(!) but you'd might imagine I might still approach such a thing as that talk-out with some gingerlyness like pains in the half-moons of my fingernails! In fact I read the 1st 15 pages & jumped out of here looking for a *drink!* In other words give me *my* time now to "suffer" the experience of it sitting here before me—meaning *only* my own need to see how much I'd have to blush!—and *nothing* whatsoever to do with yours and Bill's delicious pleasure in it.

Ok? And I'll *anyway* gloat & let people look in to it (like the original *camera oscura!*)—or Mark Riboud's photos of China!! It's great anyway to feel like at least Paulette Goddard—& hopefully I'll find out we have here what you tell me we have

(Above all, or also, don't feel at *all* put off by that sheet transposition of the poem, in the back: the whole idea of putting the poem there anyway is so good anyway no little slip can spoil it

Hope the thing sells like high pitch medicine bottles—& that we'll all be hailed for changing the dampening of all keys on the piano these days by so foolish the numbers of young cadres—and so many of their older Leaders!!!

(Ed S—Fug I—was here, saw same & proposed, on return to New York, to see that either ESP or his *new* record Co do the tape into a long player record. So *then* I shd think your transcription both might be a fold-in? or in any case announced, on the liner, & that ought, no?, to increase *sales*—(???

Also, from your husband's letter, do I gather Don Allen's now getting *into* the "Lecture" there? Or was it simply the one poem I promised you both for the next "Journal"? Will you let me know—& *please* excuse this *handwriting*—I've been sick with some flu & trying tonight to catch up a little.

Tell Bill I was *niftied* by his letter—(& also that I show off his novel every time these *damn* (too many) visitors occur here

(I think it was *Jim Lowell* the Cleveland bookstore man who saw Bill's face like Genet's! (I never *hear* that of course except as "Citizen Genet".)

Love, & more

O

(Mon. Oct 3)

140

To George Starbuck (1966)

The poet George Starbuck was on the library staff at Buffalo during Olson's time there. The following letter was in response to Starbuck's book of poems *White Paper* (1966). *Letter at Iowa.*

28 Fort Square   Gloucester
October 7th

Dear George:

      Delightful pleasure. And don't I wish I cld write like you. Sitting here groaning with envy.

Hope all is good for you all. (I curiously have now spent a year in such a detention or isolation cell I seem to have lost all manner of possibilities—as well as in fact all manners. Which leaves me, even though by salt water, neither any longer possessed of wit at all nor, to steal the rest of it from Stendhal, preferable dreaming.

I hope the book does well—& aren't you lucky in both the manufacture, and the cover by Glaser? (Buffalo seems not able—due to Rockefeller?—to change its spots (?)

Yrs with affection & respect,
Charles (Olson)

X

The great hostess and patron Panna Grady was instrumental in getting Olson to England, finally, in November 1966, and Klaus Reichert organized a visit to Berlin in December. Olson's long-standing wish to research the Weymouth Port Books for information about the founding fathers of Gloucester took him to Dorchester, Dorset, for five weeks in February and March 1967. He was no sooner back in the United States than he went off again to participate in the International Poetry Festival in London on 12 July 1967.

This was enough. But he was coaxed out again for lectures and readings at Cortland, New York (20–22 October 1967), and Beloit, Wisconsin (25–29 March 1968), with a side trip to San Francisco (April 1968).

This was certainly enough.

141
To Kate Olson and Harvey Brown (1966)

The first person Olson wrote to on disembarking at Liverpool on 4 November 1966 was his daughter, Kate, now at Cambridge School in Weston, Massachusetts, and predictably interested in the Beatles. The letters are postmarked 4 and 7 November 1966. Olson also wrote a brief note to Harvey Brown from Liverpool, and then, as soon as he was reasonably settled in London on 18 November 1966, he wrote the letter below to catch up with ongoing projects at Frontier Press.

Letter to Kate Olson in possession of Ralph Maud;
letter to Harvey Brown at Buffalo.

[letterhead]
Adelphi Hotel   Ranelagh Place   Liverpool 1

Friday

Kate love

Just cabled you. Had a very difficult passage but find *Liverpool* which is out the *window* right now the Beatles own home town marvelous. Staying a couple of days before going over to the Dorns: (miss you extremely today—I suppose because *suddenly* I *like* the English especially the *wild speech*

Love quickly
Papa

[letterhead]
Adelphi Hotel   Ranelagh Place   Liverpool 1

Kate love: just absolutely kook here (marvelous city—but will tomorrow press on to the other side (of England: the Dorns, & London.

(Bought you Liverpool latest marvelous young people's scarf—in big store here yesterday (Will send as soon as I can figure out *how* to do these things! In a *strange!!* country.

Miss you & hope you will write often to tell me how you are how school *does* go & how you feel

Quickly Sending Kisses   Papa

Harv—Delighted to have yr news (rec'd today, Friday November 18th—forwarded by Dorn, from Colchester yesterday. (Present address: two weeks anyway, possibly more: 90 Piccadilly, Apt. 9.

Might in fact be something you & Polly cld use February (?in case you aren't set? THAT IS: or *COME* DIRECT—TO *CRETE!!!!* Where I surely AM HEADED—wild! In fact have house possibility reasonably *set* there (Charles Henri Ford's no less! at Candia! So *surely* we can make it either way—either in what I still crave most, until spring; or here (by April for me—reading Aberystwyth in April May. So *only* other engagement is the Berlin reading Dec. 15th—& *then* *ZAP* XANDIA! Or if it is cold there the CATARACT HOTEL, ASWAN!

So be of full cheer—&

movement. And don't mind if my publishing advice is so thin at present. Have been *tossed* for the past three weeks like mad (don't travel well yet or anyway being simply just too big: Steve Rodefer's always been right, I need a private railway car!

Love to you both, & to K & please keep closely in touch. (I told Dorn the Drew must have come from you—& he was very excited by it. Will tell him tomorrow—he's in Devon today—that you wld welcome an introduction by him. Also both Prynne & he, the other night in a rest. in Colchester, were full of excitement over Woodward's General History (of the U.S.: which I haven't read.) I told them you planned to issue the Civil War shot.

As of Hulbert's Pathways I feel yr own plan to throw in

the 1st two, & the 1st of the Canal books (?), is very wise: simply *awake* interest in them.

OK. Rushing now to go to party tonight at Trocchi's—to meet the Sigma "bosses" in fr Amsterdam Millbrook etc: & with Burroughs Trocchi & team all in fort(e)! I shall tell you.

Been troubled by colds—but otherwise finding the shifts (despite fatigue) some freshness.

(Oh yes—wow: remember the *house* we looked at that March morning (after breakfast at the Douglases)? I *bought it* (if the City Council agreed: (I'll know tomorrow. *$1000!!!* Dig that land & two buildings. And all I have to do is cut 2½ feet off the front so the State can widen the Highway! Wow. Come see me *there*! Too!

Yrs

O

London

142

To T. L. Kryss (1966)

The following statements on behalf of Jim Lowell were solicited by T. L. Kryss after Lowell, owner of the Asphodel Bookshop in Cleveland, was arrested and charged on 1 December 1966 with possession and distribution of obscene materials—that is, books of contemporary poetry. The news came to Olson after he had gone to Berlin for talks and readings beginning on 14 December 1966.
Letters in A Tribute to Jim Lowell *(p. 10).*

Jim Lowell runs one of the 3 or 4 sole principal *interesting* bookstores in *all* of the United States.

I do not know at this distance (Berlin) what the so-called obscene item he has been charged with is, but by the law of today as well as the incredible important freedom of the United States, who in their right mind, law officers or otherwise, would wish to again offend human actions and human beings by dragging *obscenity* once more across the Scene? War Piss and Obscenity, Our Nation Shrieking!

I have known Lowell as *the* original collector of the writing of the past 15 years *all* that time; and recently as bookseller paramount, as well as "publisher" (in his subtle *useful* catalogues).

Nothing seems more calculated to be as objectionable in the writing-publishing world (as other police actions in social & personal matters) as this arrest, by officers of Cuyahoga County. (May I remind all, the Cleveland Police, Clevelanders, as well as other Americans, that it was exactly Cuyahoga County which Mr. Kennedy spoke of specifically as the one shock of the vote the night of his election to the Presidency?)

Let Cuyahoga County look at its *condition*, as well as its law and set Jim Lowell free!

ANOTHER—LATE—STATEMENT

Ridiculous. The U.S. Nation is simply an *harassment* of all active decent human beings and things like it once, & exactly in Cuyahoga County? Or at least the name is from those *Indians* whom we once treated as we now do *our own*—all are now gooks, all of us who keep our lives as real and productive as possible. Jim Lowell has done for *books* & their writers what only Lawrence Ferlinghetti (San Francisco) & Gordon Cairnie (Cambridge, Massachusetts) have, likewise—*plus* Phoenix Books, New York City. When *will* this *curse* of local ordinance & local smut-snuffers (as acrid & lousy as smog itself) CUT IT OUT? STOP? Leave the LOWELLS ALONE???

143
To Robert Creeley (1966)

Olson wrote to Robert Creeley from a hotel in Berlin, where he had, three days earlier, written a poem included in *The Maximus Poems,* "Hotel Steinplatz, Berlin, December 25 (1966)" (pp. 569–570). *Letter at Stanford.*

[letterhead]
Hotel Steinplatz

now *56* years old—1st day
Dec 28th 1966

My dear Bob—What a *happy thing*, this Berlin thing has been for me. Even though it did include, a week ago today, the scare of my life. My heart. That it had become weak! Wow. But apparently—or like you say hopefully—it has been the explanation of so much which has been draggy for me, as you'd know knowing me, for so long. And the good Herrn Doktor Mertens promised me yesterday (it was *through* Renate I got on to him last week) I shall live another 30 years!

So hail the Future! In any case it cld be if I keep my cool I might well be in yr audience the night of the 12th sitting there gloating at you knocking the ass out of these lovable—& better than any *other* European humanism (including fuckin Britain)—old-fashion dumb Berliners. But sweet, & lovable people. (Grass by the way—though you have probably met him—will simply be better, that night, because you are along. I heard him with *flute* at the same place 2 nights after myself (& a Turin Italian named Sanguineti—Wops seem always the ones *I* get put with!). And he's—even though a Dresdener—another draggy fuckin Dutchman!

Love & keep me with yr movements. If by any chance you are stopping in London 1st, let me know: that is, if you are traveling light. (In any case Lady Grady—& much of my own things—are now at 22 Mount Street there—telephone Mayfair 0187—but on Jan 5th she'll have moved to Hanover Terrace! Dig that! Nash's (terraces!

So looking altogether *forward*

Your dearest friend

Oh!

(Reichert is, will be & *was* most helpful)

[on back of envelope]

PS: Shld have added I do have to be *careful*! for 120 days! Yet —And *avoid*—"Avaunt L'hiver"!

144

To Mary Shore (1967)

At least two coincidences connected Olson and Mary Shore. One was that her grandmother had the same name as Olson's mother. The other was that she married Olson's Gloucester poet-friend Vincent Ferrini. Olson once said, "I call him and Mary Shore the only brother and sister I've had . . . that kind of family" (*Mutbologos* 1, p. 182). It is clear from other letters, as well as the one below, that Olson knew she had a good head on her shoulders as well as good shoulders for sisterly comforting. The letter was mailed on 21 February 1967 from Hanover Terrace, London, to Way Road, Gloucester.   *Letter at Storrs.*

Dear Mary,

Jean did have pictures taken—and knows the problem (and has tried to get Dick Clarke to write me more fully just what is my "*owner-ship*" situation as of my(?) "house"—and land, 106 Western Avenue; and I have had Richard Hunt board it up ($44.25!!!) to—I believe—the satisfaction of Dennen, the City's Bldg Inspector.

But, as so often in the past, I do feel you may be able to give me some one thing probably no one else can because I myself probably make them unsure just what I do want—and it is perfectly obvious it is because I am not there, as well. But if you cld write me—or might be interested, I'd be aided to have your interest or attention on

(a) what *have* I got there (I *know* the *land* as it is (*just as it is*) plus the wonderful shack at the back—both of these, are to my perfect liking

the problem—(b)—is that bloody house (which I am supposed to *move!*): what actually is its worth, or, what wld it cost—& wld it be worth it, & move it too to make it into something with at least a decent *face* on it?? Actually the land (I), & the shack (II)—& both as is for the present, are *most* to my liking—

Altho I *cld* use the house if it were *tight*, & had a decent outside, use it at least as a *base* of *future development*

(*That* seems to make sense, altho the *2nd* condition apparently by the City Council is that I have only 6 months from December something—say until *June 15th* and then that damn Historical Society or *Commission* I guess it is takes over.

What I *guess* I am asking *is*
1) wld you feel and think in my absence as though you were me; &
2) advise me hard headedly what you think: my *own* impression is,
    (1) *to make sure I hold the property*
    & (2) either *satisfy them in some easiest way before June 15th*—or get them to give me an extension to face *all* the architectural and cost problems.

In any case if you *were* interested and cld survey the matter at least, I'd gain from hearing from you. (I think Vincent wld know I want actually to do the *least* change possible; in other words to keep it *neat*, & clean, to start with; and *then*, over the immediate next few years, develop it into *something!* And I mean *something* something *very quiet & nice!!*

          Love—& delighted to hear our "children"
          have again been your guests!
              Love to you both,
                    Charles

Monday
February 20th

145

To Chad Walsh (1967)

Chad Walsh, the hardworking poet-professor of Beloit College, Wisconsin, had invited Olson to give a series of lectures there. The plan was to tape the events and make them into a book. Olson reacted with some reluctance to the idea, and his misgivings possibly marred his lecture performance during his week at Beloit, 25–29 March 1968. *Letter at Storrs.*

Dear Chad Walsh:

Many thanks for letting me see your Book-World article. (I shld of course warn you—or urge you to *abjure*(!) tape or dictaphone if, as 'tis claimed—& therefore he claimed it as "projective"(!)—you take Ginzy's latest, or later work (example, Wichita Vortex Sutra) as any evidence of what you are there talking about!

Anyway, one thing which wld make it all more promising wld be if you cld—& if it means any special arrangements, at my cost, of course—make it possible for those lectures to be taped—or even finer, as good copy as dictaphone, say. And that any such mechanics be as inconspicuous, to me actually, I don't mean the people, as it can be.—I am therefore freeer to invent, if that shld happen Etc—And we'll be the more certain to have our book out of it, equally.

I dare say this may be a matter of course but I mention it as it comes into my mind today, actively thinking of the occasion.

I *also* in faith ought to mention that like Dehn the German mathematician who solved the problem of the clover leaf knot I hardly believe thought is anywhere near as good in the morning—at least in the 20th century—as in the evening; though I despair that you Beloit or anywhere can marshall the same 500 at 8:30 P as you do at 10:30 A. Is it sadly so?

In any case greetings & any results or assurances you can give me all to the good,

Charles (Olson)

Gloucester October 6th (1967)

On 29 February 1968 Olson wrote to Walsh that the subtitle of the lectures could be "The dogmatic nature of experience" and that they could be titled "Cosmology," "Belief 1," and "Belief 2" (letter at Storrs). The tapes were transcribed after Olson's death by George Butterick and published by Donald Allen as *Poetry and Truth* (1971), with a reminiscence by Chad Walsh.

146

To Harvey Brown (1967)

Olson was invited to speak at a convocation of poets at the state college in Cortland, New York. Several people were expected to come down from Buffalo, including John Wieners, whom Olson had not seen since the estrangement caused
by the fact that Panna Grady took Olson to Europe and not John. In these letters
to confidant Harvey Brown before and after the event, Olson expresses his ap-
prehension and relief. More details are to be found in Duncan McNaughton's introduction to a revised transcript, "Charles Olson's 'Talk at Cortland,'" *Minutes
of the Charles Olson Society,* no. 4 (March 1994). *Letters at Buffalo.*

Harv
    Whatever that poem is of course use it if *you* want to (I am advised
when you choose something!

    Things going ok, though they got a little bunched earlier in the week
(simply, for one thing, that I got into continuing all sorts of oversensi-
tive problems buying a refrigerator! The other one suddenly over Sunday night went dead, and awful.

    Also made off to see you both Wednesday night—remember that
beautiful blowing wind, & then rain, but eating, on the way, simply
knocked me out & I regretfully turned back, at Ipswich (had in fact nice
hot clams for you both, on the chance you like good fried clams. Do
you?

    Off today to do that stint before 70 New York State (College I sup-
pose poets—including I hear one John Wieners. So hold your breath—
I'm not sure I shldn't have you along as my bodyguard, at least to frisk
him unnoticeably!

Love & back Sunday

(Charles

Friday October 19th—

Thursday

Harv—

Saw John & he was just as usual too much. Read marvelously—&
was more than ever my Admired One! Though his hair is now Henna
Bardol I mean Clairon I mean Neponset Bleach—& there are three
teeth hanging in his front mouth.—He *is* sharp-tongued & swollen
with hurt-pain & feeling, but anybody who can't see he is quicker &
more profound than ever are themselves fools!

Bob Hogg & Butterick were there with whom I spent much
time—& the new Contingent, McNaughton & MacAdams. Plus
Creeley's Kirsten who's now traveling with a quick Batavia-Buffalo
potato—the Shatovs too have their Myshkins these days—named Jim
Roberts.

Hope you people are all right—Not hearing from you it comes out
now *I'm* the worrier! Hope no further problem for Polly,

Yrs

Charles

147

To Donald Sutherland (1967–1968)

When Olson received, presumably from the publisher New Directions, a clipping of a review of the *Selected Writings* that appeared in the *New Leader* on 22
May 1967, he wrote to the reviewer, Donald Sutherland, who was identified only
as the author of *Gertrude Stein: A Biography of Her Work*. Sutherland taught
classics at the University of Colorado, Boulder, but Olson apparently did not
know that. Sutherland subsequently sent him a copy of his new translation of
The Bacchæ of Euripides in exchange for Olson's *Proprioception*, which was sent
with the first letter.   *Letters at Storrs.*

Saturday night October 28th
28 Fort Square Gloucester
Massachusetts

Dear Mr Sutherland,

I certainly don't wish to embarrass you in any further experience or comment. I can't though not acknowledge that your review of the New Directions Selected is such a pleasure of recognition and comprehension I hope you won't mind if I simply tell you. Also of course that it is unique, in that respect. No one else reviewing either that or the Grove essays comes anywhere near what you so see & lay out.

It is in fact my first *public* judgment of any relevancy. I hope you won't therefore mind if I slip in to this letter a *later* prose—not at all to push it at you but because I think you deserve to know where I had gone *since* those developments you so more than anyone connect & reveal.

I wish also I had a small book of five poems, printed in London & called *'West'* the past year to send too, just likewise even on the verse to win or lose you in the progress! (But there were only a few copies & long gone.)

Anyway very real pleasure to have you speak out.

Cordially

Charles Olson

———————

Sunday January 7th (1968)

My dear Donald Sutherland—

It meant so much to me to have both of your letters I hope you will forgive me to have been so slow to acknowledge them. —And to thank you, for my form of life—cold-water flat still, and jutting out here the farthest point of the land—is no place to be from December on. And I therefore spend too much time & thought on simply living: I *guess* I'm doing it, this year, because of what also detains me, an invitation to Beloit in Wisconsin in March. (Which actually seems to go so badly—it *is* an unconscionable time, isn't it, the present, in this world or at least in this nation—what *was* a nation—in this period?—that I *think* I know all which *was*, it occurred to me just now (and your own public, and now private recognition at least of some of those things I *have* felt and, too few times, have managed to recapitulate—I was terribly pleased that it was "Theory of Society" you did like they now say dig in *Proprio-ception:*

but you will yourself know that any negative today almost too is taken like a swallowed bait. And it is exactly negative I *had* at least thought, in *some* such contextual balances as I did feel *Proprioception* had (enough of course to send to you so that as I said I might—or at least risk—having your confidence into the future) that I have still some hope to achieve for Beloit. But the thought of speaking before 500 of today's young chills me as a day like today with my own two children "failures" in my own hands—because like there's, say, no food in the house. They are young, 12 & 16, and both live with other mothers (one a wife's *sister*), and I have them here & together in this flat rarely.

Well, hopefully, in some sort of way to write you—hopefully decently—on those things which *are* close, it would seem, to your concerns as well as my own—& I hope terribly much you do go on with the Hesiod book. He bears home where it seems to me the Huge Division of today itself does (not) reach.—If I was to say, in March, I stand here to offer what was, I shld *hope* I might manage (or I did until today—I *did* last night! zero weather blizzard schools Mass etc) to forecast or what at least has made Hesiod a comfort at least for poets even as young as my most interesting youngest new one, Ed Sanders, 28, is (as Sanders particularly has capted Egyptian hieroglyph out of the blue) Hesiod gives that *other side*

I am too obviously hungry to write to ask more of your patience. Please if this (plus my handwriting) is not too intolerable let me hear from you again. In any case you are like my star I can look to at morning or and evening and feel somewhere I do have that sense I can write to!

Very luckily,

yours

Charles Olson

28 Fort Square Gloucester
Massachusetts)

148

To Martin Duberman (1967)

"I never met Olson, though I tried to for several years," writes Martin Duberman in his large book *Black Mountain: An Exploration in Community* (p. 368). "I wish we had met. Because not only have I gone through the ordeal with Black Mountain that he suspected I would, but also in process, have developed great affection for him. . . . He wrote me long letters when he heard I was going to do a book on Black Mountain, put in an occasional phone call to say he *might* feel ready to talk at some point soon—but not just yet." One of the long letters survives; it was mailed on 19 November 1967.   *Letter at Kent State.*

My dear Mr. Duberman:

It suddenly strikes me, the real reason why as you say you find little files on the place as of the 50's, that in fact in those last days of 1949 (in case Albers may have told you that once I arrived when he himself had no voice left, from talking for days with that inside-outside Committee he & Ted hoped wld lift, somehow, the weight of finance off the place, Albers asked me to speak for him—! I mean solely to use my voice, to say his piece, he was so literally, out of voice!

that in fact from some point like that on, Black Mountain was *expelled* from itself

—and that the Black Mountain which we who did finally inherit in 1951 I believe it was, or that that Black Mountain which you rightly call the one of the 50s was indeed that very core of the old apple which Rice himself had said—& I think thereby gave himself, & made her (as *who* wrote me from Columbia when Eisenhower was her President, that Black Mountain's charter was unique, in education—a known sociologist, asking for a copy for Columbia's tercentenary celebration, Louis Hatchy? cld it be?—I come back: that what Rice sd, in the 1st catalogue, was to be her aim—"that the arts shall share the center of the curriculum with the more usual studies"—that something just that was what the LAST BLACK MOUNTAIN was—and was therefore in that sense gone, from say take Rauschenberg as *freshman*—or I'd say Nick Cernovich or Mary Fiore or Michael Rumaker or I cld name others—Edward Dorn for example—or for graduate students John Wieners—or for primary-remedial type (child-type) the *oldest* student we ever had, Flola's Benton Pride!

Or Huss' theater becoming Robert Duncan's personal—as playwright—Company, San Francisco

not to mention Franz Kline's effects upon so many

—or Joel Oppenheimer learning printing & getting literally a job at Judd & Detwaler Washington direct out of— & then Bloomingdales

> (as say the weavers used to, to Forstman's Woolens
> or get me sometime to tell you when Dehn & I
> were trying to replace him what Lerschitz of
> your university—who Lerschitz proposed we hire:
> Alex Kemeny—no, who was our own recent graduate?
> Yes: *Peter Nemenyi*   Even in other words in the
> more *usual* studies!   Or Eric Weinberger (Wier,
> his stage name) becoming the earliest(?) leader
> of white action in the early 60s in the south?

—a whole *going-away* by training from

Something like that at least to give you a later result of having written you earlier yesterday (today

Yrs
When
O

PS

As well of course the extraordinary existence (leaving out of acct. B. Fuller's Architech-gang of 35 was it freeloaders living while—when the Air Force had missed it—his Grapefruit or as he called it geodesic beanie etc) of *another* fantastic "Company" there, the 1st actual productions of the Merce Cunningham dance company—or David Tudor *playing* Sunday afternoon 1951 (or 1952?—no, maybe—*yes,* 1952 (?) Boulez   Stockhausen etc! Zowie!

Expelled—& imploding!

Plus Dan

Rice etc   I shldn't even know how to culminate (cull the core(s)

(includ-
ing that baseball team which *1962* hit top NYU New York City beating
the shit out of of a Sunday afternoon with only 2 ringers added—Leroi
Jones in L.F.—& Paul Blackburn in R.   otherwise intact beating the
shit out of a whole *blonde* Columbia or Mad Avenue bunch of suckers!
1962 mind you! New York City

PS—4(!)
    You may in fact have heard—or you will see in the Board Minutes
are probably in that box here—of Tony Landreau's much debated proposal one day in those 50's that she become anyway a *mobile university!*

    Or did Bobbie Dreier tell you that on one of my last—yes *last* at-
tempts to scare up anything Boston area she suggested at dinner one
night in the Newtons with Andy Oates present, & one other fellow, why
didn't I move her to become Channel 2's U of the —Air!
                                                    Crazy man: as
indeed you *must* know Paul W was perfectly prepared to rent a sky-
scraper floor Mid Manhattan to place her there too
                                            I tell you I'll drive
you *MAD*! Only because *it* probably *DID!*
                        With *sympathy*
                            Yrs
                                the Final W(Rec(er tor,
                                                    O

    I better not see you at all! It's too much for me! Or it might be better
for *you* to write your book first! And then we meet & have a good time
getting drunk as two such men in the 60s might! After what you are
going to do—& I *had* done

    Mr. Williams, by the way, the Old Man—the founder of the firm. I
don't mean at all his son. He doesn't know anything about it. It's the
old boy, Red Wms—or Judge Wms as he was known around the Court
House Asheville—who I mean, former Representative, Raleigh

    How, by the way, does the place look—or what interests me alto-
gether much more, what in *hell* did you find John Rice was like? God

love him, you are the 1st to my knowledge among any of us late comers to have ever seen him—or maybe yes MC *did* tell me she had seen him. But won't you please give me your impression—& a present report on him his condition & everything else

—And *did* Wesleyan offer him that proposal I made to them, to get *him* to do a book too on Black Mountain? ? ?

OK. Enough—for ever(?) Probably.
The Afterwards,
or the Original Damsel Re'deemed
you might call 1951 on
—with no End date known or in sight!
(I can say that, dating myself, originally, from 1948!)
Or the whole book—Boating on Lake Eden
or   What Big Carp You Have, Beautiful Eyes

And that barefoot genius Tommie Jackson descendant of the original Reverend Higginson who established with Dick Bishop that farm afterwards near South Royalton & right where Mormonism itself started called—& the sign is probably still there:

BLACK MOUNTAIN NORTH!

Seriously, though, *renting* was Rice's first belief—and here too I think he was so right—even to the meals as *served* by others than any of us and the last dishes, of coffee & dessert, never picked up until the following morning! What that man—have you read yet his piece in Harper's 1934 or 5 wld it be? anyway when Chicago was starting *Fundamentalism in Higher American Learning??!* I used to even use it there as a text!

149

To Robert Duncan (1968)

A year had gone by without an exchange of letters between Olson and Robert Duncan. "I do wish you would tell me more of Duncan," Olson wrote to Robert

Creeley in a letter of 14 December 1967, "and equally tell him, if you are in touch how I miss being so myself" (letter at Stanford). Creeley passed on the message, but Duncan had already started the warm letter to which the following is Olson's warm reply. Olson was particularly intrigued by Duncan's sense of his body's changing every seven years and remarked on it here and elsewhere. Also, Duncan had typed out "Passages" 31 and 32 to bring Olson up to date. Olson wrote a postscript on the front of the envelope: "Hail your line. You do find yourself learning to believe everything. Isn't it beautiful?"   *Letter at Buffalo.*

My dear Robert—

It is *remarkable,* how much my soul correlates to such temporal matters as your mind & thought both supply me with—as here, in your delicious welcome letter (of your 1st hours of 50th year) of 7's (it is like that letter I wrote you once years ago & baldly, out of the blue, sd something like 1224, I have yet no reason to change that sense, by sitting down & writing to you I established a time-in-the-world I am still finding enough to do to find out what it is—and this *beautiful* thing you place in my hands, of the error of eternal youth so rocks my soul in my own present striving to be able to succeed in living, I hasten to acknowledge it—before even continuing to read your letter.—It is remarkable, in that sense that the "clash" of our souls (I was thinking of that musical instrument) on this matter of time: again I think of your own apercu of 1904 I think it was—or 1903 (1907)   what in fact you *probably* raised The Maiden matter on. But I got from a lecture or piece of writing by you on the 20th century writing—Miss Stein as a chronological fox.

I *usually* think of ourselves (or write of you, as in 'West',) with a great psychic aura and yet when it comes right down on the track it isn't the substantive experience (alone at least) it is also this crazy wild time-thing I almost must dry-up about without such sudden in-ways or outbreaks (to you) of this pattern of time I swear we share in some fashion uniquely. It is like when I used to do the Tarot cards—*not the same at all*—I only mean the *mathematics* that I am speaking of in this extraordinarily *new* thing to me, your life by sevens: wow it's snake-body skin-shedding truth! And of course what "*frees*" me like in fact 1st reading or coming on to Cabeza de Vaca, is the region abt the Heart: there certainly is love (in Time) which is mathematical—fore-sight whatever a whole series of qualities we cld spell out, I only (again here) want to specify rather the mysterium of that it is yourself whose soul causes my own to awaken & spit, practically, the same "truths" of when a fire-crackers

a squealing or screaming kitchen-maid the Germans have a fantastic "salute" I fired myself a year ago New Year's Eve at & from Renate Gerhardt's apartment right near the Wall! Screaming kitchen-maid was the translation of this wonderful fire-works.

All love to you, & excuse please this *scrabble* to get back to you as soon as caught practically thanks, both for writing & so far already for your grand formula of—living life's outliving on-living its self

Charles (Friday January 19th (1968)

And to Jess—& will be back—(I *hope* directly AND GREETINGS OF COURSE ON HAVING BEEN 7×7—AND NOW ON "OUR" SIDE, God help us!

[on back of envelope]

PS: (further thought, on same

My dear Duncan, it is like the hoop and the circle, I must know nothing when I am *not* in touch with you(! Isn't it incroyable to be so slow to have *known* this powerful consciousness?   Love, I

PS2: You might even, make me a *poet* again, it is so beautiful to read the *Passages* you have sent me, I am reading now (too, in the midst of them.

Charles.

150

To Joel Oppenheimer (1968)

The poet Joel Oppenheimer was one of the Black Mountain College stalwarts, a student there from 1950 to 1953, with work published in the *Black Mountain*

Review. He moved to New York and was associated with *Kulchur* magazine and the avant-garde generally. The letter below is Olson's reply to an invitation to read at St. Martin's in the Bowery during the 1968 winter season. Oppenheimer has apparently moved to Greenwich Village, and Olson begins by remembering his own time there in spring 1942.   *Letter at Storrs.*

28 Fort Square Gloucester

Joel,   (I used to live 1st floor 77 Washington Place—is 125 an apartment almost or at the corner of McDougal? I saw somewhere recently an ad for that overbearing restaurant which was a couple of numbers up Washington Place toward the Square from 77)

In any case to acknowledge, and thank you for your invitation but I have become so aware that winters, even though I manage them poorly, are the consistent time of the year that I have *almost* got wise enough to read only in the summers! Almost. Not altogether successfully. So *don't* mind if I ask you to ask me again. (I hope very much you will.)

How are things? I hate to be so slow in welcoming your marriage (and tell your wife I have heard nothing but praise & excitement at her and her beauty), and hope you are both very happy. And that what you *are* doing is to your taste. (I of course miss you as a printer in the world: that even made Black Mountain more digestible—I mean its reputation: you'd have been surprised, in Berlin, a year ago, in the Eden Saloon the big night thing there the kids like you call them wanted only or practically exclusively to hear about that place! And with what longing really—which of course turned me off, thinking of what reality is when people only have heard of something (!) Yet we do, as a "race," increase like Abal da Mare or whoever that was: has the fellow (who wrote some play) and is now doing a book on the place been in touch with you?

Greetings altogether—and Happy New Year *too*. Write me when you can, & catch me up on your own self. (I have become like a True Nearctic one, & almost now live on a floe far far into those currents which I suppose cld just as well be the Early Nile. In fact I know they cld, & feel as close to the sun as (more than) I ever had before.

Love & your own virtues to you

Charles

Sunday January 21st (1968)

Oppenheimer wrote in an obituary of Olson for the *Village Voice*, 15 January 1970:

> The last time I saw him, New Year's Day, he was still lucid, still fighting, preparing a paper for the doctors, planning to tell them patiently that he was not Zeus, he was Prometheus, and you had to believe him even while they picked at his liver.

151

To the *Gloucester Daily Times* (1968)

As so often in the later poems of the *Maximus* poems, Olson in the following letter to the editor is simply a figure of his city, looking, listening, and feeling the value of his life. He once said in conversation: "Wasn't I right to come back here when I did?" It was what he termed "terrestrial paradise," even though he found things to complain about. The letter was written on 7 February 1968 and printed in the *Gloucester Daily Times* five days later.　*Letter in* Maximus to Gloucester.

Dear Editor:
happy poet like my friend Stephen Jonas the Boston poet says. I was raised over the Cut and except for the Parsons-Morse house I tried to buy last year and a gambrel Ray Morrison covered up a few years back, there never has been any reason to talk about the light, or at least the houses as fixing it, by texture or color or by their dignity or loveliness in shape or bearing—what arrests one this side of the River, at so many turns of heights and streets and lying of the land and abruptness small-ness a little street like lower Hancock which not so many years ago was simply Sea Street. Or Short is still Short. And Mansfield Place—or equally (coming into Western at the Boulevard Grocery) Mansfield Way.

I'm up this morning at dawn and my whole soul cries out again, looking out my door and seeing the early morning sun so differently striking the (Puritan) Hotel I better call the ancient Gloucester House brick—how rosy red that is brick as against the Mansfield house   dark red   blood red   brick.

Or I was away most of last week and on Saturday, in the morning, walk up again into town, cutting through Tallys to swing on to Main, cross over into the sun on the northerly side and go along to post my letters at the Bob's Haberdashery box—and up upper Hancock to my doctor's. Returning, stop in Connors for a gingerale and then equally paced start home.

And that shore-path, curving still right now as she was laid out 326 years back gave me again as I think it has never failed, a sense of auspice of life and being I don't even know the equivalent of, down and over the Earth's cities in Central America. Or Rome West Berlin London. San Francisco New York. Washington, New Orleans, Montreal, Seattle—West Newbury—Dorchester England Weymouth England both of which latter places Gloucester principally sprang from.

And I have objective proof I do not speak alone personally: on Pleasant Street in a house there is a painting of exactly those differences of light on brick, and in the cluster as the width and winding of Main Street still holds and shows it—and of course the light on the white shapely houses too, this rarest of all paintings of just this *gloire* of Gloucester I can look out or walk out and find

and for all pious people who think that history is problems, and that we must now live, and with problems, Fitz Hugh Lane's immaculate re-tention in paint of what is still my eye awakened this morning, out my door, or my blood, Saturday morning, walking it until I have lived on an ability and plane of 48 hours of maximum production and human joy (it is now Monday AM 7.45) I say shoo: this is, and can't be bettered. Kiss Joy, as it flies a greater poet than I can ever be said just when just what happily in Gloucester is still at stake was being rifled in the world, from each of us, for the first time.

Charles Olson

He also said, some years later, in his preface to his poem "Milton" (I owe the knowledge of this quote to another friend, & poet, a London poet Michael Horovitz)

"Rouze up, O Young Men of the New Age! set your foreheads against the ignorant hirelings! For we have Hirelings in the Camp, in the Court & the University, who would, if they could, for ever depress Mental & prolong Corporeal War. Painters! on you I call. Sculptors! Architects! Suffer not the fashionable Fools to depress your powers by the prices they pretend to give for the contemptible works, or the expensive advertising boasts that they make of such works; believe Christ & his Apostles that there is a Class of Men whose whole delight is in Destroying."

It is like a whole alphabet: when Gloucester loses her alleys, and masses of buildings (which carry these incrementals, as well as like dishes and spoons receive each day now as they have often before the same shovelfuls of snow etc—I actually mean of course as much more as well, the violets of light) the way a pansy joins its stalk, and nods there, in its head, so very rarely, as human heads can do. There was a kitchen garden by a house right next to Birdseyes just recently removed where each early summer I cld be sure, one day, to be bombed right out, walking up Commercial Street, by suddenly a poppy, maybe one or two more, lying there up on its stalk like crepe paper, and swinging, in the least of all possible air, in a mad dance of toss and tremor. And the woman who had those seeds there, as well as tomatoes, knew it.—It's a million worlds is tied up in what's being dolled-up—and that I am talking about.

28 Fort Square
February 7, 1968

152

To George Butterick (1968)

George Butterick had visited Olson in Gloucester in January 1968, checking on details for what became a Ph.D. dissertation at Buffalo (January 1970) and later the published *Guide to the Maximus Poems.* Perhaps as a consequence of their discussion about the inchoate existence of the "Institute of Further Studies" at Buffalo, Olson drafted "A Plan for a Curriculum of the Soul" and sent it to Butterick for the *Magazine of Further Studies,* no. 5 (July 1968), where it was printed with the requested correction. *Letter at Buffalo.*

Monday February 26th
(fantastick!

Dear George: Shrove Monday

Dear George—Just for further accuracy please change word drugs in 1st line of Plan for a Curriculum of the Soul to the Mushroom.

 I find your objection, that there isn't anything new in the above, a curious demand, and not actually relevant, I don't think, to the proposal. That is, the need, in fact—or at least what seemed to me the gain of this particular separation, was to have a congestion which ought to be including and likewise exclusive.
                    Or at least that, so placed, it can then be tested for its thoroughness. In fact what new is as interesting now as condensation?

 All right—and again hope your work & situation is satisfactory. (If you need, at any time, a letter or testifying by me I hope you realize I am one of your witnesses.

Charles

153

To Thorpe Feidt (1968)

Thorpe Feidt was an artist living in New York City when, answering to what he has called the "charge" of Olson, he moved to the neighborhood of Gloucester to work and, in 1969, to edit a magazine of the arts, *Mail.* The letter below, printed in the second issue of the journal, draws on Olson's ongoing concern with Hesiod's *Theogony* and with the Hopi worldview that he obtained via Benjamin Whorf, the anthropological linguist. The book described as the one that "I most believe in" is *The Secret of the Golden Flower: A Chinese Book of Life.* The letter picks up on one Olson sent a few days earlier in which he wrote "one is now 'free' to be or go anywhere—or specifically just where *one can get.* And thereby arises a wholly livelier universe" (printed in *Mail* 3 [summer 1970]: 2).

Letter in possession of the recipient.

Tuesday February 27th 1968

Thorpe Feidt:

That is, one can't stand around in wonder like in a city like the ape Godzilla or simply go on naming places. They have to be something to one self like flowers can be if one happens to fall in to one as one can and does once in a while.—"In natural things there is a. . . ."

Actually I think there is Earth and Heaven (and Hell of course. But Hell is simply missing out, and won't, though I suppose we all know it or more or less all the time are out of Heaven at least, help at all except to wear one down like leather or the fires of it proper.

It comes then to a good part of Earth herself unless Heaven suddenly renews itself in us which can happen. Or Earth & Heaven are the married pair as they were in mythological society, husband and wife, and the father and the mother of *every* primary thing—Night, and Day, and so forth, and so they do differ from Hell even if that is wealth, though the Book I most believe in, a Chinese book, says the real aim is to even be beyond Heaven & Earth as well as Hell in order to be anything which really counts at all. So there's a way for the universe to come home in the Hopi sense!

yrs,

O

154

To Barry Hall (1968)

After the beautiful work Goliard Press had done in producing the small pamphlet of poems titled *'West'* in June 1966, Olson felt he could release to that press the *Maximus IV, V, VI* that he had long withheld from his American publishers because of his dissatisfaction with the format that was being offered him. The much-attended-to manuscript of *Maximus IV, V, VI* was finally sent to England on 4 December 1967 with a "Note on type-setting" (letter at Simon Fraser):

> The problem here is the *disparateness* of the whole work: the book *depends* upon these *kooked balances* throughout.
>
> Each poem needs to be set individually for itself on each page, irregularly though that may seem, and going against normal justifying.
>
> I have in as many instances as possible included or had xerox'd my original mss. so that *all spaces both between words as well as between lines*—as well as *location on the page* may be followed.
>
> Ok. Thank you. It will save us all a lot of trouble on proofs.

The following letters indicate some (but by no means all) of the concerns the worried poet put to Barry Hall, the patient printer.   *Letters at Simon Fraser.*

Friday July 12th

Barry—Simply so that you know where we are (by July 15th as you requested) on the proofs:

actually the typos are very few, and the main job has turned out to be to re-paste most every page for the reason you also yourself have stated: that the Bembo type chosen so shortens my lines *that that "flat" literal effect those poems require,* has had to be achieved (so far as it is possible, given the shortening of the line (plus reason 2, below)) by re-organizing (as against both my original & your fair attempt to duplicate it) the position of each poem, (1) on each page, & (2) compared, on the left & the right page, in each pair, facing each other, to each other.

The *real* agony—what I mean above by Reason 2, is the bloody Bembo double-space (actually also *the leading of single-space* is too open for my harder taste) either in this font—or in some necessity of modern type-setting I don't understand.

That is, *that same flatness* (& *strung-out quality* I want, & *require,* to make my staves show any reader what is the exact condition of these letters, syllables words, &

how they "sound" to the silent ear) is be-devilled throughout by too wide a space between single-space lines, in the 1st place—& havoc & hell itself where my double-space has been duplicated by your Bembo d.s.

I have adjusted, as best I could—crying, in some cases, on page after page (in notes to yourself) out to you if there isn't some 1½ space or some way to shrink or sweat the leading. (In most cases I have just had to abandon double-space.)

So you will see—& I shall have the whole thing mailed to you just the very moment I finish. (It's devilish work—I average at best 33 pages a day—& as you know I was somewhat held up by that hospital spell. *PS:* If I am not interrupted it ought to be on the heels of this letter.

I. But for god's sake *please* dear friend *twist your whole shop around to keep us on schedule:* I want this book out, *on schedule.* I equally of course want the book you promised me, & I *require*—the best looking book in the business.

The problem then is mainly this leading—& *anything* you can possibly do to improve it—to "dry out" the over-distance between lines, will give us both a better press and, for me, a longer life of my poems.

Yours, to be on to you,

Charles

September 21st

My dear Barry—

That seems so cold (& dry) that inscription I cabled you—and I want something so moving & expressive,

that I enclose to you what I found out afterwards I had written on the back of a letter preparing to send you the cable. I believe that if it were set *down page right* in a very close straight careful vertical, that, in fact, it does what I wld want this statement to do

Please give it your *carefullest* care.

Love

Charles

Single space—narrower
(& *not* that s.s. of the book's type
except a *(equally narrow double space)* before the last line

[enclosed]

Bet

for Bet

for

Bet

For Bet

155

To Gordon Cairnie (1968)

On the flyleaf of his copy of Bernard Lewis's *The Assassins: A Radical Sect in Islam* (1968) Olson wrote: "bot before Labor Day via Gordon & rec'd Sept *19th!*"—a comment on the postal service. The other book mentioned below, expected from Oyez, was *Olson/Melville: A Study in Affinity* by Ann Charters, with photographs taken during the author's visit to Gloucester 13–14 June 1968.

Letter at Harvard.

Sept 23rd 1968
Enclosed check
catching me up
to date   by god
Cheers *yrself.* Everything seems worth doing—at least some of the time! (Tho I dig what you mean abt being 72, and feeling a 1000: isn't it wonderful-----? some of the time?

(I feel as though I'm writing to you like Stefansson from his 1st igloo just West of the mouth of the Mac-Kenzie the 1st winter he tried to get into the Arctic—and had to hole up, he & his friend, with, luckily, two Eskimo families they ran into by luck also caught west of the mouth of the River by a sudden freeze-in.

Love

this fellow

PS I got the *Assassins* by the way about 4 days ago! So you see how America does win the Space-Race—wow how right C. P. Snow was, that when the Post Office & the Railroad conductors decline-------

Keep your eye peeled for a new book coming *Oyez* Berkeley—not mine but on himself, and with an advertising spread I hope they send you in which the rocks are good even if I look like the grampus himself just hauled out, of the green slime.

156

To Joseph Garland (1968)

Joseph Garland, an author of Gloucester, and Peter Smith, a publisher also of Gloucester, had approached Olson with a project: to redo Babson's *History of the Town of Gloucester.* Below is his response. *Letter at Storrs.*

28 Fort Square, City

My dear Joe,
   Admittedly I'd like to get in on that re-edition of Babson. I bought him from Choate Alderman 21 years ago, and in the past 11 years have invested, in untaken salaries over that time—or at least 9 years of it—and therefore in remedial living as a result (for myself & family for several years of that time) something in the neighborhood of $250,000.

   It is true I also have realized other ends. Yet, *specifically John Babson* has been to me like a 3rd rail (inside me & my own two tracks) and I regard him as a *daily* matter. Almost literally: he is of such value—and it is a great deal more than a simple Gloucester matter (it is 250 years of the nation's life, because it was Gloucester he was the historian of) I better either stay altogether out of your project with Peter Smith or (what *does* occur to me, and because I imagine this re-edition is probably the only one we shall see in our lifetime, I *might* (if you & Smith would welcome it) seek to bring to bear an examination of the "History" in the light of my own researches. I mean literally to write a critique of his *proportions* and of his *"difficulties"* (is probably the best word in the light of his enormous labors, and successes) at points where the information was so devilish—or *is* devilish, and remains so unless one tackles it in a way almost precisely as good at least as his own.

I wld then want billing practically the same as yourself—because these proportions & problems in Babson's History are "Commons" and tantamount to the very bases of what now plagues and destroys this City.

Why don't we do this? You go ahead and if you'd like, when you have finished your Introduction, if you & Peter Smith would want me to examine that too (as I have the History over this long period of time) I cld then try to do some such "Additional Note on the History Itself" as above proposed.

(I have given considerable thought to the problem of the materials of Gloucester, and their publication—and *certainly* the Babson is altogether central. I'm just not that easily convinced that PS's re-editions of things are in fact that useful *unless* either just what you could do with such an Introduction as you are planning does bring John Babson up out of simply that old style & text—*or* what I think you are *already* doing (and *propose* even in this *specific* study of Eastern Point—or in that *further* study of the 1830's I urged on you so strongly after the *Patillo* book—

Well, simply, and quickly to get back to you on whatever you did mean by your question to me—is this catalyzing?

Yrs

O

Thursday September 26th
('LXVIII)

2nd letter: 1st letter enclosed

Actually, what wld be an enormous service to Gloucester wld be if you cld argue Peter Smith into another greater project: that, to be prepared & ready for issue 1972 (doesn't give you much time) wld be a Full

History of Gloucester, and which I think is entirely practicable: that is
my hunch is you have continued more than anyone (with the peculiar
difference of Gordon Thomas' special attention to schooners) to keep
your eyes on to that *last 150 years* (which Pringle & his recent pathetic
chummy equivalents have given nothing but their cute & equally un-
written ability to (exceptions, Charlie Lowe—& Brooksie, in his attractive way—but Charles Mann also the moment some member of the
Day family in Newton put him straight on what really was available
in the Dogtown Matter)

So why don't *I revise* Babson's History as a Part I of some such General History of Gloucester to Now—and you do the major task, write
the fucking thing (& these shld properly be an overlap, with the Babson, from a date abt 1830 or so on—as I sd to you when we talked about
your Patillo

That wld be a live thing—& Smith's got the money squirrelled away
somewhere: he could even—or I'd have to ask him, & demand it—*reset*
the Babson.
Love & really offering you catalysis, your

Catalysis Olson Him Self

The 350th anniversary edition of Babson's *History of the Town of Gloucester*, with
an introduction by Garland, was published by Peter Smith in 1972, after Olson's
death.

157

To Donald Allen (1968)

On 14 November 1968 Olson thanks Donald Allen for a gift: a copy of Carlos
Castaneda's *The Teachings of Don Juan*. Charles Boer in *Charles Olson in Connecticut* (p. 103) says that Olson recommended this book to many people and
quoted it in his University of Connecticut classes. He did not live to have to face
the sequels. *Letter at Storrs.*

Don,

    Did, yesterday, for the 1st time, open up Castaneda's very remarkable book—and hereby thank you for thinking of me for it: I jumped in where he is returning to Mr. Mescalito in order to have out that confrontation he does seek with him—and it's as true & wonderful as anything can be: the long voice coming into his ear like a tube to tell him the secret name—& dancing again twice (in front of him) like a stick yellow of light

            Wow

Well, there *ain't* much like that around—except anciently—anywhere

                                    So

the *more* my gratitude to have had it made known to me,

                         Yrs quickly

                              Charles

XI

The last year of Olson's life contained dire premonitions that were not entirely submerged in the enthusiasms of the moment.

Olson was under no illusion about his health, but he chose to leave Gloucester and visit Charles Boer at the University of Connecticut. This was on 26 September 1969. Early in October he made a quick trip back to Gloucester to get books needed for the teaching he had embarked upon at the university.

His cancer overcame him on 1 December 1969, and he was admitted to a local hospital. Having been moved to an intensive care unit in New York City on 19 December 1969, he died there, ten days into the new year, surrounded by family and friends.

158

To Robert Creeley (1969)

This New Year's greeting is apparently Olson's last letter to Robert Creeley. The telephone was becoming more and more a means of communication.

Letter at Stanford.

Robert Creeley: How
are *you?*   And
yours?
          I am
surviving
blasts
          winter—& myself.   All love,
                                                      & wishes etc (to all there—
                                                                Yrs
                                                                          Charles

Monday January 6th
1969

159

To Anna Shaughnessy (1969)

Olson here contacts his old Worcester Classical High School teacher, who might be able to fill in some gaps in his knowledge of the Irish side of his family.

Letters at Storrs.

                                        Saturday night, March 29th (1969!)
                                                                -28
                                                                41!

My dear Anna S:
    You shldn't at all be surprised I've carried you as close to my heart as the first days I ever sat in your class. And what a class both it was and

those bright girls who were in it, Helen Mason and the other lovely Jew
from Providence Street (Of course *I* was the only boy (-man I remember!

No but I mean you *wld* know to teach high school, and be you,
was for each one of us then, and there then, enough to feed us for the
rest of our lives. (I believe it *was* Macbeth and that I remember now
every facial expression, and condition of the air—as well as every move,
& thing you said. That's the glory of learning just at *that* moment—was
I 16 or 17 & they too—and you new too yourself for us anyway—Wow.

So. Happy I am to be literally in touch with you again. And actually
what I did want was your address. For suddenly I had noticed that the
Shaughnessys were almost neighbors in Galway to Gort where the
Hines—my mother's name was Mary Theresa H, and my grandfather,
the migrant was John ——? (if any) Hines (In fact a few years back I
won the *only* prize in poetry I ever have—the Levinson, from Poetry
Chicago—for a poem on him!) And his being a fireman at the old
South Works of U.S. Steel.

What I actually had hoped was not that you'd know necessarily my
family in Worcester—rather, anything (via your own Shaughnessys) in,
if that close, in that small part of Galway I had noticed—in Yeats or Lady
Gregory—that was parts of kilometres from my own direct ancestress:
my grandfather's father's
sister. Was
Mary
Hines. *The*
Mary
Hines,
Whom Raftery
met
"going to Mass by the will of God," he says, "at the cross of Kiltartan."

It's a very sober flat poem—for the Irish! And even Yeats has to dislike it a bit: "The poem," he says, "is not as natural as the best Irish
poetry of the last century, for the thoughts are arranged
in a too obviously traditional form, so the old poor half-
blind man who made it has to speak as if he were a rich

farmer offering the best of everything to the woman he
loves . . . etc"

I read it differently even in the translation it may be Lady Gregory,
"and some of it has been made by the country people themselves."

But maybe all this for you too has not been of your interest (? Any
more than it has been particularly mine. Though I wish I had caught
up with it earlier—in 1950 in fact, when, still Katherine Degnan (who
seemed to know a great deal of my family's Worcester life anyway—
Katherine Tarbidy (married Powers), and my grandfather's sisters married Torpeys & Higginses (one of those latter Bridget, who worked in
the mills all her life, & lived with a Mary Schary (?) Sherry? as late as
1950 down on Mitchell Street—(wld you have ever known Clarence
Graham, who taught physio-psychology at Clark when I taught there?
His family also came from that earliest Irish enclave: I was myself born
on Middle Row Road (where Holy Cross Stadium was built etc.

Anyway, actually I suppose I am equally interested to know if you
have been in touch with all those attractive students in "our" class with
you, in I think it must have been, *senior* English—Macbeth?—1928:

& finally yourself: I was so pleased, when Percy Howe came by here
last summer, to have news of you. For Miller—Phil(?) had a sister—
they lived on Chandler Street—'member him? Amherst, & a somewhat
crippled boy who loved you too. As we all did. Admired, and loved you.
And *learned* from you hard. In that beautiful spring time—& *last* equal
green-time *of* learning—when one is still "home"—the *last year* the *old*
world (before the new one which never ends, and never does one know
with such imprinting as that 2-18 one, the 16 years of which the rest of
life is making "book", I shd think (?

Love, & please feel free to write as much (or little as your will wishes.
I have myself in writing you already had a long long overdue regard to
place at your feet.

                              Your fondest student—or
                              one of them,
                                        Charles
                                        (Olson

And do forgive my wretched
penmanship: I long now have gotten
impossible, in that respect.

Postscript March 31st

My dear Anna:

What led me into all this was the following, from Muirhead's "Blue
Guide" to Ireland (which I had used originally years ago in identifying
the hill of Many (Menes—Minos) in Tyrone (KNOCKMANY), as the
"site" of the landing, & the death—from the bite of a bee—of one aspect of the "hero" of that poem of mine you may mean as one of those
which "lost" you in its verse (!) *(The Maximus Poems)*:

after having got the traveler to Gort, & telling how shabbily now Coole
Park is, and that Yeats'—& Mary Hines'—Ballylee *Thor Ballylee* is now
a shell, it reads—

At *Kilmacduagh*, 3m. S.W. of Gort, is a very interesting group of eccle-
siastical ruins. It was here that St Colman *MacDuagh* founded an
episcopal see c. 610 . . . and the original church was built for him by
his kinsman Guaire Aidhne, King of Connaught. The present Cathedral, a 14th-15th cent. rebuilding, incorporates the 10th cent. W. doorway with its massive lintel. The *N.* chapel contains *16-18th cent.
O'Shaughnessy tombs,* a figure of St. Colman, and two Crucifixions.
More interesting is the church of *O'Heyne's* Abbey [Irish *Hines*], to
the N.W., a *13th* cent. foundation *with evidences of earlier occupation*
(? *10th cent.*) The piers of the chancel arch and the two-light *E.* windows are in the mature Irish Romanesque style (c. *1266*); the vaulted
sacristy and chapter house remain on the *S.* The little *Oratory of St.
John, N.* of the cathedral, may date from St. Colman's time [i.e. 610].
Beyond it is the 14th cent. *Bishop's Castle*; while the *Roman Tower* is a
magnificent specimen 112ft high, restored in 1877-79. It leans c. 2ft out
of the perpendicular and the doorway is 26ft from the ground [where
muzzin was cried at evening time]. *Team pull Maire* [Mary's Temple]
(*E.,* beyond the road) preserves two round-headed windows and a
doorway. *Fiddane Castle, 2½m. S., is a well preserved stronghold of the
O'Shaughnessys*

So you will see it wld seem *O'Heynes* & the *O'Shaughnessys* the *Hines &*
the Shaughnessys seem to have overlayed *the very same narrow piece of*
Irish land! And (as I found out some 7 yrs ago in Salem) the O'Heyne
land is still clan-owned, we may in turn share blood as well—(?)—
Which wld be *delightful, I'd think. (!)* Anyway—IN-FORM-A-TION!

I add, hopefully for your delectation, a "late" Maximus poem—
which seems to fit all I fear I may be only troubling you with (!):

flower of the underworld

to build out of sound the walls of the city & display
in one flower the underworld so that,
by such means the unique
shall be made known

160

To Barry Miles (1969)

Barry Miles came over from London in January 1969 to record Olson for the
spoken-word series planned by Apple Records. In the nitty-gritty business letter
below Olson overrides the contract with Cape, which presumably had a clause
about residuals.   *Letter at Columbia.*

Thursday April 10th

My dear Miles:
    You pay me direct, and *ignore that contract:* & tell Tom I sd so.

This is the most absurd example of the *slavery* of a writer to companies with all their secretarial & legal—& commercial crap I am finally
sick of:
        that book cost me to write at least $100,000—& my payment so
far from Cape is abt $167. So like *until* some equity occurs on this end
of the equation—of which my earnings from this record will at least increase those small amounts, fuck anybody.

I (1) have to live on something; & (2) what Cape forgets is the *sale* advantage of the Apple record (haven't they any *personal-business* sense?

OK. (And I will send you a copy of the contract *if* I can lay my hand on it—but *any way: go ahead on my word—& to my interest,*

O

The Apple series did not materialize. Miles turned to Folkways Records and produced in 1975 *Charles Olson Reads from Maximus Poems IV, V, VI* (FL 9738).

161

To Kate Olson (1969)

The letter below is presumably a draft copy of what was actually sent. Olson wrote at the end: "Letter for Kate   Friday May 2nd 1969."

Letter (draft) at Storrs.

Kate,

This adoption thing appears to have come up, and as I've written to your mother (as I had previously indicated to George, when he called me on the telephone back about three months ago, I shld suppose) I'm going to find this thing a very hard or possibly impossible thing to do.

At least this will announce to you that I'm going to have to start living with the thing as something which now—for the first time, for me—is presented as a requested thing. And it seems, now that it does so present itself, as something I have no belief in, whatsoever. I feel like your father, my nature has no recognition of any accommodations, realistic or otherwise, of such primary things—and I fear my belief here is of such proportions that I'm going to be, if that's what it comes out as, a lot of trouble.

That is, if my agreement to permit you to be "adopted" is the point on which all these "advantages" to you hang, it does seem a hell of a lot both to deny you as well as to place on such a "feeling" or belief thing—and I hardly seem the best example of one to take such a position—or, for that matter, deny either you, if you want it, nor certainly to throw into any question what I take to be both George's and your Mother's best wishes on your own behalf.

I can only say this—that I've never known any of these real things to be anything but just this way, and if, in the end, I come out without having been able to agree to lessen or remove my relationship to you as father no more nor less & solely only as per se, I pray God it may life-wise be both a true thing to do—and a real one, in the end for your own life. For certainly I have no right to be a sticker here, if you and both your mother & George wish it (and it even does have only this sticker in it of the twist of George's father's will to bring it up even) unless I do believe there is something in which I am balking on which is of the highest importance.

In any case, right off (Friday May 2nd, the day I rec'd your mother's letter, & some legal paper in it) to record to you my first & fullest response.

My dear love, your

own

Father

for better or for worse.

162

To Frances Boldereff (1969)

This letter of 28 May 1969 was Olson's last letter to the woman who had been so much in his mind and heart from the time she wrote to him in 1947.

Letter at Storrs.

My dear sweet Frances—Just in another burst of love for you (they come in such gusts my whole nature at this moment (as I write) bursts on you)

                                    Love
                                          Charles
PS
    I adore you

                             163

          To John and Mary Clarke (1969)

In the letter below, Olson responds to an invitation to the wedding of his close
Buffalo friend, Jack Clarke, and Mary Leary, a university student. The date of the
ceremony was 28 June 1969 (in Oxford, New York). This letter, according to a
marginal note Olson made in his copy of Whitehead's *Process and Reality,* was
written on 23 June. The word *transmission* in the letter is taken from page 517 of
the U.S. edition.   *Letter (photocopy) supplied by the recipient.*

Dear Jack & Mary,
    I hope you both will forgive me but I won't be able to come Satur-
day simply because my system has become nothing but a tuned fork,
so I have to use it as such and behave in some such peculiar fashion. So
perhaps that is what I better be or send you as a—as though it were
some present—the idea that I am almost unable to move! It isn't at all
true in any immobile sense—I even had a marvelous day Friday June
6th, going across the City line for the 1st time in a year (exception, a
visit or two to Harvey & Polly's, but then, I met them here together for
the 1st time when I was walking into the Fort on the day of my original
return from New York in 1964. So they are the same belt as I am talking about—transmission, I suppose one wld call it. It was my daughter's "high school" graduation, and Mary drove me there—and Vincent who happened to be on Boston television that day, having read a
poem on RFK's shooting, also came. It was such a holiday I was re-
freshed as I have rarely been—or was last Tuesday having washed &
shaved & put on the finest duds I cld haul together—dun-colored
Harry Martin sd I looked, from his window!—just to go walking up
Main Street. No, I did have a purpose: I needed more of the smaller
yellow pad than this one—but as you see I so malingered or Malanga'd

(who courts only Court ladies!) along Main Street, visiting, that I got
to the new stationer's store 10 minutes too late (They close, at 5.

So every possible form of happiness and all the other joys life car-
ries along with everything else in (I mean *under*) her robes (I was
aware I was thinking of a Queen of Spain—or was it Portugal—
Catherine of Aragon, was it? (? no, a Catherine, though, I *think*)—
whose husband was so bad a ruler or times were so cruel, in any case
became a saint or was severely punished (?) for coming out of the Castle loaded with food—oh yes, when she was caught, if you remember,
it was a miracle, the bread all turned to roses so that she wasn't discovered, wasn't it?

> Love & *her* kinds of blessings & miracles! (as well as
> my own personal ones, (I mean, blessings
> > Yours the Old Caretaker of Fort Square,
> > for Saturday June 28th 1969
> > > Charles

In the last paragraph of this letter Olson is recalling a story he had told much
earlier, in a letter to William Radoslovich of 14 May 1959, about the widowed
Queen Isabella of Portugal. Her son Alphonso, the "stinker," had his eye on her
because "he heard she was slipping loaves of bread to the poor, from the palace
kitchen." One day he "nabbed" her as she was going out with plenty of bread
under her cloak. He asked what she was carrying, and she said roses. "Whereupon he tore her cloak off and bingo, there were roses indeed." See letter in *Minutes of the Charles Olson Society*, no. 16 (May 1996): 9–11.

164

To James Laughlin (1969)

The letter below is apparently in response to a letter received by New Directions
that made Olson feel "notorious" (the details are not known). The poet took the
opportunity to ask James Laughlin for a copy of Ezra Pound's *Thrones*, published
by New Directions in 1959 and now out of print.

Letter in possession of the recipient.

My dear Jas—

Am sending both yr letter & "theirs" off immediately to my great bibliographer (& biographer) at Chambersburg, George Butterick, whom I know will instantaneously supply you faster than I can all that you will need.—At the same time *please* keep me in touch with any final results direct: it is *marvelous* finally to become notorious.

Black Bart the
Po-8!

Item #1:

And while I think of it, the reason you haven't had that check-out of yr question on a typo apparently in our "Selected" is that I don't *have* one! (Probably due to that London-time I have *never* owned the *book!*

Also please have one of yr people repeat the page etc—my correspondence is a snow-pile now (like last winter's great *storms* here (February—they were by far the greatest ever even backing back to 1707! And the "Russians" (US Corps of Engineers) suddenly were outside clearing off the fresh beautiful stuff with a front-loader

Sat Jly

—*Item #2:*

Can you give me—to celebrate our *new* notoriety—a copy of *Thrones* (the one missing piece of the Cantos I don't have? Thankyou—& *belated* thanks both for the gift of the new *Cantos* vol.—and *as well* for that *happiest* of *all* royalty checks I ever cashed! The last New Directions one for *$375 for the "Selected"!*

O

NOW SAT. JLY 26th—so all this *done* but please read for items 1 & 2.

Laughlin found a copy of *Thrones* and also passed on a significant item of news for Olson, who thanked him with a postcard: "thank you altogether for both letter & books (including invaluable copy of *Thrones*—& news EZ did *look* at least at the Maximus Poems" (postcard of 20 August 1969 in possession of the recipient).

165

To Vincent Ferrini (1969)

On a picture postcard of Wingaersheek Beach, Gloucester, Olson sent on 28 August 1969 a note across town to his old friend, Vincent Ferrini. This would be his last note to Ferrini, except for the inscription that Olson wrote on a copy of *Human Universe* when Vincent and Mary Ferrini went to his hospital bed in New York on 1 January 1970, about a week before he went into a coma. The inscription reads: "for my oldest Lovers and Believers, Mary probably actually a relation and Vincent at every point throughout the creation—Charles."

The poem referred to below is "*From* the Song of Ullikummi," which Olson thought had fallen flat when he read it in honor of Ezra Pound in Spoleto; hence Olson's pleasure at Ferrini's appreciation of it. *Postcard at Storrs.*

Vinc—I was *so pleased* you dug that Hurrian masterpiece (crazy thing is, the man I took it from Mr. Hans Güterbock says he can't understand Charles Olson's poetry!

Love

Olson had received from the author at the time it came out Hans Güterbock's "The Song of Ullikummi: Revised Text of the Hittite Version of a Hurrian Myth," a reprint from the *Journal of Cuneiform Studies* (1951, 1952). The poem Olson made from the transliteration of the ancient text is found in *The Collected Poems*, pp. 600–602.

166

To Donald Allen (1969)

Donald Allen had published *Proprioception* in 1965 as the sixth in the Four Seasons Foundation Writing series. He has now proposed a reprinting. *Letter at San Diego.*

Wed. Sept 10th
1969

Don—That *seems* acceptable (I shld at the same time ask you as my personal agent is it?!)

And *delighted* you are enclosing it *(Proprioception)* as one full self: will you kindly inscribe it to the *right* of the 1st use of the title, & in *italics:*

> for Leroi Jones
> who first published
> all of these pieces, and
> fast, in *Yugen, Floating Bear,* & *Kulchur,*
> 1961 and 1962

in other words
5 lines of
inscription

When *Proprioception* was included in *Collected Prose,* the editors Donald Allen and Benjamin Friedlander added the inscription "p. 180" in keeping with Olson's request.

167

To Joyce Benson (1969)

In June 1969, Joyce Benson wrote to Olson from Oxford, Ohio, praising *Maximus IV,V,VI.* Olson wrote in return: "tell me *more!*" So she sent a poem. Olson responded with practical criticism, quoting with approval the last lines of the poem. *Letter at Storrs.*

> —which is why
> at this point in his space
> running from it so hard
> no land in sight
> he sits still and,
> will

I just wanted thus to register (for what use it might be, trusting my own instinct here and happily your own trust in my instinct) what strikes me does harmonize in your poem—coagulate properly in that "critical" sense of the metric or congruence occurring with total satisfaction too, to both syntax & feeling—Or like they say (or *I* do, & the Chinese—in one known text—the *logos* is at work!

That is, otherwise—the rest of the poem seems to prolong itself &
therefore or thereby has that unhappy effect (not logic's) of explanation—
Or in this instance preparation. So I am led to think your poem begins
where you end it—that, whatever is or was, for yourself valuable in what
precedes the above then does beyond tucked in if it shld at all be called for
the moment you departed from what certainly is the "beginning"

Ok? And don't god help us be bothered at this sharpness of our explica-
tion de   la   du? texte. I love to do it & to have the chance once again to do
it and for you wow what a plaisir

                            —And I *hope* you feel a good reason!
                Love & over
                                        the continuing love
                                                    Charles

                    [on back of envelope]
PS
    By the way this *"problem"* (inside) seems practically the *only one*
which "counts" any more in & of, like they say, "composition."

So count it
Something I hope

                                        September 10th

It does in fact—& I myself know hardly at present how to do it—any
more!
                    (Sed note not sad!) (Just, like, present news!)

168

To Wilbert Snow (1969)

This letter of 11 September 1969 is the last of the many letters Olson wrote to his
old college professor, although there was after this, Charles Boer records in
Charles Olson in Connecticut, a telephone conversation with Snow, as well as
with Carl Sauer, two of Olson's "fathers" (p. 87).   *Letter at Wesleyan.*

My dear Bill—Delighted to have your letter. And news—particularly of the autobiography. Which is good news indeed—how I look *forward* to it!

Regretfully I *didn't* get to Spruce Head (tho, curiously, one of my "Greater Boston" girl friends *did* unknown to either of us ahead of time stay at that "hotel" there I had noticed when Bet & Chas Peter & I were visiting those years back—& always wanted to come stay there & visit you!)

I *was* to the eastward (with my daughter Kate, to "her" island—Islesford—but only by plane via Bangor both ways due to push at each end. And longed actually for my own helicopter to come sit down in *yr* private water

Am back here having a hell of a time getting my feet back on to life but a day like this feels more like it

Keep me posted—& God knows, we ought somehow to see each other soon (I'm thinking of visiting one of my own men at Storrs, so possibly even that might work when you are back in October

In any case love to you both—& the best of news,

                               Charles,   Gloucester

Olson sent Snow a copy of Ann Charters's study *Olson/Melville* with the following inscription to express his long-standing indebtedness:

> for Bill, & though it looks so hidden (cf. p. 7)
> it is at last in *print* where it long
> should have been,
>   love
>   from your (long)
>   "Charlie"

Gloucester,
    September 11th '*LXIX*

169

To Peter Anastas (1969)

Olson had been discussing James W. Mavor's book *Voyage to Atlantis* (1969) with Peter Anastas, a local writer whose father is mentioned in the *Maximus* poems.

Anastas found an old copy of the *New Yorker* (13 August 1966) with a "Reporter at Large" piece by Joseph Alsop on the same subject, and passed it on to Olson.

Letter at Storrs.

Thurs September 11th
(later:

   Suddenly of course *sense*, that Joseph Alsop's—like *the Sedg-wicks!*—natural reaction wld indeed lead exactly to enthusiasm over such classicalness as even Blegen's—or here (Zakros) by the "Pomer-ances, of Great Neck, New York" it turns out are Mavor's friends! Howdee Doo-de as they say in *recent* Greek: (I had even sd to Mavor what abt Judge Pappas(!?) last night! And suddenly think of my pal's brother—also a Pappas—who has made 50M. Million that is in—like—*fish!*
  So there's hope
             for all us like
                  Gurreeks!
                    Love
          Your Ancient Friend from Over
             the Corinthian Canal

170

To Harvey Brown (1969)

This postcard was sent to West Newbury from Storrs, Connecticut.

Postcard at Buffalo.

(Tuesday October 7th
Harvey—I have had to make a hell of a lot of moves fast, and I hope you will allow me to catch up with our own affairs as soon as I can—certainly by or during the week following this,
                Charles

171

To Inga Lovén (1969)

Inga Lovén, a Swedish journalist, did a taped interview with Olson in Gloucester over a two-day period in August 1968 (see *Muthologos* 2, pp. 84–104). Previously a translator of William Carlos Williams's poetry, she was clearly knowledgeable about Olson's work and brought out the best in him. Olson refers to her in the "Paris Review Interview" (16 April 1969) as "a woman in Stockholm whom sort of like I fell in love with during this past year, and I tried to meet her in London, but that didn't work out either; so I then wrote her a letter, as I told Brown, and it was in Icelandic, which is why she's been staying in Stockholm studying it all this year. And I've never had an answer" (*Muthologos* 2, p. 135). He apparently did receive an answer eventually; the letter below is a reply to hers. The text is the draft or a copy written by Olson in the flyleaf of a book he had brought to Connecticut from Gloucester, *Early English and Norse Studies* (1963). It is dated 11 November 1969, less than three weeks before he enters the hospital.

Letter at Storrs.

Inga,

I do & I don't know. I've taken a job here. And it's holding me to-gether. But my strength, which seems enormous sometimes, for moments or sometimes more, is still weak—or doesn't stay steady and long enough for what my whole spirit more & more wants, and feels it knows, what to do.

I was so grateful for your letter and you musn't mind if you seem the answer to all which I mean by the above—and the future. You came to me as Ahab, you sd, and I hope for God's sake if at all you are prompted to come come too as Ahab whatever allusion that has, don't let anything in this world, or hurt or harm to yourself, keep you from me. I love you onely & solely, & I am now so prescient & suffered (almost to death's door) that I wldn't want anything to keep us apart if you were of that mind. So *please* hear me: love me (if you do) enough to trust us with anything. And everything it wld burn me alive. Let *NOTHING* BUT NOTHING keep you back.

Write me here care Altnaveigh Inn,

Spring Hill, Rte 195,
Storrs, Connecticut
       Love Charles   Tuesday November 11th
       LXIX

172

To Nimai Chatterji (1969)

This last known letter penned in Olson's hand is obviously a response to a query from an Indian student working on a dissertation. It is dated 5 December 1969, the fifth day of Olson's hospitalization. He had handed his University of Connecticut seminar over to Charles Boer, but he is here continuing as a teacher.

Letter at Storrs.

I am astonished actually that Ezra shld have had any particular knowledge (other than rubbed off from Yeats' of Rabindranath Tagore.

Which only shows my ignorance as you'd hardly have the subject.

From my own side (of the pickle) I can say I hardly think Tagore wld have been much ZP's dish. And at least I can give you back (for your inquiry) a story of Ezra's (in another context) which I *very* much suspect must have been somewhere where he could have playing along on the Tagore flute: he told me once in St Elizabeth's (early, when I was visiting him when he was still in Howard Hall, the Federal pen proper) that Yeats used to pester him so much when the Yeatses wld visit Rapallo hoping & asking Ezra to be a 4th at table-wrapping! (Which Ezra wld tell with exact American impatience at the time wasted, and equally with his own marked & particular graciousness, that I'm sure he often gave in.

                    Regards
                    Charles Olson

and of course (in addition to my not knowing anything abt the Tagore attention) I equally am and always been impressed by his searing lump-ing of Hindooism & Hebraism in that slashing attack upon Greekism as well, in the essay called "Medievalism" (is it not ?) in the Cavalcanti essays?

Regards—& excuses for the handwriting. I am getting it off to you as soon as possible from a hospital bed!   Friday December 5th 1969.

Bibliography

Cited Publications by Charles Olson

"ABCs(2)." In *Collected Poems.*

Additional Prose: A Bibliography on America, Proprioception, and Other Notes and Essays. Ed. George F. Butterick. Bolinas, Calif.: Four Seasons, 1974. In *Collected Prose.*

"Against Wisdom as Such." *Black Mountain Review* 1 (spring 1954): 35–39. In *Collected Prose.*

Archaeologist of Morning. London: Cape Goliard, 1970; New York: Grossman, 1973. In *Collected Poems.*

A Bibliography on America for Ed Dorn. San Francisco: Four Seasons, 1964. In *Collected Prose.*

Call Me Ishmael. New York: Reynal & Hitchcock, 1947; reprint, New York: Grove Press, 1958; San Francisco: City Lights Books, 1967; Baltimore: Johns Hopkins University Press, 1997. In *Collected Prose.*

"Captain John Smith." *Black Mountain Review* 1 (spring 1954): 54–57. In *Collected Prose.*

Causal Mythology. San Francisco: Four Seasons, 1969. In *Muthologos.*

Charles Olson and Ezra Pound: An Encounter at St. Elizabeths. Ed. Catherine Seelye. New York: Grossman, 1975.

"Charles Olson's Talk at Cortland." *Minutes of the Charles Olson Society,* no. 4 (March 1994): 15–23.

The Collected Poems of Charles Olson: Excluding the Maximus Poems. Ed. George F. Butterick. Berkeley and Los Angeles: University of California Press, 1987.

Collected Prose. Ed. Donald Allen and Benjamin Friedlander. Berkeley and Los Angeles: University of California Press, 1997.

"The Company of Men." *Evergreen Review* 2 (spring 1959): 119–20. In *Collected Poems*.

"David Young, David Old." *Western Review* 14 (autumn 1949): 63–66. In *Collected Prose*.

"A Day's Work, for Toronto." *Minutes of the Charles Olson Society*, no. 6 (October 1994): 28–33.

"The Death of Europe." In *Collected Poems*.

The Distances: Poems. New York: Grove Press, 1960. In *Collected Poems*.

"Dostoevsky and the Possessed." *Twice A Year* 5–6 (fall–winter 1940; spring–summer 1941): 230–37. In *Collected Prose*.

"Enniscorthy Suite." In *Collected Poems*.

"Equal, That Is, to the Real Itself." *Chicago Review* 12 (summer 1958): 98–104. In *Collected Prose*.

The Fiery Hunt and Other Plays. Bolinas, Calif.: Four Seasons, 1977.

"The Fish Weir." *Minutes of the Charles Olson Society*, no. 34 (January 2000): 1–10

"flower of the underworld." In *The Maximus Poems*.

"For a Man Gone to Stuttgart Who Left an Automobile Behind Him." In *Collected Poems*.

"For K." *Harper's Bazaar* 80 (February 1946): 227. In *A Nation of Nothing But Poetry*.

"*From* the Song of Ullikummi." In *Collected Poems*.

"The Gate and the Center." *Origin* 1 (spring 1951): 35–41. In *Collected Prose*.

"Glyphs." In *A Nation of Nothing But Poetry*.

"The Grandfather-Father Poem." *Poetry* 106 (April–May 1965): 90–96. In *Collected Poems*.

"The Growth of Herman Melville, Prose Writer and Poetic Thinker." Master's thesis. Middletown, Conn.: Wesleyan University, 1933.

"Hector-body." In *Maximus Poems*.

"Hotel Steinplatz, Berlin, December 25 (1966)." In *Maximus Poems*.

Human Universe and Other Essays. Ed. Donald Allen. San Francisco: Auerhahn, 1965; reprint, New York: Grove Press, 1967. In *Collected Prose*.

"The Hustings." In *Collected Poems*.

"I, Maximus of Gloucester, to You." *Origin* 1 (spring 1951): 1–4. In *Maximus Poems*.

"In Cold Hell, in Thicket." *Golden Goose*, series 3, no. 1 (1951): 34–40. In *Collected Poems*.

In Cold Hell, In Thicket. Mallorca: Divers Press, 1953; reprint, San Francisco: Four Seasons, 1967. In *Collected Poems*.

"I weep, fountain of Jazer." In *Collected Poems*.

"The K." In *y & x* and in *Collected Poems*.

"The Kingfishers." *Montevallo Review* 1 (summer 1950): 27–32. In *Collected Poems*.

"Lear and Moby-Dick." *Twice A Year* 1 (fall–winter 1938): 162–89.

"Letter 5." In *Maximus Poems*.

"Letter 10." In *Maximus Poems*.

"Letter 23." In *Maximus Poems*.

Letter for Melville 1951. Black Mountain, N.C.: Black Mountain College, 1951. In *Collected Poems*.

"Letter to Elaine Feinstein." In *Collected Prose*.

"The Librarian." *Yugen* 4 (1959): 2–3. In *Collected Poems*.

"like a fold-out." *Wild Dog* 16 (30 April 1965): 21. In *Collected Poems*.

"A Lion Upon the Floor." *Harper's Bazaar* 80 (January 1946): 156. In *Collected Poems*.

"The Lordly and Isolate Satyrs." *Evergreen Review* 1 (1957): 5–8. In *Collected Poems*.

"Lustrum." In *A Nation of Nothing But Poetry*.

"The Materials and Weights of Herman Melville." *New Republic* 127 (8 September 1952): 20–21; (15 September 1952): 17–18, 21. In *Collected Prose*.

Maximus, from Dogtown—I. San Francisco: Auerhahn, 1961. In *Maximus Poems*.

"Maximus, from Dogtown—IV." *Psychedelic Review*, vol. 1, no. 3 (1964): 347–53. In *Maximus Poems*.

"Maximus, in Gloucester, Sunday, LXV." In *Maximus Poems*.

The Maximus Poems. Ed. George F. Butterick. Berkeley and Los Angeles: University of California Press, 1983.

The Maximus Poems. New York: Jargo / Corinth, 1960; reprint, London: Cape Goliard, 1970.

The Maximus Poems 1 - 10. Stuttgart: Jonathan Williams, 1953.

The Maximus Poems 11 - 22. Stuttgart: Jonathan Williams, 1956.

Maximus Poems IV, V, VI. London: Cape Goliard, 1968.

Maximus to Gloucester. Ed. Peter Anastas. Gloucester: Ten Pound Island, 1992.

"Maximus, to Gloucester: Letter 15." In *Maximus Poems*.

"Merce of Egypt." *Montevallo Review* 1 (summer 1953): 20–21. In *Collected Poems*.

"The Morning News." *Origin* 10 (summer 1953): 122–28. In *Collected Poems*.

Muthologos: The Collected Lectures and Interviews. Ed. George F. Butterick. 2 vols. Bolinas, Calif.: Four Seasons, 1978–1979.

A Nation of Nothing But Poetry: Supplementary Poems. Ed. George F. Butterick. Santa Rosa, Calif.: Black Sparrow Press, 1989.

"The New Empire. . . ." Preface to *The New Empire* by Brooks Adams. Cleveland: Frontier Press, 1967.

"November 20, 1946." *Olson* 5 (spring 1976): 20–21.

"On first Looking out through Juan de la Cosa's Eyes." In *Maximus Poems.*

O'Ryan 1 2 3 4 5 6 7 8 9 10. San Francisco: White Rabbit Press, 1965. In *Collected Poems.*

O'Ryan 2 4 6 8 10. San Francisco: White Rabbit Press, 1958. In *Collected Poems.*

"Paris Review Interview." In *Muthologos.*

"A Plan for a Curriculum of the Soul." *Magazine of Further Studies* 5 (July 1968): 31–32.

Poetry and Truth: The Beloit Lectures and Poems. Ed. George F. Butterick. San Francisco: Four Seasons, 1971. In *Muthologos.*

The Post Office: A Memoir of His Father. Bolinas, Calif.: Grey Fox Press, 1975. In *Collected Prose.*

"The Praises." *New Directions* 12 (1950): 86–91. In *Collected Poems.*

"La Préface." *Vou* 33 (November 1949): 35. In *y & x* and *Collected Poems.*

"The Present Is Prologue." *Twentieth-Century Authors (First Supplement).* Ed. Stanley J. Kunitz. New York: H. W. Wilson, 1955. Pp. 741–42. In *Collected Prose.*

Projective Verse. New York: Totem Press, 1959. In *Collected Prose.*

"Projective Verse." *Poetry New York* 3 (1950): 13–22. In *Collected Prose.*

Proprioception. San Francisco: Four Seasons, 1965. In *Collected Prose.*

"Quantity in Verse, and Shakespeare's Late Plays." In *Collected Prose.*

Reading at Berkeley. Ed. Zoe Brown. San Francisco: Coyote, 1966. In *Muthologos.*

"The Resistance." *Four Winds* 4 (winter 1953): 20. In *Collected Prose.*

Review of *Cape Ann: A Tourist Guide* by Roger W. Babson and Forster H. Saville. *New England Quarterly* 10 (March 1937): 191–92.

"A *Scream* to the Editor." *Gloucester Daily Times* (3 December 1965): 6. In *Collected Poems.*

Selected Writings of Charles Olson. Ed. Robert Creeley. New York: New Directions, 1966.

"Siena." *Western Review* 13 (winter 1949): 100. In *Collected Poems.*

"Some Good News." In *Maximus Poems.*

"The Songs of Maximus." *Four Winds* 4 (winter 1953): 25–26. In *Maximus Poems*.

Spanish Speaking Americans in the War. Washington, D.C.: Office of the Coordinator of Inter-American Affairs, 1943.

The Special View of History. Ed. Ann Charters. Berkeley: Oyez, 1970.

"Stocking Cap." *Montevallo Review* 1 (summer 1951): 16–21. In *Collected Prose*.

The Sutter-Marshall Lease. San Francisco: Book Club of California. In *Collected Prose*.

"Theory of Society." In *Proprioception* and in *Collected Prose*.

"There Was a Youth Whose Name Was Thomas Granger." *Western Review* 11 (spring 1947): 173–74. In *Collected Poems*.

"These Days." In *Collected Poems*.

This. Black Mountain, N.C.: Black Mountain College Graphics Workshop Broadside no. 1, 1951. In *Collected Poems*.

"This Is Yeats Speaking." *Partisan Review* 13 (winter 1946): 139–42. In *Collected Prose*.

"Trinacria." In *y & x* and *Collected Poems*.

"Troilus." In *The Fiery Hunt*.

"Variations Done for Gerald Van De Wiele." *Measure* 1 (summer 1957): 2–5. In *Collected Poems*.

"*The Vineland Map* Review." *Wivenhoe Park Review* 1 (winter 1965): 100–111. In *Collected Prose*.

'*West.*' London: Goliard Press, 1966. In *Collected Poems*.

y & x. Paris: Black Sun Press, 1948; reprint, Washington, D.C.: Black Sun Press, 1950. In *Collected Poems*.

Collections of Correspondence
(Listed alphabetically by correspondent)

Benson, Joyce
"First Round of Letters." *boundary 2*, vol. 2, nos. 1–2 (fall 1973–winter 1974): 358–67.

Blaser, Robin
"Charles Olson to Robin Blaser, Part I: Robin Blaser in Massachusetts." *Minutes of the Charles Olson Society*, no. 8 (June 1995): 15–33.

Boldereff, Frances
Charles Olson and Frances Boldereff: A Modern Corespondence. Ed. Ralph Maud and Sharon Thesen. Middletown, Conn.: Wesleyan University Press, 1999.

Bronk, William

"The William Bronk–Charles Olson Correspondence." Ed. Burt Kimmelman. *Minutes of the Charles Olson Society,* no. 22 (January 1998): 1–30.

Brown, Bill and Zoe

"Background to Berkeley—VII: Zoe Brown's Transcription." *Minutes of the Charles Olson Society,* no. 7 (March 1955): 17–23.

Clarke, John

Pleistocene Man: Letters from Charles Olson to John Clarke during October 1965. Buffalo, N.Y.: Institute of Further Studies, 1968.

Corman, Cid

Charles Olson and Cid Corman: Complete Correspondence, 1950–1964. Ed. George Evans. 2 vols. Orono, Maine: National Poetry Foundation, 1987, 1991.

Letters for Origin. Ed. Albert Glover. New York: Grossman, 1970.

Creeley, Robert

Charles Olson and Robert Creeley: The Complete Correspondence. Vol. 1–8 ed. George F. Butterick; vols. 9–10 ed. Richard Blevins. Santa Rosa, Calif.: Black Sparrow Press, 1980–1996.

Mayan Letters. Ed. Robert Creeley. Mallorca: Divers Press, 1953.

Dahlberg, Edward

In Love, In Sorrow: The Complete Correspondence of Charles Olson and Edward Dahlberg. Ed. Paul Christensen. New York: Paragon House, 1990.

Gloucester Daily Times

Maximus to Gloucester: The Letters and Poems of Charles Olson to the Editor of the Gloucester Daily Times, *1962 - 1969.* Ed. Peter Anastas. Gloucester: Ten Pound Island Book Co., 1992.

Glover, Albert

"Charles Olson: Recollections." *Minutes of the Charles Olson Society,* no. 19 (April 1997): 3–25.

Layton, Irving

" 'The North American States': Charles Olson's Letters to Irving Layton." Ed. Tim Hunter. *Line* 13 (spring 1989): 123–52.

McRobbie, Kenneth

"Charles Olson: Recollections and Reflections, with Documentation." *Minutes of the Charles Olson Society,* no. 6 (October 1994): 11–33.

Mowat, Suzanne

"Background to Berkeley—VI: The Suzanne Mowat—Charles Olson Correspondence." *Minutes of the Charles Olson Society,* no. 7 (March 1995): 9–16.

Olson, Charles Joseph, and Mary Olson

"Olson's European Trip—1928." *Minutes of the Charles Olson Society,* no. 33 (January 2000): 4–30.

Payne, Robert

"Montevallo and Montenegro: The Correspondence of Robert Payne and Charles Olson." Ed. Ralph Maud. *Minutes of the Charles Olson Society,* nos. 14 and 15 (April 1996): 1–90.

Sauer, Carl O.

"The Correspondences: Charles Olson and Carl Sauer." Ed. Bob Callahan. *New World Journal* 1, no. 4 (spring 1979): 136–68.

Sealts, Merton M., Jr.

"A Correspondence with Charles Olson." In Merton M. Sealts, Jr. *Pursuing Melville, 1940–1980.* Madison: University of Wisconsin Press, 1982, pp. 91–151.

Recordings

Charles Olson Reads from Maximus Poems IV, V, IV. Folkways Records, 1975.

Works by Other Authors

Adams, Brooks. *The New Empire.* New York: Macmillan, 1902: reprint, Buffalo, N.Y.: Frontier Press, 1967.

Allen, Donald M., ed. *The New American Poetry, 1945–1960.* New York: Grove Press, 1960.

Alsop, Joseph. "Reporter at Large." *New Yorker,* 13 August 1966, 32–95.

Anderson, Charles R. *Melville in the South Seas.* New York: Columbia University Press, 1939.

Babson, John J. *History of the Town of Gloucester, Cape Ann, Including the Town of Rockport.* Gloucester, Mass.: Procter Brothers, 1860.

Babson, Roger W., and Forster H. Saville. *Cape Ann: A Tourist Guide.* Rockport: Cape Ann Old Book Shop, 1936.

Baird, James. *Ishmael.* Baltimore: Johns Hopkins University Press, 1956.

Barr, Stringfellow. *Pilgrimage of Western Man.* Philadelphia: Lippincott, 1949.

Benardete. M. J. *Waldo Frank in America Hispania.* New York: Columbia University Press, 1929.

Benedict, Ruth. *The Chrysanthemum and the Sword.* Boston: Houghton Mifflin, 1946.

———. *Patterns of Culture.* Boston: Houghton Mifflin, 1946.

———. *Tales of the Cochiti Indians.* Smithsonian Institution Bureau of American Ethnology Bulletin 98. Washingon, D.C.: U.S. Government Printing Office, 1931.

Bentley, William. *The Diary of William Bentley, D.D., Pastor of the East Church, Salem, Massachusetts.* 4 vols. Gloucester: Peter Smith, 1962.

Bérard, Victor. *Did Homer Live?* New York: Dutton, 1931.

Berkson, Bill, and Joe LeSueur, eds. *Homage to Frank O'Hara.* Bolinas, Calif.: Big Sky, 1978.

Blackburn, Paul. *Proensa.* Mallorca: Divers Press, 1952.

Blegen, Carl W. *The Mycenaean Age.* Cincinnati: University of Cincinnati Press, 1962.

Blom, Franz. *The Conquest of Yucatan.* Boston: Houghton Mifflin, 1936.

Boer, Charles. *Charles Olson in Connecticut.* Chicago: Swallow Press, 1975. Reprint. Rocky Mount, N.C.: North Carolina Wesleyan College Press, 1991.

Boldereff, Frances. *A Primer of Morals for Medea.* Woodward, Pa.: Russian Classic Non-fiction Library, 1949.

Bowering, George. *Touch: Selected Poems, 1960–1970.* Toronto: McClelland and Stewart, 1971.

Boyd, William C. *Genetics and the Races of Man.* Boston: Little, Brown, 1950.

Braidwood, Robert J. *Prehistoric Men.* Chicago: Chicago Natural History Museum, 1948.

Braswell, William. "Melville as a Critic of Emerson." *American Literature* 9 (November 1937): 317–34.

Bredius, A. *The Paintings of Rembrandt.* Vienna: Phaidon, 1937.

Brown, Arthur, and Peter Foote, eds. *Early English and Norse Studies, Presented to Hugh Smith in Honour of His Sixtieth Birthday.* London: Methuen, 1963.

Butterick, George F. *Editing* The Maximus Poems: *Supplementary Notes.* Storrs: University of Connecticut Library, 1983.

———. *A Guide to the* Maximus Poems *of Charles Olson.* Berkeley: University of California Press, 1978.

Butterick, George F., and Albert Glover. *Bibliography of Works by Charles Olson.* New York: Phoenix Book Shop, 1967.

Cairns, Huntington. *The Limits of Art.* Princeton, N.J.: Princeton University Press, 1948.

Campbell, Joseph. *The Hero with a Thousand Faces.* New York: Pantheon Books, 1949.

Castaneda, Carlos. *The Teachings of Don Juan: A Yaqui Way of Knowledge.* Berkeley: University of California Press, 1968.

Charters, Ann. *Olson/Melville: A Study in Affinity.* Berkeley: Oyez, 1968.

Chase, Richard. *Herman Melville.* New York: Macmillan, 1949.

Cheney, Sheldon. *Men Who Have Walked with God.* New York: Knopf, 1945.

Clark, Tom. *Charles Olson: The Allegory of a Poet's Life.* New York: Norton, 1991.

Connolly, James B. *The Book of the Gloucester Fishermen.* New York: The John Day Company, 1927.

Cook, Albert. "I Remember Olson." *boundary 2,* nos. 1–2 (fall–winter 1974): 13–15.

Corman, Cid, ed. *The Gist of Origin: An Anthology.* New York: Grossman, 1975.

Cornell, Julien. *The Trial of Ezra Pound: A Documented Account of the Treason Case.* New York: The John Day Company, 1966.

Coxeter, H. S. M. *Non-Euclidean Geometry.* Toronto: University of Toronto Press, 1942.

Crosby, Caresse. *The Passionate Years.* New York: Dial Press, 1953.

Dahlberg, Edward. *The Flea of Sodom.* London: Peter Nevill, 1950.

Davidson, H. R. Ellis. *Gods and Myths of Northern Europe.* Baltimore: Penguin Books, 1964.

Davie, Donald. *Ezra Pound: Poet as Sculptor.* New York: Oxford University Press, 1964.

Dawson, Fielding. *The Black Mountain Book.* New York: Croton Press, 1970. New edition. Rocky Mount, N.C.: North Carolina Wesleyan College Press, 1991.

DeVoto, Bernard. *The Year of Decision: 1846.* Boston: Houghton Mifflin, 1943.

Dorn, Edward. *The Rites of Passage: A Brief History.* Buffalo, N.Y.: Frontier Press, 1965.

———. *Views.* Ed. Donald Allen. San Francisco: Four Seasons Foundation, 1980.

―――. *What I See in the Maximus Poems.* Ventura, Calif.: Migrant Press, 1960.

Dostoevsky, Fyodor. *The Eternal Husband and Other Stories.* New York: Macmillan, 1917.

Duberman, Martin. *Black Mountain: An Exploration in Community.* New York: Dutton, 1972.

Duncan, Robert. *Heavenly City Earthly City.* Berkeley: Bern Porter, 1947.

―――. "Pages from a Notebook." *The Artist's View* 5 (1953): 2–4.

―――. *Opening of the Field.* New York: Grove Press, 1960.

―――. *Passages 22–27 Of The War.* Berkeley: Oyez, 1966.

Eisenstein, Sergei. *The Film Sense.* Trans. and ed. Jay Leyda. New York: Harcourt, Brace, 1942.

Euripides. *The Bacchæ of Euripides.* Trans. Donald Sutherland. Lincoln: University of Nebraska Press, 1968.

Evans-White, W. Y. *Tibetan Yoga and Secret Doctrines.* 2d ed. London: Oxford University Press, 1958.

Fenichel, Otto. *The Psychological Theory of Neurosis.* New York: Norton, 1945.

Ferrini, Vincent. "A Frame." *Maps* 4 (1971): 47–60.

―――. "The House." *Imagi* 4 (spring 1949): 4.

―――. *In the Arriving.* London: Heron Press, 1954.

Finch, John. "Dancer and Clerk." *Massachusetts Review* 12, no. 1 (winter 1971): 34–40.

Frankfort, Henri. *The Birth of Civilization in the Near East.* Bloomington: Indiana University Press, 1951.

Fox, Douglas. "Frobenius' Paideuma as a Philosophy of Culture." *New England Weekly* 9 (3 September–5 October 1936).

Frobenius, Leo. *The Childhood of Man.* London: Seeley, 1909.

Frobenius, Leo, and Douglas Fox. *African Genesis.* London: Faber & Faber, 1938.

―――. *Prehistoric Rock Pictures in Europe and Africa.* New York: Museum of Modern Art, 1937.

Garland, Joseph. *That Great Pattillo.* Boston: Little, Brown, 1966.

Gates, Reginald Ruggles. *Human Ancestry from a Genetic Point of View.* Cambridge, Mass.: Harvard University Press, 1948.

Ginsberg, Allen. *Allen Verbatim: Lectures on Poetry, Politics, Consciousness.* Ed. Gordon Ball. New York: McGraw-Hill, 1974.

Gruber, Frank. *Buffalo Box.* New York: Bantam Books, 1946.

Güterbock, Hans Gustav. "The Song of Ullikummi: Revised Text of the Hittite Version of a Hurrian Myth." *Journal of Cuneiform Studies* 5 (1951): 135–61; 6 (1952): 8–42.

Harris, Mary Emma. *The Arts at Black Mountain College.* Cambridge, Mass.: MIT Press, 1987.

Havelock, Eric A. *Preface to Plato.* Cambridge, Mass.: Harvard University Press 1963.

Hawkes, Sonia Chadwick, H. R. Ellis Davidson, and Christopher Hawkes. "The Finglesham Man." *Antiquity* 39 (March 1965): 118.

Heezen, Bruce C., and Marie Tharp, eds. *Physiographic Diagram: Atlantic Ocean.* Geological Society of America, n.d.

Heraclitus. *The Cosmic Fragments.* Ed. G. S. Kirk. Cambridge: Cambridge University Press, 1954.

Hesiod. *The Homeric Hymns and Homerica.* Trans. Hugh G. Evelyn-White. New York: G. P. Putnam's Sons, 1926.

Hollo, Anselm. *Tumbleweed: Poems.* Toronto: Wildflower Press, 1968.

Humphries, Rolph. *Review of y & x. The Nation* 12 (12 February 1949): 191–92.

Hyman, Stanley Edgar. "The Deflowering of New England." *Hudson Review* 2 (winter 1950): 600–612.

Hymes, Dell. *Language in Culture and Society.* New York: Harper & Row, 1964.

Innis, Harold A. *The Cod Fisheries.* Toronto: University of Toronto Press, 1954.

Jaeger, Werner. *Paideia.* Oxford: Basil Blackwell, 1947.

Jakobson, Roman, and Morris Halle. *Fundamentals of Language.* The Hague: Mouton, 1956.

Jonas, Hans. *The Gnostic Religion.* Boston: Beacon Press, 1958.

Jones, LeRoi. *Blues People: Negro Music in White America.* New York: William Morrow, 1963.

———. *Home: Social Essays.* New York: William Morrow, 1966.

Jung, Carl G. *The Integration of the Personality.* Trans. Stanley M. Dell. New York: Farrar & Rinehart, 1939.

———. *Psychology and Alchemy.* New York: Pantheon Books, 1953.

———. *Psychology and Religion.* New Haven, Conn.: Yale University Press, 1946.

Kittredge, George Lyman. *Chaucer and His Poetry.* Cambridge, Mass.: Harvard University Press, 1915.

Knight, Richard Payne. *A Discourse on the Worship of Priapus.* London: Privately printed, 1865.

Kramer, S. N. *Lamentation over the Destruction of Ur.* Chicago: Oriental Institute of the University of Chicago, 1940.

Kryss, T. L. *A Tribute to Jim Lowell.* Cleveland: Ghost Press, 1967.

Kunitz, Stanley. *Twentieth Century Authors: A Biographical Dictionary of Modern Literature—First Supplement.* New York: Wilson, 1955.

Landes, George M. "The Fountain at Jazer." *Bulletin of the American Schools of Oriental Research* 144 (December 1956): 30–37.

Lange, Oscar R. *Price Flexibility and Employment.* Bloomington, Ind.: Principia Press, 1944.

Levi, Carlo. *Christ Stopped at Eboli.* New York: Farrar, Straus, 1947.

Lewis, Bernard. *The Assassins: A Radical Sect in Islam.* New York: Basic Books, 1968.

Leyda, Jay. *The Melville Log: A Documentary Life of Herman Melville, 1819–1891.* New York: Harcourt, Brace, 1951.

Linton, Ralph. *Archaeology in the Marquesas Islands.* Honolulu: Bishop Museum, 1925.

Lobeck, A. K. *Physiographic Diagram of the United States.* New York: Geographical Press, Columbia University, c. 1932.

Lossing, Benson J. *A History of the Civil War.* New York: The War Memorial Association, 1912.

Lounsbury, Ralph Greenlee. "Yankee Trade at Newfoundland." *New England Quarterly* 3 (October 1930): 607–26.

Lowell, Robert. *Life Studies.* New York: Farrar, Straus, and Cudahy, 1959.

Lowenfels, Walter, ed. *Where Is Vietnam? American Poets Respond.* Garden City, N. Y.: Anchor Books, 1967.

Mann, Charles. *In the Heart of Cape Ann, or the Story of Dogtown.* 2d ed. Gloucester, Mass.: Procter Bros., 1906.

Mason, Ronald. *The Spirit Above the Dust: A Study of Herman Melville.* London: J. Lehmann, 1951.

Mathews, John Joseph. *Wah' Kon-tah: The Osage and the White Man's Road.* Norman: University of Oklahoma Press, 1932.

Matthiessen, F. O. *American Renaissance: Art and Expression in the Age of Emerson and Whitman.* London: Oxford University Press, 1941.

Maud, Ralph. *Charles Olson's Reading: A Biography*. Carbondale: Southern Illinois University Press, 1996.

———. *What Does Not Change: The Significance of Charles Olson's "The Kingfishers."* Madison, N.J.: Fairleigh Dickinson University Press, 1998.

Mavor, James W. *Voyage to Atlantis*. New York: Putnam, 1969.

Mead, G.R.S. *Apollonius of Tyana*. London: Theosophical Publishing Society, 1901.

Melville, Herman. *Billy Budd*. Ed. F. Barron Freeman. Cambridge, Mass.: Harvard University Press, 1948.

———. *The Complete Stories of Herman Melville*. Ed. Jay Leyda. New York: Random House, 1949.

———. *Moby-Dick, or the Whale*. Ed. Luther S. Mansfield and Howard P. Vincent. New York: Hendricks House, 1952.

———. *Pierre, or, the Ambiguities*. Ed. Henry A. Murray. New York: Hendricks House, Farrar Straus, 1949.

Merk, Frederick, ed. *Fur Trade and Empire: George Simpson's Journal*. Cambridge, Mass.: Harvard University Press, 1931.

Merleau-Ponty, Maurice. *Phenomenology of Perception*. Trans. Colin Smith. New York: Humanities Press, 1962.

Millward, Pamela. *The Route of the Phoebe Snow*. San Francisco: Coyote, 1966.

Moloney, Francis X. *The Fur Trade in New England*. Cambridge, Mass.: Harvard University Press, 1931.

Morison, Samuel Eliot. "The Dry Salvages and the Thacher Shipwreck." *American Neptune* 20, no. 4 (October 1965): 233–47.

Morley, Sylvanus Griswold. *An Introduction to the Study of the Maya Hieroglyphs*. Washington, D.C.: Smithsonian Institution, 1915.

Muirhead, L. Russell, ed. *Ireland*. London: Ernest Benn, 1962.

Mumford, Lewis. *Herman Melville*. New York: Harcourt, Brace, 1929.

Murray, Henry. "In Nomine Diaboli." *New England Quarterly* 24 (December 1951): 435–52.

Nasr, Seyyed Hossein. *Three Muslim Sages: Avicenna-Suhrawardi-Ibn 'Arabi*. Cambridge, Mass.: Harvard University Press, 1964.

Oppenheimer, Joel. "Charles Olson, 1910–1970." *Village Voice*, 15 January 1970, p. 9.

Payne, Robert. *The Tormentors*. London: Gollanz, 1949.

———. *Zero, The Story of Terrorism*. London: Wingate, 1951.

Pease, Zephaniah W. *Visit to the Museum of the Old Dartmouth Historical Society.* N.p., 1947.

Perkoff, Stuart Z. *The Suicide Room.* Karlsruhe, Germany: Jonathan Williams, 1956.

Plutarch. "On the E at Delphi." In *Plutarch's Morals.* Trans. C. W. King. London: George Bell and Sons, 1882.

Pound, Ezra. *The Cantos of Ezra Pound.* New York: New Directions, 1948.

―――. *Drafts and Fragments of Cantos CX–CXVII.* New York: New Directions, 1968.

―――. *Make It New.* New Haven, Conn.: Yale University Press, 1935.

―――. *Personae.* New York: Boni & Liveright, 1926.

―――. *Thrones: 96-109 de los cantares.* New York: New Directions, 1959.

Prescott, William Hickling. *History of Conquest of Mexico and History of the Conquest of Peru.* New York: Modern Library, n.d.

Pringle, James R. *History of the Town and City of Gloucester, Cape Ann, Massachusetts.* Gloucester, Mass.: self-published, 1892.

Rice, John A. "Fundamentalism and the Higher Learning." *Harper's* 174 (May 1937): 587-96.

Rosenstock-Huessy, Eugen. *The Christian Future; or, The Modern Mind Outrun.* New York: Scribner's, 1946.

Rose-Troup, Frances. *John White, the Patriarch of Dorchester (Dorset) and the Founder of Massachusetts, 1575-1648.* New York: G. P. Putnam's Sons, 1930.

Rumaker, Michael. "The Use of the Unconscious in Writing." *Measure,* no. 2 (winter 1958): 2-4.

Sanders, Ed. *Peace Eye.* Buffalo, N.Y.: Frontier Press, 1965.

Sauer, Carl O. "Environment and Culture in the Last Deglaciation." *Proceedings of the American Philosophical Society* 92 (1948): 65-77.

―――. *Man in Nature.* New York: Scribner's, 1939.

―――. *The Road to Cibola.* Berkeley: University of California Press, 1932.

Sealts, Merton. *Melville's Reading: A Check-list of Books Owned and Borrowed.* Madison: University of Wisconsin Press, 1966.

The Secret of the Golden Flower: A Chinese Book of Life. Trans. Richard Wilhelm. London: Kegan Paul, 1945.

Seler, Eduard, et al. *Mexican and Central American Antiquities.* Washington, D.C.: Smithsonian Institution, 1904.

Simpson, William. *The Buddhist Praying-Wheel.* London: Macmillan, 1896.

Skelton, R.A. et al. *The Vinland Map and the Tartar Relation.* New Haven: Yale University Press, 1965.

Smith, Bradford. *Captain John Smith: His Life and Legend.* Philadelphia: Lippincott, 1953.

Smith, Henry Nash. *Virgin Land.* Cambridge, Mass.: Harvard University Press, 1950.

Snodgrass, W. D. *Heart's Needle.* New York: Knopf, 1961.

Snow, C. P. *The Two Cultures and the Scientific Revolution.* New York: Cambridge University Press, 1959.

Snow, Wilbert. *Collected Poems.* Middletown, Conn.: Wesleyan University Press, 1963.

———. "A Teacher's View." *Massachusetts Review* 12 (winter 1971): 40–45.

Sorrentino, Gilbert. "Some Notes Toward a Paper on Prosody." *Yugen,* no. 7 (1961): 34–37.

Souster, Raymond. *For What Time Slays.* Toronto: Contact, 1955.

Spengler, Oswald. *Decline of the West.* New York: Knopf, 1926.

Starbuck, George. *White Paper: Poems.* Boston: Little, Brown, 1966.

Stefansson, Vilhjalmur. *My Life with the Eskimos.* New York: Macmillan, 1913.

Stonor, C. R., and Edgar Anderson. "Maize Among the Hill Peoples of Assam." *Annals of the Missouri Botanical Gardens* 36 (September 1949): 355–404.

Sutherland, Donald. *Gertrude Stein: A Biography of Her Work.* New Haven, Conn.: Yale University Press, 1951.

Thomas, Gordon W. *Fast and Able: Life Stories of Great Gloucester Fishing Vessels.* Gloucester: William G. Brown, 1952.

Thompson, Lawrance. *Melville's Quarrel with God.* Princeton: Princeton University Press, 1952.

Thomson, J.A.K. *The Art of the Logos.* London: Allen & Unwin, 1935.

Tillich, Paul. *The Interpretation of History.* New York: Scribner's, 1936.

Turner, Frederick Jackson, and Frederick Merk. *List of References on the History of the West.* Cambridge, Mass.: Harvard University Press, 1930.

Vincent, Howard P. *Trying-Out of Moby-Dick.* Boston: Houghton Mifflin, 1949.

Walt Whitman of the New York Aurora, Editor at Twenty-Two: A Collection of Recently Discovered Writings. Ed. Joseph Jay Rubin and Charles H. Brown. State College, Pa.: Bald Eagle Press, 1950.

Wasson, Valentina Pavlovna, and R. Gordon Wasson. *Mushrooms, Russia, and History.* 2 vols. New York: Pantheon Books, 1957.

Wauchope, Robert. *Modern Maya Houses: A Study of Their Archaeological Significance*. Washington, D.C.: Carnegie Institution of Washington, 1938.

White, Bouck. *The Book of Daniel Drew*. New York: Doubleday, Page, 1910; reprint, New York: Frontier Press, 1969.

Whitehead, Alfred North. *Process and Reality: An Essay in Cosmology*. New York: Macmillan, 1929.

Williams, William Carlos. "Against the Weather." *Twice A Year* 2 (spring–summer 1939): 53–78.

———. *In the American Grain*. New York: Boni, 1925.

———. *The Autobiography of William Carlos Williams*. New York: Random House, 1951.

———. *The Desert Music*. New York: Random House, 1954.

———. "The Ivy Crown." *Beloit Poetry Journal Chapbook* 3 (1954): 33–36.

———. *Paterson (Book Five)*. New York: New Directions, 1958.

———. "The Present Relationship of Prose to Verse." In *Seven Arts*. Ed. Fernando Puma. Garden City, N.Y.: Permabooks.

———. "With Forced Fingers Rude." *Four Pages*, no. 2 (February 1948): 1–4.

Wind, Edgar. *Bellini's Feast of the Gods*. Cambridge, Mass.: Harvard University Press, 1948.

Wingert, Paul S. *Prehistoric Stone Sculpture of the Pacific Northwest*. Portland, Ore.: Portland Art Association, 1952.

Woodroffe, John [pseud. Arthur Avalon]. *The Serpent Power*. Madras: Ganesh, 1964.

Woodward, W. E. *Years of Madness*. New York: Putnam, 1951; reprint, New York: Frontier Press, 1967.

Wright, Nathalia. *Melville's Use of the Bible*. Durham, N.C.: Duke University Press, 1949.

Wright, Richard. *Black Boy*. New York: Harper, 1945.

Zimmer, Heinrich. *Myths and Symbols in Indian Art and Civilization*. Ed. Joseph Campbell. New York: Pantheon, 1947.

Annotated Index

This index lists persons, places, languages, periodicals, organizations, and certain concepts occurring in the letters. Also indexed in their alphabetical place are abbreviations, some of the foreign phrases, and other possibly puzzling usages.

The index indicates recipients of letters with page numbers in bold type. Where *n* follows a page number, the item will be found in the headnote or endnote on that page.

As for annotations, a word or two is usually offered to identify the person, place, etc. Any further comment, the equivalent of a brief footnote, will arise in elucidation of a potential problem in a letter.

The poet's published or unpublished writings referred to in the letters appear under "Olson, Charles John." Fuller bibliographical information on Olson's and other authors' publications is to be found in the separate Bibliography section.

Chase, Richard (author of *Herman Melville*), 148, 155, 167

Chase National Bank, N.Y., 31

Chasles, Philarète (Melville scholar), 115

Chatterji, Nimai (student of Tagore), **431–32**

Chatterley, Constance (of D. H. Lawrence's *Lady Chatterley's Lover*), 335

Chaucer, Geoffrey, 172, 201, 241, 281n, 282, 291

Chelsea, 267n, 271n

Chester (medieval play cycle), 67

Chevaux-de-frise (French: "Friesland horses"—a sharp-pointed obstacle), 365

Cheyney, Russell (artist, F. O. Matthiessen's companion), 25 ("Russell")

Chiang Kai Check (general), 85

Chicago, Illinois, 52, 84, 226, 396

Chicago Review, 353

China/Chinese, 96, 139, 306, 337, 376, 404, 426 ("one known text" = *The Secret of the Golden Flower*)

Chirico, Giorgio de (Italian artist), 86

Chisholm, Hugh (of the Bollingen Foundation), 181

Chorley, Ken (friend of Ben Shahn's), 138

Chou (Chinese dynasty, 1122–256 B.C.), 76

Christ/Christian, 58, 67, 68, 84, 104, 153, 244 ("Xty"), 255, 256 ("Xst")

Chun-Can (archaeological site), 131, 132

Cid = Cid Corman, 237

CIO = Congress of Industrial Organizations, 136n

Circle, 207 (Olson means *Contour* magazine)

Citizens of the World (organization led by Caresse Crosby and Rufus King), 85, 326, 340 ("citoyen du monde")

City Lights Books, San Francisco, 350n

Civil War (U.S.), 148, 364

Clancy's = the Harvard pub, Cronin's, 161

Clark, Tom (author of *Charles Olson: The Allegory of a Poet's Life*), 13n, 30n, 317n, 366n

Clark University, Worcester, Massachusetts, 13n, 16n, 417

Clarke, Dick (Gloucester lawyer), 386

Clarke, John (of Buffalo English Department), 318 ("Jack"), **332–35, 422–23** (with wife, Mary)

Classic Myths (Worcester Classical High School Yearbook), 184

Classics/classical, 259, 260, 265, 299, 300, 360n, 429

Claude of Lorraine (French landscape painter), 86

Clement of Alexandria (church father, quoted in Kirk's edition of Heraclitus), 355, 357, 370

Cleopatra (of Egypt), 56, 227

Cleveland, Ohio, 52, 377, 383n, 384

Clouds, 365 (referring to the photograph of Red Cloud in '*West*')

Clynman, James (frontiersman), 362

Cochiti (New Mexico Indian tribe), 57, 58, 59

COL = government department, not traced, 37

Colby College, Waterville, Maine, 352

Colchester, England (University of Essex), 382

Colt (revolver), 242

Columbia River, Oregon, 195

Columbus, Christopher, 363 ("Columbo")

Olson, Charles John *(continued)*
  "History" (prose manuscript), 159
  "Hotel Steinplatz, Berlin, December 25 (1966)" (published posthumously as a *Maximus* poem), 384n
  Human Universe (collected essays), 277n, 339, 391 ("Grove essays"), 425n
  "The Hustings" (posthumously published poem), 322
  ICH = *In Cold Hell, In Thicket,* 187
  "I, Maximus of Gloucester, to You" (published *Maximus* poem), 194n, 195 ("#1"), 197 ("Max #1")
  "In Cold Hell, in Thicket" (published poem), 109n
  In Cold Hell, In Thicket, (selected poems), 187 ("ICH"), 207 ("both of the books")
  In Love, In Sorrow: The Complete Correspondence of Charles Olson and Edward Dahlberg, 67n
  ISH or ISHMAEL = *Call Me Ishmael,* 27, 55, 90, 113, 115, 149
  "*I weep, fountain of Jazer*" (poem published posthumously), 244, 246n
  "The K" (published poem), 107 ("*K*")
  "The Kingfishers" (published poem), 92n, 95n, 99n, 100, 101 ("THE KS"), 126
  La Cosa = "On First Looking Out Through Juan de la Cosa's Eyes," 259
  "La Préface" (published poem), 95n, 97n, 107
  "Lear and Moby-Dick" (published essay), 21n, 23 ("Melville essay"), 24n
  Lecture = *Causal Mythology,* 377
  "Letter 5" (published *Maximus* poem), 229n, 230n
  "Letter 10" (published *Maximus* poem), 195
  "Letter 15" = "Maximus, to Gloucester: Letter 15" (published *Maximus* poem), 190n, 274 ("Letter something or other")
  "Letter 23" (published *Maximus* poem), 203n
  Letter for Melville 1951 (broadside, "written to be read AWAY FROM the Melville Society's 'One hundredth Birthday Party' for MOBY-DICK at Williams College, Labor Day Weekend, Sept. 2–4, 1951"), 147n
  "Letter to Elaine Feinstein" (published essay), 264n, 353
  "The Librarian" (published poem), 246n
  "like a fold-out" (published poem), 323
  "A Lion Upon the Floor" (first published poem), 63n
  lobgesange = "Die Lobgesange" (Rainer Gerhardt's translation of "The Praises"), 128
  long poem = "The Hustings," 322
  "The Lordly and Isolate Satyrs" (published poem), 273n
  "Lustrum" (posthumously published poem), 42n
  "The Materials and Weights of Herman Melville" (review essay), 173n, 197n
  M.A. thesis = "The Growth of Herman Melville," 27n, 114, 115, 160n
  max = *The Maximus Poems 1-10,* 207

Text and Display Type:	Minion
Design:	Terry Bain
Composition:	Impressions Book and Journal Services
Printing and binding:	Edwards Bros.

DATE DUE

Demco, Inc 38-293